GOVERNMENT AND POLITICS IN *West Virginia*

READINGS CASES & COMMENTARIES

FIFTH EDITION

EDITED BY
JAMES R. FORRESTER

Pearson
Custom
Publishing

D1366464

Cover photo: Courtesy of West Virginia State House.

Copyright © 2002, 2000 by Pearson Custom Publishing.
All rights reserved.

This copyright covers material written expressly for this volume by the editor/s as well as the compilation itself. It does not cover the individual selections herein that first appeared elsewhere. Permission to reprint these has been obtained by Pearson Custom Publishing for this edition only. Further reproduction by any means, electronic or mechanical, including photocopying and recording, or by any information storage or retrieval system, must be arranged with the individual copyright holders noted.

Printed in the United States of America

10 9 8 7 6 5 4 3 2 1

Please visit our web site at www.pearsoncustom.com

ISBN 0–536–68317–4

BA 995287

PEARSON CUSTOM PUBLISHING
75 Arlington Street, Suite 300, Boston, MA 02116
A Pearson Education Company

Copyright Acknowledgments

Grateful acknowledgment is made to the following sources for permission to reprint material copyrighted or controlled by them:

"Statehood for West Virginia an Illegal Act?" by Sheldon Winston, reprinted by permission from *West Virginia History*, Vol. 30, No. 3, April 1969, pp. 530-534. Copyright © 1969 West Virginia History.

"What Should a Model Constitution Contain?" by Albert L. Sturm, reprinted by permission from *West Virginia Law Review*, Vol. 71, 1969, pp. 238-252. Copyright © *West Virginia Law Review*, West Virginia University.

"A Case in Constitutional Reform, The West Virginia Governor's Succession Amendment," reprinted by permission. Copyright © Donald R. Andrews.

"The West Virginia Mine War," by Cabell Phillips, *American Heritage*, Vol. 25, No. 5, August, 1974, pp. 58-61; 90-94. Copyright © *American Heritage* Magazine. Reprinted by permission.

"The Primary That Made a President: West Virginia 1960," by Harry W. Ernst, reprinted by permission from *Eagleton Institute Cases in Practical Politics*, McGraw-Hill Book Company, Inc, 1962. Copyright © Eagleton Institute, Rutgers University, New Brunswick, New Jersey.

"Was the Press Unfair to Charlotte?" by John David Rausch, Jr. Paper presented at the Annual Meeting of the West Virginia Political Science Association, Morgantown, WV. Copyright © by John David Rausch, Jr.

"On Guns, Coal, and Electoral College Victory Margins: West Virginia in the 2000 Presidential Campaign," Copyright © by Allan S. Hammock and Lawrence J. Grossback.

"Humor in West Virginia Politics," reprinted by permission. Copyright © The Charleston Gazette.

"A Guide Through the Legislative Process," reprinted by permission. Copyright © Donald R. Andrews and James A. Hoyer.

"Problems and Prospects Facing the Republican Party in the House of Delegates," reprinted by permission. Copyright © David B. McKinley.

"Some Thoughts on my Experiences as a Woman in the West Virginia House of Delegates," reprinted by permission. Copyright © Patricia Bradley Pitrolo.

"Does the West Virginia Legislature Really Have Two Political Parties?" reprinted by permission. Copyright © Thais Blatnik.

"Dear Ronald Letter," reprinted by permission. Copyright © The Charleston Gazette.

"1984 Gubernatorial Transitions in West Virginia: Rockefeller to Moore," by David J. Webber, reprinted by permission. Copyright © Duke University Press.

"Coal, Taxes and Political Suicide: Governor Marland's Abortive Severance Tax Proposal of 1953," reprinted by permission from *West Virginia History*, by Paul F. Lutz, Vol. 40, Fall 1978, pp. 13-27. Copyright © West Virginia History.

"Why West Virginia Needs a Secretary of State," reprinted by permission. Copyright © Ken Hechler.

"Office of the Attorney General," reprinted by permission. Copyright © Mario J. Palumbo.

"The Impact of Institutional Role on Judicial Decision-Making in the Supreme Court of Appeals," reprinted by permission. Copyright © Ancil G. Ramey.

"West Virginia Jehovah's Witnesses and the Expansion of Legal Protection for Religious Liberty," by Chuck Smith. Copyright © Chuck Smith.

"Historic Bridge Case Spanned Years," reprinted by permission of the author, Douglas McKay and publisher. Copyright © Wheeling News-Register.

"Who Owns West Virginia?" reprinted by permission. Copyright © Tom D. Miller.

"Problems of Church and State in Property Tax Exemptions: Hare Krishna versus the Marshall County Tax Assessor," reprinted by permission. Copyright © Alfred "Pinky" Clark.

"Consolidation in the Kanawha Valley—Is a 'Skinny City' Possible?" reprinted by permission. Copyright © Evelyn L.K. Harris.

"West Virginia's Declaration of Independence," reprinted by permission. Copyright © State of West Virginia.

"A Summary of the *West Virginia Governmental Ethics Act*," reprinted by permission. Copyright © West Virginia Ethics Commission.

**DEDICATED TO THE MEMORY OF
MY PARENTS**

FOREWORD

It is very refreshing to have a textbook which makes a happy combination of the basic academic approach with its application. Both the serious student and the general reader (as well as the practitioner) will find in this useful text a wealth of material presented in an interesting and provocative way.

As one who has migrated back and forth from the academic world to elective politics at both the national and state levels, I am fascinated by the new material which provides fresh new insights into the jobs of practitioners and those academics who are experts at objective analysis.

Of course there are some points of view with which both students and the general public will strongly disagree. Personally, I find this to be very healthy because it will stimulate the kind of class discussions which are essential to the learning process.

Even though some of the references in a book as contemporary as this may be out-of-date within a short time, this volume furnishes an accurate snapshot of West Virginia government and politics in a fascinating and stimulating fashion.

Ken Hechler
Secretary of State, 1985—2001

CONTENTS

CHAPTER ONE THE FEDERAL CONSTITUTIONAL FRAMEWORK: WEST VIRGINIA AND THE NATION

CHAPTER TWO POLITICAL PARTICIPATION AND POLITICAL PARTIES

CHAPTER THREE LEGISLATIVE POLICY-MAKING

CHAPTER FOUR EXECUTIVE LEADERSHIP

CHAPTER FIVE JUDICIAL POLICY-MAKING

PREFACE TO THE FIFTH EDITION

It has been thirteen years since the first edition of this book was published. In each of the four previous editions I noted various themes: the paucity of research on government and politics in West Virginia, political corruption, the sluggish economy, slow economic development and the need for political and educational reform. The earlier editions also noted that considerably more research has been conducted on West Virginia and the body politic has steadily improved in its capacity to deal with its problems.

An important theme in this fifth edition is the 2000 presidential election which highlighted the fact that George W. Bush could not have won the presidency without carrying West Virginia. Could it be that the state's 2 to 1 majority Democratic voters are starting to slowly break loose from their party moorings and vote Republican at both the presidential and congressional levels? The presidential election was not even close, George Bush won in a state that was considered a "lock" for the Democrats with 53% of the vote to Al Gore's 47% and former governor Arch Moore's daughter, Shelly Moore Capito, in the second congressional district race, overcame great odds to also win. Finally, current voter registration data reveal that there are now more independent voters in West Virginia than ever before. Yet, these same voters in the 2000 election defeated a moderate, reform minded, Republican governor, Cecil Underwood by electing the Democrat, and former congressman, Bob Wise. It should be recalled that Underwood tried to reform the state's archaic "unfair" tax system with his Governor's Commission on Fair Taxation. To underscore the point that political change comes slowly in West Virginia, the Democrats retained their lopsided party dominance over the Republicans in the 75th Legislature.

This fifth edition features significant chapter revisions and incorporates the 2000 Census in its tables and figures. World Wide Web addresses at the end of the chapters are updated so that readers can continue to surf the net and obtain new information about West Virginia.

An important new selection is added to this edition, "On Guns, Coal, and Electoral College Victory Margins: West Virginia in the 2000 Presidential Campaign" written by two West Virginia University political scientists, Allan S. Hammock and Lawrence J. Grossback who read my revisions, made suggestions for improvement and provided their encouragement for this edition. They have my gratitude.

Two scholars, who encouraged me when I was first writing this book, deserve my continuing admiration: Evelyn L.K. Harris, Professor Emeritus of the University of Charleston and Ken Hechler, former secretary of state, who recently retired after many years of service to the people of West Virginia.

The completion of this fifth edition, in some ways easier for my family, still required their support and patience, and for that they have my love.

James R. Forrester

PREFACE

The genesis of this book is as varied as the topics contained within. For many years now, the West Virginia Political Science Association (WVPSA) has called for more research on West Virginia government and politics and a scholarly updating of the standard texts. During approximately the same time, I have frequently taught the general survey course, American State and Local Government, to moderately interested students at West Liberty State College. I have attempted to provide relevance for the potentially dry and outdated West Virginia text material with interesting supplemental library readings. As an instructor knows, such a procedure frequently lacks conceptual clarity and is frequently inconvenient.

Moreover, the old tension between practitioners (insiders) and academicians (outsiders) becomes evident in using supplemental readings as the most interesting readings from the student's perspective are, more often than not, written by practitioners. This is because the practitioners frequently reveal as much about themselves in their writings as they do about politics.

I have had many conversations with practitioners (elected and appointed) through the years and have realized that their colorful views of politics are not reported in the few texts that deal with West Virginia government and politics. This is not to say that the available texts are inaccurate, rather the perspectives advanced in them differ markedly from the practitioners' views. The scientifically trained academician who writes a text is usually interested in theory building, testing hypotheses and carefully summarizing his findings from data that were painstakingly collected.

The practitioner conversely is not interested in scientific generalizing and instead reports on his "practical experience" much as the craftsman demonstrates his trade.

The readings, cases and commentaries reported in this reader provide insights into both the practical and the theoretical side of politics in West Virginia. The selections are not intended to be typical or comprehensive, although some are of necessity original, most are hopefully interesting and will provide enrichment to courses dealing with West Virginia government and politics.

The non-collegiate reader of this book likewise should find the selections interesting and informative as they show how the state was carved out of Virginia, and provide insights into its unique culture and political institutions.

The selections are organized into six chapters, with each chapter subdivided into an introduction, readings (research findings reported by political scientists), cases (story narratives that reveal lessons about West Virginia government and politics) and commentaries (discussions by practitioners or office holders as the way things are from the inside of government).

With the completion of a project such as this, I find myself indebted to more persons than I can name, particularly the inquiring students in my American

State and Local Government classes at West Liberty State College and many colleagues at West Liberty and elsewhere who provided advice and encouragement.

A grant from the West Liberty State College Foundation was generously provided at the beginning of this project.

The project at a crucial juncture was helped along its way by the support and encouragement of three individuals especially interested in West Virginia politics: Julius Jay Stern of Parkersburg, West Virginia; David Williams, Department of Public Administration, West Virginia University and David Webber, Department of Political Science, University of Missouri-Columbia.

The contributors, who are profiled in the Appendix, deserve my special thanks because they made the book possible. Evelyn L.K. Harris, of the University of Charleston, and Richard Rosswurm, Administrative Office, Supreme Court of Appeals also have my gratitude. Evelyn in addition to contributing an article, advised me on selections, sent me materials, read all of my introductions and made helpful suggestions. Richard provided advice, counsel and patiently corrected the errors in Chapter Five, "Judicial Policy-Making."

Finally, I must acknowledge my wife, Carolyn, who tirelessly proofread the manuscript and arranged her schedule to accommodate mine and my many hours with the word processor. Through all of this she and our daughters Suzanne, Kimberly and Carrie rarely complained. For these and many other reasons they have my love.

James R. Forrester
West Liberty State College

LIST OF TABLES

LIST OF FIGURES

FIGURE   PAGE

CHAPTER ONE

The Federal Constitutional Framework: West Virginia and the Nation

---

INTRODUCTION

The 1987 bicentennial celebration of the United States Constitution reminds us of the importance of constitutions. In fact, most political organizations have constitutions or rules that distribute political power. Sometimes these "rules" or constitutions are unwritten and have come to be accepted informally over time. In the American political tradition the tendency is to have formal sets of central rules that both limit the power of governments and guarantee citizens certain rights.

A more inclusive idea than the notion of written or unwritten rules governing our behavior is the concept of "constitutionalism." Given the fact that each state in the United States, including the national government, has a constitution, the idea is that the American "states" should faithfully follow their constitutions. American constitutionalism is further complicated by the "federal arrangement" of power. This means that state constitutions take precedence over state and local law, but state constitutions in turn are subordinate to the U.S. Constitution and laws passed pursuant to it by Congress.

This hierarchy of constitutional law is asserted in Article VI of the U.S. Constitution:

> "This constitution, and the laws of the United States which shall be made in pursuance thereof; and all treaties made, or which shall be made, under the authority of the United States, shall be the supreme law of the land; and the judges in every state shall be bound thereby, anything in the constitution or laws of any state to the contrary notwithstanding."[1]

It should be noted also that the U.S. Constitution is "incomplete." Many key constitutional issues are left to the states, including education, the organization of state and local government, privacy rights, etc.[2]

The constitutional place of West Virginia[3] in the federal system is revealed by clauses in the West Virginia and federal constitutions. These clauses limit or guarantee the power of West Virginia in its relationship with the federal government. At the same time, the federal constitution provides West Virginia a role in the makeup of the national government. These "constitutional relations" are interpreted by the West Virginia Supreme Court and most particularly by the United States Supreme Court.[4]

Figure 1.1 lists the major guarantees and limitations of West Virginia's powers concerning the categories of Integrity, Sovereignty, Military Affairs, Defense, Commerce, Taxation, and Administration of Justice.[5]

Figure 1.1 Federal Constitutional Provisions that Guarantee or Limit West Virginia's Powers

Guarantees	Limits

A. West Virginia's Integrity and Sovereignty

Guarantees	Limits
WV is protected from division or consolidation without its legislative consent (IV-4).[6] Republican form of government (IV-2). Protection against invasion (IV-2). Protection against domestic violence when requested by proper state officials (IV-2). Powers are reserved to the states by the Constitution when not prohibited by it to the states (Amend. X). WV cannot be sued by citizens of another state or foreign country (Amend. XI).	WV cannot enter into treaties, alliances, or confederations (I-10). No separate coinage (I-10). No grants of titles of nobility (I-10). No interstate or foreign compacts without congressional approval (I-10). Constitution is supreme law and binds WV and other states (VI). Slavery is prohibited (Amend. XIII). WV's state executive, legislative and judicial officers including reps. in Congress are bound by the Constitution (VI). No abridgement of privileges and immunities of U.S. citizens (Amend. XIV). Reduction of reps. in House of Representatives for denial of franchise to U.S. citizens (Amend. XIV). No payment of debts incurred in aid of insurrection or rebellion against U.S. or for emancipation of slaves (Amend. XIV). No denial of franchise on basis of race, color, or previous condition of servitude (Amend. XV). Popular election of U.S. Senators (Amend. XVII). No denial of franchise on account of sex (Amend. XIX). No poll tax in national elections (Amend. XXIV).

B. West Virginia's Military Affairs and Defense

Guarantees	Limits
WV has power to maintain militia and appoint officers (I-8, Amend. II).	No letters of marque and reprisal (I-10). No maintenance of standing military forces in peacetime without congressional consent (I-10). No engagement in war without congressional consent, except for the purpose of repelling invasion (I-10).

Figure 1.1 (continued)

Guarantees	Limits

C. West Virginia's Commerce and Taxation

Equal apportionment of direct federal taxes (I-2, 9; Amend. XVII). No federal export duties (I-9). No preferential treatment for ports of one state (I-9). Reciprocal full faith and credit among states for public acts, records and judicial proceedings (IV-1). Reciprocal privileges and immunities for citizens of the several states (IV-2). Intoxicating liquor may not be imported into states where its sale or use is prohibited (Amend. XXI-2).

No levying of duties on vessels of sister states (I-9). No legal tender other than gold or silver (I-10). No impairment of obligations of contracts (I-10). No levying of import or export duties without Congress' consent except when levying reasonable inspection fees (I-10). No tonnage duties without congressional consent (I-10).

D. West Virginia's Administration of Justice

Federal criminal trials to be held in state where crime was committed. Extradition for crimes (IV-2). Federal criminal juries to be chosen from state and district in which crime was committed (Amend. VII).[7] Federal judicial power extends to controversies between two or more states; between a state and citizens of another state when state is plaintiff; and between a foreign nation or its citizens, with original jurisdiction vested in the U.S. Supreme Court (III-2).

No bills of attainder (I-10). No *ex post facto* laws (I-10). Supreme Court has original jurisdiction over all cases in which a state shall be a party (III-2). Judges in every state bound by U.S. Constitution, all laws and treaties made under it, notwithstanding the constitutions or laws of any state (VI). No denial of life, liberty or property without due process of law (Amend. XIV). No denial of equal protection of state laws to citizens within its limits (Amend. XIV).

The federal constitution also provides West Virginia and its sister states a role in the make-up of the national government. Article I, section 2, of the U.S. Constitution guarantees each state at least one representative in the U.S. House of Representatives[8] and representatives, in addition to being inhabitants of the state, must be apportioned among the states every ten years according to population. The governor has the authority to fill vacancies when they might occur (I–2).

Article I, Section 3 relates that each state is guaranteed two senators "who are chosen by the people qualified to vote for the most numerous house of the state legislature . . . with vacancies to be filled as prescribed by state legislation (Amendment XVII)."[9]

Similarly to congressmen, U.S. senators must be inhabitants of the states that they represent. The West Virginia and other state legislatures determine the times, places, and manner of holding elections for representatives and senators (I–4).

Article II, Section 1 provides that each state has a role in determining the electoral vote for President of the U.S. The states are allocated as many electors as they have in their congressional delegations (congressmen and senators). Since West Virginia has three congressmen and two senators it has five electors in presidential elections. In case there is no majority of the electoral college vote for President, each state is guaranteed one vote if the election is decided in the U.S. House of Representatives.

Many of the state constitutions are silent concerning state-federal relations. The exceptions to this are the reconstructed constitutions of the southern states that acknowledge federal supremacy (no right to secede) and Article I of the West Virginia Constitution which elaborates its relations to the U.S. government:

". . . . Relations to the Government of the United States"

1. The State of West Virginia is, and shall remain, one of the United States of America. The Constitution of the United States of America, and the laws and treaties made in pursuance thereof, shall be the supreme law of the land.

Internal Government and Police

2. The government of the United States is a government of enumerated powers, and all powers not delegated to it, nor inhibited to the states, are reserved to the states or to the people thereof. Among the powers so reserved to the states is the exclusive regulation of their own internal government and police; and it is the high and solemn duty of the several departments of government, created by this constitution, to guard and protect the people of this state from all encroachments upon the rights so reserved.

Continuity of Constitutional Operation

3. The provisions of the Constitution of the United States, and of this state, are operative alike in a period of war as in times of peace, and any departure therefrom, or violation thereof, under the plea of necessity, or any other plea, is subversive of good government, and tends to anarchy and despotism. . . . "[10]

In the articles that follow are the "roots" of an unique relationship between West Virginia and the federal government. First, Sheldon Winston in his "Statehood for West Virginia: An Illegal Act?" questions whether the creation of West Virginia from the western counties of Virginia during the Civil War[11] had a basis in law. Winston gathers historical evidence that disputes the claim that the so-called Restored Legislature of Virginia really represented the will of loyal Virginia.

Albert L. Sturm in his article, "What Should a Model Constitution Contain?" presents the salient features of a reform constitution and these are compared through editorial updating with the (1872) West Virginia Constitution. The West Virginia Constitution has come a long way in the 26 years since Sturm wrote his article. Finally, Donald R. Andrews, a political scientist formerly with

Legislative Services, reveals the historical background and the politics of The Citizens' Advisory Commission on the Legislature of West Virginia which created a number of significant constitutional reforms including the Governor's Succession Amendment.

Notes

[1] *United States Constitution*, Article VI, Section 2.

[2] See Donald S. Lutz, "The United States Constitution as an Incomplete Text," *Annals of the American Academy of Political and Social Science*, 496 (March, 1989), 23-32.

[3] For a fuller discussion see Daniel J. Elazar, *American Federalism: View From the States*, third edition, (New York: Harper & Row, Publishers, 1984), 31-51.

[4] *Ibid.*, 42.

[5] Figure I is adapted from Elazar, 42–43.

[6] Numbers in parentheses depict the article and section of the U.S. Constitution that contains the provision.

[7] Guarantees the integrity of each state's common law in federal cases.

[8] Article 1, section 4, *West Virginia Constitution* mandates that West Virginia shall have Congressional Districts that are formed of contiguous counties, compact and "as nearly as may be, an equal number of population."

[9] Elazar, *op cit.*, 44.

[10] *West Virginia Constitution*, Article I, Sections 1–3.

[11] Brisbin et al., note that . . . "from 1775 to 1861 West Virginia was governed under three different constitutions of Virginia . . . the Constitution of 1776 generated sectional controversy in Virginia because it included slaves in the population figures to apportion the state legislature. It also limited suffrage to white males in possession of at least fifty acres of improved land. These provisions ensured that the legislature would be dominated by the eastern counties. The Constitution of 1830 contained the property-holding restrictions on suffrage and retained an apportionment scheme that favored the eastern counties . . . The Constitution of 1851 included universal white male suffrage . . . <and> although the extension of suffrage did provide western counties with more influence in the legislature, the **state's history of sectional conflict did set the stage for the west's secession during the Civil War**." <emphasis added> See Richard A. Brisbin, Jr., et al., *West Virginia Politics and Government* (Lincoln & London: University of Nebraska Press, 1996), 73, 69–70.

Web Sites

http://its2.ocs.lsu.edu/guests/pols/public_html/const.html (constitution page, contains constitutions of the world, state constitutions, bills of rights, etc.)

http://lawyers.about.com/jobs/lawyers/msubuswv.htm (U.S. State Resources: West Virginia, contains the West Virginia Constitution)

Web sites are provided for information only. The sites that follow in the chapters are not endorsed by the editor and authors of articles or Pearson Custom Publishing.

STATEHOOD FOR WEST VIRGINIA: AN ILLEGAL ACT?

Sheldon Winston

The admission of West Virginia in the midst of a war was an unusual event in the history of our nation. The circumstances of its admission leaves doubt as to whether the granting of statehood to West Virginia had a basis in law.

A relatively unknown political entity played a key role between June 17, 1861 and October 24, 1861 in the creation of West Virginia. We must look to the history of that government to determine the legality of West Virginia statehood. The restored Union-oriented government of Virginia lived briefly and with little notoriety during the War Between the States. Its fragile existence, however, was crucial in the dismemberment of Virginia and the admission of West Virginia to the Union.

The original State of Virginia was a state zealously sought by both the federal government and the emerging confederacy prior to the outbreak of hostilities at Fort Sumter, South Carolina.

Under the impact of events at Fort Sumter, however, and President Lincoln's request for 75,000 troops, Virginia cast its lot with the Confederacy.[1]

During the debate prior to the vote on secession, Waitman T. Willey, who became a United States Senator from the Restored Government of Virginia and later United States Senator from West Virginia, enunciated the position of those delegates from the mountainous western counties of Virginia.

> "I am for Virginia, as she is and was; as our forefathers created her, one and indivisible . . . . But if we are to be dragged into secession or dissension; become a mere appendage of a southern confederacy . . . our oppression may become intolerable, and I for one will be ready to accept the only alternative."[2]

Once the convention voted to leave the Union many delegates from the northwest counties left. Out of the 47 delegates from the territory that ultimately formed West Virginia, 32 voted against secession.[3] The pro-Union delegates returned to their homes and then assembled in Clarksburg on April 23rd. The hastily formed gathering recommended that each dissident county have five Representatives meet in Wheeling on May 13th.

On May 13, 1861, the first Wheeling Convention convened in Washington Hall for the purpose of reorganizing the government of Virginia and remaining in the Union.[4] Delegates from 25 counties were represented but no one individual led the convention.[5]

A committee of State and Federal Relations chaired by Francis H. Pierpont, who later became Governor of the re-organized Virginia government, was established. Under his leadership the committee submitted a report to the rebellious northwest counties.

> "1. Policy of state authorities was unwise and utterly subversive and destructive of our interests and efforts should be made to defeat the ordinance of secession in the special referendum.

> 2. If people of the state should ratify secession, a special election should be held in the northwest counties to choose delegates to meet at a second Wheeling Convention.

> 3. People of the northwest counties might appeal to Virginia to let them leave peacefully."[6]

Shortly thereafter, on May 23, 1861, the Secession Ordinance was ratified overwhelmingly by the people of Virginia. Only 20,373 Virginians voted to stay with the Union, while 125,950 cast votes to join the Confederacy.[7]

The dissident group of Virginians met again in Wheeling on June 11, 1861 and selected Arthur Boreman as Chairman. He later became West Virginia's first Governor. Delegates to the Second Wheeling Convention signed a declaration of rights on June 17th calling all state offices of Virginia vacant, and all actions of the General Assembly in Richmond to be null and void. Its acts of attempting to force "the people of Virginia to separate from and wage war against citizens of neighboring states, were therefore declared to be without authority."[8]

This same convention, on June 20th, called for the government of Virginia to be restored to the people and elected Francis Pierpont as the new Governor until such time as a new election could be held. In order to have a "restored legislature," all loyal individuals who had been elected the previous May were declared to be "The Legislature of The State."[9]

The Second Wheeling Convention assumed power, in an arbitrary fashion, by calling the existing government in Virginia illegal! The government in Virginia, in the eyes of the Second Wheeling Convention, had been restored to the Union even though Virginia as a state had overwhelmingly voted for secession.

The question arises was this new government a sincere effort on the part of loyal Virginians, or was it a subterfuge to enable separatists to set up an entirely new state separate from the parent state?

The connection between the Union-oriented Virginia government and the emergence of West Virginia becomes very clear when one considers the fact that four of the five restored Virginia Representatives in Congress later served in West Virginia's first Congressional delegation.

On October 24, 1861 the inhabitants of the Restored State of Virginia approved statehood for those living in the counties that were to become West Virginia. Loyal Virginians approved West Virginia statehood by a vote of 18,408 to 781!

In order to give West Virginia statehood a legal edifice, the consent of the restored government was of paramount importance. Article 4, Section 3 of the Federal Constitution provides that "no new state shall be formed or erected within the jurisdiction of any other state; nor any state be formed by the junction of two or more states, or parts of states, without the consent of the legislature of the states concerned, as well as of the Congress."

Actual statehood did not occur until June 20, 1863 but the creation of West Virginia was just about assured three and one-half months after the formal birth of a loyal Virginia government.

Most of the individuals consenting to the creation of West Virginia would later live in and be actively involved in its affairs. The overwhelming majority of individuals voting for the separation lived in that area that was to be torn from the "Old Dominion."

The dubious constitutional authorization for West Virginia came up often during the debate leading to statehood. Senator Powell of Kentucky questioned whether the restored legislature of Virginia represented the will of loyal Virginia.

> Out of the 160 counties that comprise the state of Virginia, less than one-fourth have assumed to act for the entire state, even within the boundaries of the new state more than half of the voters have declined to take part in the election. No Senator could pretend to claim that even a 3rd part of the people of Virginia ever had anything to do with rendering their assent to the making of this state within the territorial limits of the ancient commonwealth.[10]

Representative Joseph Segar of Virginia was alone in his delegation opposing West Virginia statehood. He maintained in a House debate that "there is no evidence that the majority of people within the counties which were to compose the new state had ever given their assent to its formation."[11] He called the statehood bill a punitive measure chastening Virginia.

In the same theme Representative James Blaine of Maine argued that "essentially the government of West Virginia was giving permission to the formation of a new state of West Virginia."[12]

Representative Thaddeus Stevens of Pennsylvania expressed an opinion held by many:

> "We may admit West Virginia as a new state, not by virtue of any provision of the Constitution, but under an absolute power which the laws of war shall give us. I shall vote for this bill upon that theory, for I will not stultify myself by supposing that we have any warrant in the constitution for this proceeding."[13]

Even after West Virginia was admitted to the Union, Senator Davis of Kentucky objected to seating its Senators in the upper house.

> "I hold that there is, legally and constitutionally no such state in existence as the state of West Virginia and consequently no Senators from such a state. My object is simply to raise a question to be put upon the record, and to have my name as a Senator recorded against the recognition of West Virginia as a state of the United States. I do not believe that the Old Dominion, like a polypus, can be separated into different segments, and each segment become a living constitutional organism in this mode. The present state of West Virginia as it has been orga-

nized, and as it is seeking representation on the floor of the Senate, is a flagrant violation of the Constitution."[14]

To the present day Virginia does not recognize the Restored Government of Virginia in its list of state administrations, or the validity of the secession by West Virginia.[15]

> "Virginia had lost a third of its area when in entire violation of the Federal Constitution, its western part had been torn away, organized and admitted to the union as the state of West Virginia."[16]

Jefferson Davis in his memoirs wrote, with considerable bitterness, on the creation of West Virginia:

> "When the state convention at Richmond passed an ordinance of secession, which was subsequently ratified by a 60,000 majority, it was as valid an act for the people of Virginia as was ever passed by a representative body. The legally expressed decision of the majority was the voice of the state. When, therefore, disorderly persons in the northwest counties assembled and declared the ordinance of secession 'to be null and void,' they rose up against the authority of the state. . . . The subsequent organization of the state of West Virginia and its separation from the state of Virginia were acts of secession. Thus we have, in their movements, insurrection, revolution and secession. . . . To admit a state under such a government is entirely unauthorized, revolutionary, subversive of the constitution and destructive of the Union of States."[17]

Even President Lincoln had doubts about the legality of admitting West Virginia to the Union.

> . . ."We can scarcely dispense with the aid of West Virginia, much less can we afford to have her against us, in Congress and in the field. Her brave and good men regard her admission into the union as a matter of life and death. They have been true to the union under many severe trials. The division of a state is dreaded as a precedent but a measure made expedient by a war is no precedent for times of peace.
>
> It is said that the admission of West Virginia is secession, and tolerated only because it is our secession. Well, if we call it by that name, there is a difference enough between secession against the constitution and secession in favor of the constitution. I believe the admission of West Virginia into the union is expedient."[18]

The restored government of Virginia existed for a brief time as a weak impotent political entity. This fragile government did make it possible, however, for West Virginia to eventually enter the Union with a modicum of constitutionality. The people of West Virginia had utilized a national crisis to acquire statehood.

The legality of West Virginia's creation and admission was obviously in doubt. Perhaps granting statehood to West Virginia was illegal, but its existence today attests to the durability of that very disputed decision.

Notes

[1] Beverly Mumford, *Virginia's Attitude Toward Slavery and Secession* (Richmond, Va.: L.H. Jenkins Inc., 1909), 271.

[2] John T. Favio, *Romance of the Boundaries* (New York: Harper & Brothers, 1926), 265.

[3] Homer F. Fansler, *History of Tucker County West Virginia* (Parsons, West Virginia: McClain Printing Company, 1962), 129.

[4] Ibid., 130.

[5] Edward Smith, *Borderland in the Civil War* (New York: MacMillan Company, 1927), 194.

[6] Ibid., 198.

[7] Charles H. Ambler, *Francis H. Pierpont* (Chapel Hill: University of North Carolina Press, 1937), 94.

[8] _____, *West Virginia* (New York: Prentice-Hall, Inc., 1940), 333.

[9] Ibid., 333.

[10] James G. Blaine, *20 Years of Congress* (Norwich, Conn.: Henry Bill Publishing Company, 1884), 462.

[11] *Ibid.*, 465.

[12] *Ibid.*, 458.

[13] *Ibid.*, 266.

[14] U.S., Congressional Globe, 38th Congress, 1st session, 1863, Part I, 1.

[15] *Hornbook of Virginia History* (Richmond, Virginia: Division of History, Virginia Department of Conservation & Development, 1949), 8.

[16] *Ibid.*, 116.

[17] Jefferson Davis, *The Rise & Fall of the Confederate Government*, 2 vols. (New York: D. Appleton and Company, 1881), II, 306.

[18] John C. Nicolay, ed., *Abe Lincoln*, 2 vols. (New York: The Century Company, 1894), II, 286.

Reprinted with permission of *West Virginia History*, State Division of Archives and History, Charleston, West Virginia, from Sheldon Winston, "Statehood for West Virginia: An Illegal Act," *West Virginia History*, Vol. 30, (April 1969), 530-534.

WHAT SHOULD A MODEL CONSTITUTION CONTAIN?

Albert L. Sturm

The major focus of this paper is on the proper contents of a state constitution as viewed by authorities on the subject . . . as a preface for further discussion it appears appropriate . . . to summarize the salient characteristics of present state constitutions with particular attention to the 1872 West Virginia document.

Nature of State Constitutions

As fundamental laws, all American state constitutions embody the basic principles of political democracy, such as popular sovereignty, and especially limited government, which is implemented through the familiar tripartite separation of powers, checks and balances, bills of rights, and by other restrictions. In addition to providing the basic structural framework of government, state constitutions express in varying detail both positive and limiting provisions for the exercise of governmental powers. They define boundaries, specify suffrage qualifications and the manner of conducting elections, and provide methods for amendment and revision. Much verbiage in these documents is accounted for by articles reflecting the complexity and diversity of functional growth—local government, finance, education, highways, corporations, welfare, agriculture, labor, and other areas of governmental activity. Unlike the makers of the Constitution of the United States, the framers of state organic laws traditionally have been much more concerned with limiting government than with enabling and vitalizing it as an effective instrument for accomplishing social objectives.

- **Number.** Until the flood of new countries achieved nationhood during the last decade, American states had more collective experience in constitution-making than the rest of the world combined. . . . American states have operated under at least 147[1] constitutions since the Declaration of Independence.[2] Louisiana leads all states with 11 constitutions; Georgia ranks second with 9; South Carolina has had 7, and Alabama and Florida have had 6 each.[3] . . . Eight states, including West Virginia have had two constitutions. . . . Thus, with almost two centuries of experience, the United States has been the world's principal potential laboratory for experimentation in constitution-making.

- **Age.** The average age of state constitutions . . . is 90.7 years.[4] Oldest is the Massachusetts document dating from 1780; the newest is the Georgia Constitution, which became effective in 1983.[5] Effective since 1872, the West Virginia Constitution is 123 years old.[6] . . . The West Virginia document is one of 36 state constitutions now effective that antedate 1900, and one of 23 adopted during the 35 years from the Civil War to 1900. This group of state organic laws, probably more than any other, reflects the general distrust of government characteristics of the period in which they were formulated.

- **Length.** State constitutions range in length from the estimated 33,387 word Louisiana document to Vermont's 6,600 word instrument. The constitution of West Virginia, with an estimated 25,550 words, ranks 21st in length among the basic charters of the 50 states . . .the West Virginia document is more than three times as long as the Constitution of the United States with its 27 amendments.[7]. . .

State Constitutional Weaknesses

Most state constitutions, like the basic charter of West Virginia, were written to provide the legal foundation of government in a far simpler society than that of today. Although most have been amended numerous times, they have failed to keep pace with the times... In my 1961 monograph on Major Constitutional Issues in West Virginia, I listed the following typical weaknesses. . . .

1. A cumbersome, unrepresentative legislature inadequately staffed[8] to perform the lawmaking function intelligently, with excessively restricted powers, often unresponsive to public needs, especially in urban areas, and subject to manipulation by selfish interests.

2. A disintegrated and enfeebled executive with power widely dispersed and responsibility divided among a large number of elected officials on all levels, and an administrative structure of great complexity featured by duplication, overlapping, inefficiency, and waste.[9]

3. A diffused, complicated, and largely uncoordinated judiciary,[10] often lacking in independence, with judges selected on a political basis and frequently without professional qualifications on the lower levels.

4. Rigid restrictions on local government that seriously impede home rule.

5. A long ballot listing a bewildering array of candidates and issues and rendering the task of even the most intelligent voter exceedingly difficult.

6. Provisions for amendment and revision so rigid, in some constitutions, as practically to deprive the people of the opportunity to alter their basic law, and, in others, so lax as to encourage too frequent changes.

7. Inclusion of a mass of detail in the constitution, blurring the distinction between constitutional and statutory law, and necessitating frequent amendments.

Anyone who is at all familiar with the 1872 West Virginia Constitution must acknowledge the applicability of these several categories of deficiencies to the document. . . .

Considered as a whole, state constitutional weaknesses can be classified in these broad categories: first, general documentary infirmities relating to style, form, and manner of presentation. Of these, probably the greatest defect is excessive detail. . . . The West Virginia constitution contains many examples of excessively detailed provisions that are predominately statutory in character.[11] Obsolete sections also clutter up much of the document—exemplified in provisions relating to heredity emoluments (III, 19), fighting of duels (IV, 10), ineligibility of salaried railroad officials for the legislature (VI, 13), and participation in the Civil War (VIII, 20). Some provisions have been rendered obsolete and invalid because of changes in the national constitution—e.g., restriction of suffrage to males (IV,1) and segregated public schools (XII, 8). Other documentary weaknesses include sundry inconsistencies resulting mainly from failure to reconcile additions with other conflicting provisions.[12]

The second principal category compromises the many substantive deficiencies which are exemplified in a disintegrated, enfeebled executive with widely dispersed powers and divided responsibility . . . and in rigid restrictions on local home rule. . . .

. . . Although no "ideal" constitution exists for all the states, and probably never will because of great geographical, demographic, social and other differences, there is general agreement on some basic common qualities. Here is a representative list.[13]

1. *Consistency with the Constitution of the United States.* Under the American federal system the national constitution, laws of the United States are the supreme law of the land. All state law, both constitutional and statutory, that is contrary to valid national law, as interpreted by the United States Supreme Court, is unenforceable and invalid. . . .

2. *Provision of a sound basic framework of government with a proper balance among the three branches. . . .*

3. *Extension of ample power to governmental organs to discharge their proper functions, but with appropriate controls to curb abuse of power.*

4. *Inclusion of a bill of rights.* The national constitution affords some protection to basic personal and property rights, but this is usually minimal and is sufficient to prevent encroachment by state authority on human liberties.

5. *Provision for orderly procedures for changing the constitution that strike a balance between extremes of rigidity and laxity.* Some state constitutions have gone unchanged for decades because of a rigid amending procedure; others, can be so readily altered that they contain a great volume of extraneous matter.

6. *Inclusion in the document of fundamental matters, excluding substance of a temporary or detailed nature characteristic of statutory law.* . . . A constitution containing only fundamentals is flexible because its phraseology is necessarily general. General language is capable of interpretation that is necessary to meet changing conditions. Herein lies the strength of the national constitution, which has kept pace with the social order mainly through interpretation and adaptation rather than formal amendment.

7. *Use of clear, direct, simple language readily intelligible to the average citizen, and arrangement of provisions in logical order; conversely, avoidance of obscure and technical phraseology, inconsistencies, obsolete provisions, and poor organization.*

These are widely recognized by students of state government as generally hallmarks of excellence in state constitution-making.

There is somewhat less agreement on the detailed substantive contents of state organic law. However, comparative analysis of provisions in the new state constitutions, the *Model State Constitution*, and the writings of specialists in the various areas of state constitutional systems indicates a substantial body of agreement. . . . Here are some of the salient features of the major constitutional areas:

- **Bill of Rights:** A set of guarantees of personal and political freedom, including both traditional substantive and procedural rights and those that have recently emerged (such as "equal treatment" or "anti discrimination" guarantees, protection of persons in the course of legislative investigations and administrative proceedings, etc.).

- **Suffrage and Elections:** Provisions for broad participation in the electoral process with minimum restriction on voter qualifications, especially regarding residence requirements for participation in presidential elections; state elections in odd-numbered years, to avoid overlapping with national elections and issues; omission of organizational and procedural details for conducting elections, which would be determined by the legislature.

- **The Legislative Branch:** A continuous body (preferably unicameral), meeting annually as provided by law, with membership based solely on population, elected in single-member districts for two-year terms (if unicameral); automatic reapportionment after each decennial census by a non-legislative agent; flexibility in legislative organization and procedure with provision for adequate staffing; minimum restrictions on legislative power; legislative post audit.

- **The Executive:** Integration of executive power in a Governor elected for a four-year term and eligible for re-election (alternative: election of the Governor and Lieutenant Governor as a team on the same ticket); extensive executive and administrative powers, including the power to initiate administrative reorganization subject to legislative disallowance, the item veto and with ample time to consider legislative bills; limitation of the number of administrative departments to a maximum of twenty into which agencies would be integrated on the basis of major purpose; clear provision for succession to the Governorship and reasonable procedure for determining disability; general provision for a merit system.

- **The Judiciary:** A unified judicial system with general provision for two or three levels of courts and legislative power to create additional courts as needed; selection of judges by gubernatorial appointment (Missouri—ABA Plan) to serve during good behavior, but with definite provision for removal; administrative direction of the courts by the Chief Justice; prescription of civil and criminal jurisdiction by the legislature; vestment in the Supreme Court of extensive rule-making power covering practice, procedure, and judicial administration.

- **Finance:** An executive budget; public expenditures only in accordance with appropriations; minimum limitations on legislative power to tax, borrow, and spend; contraction of state debt only for projects or objects authorized by law; general flexibility in financial administration.

- **Local Government and Intergovernmental Relations:** Home rule for cities and counties with provision for optional charter systems; express authorization for the interchange of powers and functions among local governmental units; broad express authorization for cooperative relationships, consolidation, and sharing and transfer of functions among units of government.

- **Other State Functions:** General rather than detailed substantive provisions on governmental functions, such as education, conservation, corporations, etc.; statement of a liberal rule of judicial construction to guard against judicial findings of implied limitations.

- **Constitutional Change:** Provision for constitutional amendment and revision that permits the people, as well as the legislature, to initiate changes; express authorization for legislative proposal of amendments and constitutional conventions (and, optionally, the constitutional initiative); automatic periodic referendum on the question of calling a constitutional convention; mandatory submission of all proposed constitutional changes to the electorate. . . .

Notes

[1] Sturm originally listed 138 constitutions with Louisiana and Georgia having had ten and eight respectively, but recent sources reveal a gain of nine new constitutions. Also Louisiana and Georgia each gained a constitution. See *Book of the States*, 1990-91 (Lexington, Ky.: Council on State Governments, 1990)... <ed.,>; John Kincaid, "State Constitutions in the Federal System," Annals, 496 (March, 1988), 12-22.

[2] Not included in this figure are Hawaii's five constitutions as a kingdom and as a republic, and the Constitution of Puerto Rico adopted in 1952.

[3] The author generated his original data from questionnaires sent to 125 correspondents in the fifty states and Puerto Rico. <ed.,>.

[4] As of November, 1987 <ed>.

[5] Sturm originally listed the Florida Constitution as the "newest"...<ed.,>.

[6] The author originally listed it as 97 years old. <ed.,>.

[7] The author's constitutional paginations have been updated. <ed.,>. The national constitution with twenty-seven amendments contains approximately 7,285 words.

[8] The West Virginia Legislature is now assisted by Legislative Services. <ed.,>.

[9] Sturm's generalization no longer completely holds for West Virginia. For example WV reorganized its executive branch in 1977. Today the executive department for-

mally consists of an elected Governor, Secretary of State, Auditor, Treasurer, Commissioner of Agriculture and Attorney General. Important new powers were given to the Governor: in 1968 with the "Modern Budget Amendment" the Governor was given sole responsibility for budget-making; his appointive powers were strengthened, etc. (Thomas Dye in his *Politics in States and Communities*, 5th ed. now lists the WV Governor's appointive powers as very strong); Dye likewise depicts the WV Governor's veto powers as "strong."

10   Article VIII was amended in November 1974 and now provides for a unified court system. Also, the justice of the peace courts and fee system were replaced with the magistrate courts thereby remedying one of Sturm's strongest criticisms of the state judiciary.<ed.,>.

11   Especially in Article VI (Legislature),... and X (Taxation and Finance); most or all parts of Article XI (Corporations), XII (Education), and XIII (Land Titles) do not belong in a "model" constitution.

12   See Albert L. Sturm, *The Need for Constitutional Revision* in West Virginia (Morgantown, WV: Bureau of Government Research, 1950), passim.

13   *Ibid.*

A CASE IN CONSTITUTIONAL REFORM, THE WEST VIRGINIA GOVERNOR'S SUCCESSION AMENDMENT

Donald R. Andrews

Arch A. Moore, Jr., was elected to his second four year term as Governor of the State of West Virginia in November 1972. He was only the third person in the State's 109 year history to serve more than one term and the first Governor to have the opportunity to serve eight consecutive years.

It was an historic moment. Such moments cannot be planned, and they do not simply happen. How did this one come about? It was politics, the desire for constitutional reform, and a planned strategy that worked for one political party, but backfired on the other.

Background

West Virginia became a state June 20, 1863, on which day Arthur I. Boreman took the oath of office as the State's first Governor. The West Virginia Constitution of 1863 set the term of the Governor at two years. It did not limit the number of terms that a Governor could serve, and was silent regarding whether a Governor could serve additional terms. Consequently, a Governor could serve any number of additional terms to which he was elected.

Boreman resigned during his third consecutive term after serving five years and eight months as Governor. No other West Virginia Governor has served three consecutive terms.[1] He was subsequently elected to the United States Senate by the West Virginia Legislature.

When Moore began his seventh year as Governor in 1975, no person had served more than six years in that office. West Virginia's fourth Governor, John J. Jacob, had the unique opportunity to serve one two-year term under the 1863 constitution, and one four-year term under the 1872 constitution.[2]

Article 7, section 1 of the 1872 constitution set the Governor's term at four years. Article 7, section 4 specified:

> "The Governor shall be ineligible to said office for the four years next succeeding the term for which he was elected." A constitutional amendment, ratified in 1902, changed that provision to: "The Governor shall not be eligible to said office for the four years next succeeding the term for which he was elected."

Although the language changed, the meaning and effect remained the same. No person could serve two consecutive terms in office as Governor. Until the Governors' Succession Amendment was ratified in 1970, this prohibition remained intact.

Term Limitations, the 1863 and 1872 Conventions

The 1863 West Virginia Constitutional Convention considered two proposals.[3] One set the term of office for a Governor at four years, but prohibited a person from serving two consecutive terms. The other provided for a two-year term of office, but allowed a Governor to serve unlimited terms. From reading the constitutional proceedings, one can only conclude that opinion on the two proposals was about equal. In the end, the latter proposal was adopted and ratified as part of the 1863 Constitution.[4]

During the 1872 West Virginia Constitutional Convention, the same proposals were considered. This time the four-year term limitation with a prohibition on serving a consecutive term won out.[5] For ninety-eight years (1872–1970), this provision remained in effect.

Why did the delegates to the two conventions want to limit gubernatorial terms? Eighty-seven years had passed since the Declaration of Independence was drafted and seventy-four from the founding of the United States; nevertheless, the fear of strong executives especially governors remained from the British treatment of their American colonies. Early Americans had faith in legislative bodies, which the people believed truly represented their collective will and interests. The goal was a strong legislature and a weak Governor.

Politics of Reform

Finally in 1970, the citizens ratified the governors' succession amendment, allowing a person to serve two consecutive terms as Governor.[6] What brought about this change 107 years after West Virginia became a state?

As the years passed, people gradually lost their fear of governors. Concomitantly, although independently, they realized the merit, and finally the need for a stronger Governor. Democrats and Republicans alike began to see the advantages in having their incumbent governors elected to a second consecutive term.

By 1950 scholars, progressive governmental leaders and some legislators had advocated the strengthening of the Governor's office. One scholar, in particular, pushed for general constitutional revision. Albert L. Sturm, Professor of Political Science, West Virginia University, in "Major Constitutional Issues in West Virginia," 1961, commented:

> "The four-year term <for Governor> is in conformity with modern practice and follows the current trend in state constitutions. West Virginia, however, is one of fifteen states in which the Governor may not succeed himself. In six states, he is limited to two consecutive terms.... The present prohibition against two consecutive terms in West Virginia guarantees disruption of state administration every four years; it deprives the state of the services of experienced leaders whose administrations may be exceptionally meritorious; it weakens party leadership; and most important, it deprives the people of the power (without amending the Constitution) to reelect their own representatives. . . . Ideally, the Governor should be eligible for as many terms as the people desire him to serve."[7]

It was finally in 1966 that constitutional reformers deemed the time favorable to amend Article 7, Section 4 of the state constitution to allow a person to serve two consecutive four-year terms as Governor. The following amendment was submitted to the voters for ratification in November 1966:

> ". . . A person who has been elected, or has served as Governor during all or any part of two consecutive terms, shall be ineligible for the office of Governor during any part of the term immediately following the second of the two consecutive terms."[8]

This first attempt to strengthen the Governorship failed. The vote for ratification was 142,265 (35.3%) and against 260,352 (64.7%).[9] In fact, all of the five constitutional amendments that were submitted to the voters were rejected. How can this defeat be explained in view of the optimism of the constitutional reformers?

The data in Table 1.1, "Amendments to the West Virginia Constitution, 1880 to 1989" show that the larger picture of constitutional reform in West Virginia is actually a success story. A majority 52% (58) of the proposed amendments to the state constitution were ratified by the voters. The reformers only had two really bad years, 1962 and 1966, where no amendments were ratified.

After the defeat of the constitutional amendments in 1966, W. E. (Ned) Chilton III, publisher of the *Charleston Gazette* and former member of the House of Delegates (1953–1961), declared that the public had turned against the Legislature and its proposals for constitutional revision. He said that only through a dedicated effort to improve the legislature's public image and process could one anticipate future constitutional reforms. Many governmental leaders agreed with him.

Citizens' Advisory Commission

The West Virginia Legislature during its 1967 Regular Session took a significant step toward improving its image and setting the stage for important constitutional changes. It created the Citizens Advisory Commission to the Legislature of West Virginia. The commission was comprised of thirty-two members: the President of the Senate and the Speaker of the House as ex officio members; three other senators and three other delegates; and twenty-four private citizens. The citizen members came from across the state and represented diverse walks of life. They were educators, lawyers, bankers, business executives, labor leaders, heads of statewide organizations, and members of the news media. All were well known and highly respected.[10]

Prior to the November 1968 general election, the Citizens' Advisory Commission endorsed and worked actively for ratification of the modern budget amendment. During its 1967 regular session the Legislature took the steps necessary to submit the amendment to the voters. The Commission formed a speakers bureau comprised of its members and staff, who gave speeches and appeared on television and radio panels throughout the state. They also wrote editorials and issued press releases which many newspapers printed verbatim.

Table 1.1 Amendments to the West Virginia Constitution, 1880-1989

Time Period	Proposed Amendments	Ratified	Rejected	% Approved	% Rejected
1880–88	6	3	3	50	50
1890–98	0	0	0	—	—
1900–08	7	5	2	71	29
1910–18	6	2	4	33	66
1920–28	6	4	2	66	33
1930–38	12	7	5	58	42
1940–48	7	3	4	43	57
1950–58	11	9	2	82	18
1960	3	3	0	100	—
1962	5	0	5	—	100
1964	1	1	0	100	—
1966	5	0	5	—	100
1968	2	2	0	100	—
1970	3	3	0	100	—
1972	4	4	0	100	—
1974	1	1	0	100	—
1978	2	0	2	—	100
1980	2	2	0	100	—
1981	1	0	1	—	100
1982	3	2	1	66	33
1984	5	4	1	80	20
1986	6	3	3	50	50
1988	2	0	2	—	100
1989	3	0	3	—	100
Totals	111	58	53	54	46

Source: Darrell E. Holmes, editor, *West Virginia Blue Book*, 1993, "Constitutional Amendments Submitted," (Charleston, WV: R.R. Donnelley and Sons, 1993), 530-535.

Their work, combined with the cooperation of the media and the efforts of other groups and organizations wanting better government, resulted in the passage of the modern budget amendment. It was approved by a vote of 323,560 (67%) to 159,255 (33%), a margin of 164,305 votes.[11] That was strong approval, considering that the voters had rejected ten of the previous eleven amendments submitted to them, and that the amendment concentrated all executive budget-making power in the Governor, rather than the seven-member Board of Public Works.[12]

The Governor was now responsible for budget formulation, execution and implementation. He could veto the budget bill or reduce any item it contained. The amendment also strengthened the Legislature's role in the budget process by broadening its powers to increase, strike or reduce items in the budget the Governor submitted. Finally, West Virginia had a strong executive budget system. It was a significant step toward better government in West Virginia.

Also, the voters in the November 1968 election ratified a road development amendment which authorized the sale of bonds (worth $350,000,000) to build state roads. This amendment passed by an even larger margin than the Modern Budget Amendment. Voter attitudes on approving constitutional amendments had turned around. This was due to the reputation and work of the Citizens' Advisory Commission.

In December of 1968, the Commission submitted its final report to the Legislature. It recommended that seven sections of the state constitution be amended, and had its staff prepare drafts of those sections with several alternatives. It commented that the constitutional changes were vital to the improvement of the West Virginia Legislature and that a major effort should be made to achieve these changes.

The Legislature took that to heart and started to work on these proposals during its 1968 Regular Session. During its 1970 Regular Session, the Legislature combined into one amendment the seven constitutional changes that the Commission had recommended to strengthen the Legislature. It then took the steps necessary to place the amendment on the ballot for the 1970 general election. The amendment would allow 60 day unrestricted legislative sessions every year; split sessions after gubernatorial elections every fourth year to give the incoming Governor time to prepare his own executive budget; and the creation and appointment of a Citizens' Legislative Compensation Commission.[13]

This Commission would recommend what the compensation and expenses of members of the legislature would be, and the Legislature could reject, accept or lower the recommended amounts, but could not increase them. The Legislative Compensation Commission was an innovative approach to setting legislators' compensation and expenses, and superseded two plans previously developed by the Citizens Advisory Commission.

The legislative leaders had three reasons for thinking the time was opportune to put a governors' succession amendment before the voters. First, the Citizens' Advisory Commission had prepared a favorable climate for constitutional reform. Second, they believed allowing a Governor to succeed himself would strengthen the office of Governor, result in better government, and further enhance the value to be derived from the previously ratified modern budget amendment. Third, it looked as though the gubernatorial candidates in 1972 would be the incumbent, Republican Arch A. Moore, Jr., and Secretary of State John D. Rockefeller IV, a Democrat. Both candidates had great personal appeal and popularity. Both political parties were convinced their candidate would win in a head-to-head contest. To make that possible a governors' succession amendment would have to allow the incumbent Moore to succeed himself. Such an amendment would have the greatest chance of ratification.

The Speaker of the House of Delegates, Ivor F. Boiarsky, and the Chairman of the House Judiciary Committee, J.E. (Ned) Watson, directed the Office of Legislative Services to draft a "constitutional amendment to allow a Governor to succeed himself for one additional term." The amendment rejected by the voters in 1966 had essentially the same language with one difference. The new proposal was to state clearly that the Governor who was in office when the amendment was ratified could hold one additional term of office. This new provision made a big difference in the outcome when it was put before the voters.

The amendment put before the voters in the 1970 general election read as follows:

> "None of the executive officers mentioned in this article shall hold any other office during his term of service. A person who has been elected or who has served as Governor during all or any part of two consecutive terms shall be ineligible for the office of Governor during any part of the term immediately following the second of the two consecutive terms. The person holding the office of Governor when this section is ratified shall not be prevented from holding the office of Governor during the term immediately following the term he is then serving."[14]

In the 1970 general election, the legislative improvement, the governors' succession and the abolition of the capitation tax were all ratified by the voters. The governors' succession amendment received a vote of 213,758 (57.6%) to 157,597 (42.4%), a margin of 56,161 votes.[15]

Prognostications and expectations about whom the gubernatorial candidates would be in the 1972 general election were correct. Incumbent Governor Moore was unopposed in the primary and Jay Rockefeller won easily over Lee M. Kenna and Bob Myers. The race was on between Moore and Rockefeller.[16]

Rockefeller was favored to win, but the predictions were wrong. His stand on abolishing surface mining in the state hurt him. Moore capitalized on Rockefeller not being a native of the state. Above all, Moore, as an experienced Republican in a heavily Democratic state, was a political phenomenon and the consummate politician. He had served one term in the West Virginia House of Delegates and six consecutive terms (1956–68) in the United States House of Representatives. Moore defeated Rockefeller 423,817 votes (54.7%) to 350,462 (45.3%), with a margin of 73,355 votes.[17]

Largely because these two men were expected to be the candidates opposing each other in the 1972 general election, and because each political party believed their man would win, West Virginia now has one of the seven strongest Governor's offices in the United States. The Citizens Advisory Commission also played an important role by creating a positive climate for constitutional change.

Later Jay Rockefeller also benefited from the Governors' succession amendment. He was elected Governor in 1976 and served two consecutive terms.

Notes

1 John G. Morgan, *West Virginia Governors* (Charleston, West Virginia: Newspaper Agency Corp., 1960), 9.

2 *Ibid.*, 16.

3 See Charles H. Amber, editor, *Debates and Proceedings of the First Constitutional Convention of West Virginia (1861–1863)* (Huntington, West Virginia: Gentry Brothers Printers, 1863), vol.3.

4 *Ibid.*

5 See *Journal of Constitutional Convention of 1872* (Charleston, West Virginia: Henry S. Walker, 1872).

6 See Darrell E. Holmes, Clerk of the Senate, editor, *West Virginia Blue Book*, 1993, "Constitutional Amendments Submitted," (Charleston, West Virginia: R. R. Donnelley and Sons, 1993), 530–535.

7 Albert L. Sturm, *Major Constitutional Issues in West Virginia* (Morgantown, West Virginia: Bureau of Government Research, West Virginia University, 1961), 67–68.

8 See *Acts of the Fifty-Seventh Legislature of West Virginia*, Chapter 11, 780.

9 Holmes, *loc. cit.*

10 The Citizens Advisory Commission on the Legislature of West Virginia was a thirty-two member citizen-legislator body created by Senate Concurrent Resolution No. 12, adopted by the Legislature on March 10, 1967. Legislators serving on the Commission were Senators Howard W. Carson (President of the Senate), John H. Bowling, Jr., J. Frank Deem, and Tracy W. Hylton, and Delegates H. Laban White (Speaker, House of Delegates), Wilfred L. Dickerson, Brereton C. Jones, and J. E. Watson. Citizen members included Earle T. Andrews, President, Pennsylvania Glass Sand Corp.; Thomas J. Boyd, General Manager, Follansbee Steel Corp.; W. E. Chilton, III, Publisher, *The Charleston Gazette;* James H. Davis, III, Attorney at Law; Mr. W. A. Davis, President, The Peoples' Bank of Mullins; D. Boone Dawson, Attorney at Law; William D. Davis, Editor, *The Fairmont Times;* B. W. Fertig, State Representative, Brotherhood of Railroad Trainmen; Richard E. Ford, Attorney at Law; David L Francis, Chairman of the Board, Princess Coals, Inc.; Carl M. Frasure, Dean, College of Arts and Sciences, WVU; J. Taylor Frazier, President, Bluefield Supply Company; J. Duane Gorman, Vice President, Monongahela Power Company; Harry Hamm, Editor, *Wheeling News-Register;* Herbert H. Henderson, State President, State Conference of Branches of the NAACP; Mrs. Howard J. Jackson, President, League of Women Voters of WV; Hugh A. Latimer, Vice President, The C & P Telephone Company of WV; Mrs. Delmas Miller, President, WV Federation of Women's Clubs; Ford R. Morrow, retired Public Affairs Manager, Eastern Region, Kaiser Aluminum and Chemical Corp.; Miles C. Stanley, President, WV Labor Federation, AFL-CIO; Luke E. Terry, Counsel, West Virginia Farm Bureau; C. J. Urbaniak, President, District 31, UMWA; A. Hale Watkins, Secretary-Treasurer, WV Oil and Natural Gas Assoc.; and William G. Wilson, Attorney at Law.

    The author, then a Research Assistant in the Office of Legislative Services, served as the Staff Director of the Commission.

11 Holmes, *loc. cit.*

12 Board of Public Works is comprised of Governor, secretary of state, state auditor, state treasurer, commissioner of agriculture, attorney general, and superintendent of free schools.

13 See *Acts of the Fifty-Ninth Legislature of West Virginia*, Chapter 22, 124.

14 *Ibid*, Chapter 23, 133.

15 Holmes, *loc. cit.*

16 See Howard W. Carson, Clerk of the Senate, Compiler and Editor, *West Virginia Blue Book*, 1972, "General Election Returns," (Charleston, West Virginia: Jarrett Printing Company, 1973), 537.

17 *Ibid.*, 1973, 632.

CHAPTER TWO

Political Participation and Political Parties

INTRODUCTION

The previous chapter examined some of the political events that helped shape West Virginia's place in the federal constitutional system. An important aspect of a constitutional system is the citizens' political rights to participate in the decisions of government that effect their well being. In this sense "political participation is defined as those actions of private citizens by which they seek to influence or to support government and politics."[1] Or as one influential writer put it: "Popular participation in politics is the very definition of democracy."[2]

In this chapter we will discuss electoral participation (especially the 1996 gubernatorial and 2000 presidential elections), interest group and party activity in West Virginia, and examine some of the more important explanations[3] of Democratic Party dominance since 1932.[4] We will also examine some of the possible reasons for the serious decline in West Virginia voter turnout from its all-time high in the 1960s and 1970s.

Characteristics of the West Virginia Voters

"Much of the variation in voter turnout in the states is explained by the *socioeconomic characteristics* of their population. Indeed, most of the variation in voter turnout among the states can be attributed to differences in educational level, urbanization, median family income, and percentage black or Hispanic."[5] An examination of the demographic information in Table 2.1 shows that West Virginia ranks substantially below the U.S. national average in most of these categories. Because higher socioeconomic variables tend to correlate with higher turnout rates, one would expect that West Virginians historically would participate at rates considerably *less* than their wealthier neighbors. Many of the states in the South Atlantic region have higher indices of socioeconomic development than West Virginia, yet the Mountain State's past participation rates in Presidential elections, especially in the 1960s and 1970s, were surprisingly high as shown in Tables 2.2 and 2.3.

Other variables also influence turnout in elections. The saliency of the election itself can be a factor.[6] Presidential elections due to their extensive media coverage normally generate higher turnouts. This can be seen when John F. Kennedy brought his high profile campaign to West Virginia in the 1960 Presidential Preference Primary (see Ernst article). The state's turnout rate in the presidential election for that year was an all-time high of 77.93% of eligible voters voting. An important aspect of Kennedy's success was the work of the Democratic Party county organizations which effectively mobilized Democratic voters and got them to the polls.[7]

Interparty Competition

Another variable effecting turnout is interparty competition. Studies of voter turnout show that "the more vigorous the competition between the parties, the greater the interest of citizens in the elections, and the larger the turnout."[8]

West Virginia's record of interparty competition seen in Table 2.4 shows little competition through the years as West Virginians are in the habit of mostly sending Democrats to Washington and to Charleston. Not surprisingly, West Virginia is classified by some political scientists as a "modified one-party state."[9]

Table 2.1 Selected Characteristics of West Virginians Contrasted with the U.S. Population

Characteristic	W.V.		U.S.	Year
Personal Income per Person	$19,973	(49th)	$27,279	1999
Percentage of Population Below the Poverty Level	17.8%	(3rd)	12.7%	1998
Social Security	20.8%	(1st)	15.9%	1994
Percentage High School Graduates	66%	(48th)	75.2%	1994
Percent College Graduates	17.9%	(48th)	25.2%	1999
Unemployment Rate	6.6%	(1st)	4.2%	1999
Infant Deaths per 1000	8.0%	(16th)	7.2%	1998
Heart Disease Death Rate per 100,000 people	393	(1st)	286	1994
Cancer Death Rate per 100,000 people	257	(2nd)	204	1994
Violent Crime Rate per 100,000 people	351	(30th)	525	1999
Median Age	38.9	(1st)	35.3	2000
Percent Black Population	3.2%		13.3%	2000

Source: *Statistical Abstract of the United States, 1999*, U.S. Bureau of the Census, Washington, D.C.; http://quickfacts.census.gov/gfd/states/54000.html

Table 2.2 Percent of Voting-Age Population Voting—
West Virginia and Selected States

	Percentage Voting for President						
	1976	1980	1984	1988	1992	1996	2000
U.S.	53.5%	52.6%	53.1%	50.1%	55.2%	49.08%	51.3
Southern Region							
MD	49.3	50.0	51.4	49.1	53.4	46.6	51.6
DC	32.2	35.4	43.2	39.4	42.5	44.0	49.1
VA	47.0	47.6	50.6	48.2	50.6	47.5	53.0
WV	**57.2**	**52.8**	**51.4**	**46.7**	**50.6**	**44.9**	**45.8**
NC	43.0	43.4	47.3	43.4	50.6	45.5	50.3
SC	40.3	40.4	40.6	38.9	45.0	41.5	46.6
GA	42.0	41.2	42.0	38.7	46.8	42.4	43.8
FL	49.2	48.7	48.4	44.7	50.2	48.0	50.6
Neighboring States							
PA	54.2	51.9	53.9	50.0	54.3	49.0	53.7
OH	55.1	55.4	57.9	55.1	60.6	54.3	55.8
KY	48.0	49.9	50.8	48.1	53.7	47.4	51.6

Source: *Statistical Abstract of the United States*, 1987, 1988; "State of West Virginia Office of the secretary of State Election Returns—1988," Ken Hechler, 170; Election Data Services, 1989, 1995, 1996; http://www.fec.gov/pages/2000turnout/reg&to00.htm.

Table 2.3 Presidential Elections Percentage Turnouts—
1960 Through 1996—Top 30 States and ARC States

TOP 30 (voting age population)						ARC States		
1.	MN	70.63	16.	WY	61.62 *	1.	OH	59.6
2.	SD	67.72	17.	IL	61.61 *	2.	**WV**	**59.09**
3.	UT	67.24	18.	CO	61.30 *	3.	PA	57.27
4.	ND	66.75	19.	RI	61.23 *	4.	NY	54.17
5.	MT	66.31	20.	MI	61.19 *	5.	MD	51.46
6.	ID	66.24	21.	IN	61.13 *	6.	KY	50.79
7.	ME	66.24	22.	MO	60.42 *	7.	TN	48.91
8.	WI	65.71	23.	NE	59.86 *	8.	NC	47.52
9.	IA	65.35	24.	OH	59.60 *	9.	VA	46.24
10.	CT	64.54	25.	DE	59.41 *	10.	MS	45.67
11.	OR	63.53	26.	NJ	59.39 *	11.	AL	45.62
12.	NH	62.69	27.	KS	59.32 *	12.	GA	40.69
13.	MA	62.65	28.	**WV**	**59.09** *	13.	SC	40.15
14.	VT	62.53	29.	PA	57.26 *			
15.	WA	61.75	30.	OK	56.16 *			

Source: *Election Data Services*, 1989; "State of West Virginia Election Returns—1988," ". . . 1992," Ken Hechler. http://www.FEC.gov/VOTREGIS/TURN/MINN.htm ARC States (Appalachian Regional Commission) include all of WV, 2/3 of PA, a small portion of VA, 1/4 of OH, about 1/2 of KY, 2/3 of TN, 1/4 of NC, about 1/8 of SC, 1/4 of GA, 1/2 of AL, and 1/4 of MS, about 1/4 of NY, and 1/8 MD.

Table 2.4 Interparty Competition in West Virginia

Composition of the State Legislature
(D = Democrat; R = Republican)

Elections: Year	House of Delegates		Senate	
	D	R	D	R
1978	74	26	26	8
1980	78	22	27	7
1982	87	13	31	3
1984	73	27	30	4
1986	78	22	27	7
1988	81	19	29	5
1990	74	26	33	1
1992	79	21	32	2
1994	69	31	26	8

Composition of West Virginia's Delegation in Congress
(D = Democrat; R = Republican)

Session	U.S. Representatives		U.S. Senators	
	D	R	D	R
96th	4	0	2	0
97th	4	0	2	0
98th	4	0	2	0
99th	4	0	2	0
100th	4	0	2	0
101st	4	0	2	0
102nd	4	0	2	0
103rd	4	0	2	0
104th	3	0	2	0
105th	3	0	2	0
106th	3	0	2	0

Source: *Statistical Abstract of the United States,* 1999; "State of West Virginia Office of the Secretary of State Election Returns—1992," http://thomas.loc.gov/

The extent of Democratic dominance is revealed by examining the party's electoral successes, office by office, since 1932:

> "Of the 121 terms of statewide public offices filled by election from 1932 to 1994, all but seven were captured by Democrats, and three of the seven Republican terms were won by Arch A. Moore, Jr. Moreover, Democrats have constituted a majority in both houses of the state legislature since 1930 and currently are the majority party in all but nine lightly populated counties (Morgan, Grant, Preston, Upshur, Dodridge, Tyler, Ritchie, Jackson and Roane); the Republican majorities in these nine counties are relatively slim."[10]

Figure 2.1 West Virginia's Congressional Districts

First District	Second District	Thir
Barbour	Berkley	Boo
Brooke	Braxton	Cab
Doddridge	Calhoun	Faye
Gilmer (from 2nd)	Clay	Gre
Grant	Hampshire	Linc
Hancock	Hardy	Log
Harrison	Jackson	McI
Motion	Jefferson	Mer
Marshall	Kanawha	Min
Mineral	Lewis	Mor
Monongalia	Mason	Nlc
Ohio	Morgan	2nd
Pleasants	Pendleton	Poc
Preston	Putnam	Rale
Ritchie	Randolph	Sur
Taylor	Roane	Wa
Tucker	Upshur	Wet
Tyler	Wirt	Wyc
Wetzel		
Wood		

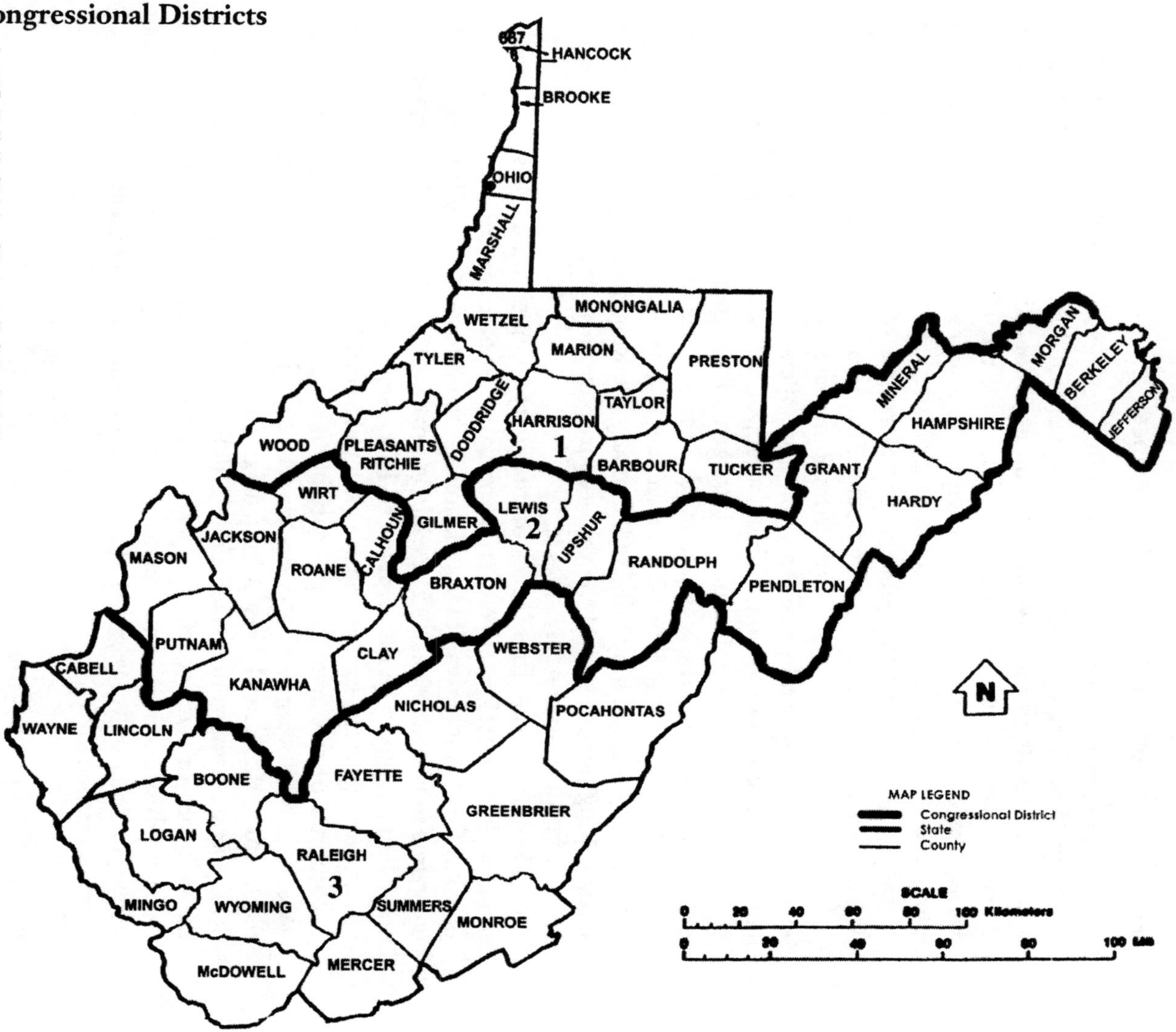

Source: Department of Commerce, Bureau of the Census, Economics and Statistics Administration.

Reasons for Democratic Party Dominance

There are at least three reasons for the Democratic Party's electoral dominance in West Virginia's politics. The first is found in the state's violent labor history, especially in the mobilization and union building efforts of the United Mine Workers in the southern coal fields (see the Phillips article). In other words, the group least likely to participate in politics—the working man—was motivated and organized to participate. This participation was enhanced by the Great Depression and the subsequent emergence of a coalition between the United Mine Workers and the Democratic Statehouse Organization.[11]

The second reason is found with the inability of the Republican Party to effectively organize and present a viable slate of candidates for the many offices contested in county elections. This "organizational inability" even extends to statewide races. For example, in the 1992 general election, the Republican Party only contested five of the seven statewide offices, seven of the open state Senate seats, and sixteen of the fifty-three circuit court judgeships.[12]

Concerning the May 9th, 2000 Primary the Republicans did a little better in contesting twenty-four of the thirty-four state senate seats and eighty-five of the one hundred state house seats.[13]

The third reason for the lack of interparty competition in West Virginia is found with the state's relatively large population of older citizens. West Virginia now has the oldest per capita population in the union with a median age of 38.6 compared to Florida's 38.3.[14] These older citizens tend to expect that the Democratic Party, rather than the Republican Party, will meet their needs with greater government services, such as, health care and Social Security maintenance. The implications of this "elderly age" variable is that older citizens who are more dependent on government services tend to be "liberal." This is supported in a recent study that found West Virginia "as the most liberal state relative to its demographic composition" (see Table 2.1).[15] The study also found evidence for the influence of state culture on party and ideological identification. That is, "state-level differences in partisanship and ideology are a function of unique state <political> cultures rather than the different group characteristics of the states' residences."[16]

Wither the Civic Culture?

Daniel Elazar, an authority on political culture, tells us that "every political system is embedded in a political culture."[17] He defines political culture "as the particular pattern of orientation to political action . . . a shared framework of values that establishes the goals of politics. . . ."[18] Within the American political culture there are important variations or subcultures in the states which Elazar feels influences the development of political institutions, and their methods of operation.

Political culture in West Virginia has historically meant that blue collar workers (especially coal miners) were politically socialized into a *civic*[19] culture through the mobilization and union building efforts of the United Mine Workers in the Southern Appalachian coal fields.

The problem, of course, with any analysis of West Virginia's political culture is that the patterns of attitudes and behavior recorded in a particular study frequently are blurred over time due to continued mobility of the population and the impact of the national culture through the media (public, commercial television and radio, movies, etc.). This idea has led some analysts to suggest a dominant national political culture—the notion of "The United *State* of America"—and significantly diminished state cultures if they exist at all.[20]

West Virginia is certainly part of the national culture. Those who argue for the diminished influence of state political cultures point to the role of the national media in shaping West Virginians' attitudes about politics. Much of what we know of politics we know through the media. There is evidence that frequency of reading about a political campaign in newspapers is positively related to voter turnout. Decreased readership is estimated to account for about 20 percent of the recent decline (1980s) in turnout.[21] Other observers of electoral politics think that television is the "cause" of much of the decline in voting. They see television teaching the potential voter to be a spectator and not a participant. Also, television newscasts create "videomalaise," cynicism, frustration and detachment from the system.[22]

During recent years television and newspaper coverage of the currupt activities of prominent West Virginia politicians[23] has contributed to negative citizen attitudes as reported in statewide West Virginia polls. The extent that these negative news stories have "caused" the decline in voting in West Virginia or the failure of the 400,000 nonregistered voters to register is unclear. These "videomalaise" studies need to be replicated.

There are a wealth of reasons why people choose not to vote[24] and West Virginians like other Americans are not immune from these reasons. Inspection of the data in Table 2.3 reveals that although the voter turnout rates have declined in recent elections and West Virginia has slipped in rank from 20th to 28th in turnout rates during the last thirty-six years, the state still ranks in the top thirty in turnout.

Before we conclude that the civic culture is alive and well, we should recall that West Virginians in the last three presidential elections had disappointing turnouts of 50.6%, 44.9%, and 45.8%, respectively. In the 2000 Presidential Election West Virginia ranked 45th in eligible voters voting. West Virginians also tend to vote the straight Democratic Party ticket and the legislative process in Charleston continues to be influenced by dominant political interest groups.

West Virginia's Dominant Interest Groups

Not surprising, a recent national study of interest groups[25] (Hrebnar-Thomas) in the states classified West Virginia's groups as "dominant." The categories ranged from "dominant," 7 states; "dominant/complementary," 21; "complementary," 17; "complementary/subordinate," 5; and "subordinate" 0.[26]

Dominant interest groups are those groups as a whole which exert an "over-whelming" and "consistent" influence on policy-making. The dominant interest groups in West Virginia[27] were listed as WV Coal Association, United Mine Workers, WV Bankers Association, Jackson & Kelly (state's largest law firm), WV Education Association, WV Federation of Labor (AFL-CIO), and the WV Chamber of Commerce.[28]

"Complementary" interest groups usually have to work in conjunction with or are "restrained" by other components of the political system. These restraining influences could be political parties, the political culture, a strong executive branch, etc.

"Subordinate" groups as the term implies, are inferior to other participants in the political system. The "dominant/complementary" and the "complementary/subordinate" group systems alternate back and forth in a kind of transition.[29]

Contrary to popular perceptions that West Virginia is mostly dominated by labor unions, the Hrebenar-Thomas data suggest that business groups share with labor and in other instances have "out hustled" labor in its influence of legislators.

It should be noted that another study of interest groups in West Virginia found more "pluralism" than the profile depicted by the Hrebnar-Thomas work. In addition to citing labor and the West Virginia Education Association as the most important players in the interest group system, the study also noted the institutionalization of formal interest interest group alliances, e.g., the United Labor Committee (UNLC) and the Business and Industrial Council (BIC). These alliances provide a united front to the legislature and the governor on issues that are dear to them. Other groups mentioned were the health care industry and the insurance industry.[30]

In conclusion, the data reveal a diminished civic political culture, i.e., a serious decline in voter turnout, a lessening of trust in political authorities[31] and a dominant interest group system that is becoming more pluralistic and competitive.

In the selections that follow we examine the historical-cultural dimension of West Virginia's relatively "high" voter turnout rates and political party activity. First, Cabell Phillips presents his dramatic account of the "Matewan Massacre" and the "Battle of Blair Mountain" which historians have called the West Virginia Mine War.

The four remaining selections examine political party activity and politics in West Virginia. John David Rausch, Jr. analyzes the 1996 gubernatorial campaign of Charlotte Pritt, which presented the state with its first opportunity to elect a female candidate governor, and contrary to all predictions lost the election that she should have easily won. Harry W. Ernst's case study of the 1960 West Virginia primary shows how John Kennedy utilized the Democratic Party county organizations and the media but most of all how he charmed West Virginians. As Robert P. McDonough, Kennedy's state campaign director, put it: "John F. Kennedy could sell eggs to chickens." Alan S. Hammock and Lawrence J. Grossback analyze the uniqueness of the 2000 presidential election in West Virginia, which made it possible for a nonincumbent Republican candidate, for the first time in seventy-two years, to carry the state giving Bush five electoral votes, one more than he needed to win the presidency.

Finally, James Dent reminds us that politics has its humorous side in West Virginia and perhaps West Virginians are at their political best when they poke fun at their political leaders.

Notes

[1] Lester Milbrath and M.L. Goel, *Political Participation, How and Why Do People Get Involved in Politics?*, second edition, (Chicago: Rand McNally College Publishing Company, 1977), 2; Sidney Verba and Norman Nie, *Participation in America, Political Democracy and Social Equality*, (New York: Harper & Row, 1972), 79–81.

[2] Thomas R. Dye, *Politics in States and Communities*, seventh edition, (Englewood Cliffs, New Jersey: Prentice-Hall, Inc., 1991), 88.

[3] In the language of political science such "explanations" may be viewed as "variables." A variable is "an observable entity which can take on more than one value or characteristic. . . . The act of recording an observation is known as *measurement.*" The variables measured during a study then become the objects . . . of statistical analysis . . . William R. Klecka et al., *SPSS PRIMER, Statistical Package for the Social Sciences Primer*, (New York: McGraw-Hill Book Company, 1975), 13. Variables concerning political participation frequently deal with individual decisions of whether or not one should act (vote); the direction of the action (to vote for whomever rather than contribute money or time), and the intensity of the action, Milbrath and Goel, 6.

[4] Richard Brisbin, et al., *West Virginia Politics and Government*, (Lincoln and London: University of Nebraska Press, 1996), 34-38.

[5] There is considerable agreement in the voting literature on this point. See Jae-On Kim, et al., "Voter Turnout in the American States: Systematic and Individual Components," *American Political Science Review*, 69 (March, 1975), 107–23; Lester W. Milbrath and M.L. Goel, *Political Participation, How and Why do People Get Involved in Politics?*, second edition, (Chicago: Rand McNally College Publishing Company, 1977), 86–122; A good survey of the current voting literature is found with Richard G. Niemi and Herbert F. Weisberg, *Controversies in Voting Behavior*, third edition, (Washington, DC: C.Q. Press, 1993), *passim*.

[6] Samuel Patterson and Gregory Caldeira, "Getting Out the Vote: Participation in Gubernatorial Elections," *The American Political Science Review*, 77 (September, 1983), 675-689; Angus Campbell, et al., *Elections and the Political Order*, (New York: John Wiley, 1966), 40-62; 63-77.

[7] See Theodore White, *The Making of a President, 1960*, (New York: Pocket Books, Inc., 1961), 115-137; Raymond Chafin and Topper Sherwood, *Just Good Politics: The Life of Raymond Chafin, Appalachian Boss*, (Pittsburgh: University of Pittsburgh Press, 1984) *passim*.

[8] See John F. Bibby and Thomas Holbrook, "Parties and Elections," in *Politics in the American States*, sixth edition, Virginia Gray and Herbert Jacob eds. (Washington, D.C.: Congressional Quarterly Inc., 1996), 108.

[9] *Ibid.*, 105.

[10] Brisbin, *op cit.*, 35.

[11] *Ibid.*, 37-38.

[12] *Ibid.*, 36.

13 WWW.Vote-Smart/org/"Candidates for State of West Virginia." But, problems still exist as the attorney general, treasurer, auditor, and commissioner of agriculture positions on the ballot are not being contested. See "Official Republican Party Ballot— Primary Election, May 9, 2000," *Charleston Gazette*, May 1, 2000.

14 *Pittsburgh Post-Gazette*, "W.Va. woos retirees home, back into politics," Saturday, July 17, 1999.

15 See Robert S. Erickson, et al., "State Political Culture and Public Opinion," *American Political Science Review*, 81, (September, 1987), 801-3.

16 *Ibid.*

17 Daniel J. Elazar, *American Federalism: A View From the States*, third edition, (New York: Harper & Row, 1984), 109.

18 *Ibid.*

19 See Gerald W. Johnson, "Research Note on Political Correlates of Voter Participation: A Deviant Case Analysis," *American Political Science Review*, 65, (September, 1971), 773.

20 See Thomas E. Patterson, *The Mass Media Election, How Americans Choose Their Presidents*, (New York: Preager, 1980), 105.

21 See Joseph Wagner, "Media Do Make a Difference: The Differential Impact of Mass Media in the 1976 Presidential Race," *American Journal of Political Science*, 27, (August, 1983), 407-430.

22 *Ibid.*

23 For example, *The Wheeling News-Register*, April 13, 1990 had banner (one inch) headlines, "Moore to Enter Criminal Plea." Wheeling, Charleston and other newspapers for about a week featured stories about the governor's legal problems as did the state's television stations.

24 Few West Virginians actually receive direct "personal and tangible" benefits with the election of one candidate over another. Instead, West Virginians, who do participate, may find intrinsic rewards in voting: patriotism (Senator Robert Byrd's argument), a sense of duty, etc. . . See J. A. Ferejohn and Morris Fiorina, "The Paradox of Voting," *American Political Science Review*, 18, (March, 1974), 523-36. Ruy A. Teixeira in pooling all the NES election studies from 1960-1980 found a number of demographic changes in American society that have worked to decrease turnout: (1) a younger eligible electorate, (2) fewer people married and living with their spouses, (3) more mobile Americans, (4) less partisan electorate, (5) fewer people reading about campaigns in newspapers, (6) decline in political efficacy feelings.

25 David Truman, *Governmental Process, Political Interests and Public Opinion* (New York: Alfred A. Knopf, 1964), 37, defines an "interest group" as: "A shared attitude group that makes certain claims upon other groups in society. If and when it makes its claims through or upon any of the institutions of government, it becomes a political interest group."

26 See Virginia Gray, Herbert Jacob, and Robert Albritton, *Politics in the American States, a Comparative Analysis*, fifth edition, (Glenville, Illinois: Scott, Foresman/Little Brown Higher Education, 1990), 147, 157; Clive S. Thomas and Ronald J. Hrebenar, "Overview of Findings from the Spring Update of Interest Group Power in the Fifty States," October 1994.

27 Hrebenar-Thomas also list the following as rising in power but not among the first rank: railroads, National Rifle Association, School Services Personnel Association, WV Surface Mine and Reclamation Association (strip mine owners), oil and gas (especially WV Oil & Gas Association, Independent Oil and Gas Association), chemical

companies (especially Union Carbide and DuPont), Georgia Pacific. See Gray, Jacob, and Albritton, *loc cit.*

28 *Ibid.*

29 *Ibid.*

30 Brisbin, op cit., 46-47.

31 See "Citizens Evaluations of Government in West Virginia: The 1992 West Virginia Political Survey," *The West Virginia Public Affairs Reporter*, Vol. 10, No. 1 (Morgantown, WV: West Virginia University, Winter, 1993), 14. The survey revealed that West Virginians have little trust in their state government: (N = 517).

> Trust the WV State Government to do what is right about all of the time: 2.5%
> Trust the WV State Government . . . most of the time: 16.2%
> Trust the WV State Government . . . some of the time: 53.8%
> Trust the WV State Government . . . none of the time: 24.8%

Job Performance:

Official	Excellent	Good	Fair	Poor	No Response
Governor	2.5%	23.6%	46.0%	25.7%	2.1%
Legislature	1.0	15.5	56.9	23.2	3.5
Judges	1.9	36.6	39.7	8.1	13.7
Local	0.8	30.0	53.6	11.8	

Web Sites

www.fedstats.gov (statistics from 100 Federal agencies)
www.vote-smart.org (good site for candidate data)
www.politicaljunkie.com (general political information including West Virginia)
www.fec.org (Federal Election Commission, good source for electoral data, campaign laws)
www.state.wv.us/sos/ (WV Secretary of State, WV voting data)
www.state.wv.us/sec/ (WV Election Commission, WV voting data)
www.arc.gov (Appalachian Regional Commission, good data source since WV is included completely in the region)
www.uky.edu/RGS/AppalCenter/ (University of Kentucky, Appalachian Center, see especially Professor Ron Eller's page)
www.wvu.edu/~appalach/index.htm (Appalachian Studies Association)

Historical Trivia

"Margarette Leach—as a WV elector in 1988 voted for Lloyd Bentsen as President and Michael Dukakis for Vice President as a way of protesting the Electoral College."

Ken Hechler
9-16-96

THE WEST VIRGINIA MINE WAR

Cabell Phillips

"Blood Flowed in the Perennially Troublesome Coalfields in 1921,
When Thousands of Miners Decided
Their Right to Organize was Worth Fighting For"

On the morning of August 1, 1921, the *Gazette* of Charleston, West Virginia, carried under an eight-column banner on its front page the following dispatch from the city of Bluefield:

> "Sid Hatfield lies in the morgue at Welch tonight, a smile frozen on his lips, eyes wide open and five bullet holes in his head and chest. On the slab next to him lies the body of his bodyguard, Ed Chambers.

> "They were shot down as they mounted the steps of the McDowell County Court House this morning, where they were scheduled to go on trial. Their wives, who were with them, ran screaming into the doorway of the building.

> "Who started the shooting nobody seems to know. The true story of how the men met their death will, in all probability, always remain a secret. . . ."

On this grim note opened the final chapter in one of the most protracted and violent episodes of civil strife and insurrection in this country's history since the Civil War.

The scene was the desolate, rugged terrain of the southern West Virginia coalfields, and the issue was the right of the miners to belong to a union.

The conflict had raged intermittently for ten years, with murder, arson, sabotage, and brutality on both sides. In its final, climactic phase thousands of armed miners, organized into squads and companies and with commissary and medical units, marched nearly seventy miles through the mountain wilderness to the relief of fellow unionists in Logan and "Bloody Mingo" counties. At Blair Mountain they locked in a week-long battle with a defending force of two thousand hastily recruited sheriffs' deputies and state militia. The stalemate was broken only by the arrival of several infantry battalions and a fleet of army bombers.

That a man of such primitive scruples and dubious attainments as Sid Hatfield should be the martyr who set in train the miners' march is ironic. He was a lanky, rawboned, semiliterate mountaineer with the high cheekbones and cold, close-set eyes that marked him as a member of the clan of old "Devil Anse" Hatfield, whose feud with the McCoys raged along the West Virginia-Kentucky border before the turn of the century. He had been born to the mines, but by the time he was twenty-six he had become police chief of Matewan, a rough-

and-tumble coal town in Mingo County, not far from his birthplace. With a silver badge on his shirt and a pair of six-guns slung around his waste, Sid Hatfield found that the life of the law suited him perfectly.

Mingo and its neighboring counties were used to violence. Though the American frontier had all but vanished by the time the twentieth century began, the code of the frontier still prevailed in this rugged, isolated mountain enclave. Fierce pride, quick suspicions, and short tempers called for the settlement of disputes on a personal basis, and human life was held to be much less dear than a mountain man's sense of his own independence and dignity. "Bloody Mingo" earned its name before the miners' union was ever heard of, but the coming of the union added a new dimension to the area's tradition of violence.

The westward thrust of empire in the fifty years between the Civil War and the First World War was powered by coal. The vast subterranean basin of "black gold" that stretched westward from the Appalachians almost to the Mississippi was sought nearly as eagerly as the yellow gold of California and the Klondike, and it inspired as much villainy, broke as many lives, and made as many fortunes. In the wake of the speculators and the engineers came the agents of the United Mine Workers of America to create a proletarian counterforce against the monopoly power of the coal barons of Pittsburgh and Wall Street. Unionization spread by a sort of slow and bloody osmosis from Pennsylvania into Indiana and Illinois, but the farther south it reached, the heavier the opposition it met. In West Virginia, by 1917, a sort of Mason-Dixon line had been established roughly along the valley of the Kanawha River; coalfields in the counties to the north were generally unionized, those to the south were not. This gave the southern operators an economic whip hand over their northern competitors; they paid lower wages, and they were immune to the shutdowns frequently enforced by the UMW in the other fields. For good reason, then, the northern operators were almost as eager as the unionists to have rich coal lands south of the Kanawha organized, and they secretly conspired to that end. For equally good reasons the southern operators were determined to keep the organizers out, and they had public opinion, which had just discovered the Bolshevik menace, in their favor.

The confrontation was a classic example of the industrial conflict that reverberated across the nation in the early decades of the century. For West Virginia the issue erupted in riots on Cabin Creek in 1912. There was a brief armistice while the war with Germany was being fought, but when it was over, the unions had gained its first precarious beachhead south of the Kananha, and over the next few years it continued to inch slowly and painfully forward.

Although they were fighting a losing battle, the southern operators, closely linked financially with the big steel and railroad empires, had the state house at Charleston and most of the law on their side. Their principal weapon was a hiring contract that forbade workers to join a union (miners called this a yellow-dog contract), and its validity was repeatedly upheld in the state courts. So was the operators' contention that anyone soliciting membership in a union was guilty of trespass. And so was their contention that miners living in company-owned houses could be evicted without notice or legal redress. This last was an impressive power, since the entire town around a mine property, including the streets, stores, and churches, if any, was actually owned by the operator. To enforce these rights the mine owners put as many deputy sheriffs on their payrolls as they felt they needed. And in times of particular stress they called on the services of the Baldwin-Felts Detective Agency, a nationwide firm of professional strong-arm men and strikebreakers for extra brawn and firepower.

The hired mine guards—"thugs" in the local vernacular—epitomized the miners' grievances, but the substantive issues went much deeper. The miners demanded the right to belong to a union and the right to bargain with their employers through that union. They wanted an eight-hour day instead of the prevalent ten-hour one, weekly instead of monthly paydays, and payment in cash instead of the local scrip that was widely employed. They demanded the establishment of two thousand pounds as the standard ton on which their pay should be based. Many companies paid by the car, the capacities of which might vary by several hundred pounds. The miners also sought the right to pick their own checkweightman to keep tabs on the company's scale operator. Above all they demanded that the hated "thugs" be stripped of their power to make arrests and ransack homes and meeting places under search warrants issued by justices of the peace who often were also in the pay of the mine owners.

The miners' leader was Frank Keeney, president of UMW District 17, whose jurisdiction covered the coal fields in the central and southern part of the state. Unlike the lank, hollow-eyed rustics and inarticulate immigrants who made up the rank and file of his following, Keeney in his mid-thirties was squat, muscular, square-jawed, and aflame with the pugnacity and accumulated resentments of his Irish forebearers. He had been born and reared in these hills and spent his early years digging coal. He had a sharp, eager mind and a fierce determination to do something about his and the other miners' plight. On the stump he was a fiery, persuasive rabble-rouser, and sitting across the table from a governor or a committee of legislators or a group of mine owners he was a shrewd, confident, resourceful negotiator. Inevitably, in the supercharged atmosphere of the time, he was a man with a double profile: a fearless and incorruptible Spartacus in one view, a dangerous troublemaker in another.

The issue of whether the miners in adjoining Logan and Mingo counties could join the union was being pushed toward an explosive climax as the 1920s arrived. Hundreds had signed up, and as promptly as they were discovered they were fired from their jobs and put out of their houses. Organizers and union representatives were clapped into jail in Williamson, the town of Logan itself, and other coal centers as soon as they stepped off the trains. The operators refused to meet with the union, and as their mines were shut down one by one they brought in strikebreakers and added more deputies and mine guards to their payrolls. Bands of miners were accused of roaming the hills at night, dynamiting coal tipples and firing at company buildings with rifles. The deputies struck back by swooping down on the tent colonies in which some fifteen hundred disposed mine families were living. They slashed the tents, threw the contents about, and arrested all the boys and men they could run down. A sense of panic spread from Logan and Mingo counties to the state house in Charleston. Governor Ephraim F. Morgan declared martial law in the area and authorized Sheriff Don Chafin of

Logan County to muster his deputies and any other recruits available into a makeshift state militia, providing them with arms and ammunition.

To the miners and their backers Chafin was the most feared and hated man in the southern coal fields. He was in quite literal sense the law in Logan County, fully backed with money and authority by the coal operators, who, in turn, controlled most other facets of the county's life. His principal mission was to keep the union out, with no questions asked about the means employed. His large corps of deputies, which included most of the Baldwin-Felts, mine guards, were openly carried on the companies' payrolls. Tales of Chafin's arrogance and brutality were legion, and in that hot, turbulent summer of 1921 the jail at Logan was jammed with more than two hundred men whose only offense was joining or talking up the union.

Sid Hatfield, the dead police chief of Matewan, had been cut from the same rough cloth, but there was a difference: he had generally used his muscle in the miners' behalf. He had attained a hero's stature among them when, on a day in May, 1920, he shot up a band of Baldwin-Felts men who had come to town to put a group of miners' families out of their homes. Seven of the "thugs," along with two bystanders, were killed, leaving behind a legacy of hate that would cost Hatfield his life a year later. But the Matewan Massacre, as it promptly came to be called, was a triumph the miners would long remember.

So it was that the news of Hatfield's slaying by three Baldwin-Felts men at Welch, preceding by a fortnight fresh rumors of atrocities by Don Chafin and his deputies in Logan, soon whipped the anger of the miners all through the Kanawha Valley into a vengeful frenzy. Calls upon the state authorities, they knew, would be unavailing (Hatfield's killers were later tried and acquitted), and as they often had done in the past, the miners determined to seek justice on their own harsh terms—to avenge Sid Hatfield's death, to crush Chafin's tyranny and liberate their brethren from Chafin's jail and to smash the anti union monopoly in Logan and Mingo counties.

To what extent this warlike spirit was encouraged by the local union leaders is unclear—certainly they were fully aware of it—but spread it did, like fire in dry grass, up and down the desolate creek bottoms and along the winding railroad spurs where the miners' shanties stood. By Saturday, August 20, 1921, between five and six hundred men had congregated in a sullen, aimless mob in a little meadow on Lens Creek, a few miles out of Charleston and some seventy miles north of where Hatfield lay buried and Chafin held sway.

Over the next few days the miners' numbers swelled to between four and five thousand. They were a tatterdemalion lot in blue jeans, worn corduroy, bits of army khaki, slouch hats, and miners' caps. Many brought their women and children along, loaded in ancient jitneys and farm wagons or trudging on foot over the hills from as far as fifty miles away. They cooked beans and fatback over open fires and slept on the ground in a cold drizzle. Most of the men were armed, some with pistols and shotguns, others with high-powered hunting and military rifles. They had gathered through a spontaneous impulse and with but a vague notion of what they were going to do. They were leaderless at the start—Keeney, Fred Mooney, Bill Blizzard, and other UMW officials denied any connection with the mobilization—but out of the turmoil of rumors, gossip, impromptu ha-rangues, and the boredom of inaction a semblance of organization began to assert itself. The miners, many of whom were World War I veterans, divided loosely into companies based on the communities from which they came. Disciplinary details were set up to take care of troublemakers and interlopers (reporters and bootleggers were sent on their way). Armed patrols kept round-the-clock vigil on the roads and mountain trails. A commissary emerged that depleted the food from stores for miles around, and a medical unit of six doctors and eight nurses was set up.

Still, no single leader emerged—none, in fact, has ever been positively iden-tified—but by Tuesday night the mounting tensions spilled over. The men had grown restless and irritable. Wild rumors of atrocities and lynchings by Chafin's men whipped their passion for revenge. They milled noisily about a dozen bon-fires, and their hoarse exhortations and rebel yells, punctuated with the erratic crack of rifles fired into the air, reverberated from the dark surrounding hills. "On to Logan!" they yelled. "Let's get the dirty thugs!" "Remember Sid Hatfield!"

At two o'clock the next morning the fire sirens in the county seat of Logan roused the startled citizens from their beds. This was the prearranged signal that brought hundreds of Sheriff Chafin's men to the courthouse, the arsenal from which the dreaded invasion was to be repelled. In Charleston, Governor Morgan was awakened by a call from the night city editor of the *Gazette* with the news that the miners of Lens Creek were on the march. The governor telephoned an order for a special detachment of state police to stand by for emergency action after daylight. At the little town of Racine, ten miles down the Logan road from Lens Creek, workmen getting ready for the day shift at the local mines stopped to cheer a plodding file of marchers, three and four abreast, that clogged their main street and stretched out of sight in either direction. All day long they came in a straggling disorganized procession, hundreds of grim-faced, weary men and ex-cited boys, each with a gun and a sack of provisions slung over his shoulder and by way of uniform, a red bandanna knotted about his neck or right sleeve. The badge gave them the name Red Necks.

A series of high ridges known collectively as Blair Mountain forms the boundary of Logan County where the main road from the north and the Coal River branch of the Chesapeake and Ohio Railroad snake in through a narrow defile. To this natural barrier Sheriff Chafin rushed about three hundred of his irregulars, deploying them in a fifteen-mile-long battle line along the crest and commanding the high passes. That night an advance party of the miners' army several hundred strong—they had commandeered a freight train up the line and pushed on ahead of the main body—tried to make their way over the mountain and ran into a defenders' patrol near Dingess Run. The two sides dug in behind rocks and trees and banged away furiously at one another in the dark. After a few hours the attackers withdrew to the base of the mountain to await daylight and reinforcements.

News of this ominous but ineffectual encounter threw Charleston into a panic that morning. Governor Morgan dashed off an urgent telegram to Washington saying the state was unable to protect itself and needed federal troops. President Harding held a hurried conference with Secretary of War John W. Weeks and dispatched General J.H. Bandholtz, commander of the Washington Military District, to West Virginia for a first-hand reconnaissance report.

The general and his aides, resplendent in gleaming puttees and Sam Browne belts, arrived in Charleston by train before daybreak. They roused the governor from his bed, summoned Keeney and Mooney from theirs, and got down to business. The minutes of the conference were not preserved. . . .

Whatever the understanding may have been, by eight o'clock that morning—Friday—the two union officials were bouncing down the Logan road as fast as their four-cylinder Dodge would take them. As they passed groups of stragglers heading south they shouted: "Go back home; the march is over!" About noon they caught up with the main body of marchers at the little town of Madison . . . Keeney herded them into the ball park, mounted the hood of his Dodge, and tore into them: (paraphrased)

> "I've told you men God knows how many times that any time you want
> to battle against Don Chafin and his thugs I'll be right there in the front
> lines with you. I've been there before and you know it. But this time
> you've got more than Don Chafin against you. You got the Governor of
> West Virginia against you (boos). You've got the *government of the United
> States* against you!". . . .

Keeney's appeal worked. There was grumbling among some of the hotheads who still wanted to storm the ramparts of Logan, but by late afternoon one group after another turned homeward, and the next morning trains began coming in to pick up the rest. Keeney called General Bandholtz in Charleston to tell him the men had turned back, and the general verified this by reports from his own scouts. At the same time Sheriff Chafin called in his defenders, and the town of Logan that night held a "peace" celebration. . . .

The peace, however, was short lived. In the predawn hours of Sunday the miners' grapevine brought a new message: *They are shooting women and children at Sharples!* Hundreds of armed men, many still on their way home from the dispersal at Madison, turned and stormed back down the Logan road. In Logan itself the sirens shrieked again, and the defenders set up machine guns and went scurrying back to their positions atop Blair Mountain.

What had happened, as nearly as it can be pieced together from many conflicting reports, is this: in spite of whatever armistice terms had been set by the Governor and General Bandholtz, Chafin and Captain J.R. Brockus of the state police planned to round up a group of men who they decided were ringleaders of the miners' march. With a force of several hundred deputies they crept across the mountain trails that night to the little town of Sharples. On a ridge just above the town they came upon a force of miners. Chafin demanded that they lay down their arms and submit to arrest. The miners answered with gunfire. For an hour there was a wild melee of shooting and hand-to-hand combat in the darkness. At last the deputies retreated in disorder over the mountain, but the miners counted five of their own dead or wounded, and many of the houses in the town had been peppered by stray bullets.

Blair Mountain became a battlefield again as thousands of miners poured into the region and scaled its northern slopes. On the opposite slope, and holding advantageous positions on the ridge, were hundreds of deputies and volunteer militia. The battle line extended some twenty miles along the serpentine crest of the ridge, from Buffalo Creek on the east to Mill Creek on the west. Throughout the day and night there were erratic bursts of rifle fire and occasionally the chatter of a machine gun. The outside world could learn little of what was going on, for telegraph wires had been cut, trains suspended, and traffic on the roadways blocked by armed patrols. An airplane from Logan, on a scouting mission of the attackers' positions, was riddled by rifle fire from the ground and forced to retire. . . .

For a week the battle of Blair Mountain raged furiously, not in a single, momentous clash but in a series of uncoordinated skirmishes, hit-and-run raids, and individual gun duels up and down the length of the thirty-mile front. The deaths on both sides have been variously estimated at from ten to thirty, but there were hundreds of lesser casualties . . . probably ten thousand men were engaged in the conflict at its height, from seven to eight thousand on the miners' side and from two to three thousand on the other. The defenders were under pseudomilitary command of the state adjutant general and were supplied with government-issue-arms, ammunition, and some communications equipment. But they were barely able to hold their own against the numerical superiority of the attackers. The miners fought under a loose form of military command (whose leadership was never fully determined) and seemed plentifully supplied with rifles and bullets. Had either side concentrated its forces for a breakthrough at one point, the consequences would have been even more bloody and disastrous. But before this could happen, the federal government moved in. . . . On Wednesday, August 31, President Harding was induced to intervene. Within two hours the news flashed that he had issued a formal ultimatum to the miners. . . .

> "Now, therefore I, Warren G. Harding, President of the United States, do hereby command all persons engaged in such unlawful and insurrectionary proceedings to disperse and retire peacefully to their respectful abodes on the first day of September 1921. . . ."

General Bandholtz was immediately dispatched to Charleston to enforce the terms of the proclamation, copies of which were dropped over the battle lines from airplanes. At the same time regiments at Camp Dix, New Jersey, Camp Sherman, Ohio, and Fort Knox, Kentucky, were put on battle alert and special trains held in readiness to take them to the scene of trouble. An air squadron at Langley Field, Virginia was similarly alerted. . . .

Shortly after midnight Bandholtz wired the War Department that the Presidential proclamation was being ignored and asked that troops be sent immediately. Within hours the regiments held in readiness began boarding trains bound for West Virginia, and soon after thirteen DeHaviland airplanes armed with bombs, machine guns, and ammunition left Langley Field to support the federal troops . . . but when the regulars moved on up to Sharples at daybreak a few hours later, the miner fighters were coming out of the hills. Their guns had been hidden, probably far back in the black recesses of old coal mines. Their red badges had been snatched off. They were simply a swarm of stubby-faced men getting out of the hills and back to their homes. . . . Similar scenes occurred at other points along the battle line, and by Sunday evening the Red Neck Rebellion had passed into history. The combatants on both sides laid down their arms and turned homeward.

One by one the mines reopened, the refugees came out of hiding, and life in the Logan and Mingo coalfields resumed its normal pattern. The soldiers remained for a couple of weeks, but in time they, too, returned to their home bases.

Peace had come to West Virginia, but it was a bitter, precarious peace that in the miners' view had been imposed by force. As so often in the past "the law" had come down on the side of their "oppressors." And in retrospect this seems to have been true. Their quarrel had been, not with the federal government, but with the private operators of the coal mines and a state administration that had conspired with them to ignore the miners' rights. Most of the miners' grievances, in fact, had specific remedies in state statutes—the private hiring of sheriffs' deputies, for example, was expressly forbidden by state law—but the governor's invariable response to such complaints was that relief should be sought through the courts. The courts were as unsympathetic toward the miners as the state house. They had repeatedly upheld the yellow-dog hiring contract and the "master and servant" tenancy relationship, both of which were subsequently upset by the federal courts. . . .

So from the standpoint of the miners the net result of the federal intervention had only been to restore an unsatisfactory status quo. Hundreds of families continued to live meagerly in tent colonies. Thousands of miners were blacklisted from employment. The Baldwin-Felts men and sheriffs' deputies were restored to authority. Keeney, Mooney, and Blizzard were dismissed from their union posts by John L. Lewis, the new UMW president, whom they had failed to consult; and the three men as well as over a hundred other leaders of the miners' uprising were indicted for, among other things, treason against the sovereign State of West Virginia.

Their trial turned out to be a farce. After elaborate maneuvers a change of venue was granted from the openly hostile atmosphere of Logan County to the more placid environs of the old courthouse at Charles Town. . . . But Charles Town did not remain placid long. When the special trainload of defendants arrived and were marched manacled through the streets, the citizens created an uproar of resentment. . . . The trial dissolved into a shambles when Harold W. Houston, the chief defense attorney, won a ruling from the bench that each defendant had to be tried separately and that there had to be two witnesses to each overt act of treason if the charges were to be sustained. This proved an insurmountable obstacle for the prosecution, and after many continuances and changes of venue the treason charges were dismissed, although ultimately a few miners were convicted on lesser counts.

For all their violence and suffering the miners got nothing in return. The Logan and Mingo fields continued to be off limits to the union, and in 1922 the UMW, having poured more than two million dollars into the cause, abandoned the effort to organize them. They remained predominantly nonunion until the passage of the Wagner Act in the early years of the New Deal.

The operators won the battle but lost the war. They preserved for a time the principle of the nonunion shop. But on the heels of their labor troubles came the depressions of the mid-twenties and of the nineteen thirties and after that the devastating competition from fuel oil. The industry shriveled and scores of operators were forced to the wall, and it remained for decades a sick industry.

As for the State of West Virginia, its harvest was a bad name among people of good conscience. Public opinion had been largely against—or at least apathetic toward—the miners, and most other unionists as well, when the decades of the twenties began. Organized labor was equated in a vague, fearful sort of way with bomb throwers and Bolsheviks. But the march on Logan, emblazoned in the newspapers and investigated by Congress, turned up another face of the coin. The human misery of the tent colonies, the harsh peonage of the mine towns and the yellow-dog contract, the shocking spectacle of a trial for treason reputedly being conducted by private prosecutors at private expense—such "discoveries" outraged thousands of citizens across the country who had virtually no opinions about the labor movement but very strong ones about injustice. West Virginia was where it happened, so West Virginia must be responsible, they reasoned. It could be because of some lingering corporate guilt that there is nowhere in the state archives at Charleston today a single official report, document, or letter relating to this historic happening, although scores of them were written. . . .

Reprinted with permission of American Heritage from Cabell Phillips, "The West Virginia Mine War," Vol. 16, No. 5, (August 1974), 58-61, 90-94.

WAS THE PRESS UNFAIR TO CHARLOTTE?

John David Rausch, Jr.

INTRODUCTION

The 1996 West Virginia gubernatorial campaign presented the state with its first chance to elect a female candidate to the office of governor. Since the candidate was also a Democrat, in a "one-party" Democratic state, it was assumed that the first female governor would be elected. However, by the end of the campaign in November, voters decided to return 74-year-old Republican Cecil Underwood to the Governor's Mansion. Underwood served as the state's youngest governor in the late 1950s and his return to office made him the state's oldest governor.

The present research analyzes the nature of local press coverage of the gubernatorial campaign. In a post-mortem, the Democratic nominee, Charlotte Pritt identified three factors that contributed to her defeat: 1), the lack of support from term-limited Governor Gaston Caperton, a fellow Democrat; 2), lack of support from women; and 3), the bias of "Republican-controlled" newspapers.[1] On the question of female vote choice, a previous study (Rausch and Rausch, 1997a) using exit poll data, found some evidence to support Pritt's claim that women did not vote for her

This research addresses the third factor identified by Pritt. It is concerned with understanding how the West Virginia press covers a statewide campaign. It also seeks to determine if press was biased against Charlotte Pritt and if such bias was due to her gender, or to her previous political activities including a bitter 1992 primary campaign against Governor Caperton, the Democratic incumbent. After her 1992 primary election defeat, Pritt complained about the "sexist bias" in the coverage of her campaign.[2] Was there "sexist bias" in the media coverage of her gubernatorial campaign?

Understanding the Media's Role in Statewide Elections

The candidacy of a woman for political office is no longer the novelty it once was. Additionally, the problems facing female candidates for office are well documented (see Kahn, 1996). While the body of research is growing, a lacuna exists in our understanding of the press coverage of female candidates (Carroll, 5;

Kahn, 1996; Mandel, 1981). The gap in knowledge is particularly wide in state and local races, and in campaigns which are most likely to involve women candidates. In 1996, the West Virginia press corps was faced with covering the campaign of a female nominee for governor, although she was a very familiar female.

Subnational elections, with or without female candidates, occur in relative obscurity. There is a significant literature on the role of the media in presidential campaigns (e.g., Joslyn, 1984; Patterson, 1980) and less attention to the media's role in congressional campaigns (e.g., Clark and Evans, 1983; Kahn, 1993). However, there is almost no literature on the role of the media in statewide campaigns (Fico, Clogston, and Pizante, 1988; Rozell, 1991; Rozell and Wilson, 1996).

Kahn (1996, 132) found that the news media is affected by the gender of candidates for statewide office. While female candidates receive about equal news coverage as male candidates (Kahn, 1993), women receive much less issue coverage than men. In gubernatorial campaigns, reporters tend to stress personalities over issues (Kohn, 1996, 132). The lack of issue coverage occurs despite the fact that women's issues are emphasized in gubernatorial campaigns (Kahn, 1993).

Charlotte Pritt's campaign presented a number of variables for reporters covering the 1996 gubernatorial race. First, in considering the lopsided two-to-one Democratic voter registration advantage, she should have won in a landslide. Second, she had challenged a reasonably popular incumbent governor in the 1992 Democratic Primary. When she lost in a close race, she refused to endorse Governor Caperton in the general election, claiming voter irregularities in the primary. She even allowed a write-in campaign to be conducted on her behalf (see Rausch and Rausch, 1997a, 2). Finally, she was nominated out of a crowded field in the 1996 Democratic Primary, which was described as an "extremely negative and rancorous primary. . . ." (Rausch and Rausch, 1997a, 3). All of these variables could contribute to the type of coverage Charlotte Pritt received in the 1996 general election campaign.

West Virginia's Gubernatorial Campaign

The 1996 West Virginia gubernatorial campaign featured an avowed "liberal," anti-establishment Democrat, former state senator and 1992 gubernatorial candidate, Charlotte Pritt, challenged by a moderately conservative Republican, former Governor Cecil Underwood. In a hypothetical match-up poll published by the Huntington *Herald-Dispatch*, about a month before the May 14 primary election, Pritt held a 20-point lead over Underwood. After she was nominated by the Democrats, most observers considered her the favorite. However, key Democratic politicians in the state, including term-limited Governor Caperton and United States Senator Robert Byrd, declined to endorse her in the primary and remained relatively quiet during the general election campaign. Pritt's most significant endorsements came from United States Senator Jay Rockefeller and President Bill Clinton.

Judging from the campaign waged by Pritt, it would appear that she counted on an "easy" general election campaign possibly explaining why she failed to bring the various elements of the Democratic Party together after the primary. While she received the endorsement of most of her primary opponents, State Senator Joe Manchin, a conservative Democrat, refused to endorse Pritt because of her tactics during the primary. Moreover, it is not clear why the Pritt campaign spent two months after the primary to find its message. During the lull, Underwood was able to define Pritt in a negative way, as someone who was anti-business instead of a moderate reformer. Former Speaker of the House of Delegates, Chuck Chambers, indicated that Pritt should have spent the first two months mounting an aggressive attack on the Underwood's plan and taking her ideas to the voters.

Underwood ran a very low-key campaign, actually stressing the successes of the previous Democratic administration in returning the state to the road of economic well-being. In short, he told voters that if they were comfortable with where the state was heading, and they did not want significant change, he was the candidate who would not make dramatic changes. Considering how Pritt challenged Governor Caperton in 1992, Underwood's message clearly resonated with the voters.

Pritt lost by more than 36,000 votes in an election marked by a low voter turnout of only 44.9 percent. Underwood claimed 51 percent of the female vote, and garnered 30 percent of the Democrats. Considering the fact that Charlotte Pritt shared a ticket with President Clinton, who received 50 percent of the vote in West Virginia, Underwood even took 21 percent of those voters who cast ballots for Clinton (see Rausch and Rausch, 1997a).

Although Underwood's victory was impressive, it should not be considered a sign that politics in West Virginia is entering a period of realignment. The governor was the only Republican to win a statewide race and the party actually lost seats in the House of Delegates.

METHODOLOGY

The analysis is based on a survey of local print media articles about the campaign (see Rozell, 1991; Rozell and Wilson, 1996). A comprehensive content analysis was conducted of four newspapers for the period beginning September 1, 1996, and ending on election day, November 5, 1996. The newspapers examined in the analysis were selected for a combination of their geographic distribution, circulation, influence, and presence within a newspaper chain (i.e., Thomson newspapers, Ogden newspapers).

The two most widely circulated and influential newspapers in the state are the *Charleston Daily Mail* and the *Charleston Gazette*. Both of these papers are distributed statewide and provide a significant level of coverage of state politics. The papers combine into one Sunday edition, the *Sunday Gazette-Mail*. For the purposes of this research, the *Sunday Gazette Mail* is considered part of the *Gazette*. The *Daily Mail* traditionally has been identified as the "Republican" paper, while the *Gazette* is "the state's largest independent Democratic newspaper."[5]

The other two papers were selected because of geographic distribution. The *Huntington Herald-Dispatch* covers the tri-state area in southwestern West Virginia, eastern Kentucky, and southeastern Ohio. It is considered to have a liberal perspective. The *Wheeling Intelligencer* is one of the Ogden newspaper chain, whose publisher is considered a conservative.

The 1996 gubernatorial campaign was covered extensively by these four papers. The data presented here were collected by a review of 276 news stories which appeared in the papers during the period studied.

The content analysis follows the approach adopted by earlier studies of the press coverage of the 1989 Virginia gubernatorial campaign (Rozell, 1991) and the 1993 Virginia gubernatorial campaign (Rozell and Wilson, 1996).

ANALYSIS

News coverage was grouped into three general categories; *subject matter*—articles which are identified as issue, horse-race, character, profile, and others; *issue coverage*—education, crime, health care, workers' compensation, among others; and *candidate coverage*—the amount of coverage given each candidate and the type of coverage (positive, negative or neutral) (see Rozell and Wilson, 1996, 30).

Subject Matter

Many studies find that the press focuses on the horse-race aspects of the campaign, rather than covering policy issues. The press has been criticized for directing attention to candidates' character and campaign gimmicks instead of providing voters with the information they need to make an intelligent vote choice. . . .

The local press coverage of the 1996 West Virginia gubernatorial campaign focused more on issues and candidate/voter group profiles than on the horse-race. Table 2.5 shows that issue coverage comprised 19.2 percent of all stories in the four newspapers. Profile coverage constituted 26.4 percent; therefore, 45.6 percent of all stories focused on issues or profiles.

A relatively small number (14.1 percent) of the stories described the horse-race aspects of the campaign. Only 8.3 percent of the articles focused on character issues. This number may have been higher had the time frame of the study been expanded. For example, in early September, a number of articles reported on Pritt's comment about Underwood's "low energy level" as a 74-year-old man. Still the total of these two categories of stories is 22.4 percent, far fewer than one would expect given the presumption that the press focuses on character and horse-race issues.

The "other" category includes articles that do not fit into one of the four thematic categories. Such articles include those reporting candidate visits to communities, interest group endorsements, and the unveiling of new campaign commercials.

Table 2.5   State Press Coverage of 1996 West Virginia Gubernatorial Election by Subject Matter

Subject Matter	Huntington Herald-Dispatch		Charleston Daily Mail		Charleston Gazette		Wheeling Intelligencer		Totals	
	Number	Percent	Number	Percent	Number	Percent	Number	Percent	Number	Percent
Issue	8	17.0	28	28.3	12	13.3	5	12.5	53	19.2
Horse-race	11	23.4	11	11.1	13	14.4	4	10.0	39	14.1
Character	5	10.6	7	7.1	5	5.6	6	15.0	23	8.3
Profile	11	23.4	25	25.3	26	28.9	11	27.5	73	26.4
Others	12	25.5	28	28.3	34	37.8	14	35.0	88	31.9
Totals	47	100.0	99	100.0	90	100.0	40	100.0	276	100.0

Issue Coverage

Relatively few issues were covered by the local press during the course of the campaign (see Table 2.6). The economy was the focus of 31.1 percent of the stories while health care was the subject of 20.8 percent. Both of these issues are among the list of important issues regularly identified by West Virginians in public opinion pols.[6] In addition, these are two of the issues around which Charlotte Pritt organized her campaign. Here Pritt should have had an advantage because as Kahn argues, "the relevant issues in gubernatorial campaigns tend to correspond to women's stereotypical strength." These issues include child care, the environment, education, and health (Kahn, 1996, 75).

State government (11.3 percent) was a significant issue for Cecil Underwood. He called for a 20 percent cut in the number of state employees. According to Underwood, state government could increase efficiency by replacing workers with technology. This was one of the more "hotly" debated issues in the campaign.

The small number of articles (5.7 percent) dealing with education is a bit misleading. All four newspapers had more articles dealing with education, but many of these fall into the "character" category. For example, several interest groups released information showing that Pritt, while a state legislator, had supported a measure to allow sex education for students including those in kindergarten.

Despite the fact that West Virginia is a socially conservative state, social, moral, or religious issues did not receive much coverage during the last two months of the general campaign. Again, this finding can be attributed to the time frame from which the articles were drawn.

A number of social issues were debated during the primary and these debates spilled over to the early part of the general election campaign. Same-sex marriages became part of the campaign discourse in large part because the U.S. House of Representatives was debating a "Defense of Marriage Act." Underwood quickly responded to questions from the press by stating that as governor he would sign a bill prohibiting recognition of same-sex marriages in West Virginia. Pritt took about ten days to reach the same conclusion. Both stories were coded in the "profile" category. After her decision, a number of staffers resigned from the Pritt campaign. Reports of the fall-out from Pritt's decision were categorized as "horse-race" stories. . . .

Charlotte Pritt's gender did not become an issue in the campaign as reflected in Table 2.6. She did not draw attention to her historic candidacy and the Republican Party did not address the issue either. In a unique situation, the Republican challenger to incumbent Democratic Attorney General Darrell McGraw was Charlotte Lane. This fact essentially prevented Pritt's opponents from making gender an issue. Of course, the positive stereotypes we hold about women also did not become a factor in the race {see Kahn, 1996).

Table 2.6   State Press Coverage of 1996 West Virginia Gubernatorial Election by Policy Issues

Policy Issue	Huntington Herald-Dispatch		Charleston Daily Mail		Charleston Gazette		Wheeling Intelligencer		Totals	
	Number	Percent	Number	Percent	Number	Percent	Number	Percent	Number	Percent
Economy	2	25.0	9.5	33.9	4	33.3	1	20.0	16.5	31.1
Education	1	12.5	2.0	7.1	0	0.0	0	0.0	3.0	5.7
Health Care	1	12.5	5.0	17.9	3	25.0	2	40.0	11.0	20.8
Workers' Comp	2	25.0	1.0	3.6	1	8.3	0	0.0	4.0	7.5
Crime	1	12.5	3.0	10.7	0	0.0	0	0.0	4.0	7.5
Corridor H	0	0.0	0.5	1.8	1	8.3	0	0.0	1.5	2.8
State Government	1	12.5	3.0	10.7	2	16.7	0	0.0	6.0	11.3
Collective Bargaining	0	0.0	3.0	10.7	0	0.0	0	0.0	3.0	5.7
Gay Rights	0	0.0	1.0	3.6	0	0.0	0	0.0	1.0	1.9
Wheeling-Pitt Steel Strike	0	0.0	0.0	0.0	0	0.0	1	20.0	1.0	1.9
General	0	0.0	0.0	0.0	1	8.3	1	20.0	2.0	3.8
Totals	8	100.0	28.0	100.0	12	100.0	5	100.0	53.0	100.0

Candidate Coverage

It should be recalled, that Pritt said one of the two "biggest factors in her loss in November [was] Republican-controlled newspapers that were biased against her."[7]

It is the case that all twelve daily newspapers in the state endorsed Underwood. However, it is difficult to support the presumption that all papers are controlled by Republicans. Clearly, none of the papers is as anti-establishment as Pritt and all seemed to favor the status quo over her proposed changes in government.

The editorials did not address her gender, only her "hostility to the corporations many West Virginians would love to work for." The leading Democratic paper in the state, the *Charleston Gazette*, argued that "Pritt is too far out of the mainstream." The editorial went on to outline the problems with Pritt's plan to establish collective bargaining for state employees. "Statehouse unions would gain the power to sway elections, endorsing candidates who promise to do most for the unions," according to the *Gazette* editorial writer. Pritt provided evidence of her lack of experience by suggesting that she could enact collective bargaining by "executive decree."[8] . . . .

The litmus test of Pritt's claim that she received more biased press coverage, is to examine the *tone* of the stories. The 269 stories were analyzed for positive, negative, and neutral content. The total number of positive, negative, and neutral stories exceeds 269 because one news story could count as positive or negative for both candidates, or even positive for one and negative for the other.

As Table 2.7 reveals, Pritt received highly negative press coverage (54.2 percent negative, 24.2 percent positive, 21.6 percent neutral). She received significantly negative coverage from the *Wheeling Intelligencer*, the reportedly Republican paper. Half of the articles appearing in the *Charleston Gazette* were negative in tone to Pritt. The *Gazette*, of all papers in the state, should have been the most supportive of the Democratic nominee.

CONCLUSION

This research finds that press coverage of the 1996 West Virginia gubernatorial campaign was substantive. While there were some stories focusing on the horse-race and character issues of the campaign, a significant number of articles provided newspaper readers with a discussion of the issues (especially the economy and health care) and candidate/voting group profiles

The data also revealed that there was indeed a negative tone in the reporting of stories about Charlotte Pritt (there were 103 negative articles to Underwood's 40). Did this negative coverage result from her gender or her platform for change? Since there is little evidence to suggest that gender "caused" the negativity, we can cautiously conclude that her perceived positions on the issues were a factor in the negative coverage. For example, her plan to repeal the sales tax on food and replace the lost revenue by revoking corporate tax credits were per-

Table 2.7　Candidate Favorability Rating in State Press Coverage of 1996 West Virginia Gubernatorial Election

Candidate	Huntington Herald-Dispatch		Charleston Daily Mail		Charleston Gazette		Wheeling Intelligencer		Totals	
	Number	Percent	Number	Percent	Number	Percent	Number	Percent	Number	Percent
Pritt										
Positive	9	29.0	24	33.3	10	15.6	3	13.0	46	24.2
Negative	16	51.6	38	52.8	32	50.0	17	73.9	103	54.2
Neutral	6	19.4	10	13.9	22	34.4	3	13.0	41	21.6
Total	31	100.0	72	100.0	64	100.0	23	100.0	190	100.0
Underwood										
Positive	14	58.3	35	55.6	19	30.6	14	66.7	82	48.2
Negative	4	16.7	15	23.8	17	27.4	4	19.0	40	23.5
Neutral	6	25.0	13	20.6	26	41.9	3	14.3	48	28.2
Total	24	100.0	63	100.0	62	100.0	21	100.0	170	100.0

ceived as more anti-business than compassionate toward working people.

Some of the reasons for the negative coverage can be also assigned to the Pritt campaign. She started late, waiting almost two months after the primary which allowed Underwood to begin defining her. The Pritt campaign was slow to respond to issues like same-sex marriages and she seemed to waiver on significant issues like the Corridor H road project.

The data show that the press was unfair to Charlotte, but nothing suggests that the lack of fairness can be attributed to her gender.

METHODOLOGICAL NOTE

The content analysis is based on a survey of print articles about the 1996 gubernatorial campaign (Labor Day to election day) from four newspapers. The articles were organized into three general areas: Subject Matter—articles are categorized as issue, horse-race, character, profile, and others; Issue-Coverage—health care, employment, education, economic development, among others; Candidate-coverage—amount of coverage given to each candidate as well as the type of coverage (positive, negative, or neutral). A news story about Governor Caperton not endorsing Charlotte Pritt was coded as a "negative" for her, for example. A story was coded as a "neutral" for both Pritt and Cecil Underwood when it reviewed their plans for health care and indicated both the costs and benefits of both plans. A similar article would be coded as "negative" for Pritt and "positive" for Underwood because it mentioned only the costs of Pritt's plan to insure children while identifying the benefits of Underwood's plan that did not include an additional cigarette tax.

In the Subject Matter area, articles were coded as "issue" if they examined a particular policy topic. "Horse race" articles discussed who was ahead in the polls or in fund-raising. Articles examining "character" reviewed the candidates personalities and/or private lives without identifying how these factors were important to their abilities to serve as governor. "Profile" stories look at the candidates' personal backgrounds as well as views of voter groups who supported or opposed one of the candidates. Articles that dealt with a policy issue, and coded as "issue" in the Subject Matter area, were further coded as to the issue that was examined in the article. If the story examined two issues equally, it was coded with a fraction of a unit.

Notes

Paper presented October 10, 1997 at the Annual Meeting of the West Virginia Political Science Association, Morgantown, WV.

[1] Associated Press, "Pritt Accuses Caperton of Helping Underwood," (Fairmont) *Times-West Virginian*, 19 February, 1997, 1b.

[2] Phil Kabler, "Group Studying Alleged Media Sexism, Pritt Says," *Charleston Gazette*, 19 June 1992, 1c. The group supposedly studying the issue for Pritt, the National Women's Caucus, has no record of the study.

³ Jack Deutsch, "Chairman Says Manchin's Comments Will Hurt Party," *Charleston Daily Mail*, 14 October 1996, 11a.

⁴ Jack McCarthy, "Anatomy of a Campaign," (Charleston) *Sunday Gazette-Mail*, 29 December 1996, lc.

⁵ John Raby, "Papers Favor Underwood," *Charleston Daily Mail*, 29 October 1996, lc.

⁶ John David Rausch, Jr., interview with Marc Harman, Cecil Underwood's campaign manager, 30 September 1996.

⁷ Associated Press, "Pritt Accuses Caperton of Helping Underwood."

⁸ Raby, loc. cit.

References

Carroll, Susan J. 1985. *Women as Candidates in American Politics*. Bloomington, IN: Indiana University Press.

Kahn, Kim Fridkin. 1996. *The Political Consequences of Being a Woman*. New York, NY: Columbia University Press.

Mandel, Ruth B. 1981. *In the Running: The New Woman Candidate*. New Haven, CT: Ticknor and Fields.

Rausch, John David, and Mary S. Rausch. 1997a. "Why Did West Virginia Voters not Elect a Woman Governor?" *Comparative State Politics* 18 (3): 1-12.

Rausch, John David, and Mary S. Rausch. 1997b. "West Virginia: In Search of the Religious Right." in *God at the Grassroots*, 1996, ed. Mark J. Rozell and Clyde Wilcox. Lanham, MD: Rowman & Littlefield.

Rozell, Mark J. 1991. "Local v. National Press Assessments of Virginia's 1989 Gubernatorial Campaign." *Polity* 24:69-89.

Rozell, Mark J., and Mary Wilson. 1996. "Press Coverage of the 1993 Virginia Gubernatorial Campaign." *State and Local Government Review* 28:28-37.

Case Study:
THE PRIMARY THAT MADE A PRESIDENT: WEST VIRGINIA 1960

Harry W. Ernst
Columnist

"Flagship West Virginia"

On July 9, 1960, "Flagship West Virginia" landed in Los Angeles. Its passengers included United States Senator John F. Kennedy. He considered it a happy omen that he had arrived on the American Airlines' plane named for the state which had made him the favored candidate for the Democratic presidential nomination. As Arthur Edson of the Associated Press, who had covered the West Virginia presidential primary that spring, wrote after the Democrats in Los Angeles had made their decision:

> "If our political disputes are ever remembered as our battlefields are now, West Virginia will become a national shrine. For it was in West Virginia's beautiful mountains, in its thriving cities, in its impoverished coal fields that the decisive battle was fought that gave Senator John F. Kennedy the Democratic presidential nomination. Everyone, including the Kennedy forces, now seems to agree this was the turning point."[1]

The 43-year-old Massachusetts millionaire, who would become the 35th President after the closest election since 1888, had been forced to take the most dangerous route to his party's nomination—the state presidential primaries. Only through decisive victories on the vote-getting trail could he hope to convince his fellow Democrats at their national convention that his Roman Catholicism would not bring them defeat in November.

Predominantly Protestant West Virginia, where Kennedy knocked United States Senator Hubert H. Humphrey of Minnesota from the race, presented the impressive proof which party leaders could not ignore. After the West Virginia primary, hesitant leaders in such key states as Michigan, New York and Pennsylvania became convinced that Kennedy was their man. They gave him the votes he needed to win the nomination on the first ballot.

The religious issue was not buried in the West Virginia hills. But the avalanche of Protestant votes for Catholic Kennedy, which surprised most journalists and their readers across the country, did submerge it at the convention. A

Protestant state, with a snugly fitting Bible Belt, made it possible for the first Roman Catholic to be elected President.

The Essential Contest

West Virginia's presidential primary which prohibits voters from crossing party lines and is not binding on delegates elected to the national conventions, was adopted in 1915. It has been seldom used by either political party, and then only for minor skirmishing. In 1928, Alfred E. Smith, the first Roman Catholic to be nominated for President by either major political party, defeated United States Senator James A. Reed, a Missouri Baptist, by almost 6,000 votes. Neither campaigned in West Virginia, and a powerful faction of the Democratic Party, then the minority party in the state, supported Smith.

But, to John F. Kennedy, what the West Virginia primary lacked in historical glitter it made up for in other qualities. Would his Roman Catholicism prevent him from becoming President? West Virginia would be a good place to find out. And a victory there on May 10th, coming on the heels of another in Wisconsin and just two months before the national convention, would be timed perfectly to sweep hesitant delegates behind Kennedy.

Another quality of West Virginia's obscure primary also appealed to him. It was a loosely run affair that the Democratic political organizations normally shied away from because of their understandable devotion to the local and state races, which are their bread and butter. A vacuum also existed in the party's state leadership. The Republicans controlled the statehouse, and five Democrats wanted their party's nomination for Governor. The statehouse, through patronage the principal source of power in state politics, could not throw its weight behind a stop-Kennedy drive.

Besides, where else could Kennedy hope to win the kind of dramatic contest he needed? Humphrey would not enter Nebraska because of Kennedy's popularity with Democratic leaders there. Kennedy would not enter South Dakota or the District of Columbia because they were strictly Humphrey land. In other states, either the threat of favorite sons or a desire to avoid a direct clash with party leaders, who did not want any primary scuffling messing up their territory, kept Kennedy away.

Kennedy and his aides had been eyeing West Virginia for several years. In 1958, they dispatched Louis Harris, the New York pollster, to feel the political pulse. The results were encouraging: 52% of those polled favored Kennedy over Richard M. Nixon. Another Harris poll in December, 1959, showed Kennedy winning over Humphrey in West Virginia with 70% of the vote (Catholics, 92% to 8%; Protestants, 67 to 33% for Kennedy).[1]

A Head-Start

Both Humphrey and Kennedy had visited West Virginia on a half-dozen occasions since 1958 to provide glamour for local Democratic fund-raising affairs. One of Humphrey's aides estimated he had met 1,500 West Virginians on visits which included the Northern Panhandle, Charleston, and Beckley. Kennedy's appearances included dinners at Parkersburg, Charleston, and Welch, a town deep in the southern coal fields.

In January 1959, Kennedy thought West Virginia might be a good place to climax his primary assault and called for a more thorough investigation. Robert P. McDonough, owner of a commercial printing plant in Parkersburg who had met Kennedy at a Democratic dinner there, was asked to set up a series of informal meetings throughout the state.

. . . . About 50 to 75 citizens active in politics and interested in Kennedy's candidacy attended each meeting. Theodore C. Sorenson, the Senator's braintruster, spoke. His pitch was this: we think the Senator has a good chance of getting the nomination if he enters the primaries because he has a good chance of winning the primaries. He is a proven vote-getter with great personal appeal. What do you think? Should he enter your primary?

Most West Virginians who attended the meetings recommended against Kennedy entering. They cited two reasons. He might lose, primarily because of his religion, and they could corral more state delegates for him by working quietly behind the scenes in the grand tradition of West Virginia politics.

But Kennedy was not interested in the state's 25 convention delegates. He wanted to demonstrate that Protestants in a heavily unionized border state would vote for a Roman Catholic presidential candidate. . . .

Robert P. McDonough was named state campaign director and was instructed to set up a West Virginians for Kennedy organization as a volunteer reserve if Kennedy decided to enter the primary. By January 1960, before either Humphrey or Kennedy had even intimated they would clash in West Virginia, McDonough had a least the framework of volunteer organizations ready in 30 of the 55 counties. . . .

Wanted: An Opponent

One big "if" remained in his plans. Kennedy had to have an opponent. An uncontested victory would prove nothing. And there was only one other Democratic presidential candidate willing to take him on in the primaries, Hubert Humphrey, whose liberalism also required a demonstration of primary popularity. Would Humphrey enter the West Virginia primary? The first step was to soft-pedal Kennedy's interest and spadework in West Virginia as much as possible, which also might keep any favorite son movement from materializing. Kennedy made no mention of the primary at his Washington press conference on January 2, 1960, when he formally announced his candidacy. . . .

Meanwhile, brothers Robert and Ted Kennedy were crisscrossing the state sampling public sentiment, getting acquainted with political leaders, and lending their prestige to McDonough's efforts to build a volunteer organization. . . .

Ted went on a grand tour of the state visiting most of its major cities. In Clarksburg, he said Senator Kennedy would decide within two weeks whether to enter. . . . It looked as if West Virginia would fall into place in Kennedy's grand design. On January 21st, he announced he would oppose Humphrey in his own backyard in the Wisconsin primary on April 5th. By January 23rd, Humphrey almost had decided to enter West Virginia. . . . On January 25th, Humphrey addressed the West Virginia Legislature in Charleston. He gave a fiery, liberal speech attacking poverty in affluent America as "a national scandal."

The pleasant reception he received, along with words of encouragement from several West Virginia political and labor leaders, convinced Humphrey. . . . With its New Deal heritage, West Virginia was an attractive place for Humphrey to preach his political gospel. . . . At the 1956 Democratic National Convention, West Virginia delegates had given Humphrey 12 of their 24 votes, compared to 5 for Kennedy, on the first ballot for the vice presidential nomination.

On February 4th, two days before the state deadline for filing, Kennedy announced at a Washington press conference that he would accept the Humphrey challenge. A short time later, Vander Zee arrived in Charleston to file for Humphrey and deposit the $1,000 fee (introduced in 1951 to chase unknown publicity seekers from the presidential primary).

Kennedy, however, used the personal touch he could afford. He flew from Indiana to Charleston in his private plane to file in the early morning hours of February 6th. After a brief interview with local newsmen, he flew west again to Bismarck, North Dakota. "What happens to me in the West Virginia primary could tell really whether I'm going to be nominated," he told newsmen.

A Prayer Is Answered

But if Humphrey were beaten in Wisconsin would he withdraw from West Virginia, leaving Kennedy without his essential opposition? ". . . We were praying that Humphrey wouldn't drop out."

Humphrey was encouraged by the Wisconsin results. His campaign got off to a disorganized start, but he had rallied to win four of ten congressional districts and had come close in several others. . . .

Part-Time Theologians

The winter of 1960 was unusually severe in West Virginia. Mountain villages remained buried in snow even through March, the coldest March on record with the most snowfall since 1914. But in April, as the Humphrey-Kennedy campaign began to sizzle, the weather warmed up, too. The trees and thick vegetation, which cling to West Virginia's hills as politicians do to election returns, covered the state with a lush coat of green.

With the arrival of spring, the primary entered its second phase. The first—pre-entry jockeying and the decisions to enter—largely had been submerged from the public view. But the second would arouse the state and turn many of its citizens into part-time theologians whose views were eagerly sought by reporters, politicians, and pollsters.

". . . It will be a miracle if the outcome in West Virginia shows that there is no religious issue which divides seriously the people of this country," wrote columnist Walter Lippmann. In their coverage of the campaign, most journalists overlooked the political forces at work and over-emphasized the Protestant heritage of West Virginians, which they confused with the intensity of their religious convictions.

In fact, church membership in West Virginia is only half the national average. About two of every three citizens are not affiliated with any church. Only 28% are actually members of Protestant churches; 5%, Roman Catholics; and less than 1%, Jews.

Gymnasiums and Rattlesnakes

Two radically different kinds of Protestantism live as uncomfortable neighbors in West Virginia. In its cities, the pursuit of salvation is pleasant and unemotional with gymnasiums often provided for the children. But in Bible Belt country, old-time religion flourishes. Baptism in cold creek water separates the saved from the damned. A few even demonstrate their faithfulness by handling rattlesnakes and copperheads.

In the coal-mining and other rural areas, where a majority of West Virginians live, hell-fire religion holds sway in hundreds of makeshift churches which may have only 100 members. What they lack in membership they make up for in devotional frenzy. To them, religion is a highly personal matter—more of an emotional outlet than a theological commitment—and each man should be left alone to worship as he pleases.

"There is enough talk about religion, but little of it has to do with application to daily living," says sociologist Roscoe Giffin of Berea (Ky) College, who has observed mountain people in the Southern Appalachian region (which embraces most of West Virginia) for years. "The social gospel is notably absent."

"A great majority of our people are categorized as Protestants, but a goodly number of them have no religious convictions at all," a West Virginia labor leader said. "They also tend to separate their religion from business and politics. It's strictly a Sunday-type religion."

There is other evidence indicating that Kennedy's religion was not as great a handicap in West Virginia as most political writers thought it would be. Dr. Giffin observed that Appalachian residents possess "less of the deep-seated racial and religious prejudices characteristic of many Americans, both North and South."

Pollster Samuel Lubell, who suggested the religious issue was being exaggerated during the primary, said he found considerable evidence to indicate there was less bigotry in West Virginia than in most other states. In other states, Lubell found one of every five Democratic voters ready to vote for the Republican nominee if Kennedy were nominated; in West Virginia, only one of nine. After the primary, he also pointed to the absence of one-sided Humphrey precincts, which he said, "is evidence of how weak was the impact of anti-Catholic feeling.". . .

Unhappy Luncheon

To probe the religious issue and neutralize the pulpit, a confidential luncheon with influential Charleston clergymen was arranged by Kennedy's aides in late March while his own energies were absorbed in Wisconsin. A dozen Protestant ministers and two rabbis met with Sorensen and Charles G. Peters, Jr., who headed the Kennedy campaign in Kanawha County.

Sorensen opened several hours of discussion with a review of Kennedy's voting record as it related to separation of church and state. He also summarized the Senator's blunt campaign statements on the importance of keeping them segregated. But the ministers remained skeptical. Only one Protestant clergyman and the two rabbis were sympathetic.

Kennedy aides came away from the meeting discouraged, but hopeful that the ministers would not snipe at their man. The ministers had left the impression the religious issue was big and probably insurmountable in West Virginia.

Two Methodist ministers who attended the luncheon went on to convince the Kennedy camp that similar meetings with other West Virginia clergymen would prove a waste of time and might even boomerang. A month later in Denver, Colorado, they and two other West Virginia ministers introduced a resolution at the Methodist General Conference which, in effect, said Kennedy's religion was a political issue because of the totalitarian nature of his church. The conference, governing body of the largest Protestant denomination in West Virginia and the nation, promptly rejected their resolution without even giving it a committee hearing. But the views of the four Methodist ministers from West Virginia made headlines back home to blend with those of the Humphrey-Kennedy primary.

On April 12th, Dr. Norman Vincent Peale came to Charleston to address a group of salesmen on his favorite subject, "The Amazing Results of Positive Thinking." But his thoughts on Kennedy's candidacy were not very positive. Dr. Peale told John Weyland of the Associated Press that he had doubts about Kennedy's candidacy because of his religion, citing a 1950 incident when Kennedy declined to attend a Philadelphia fund-raising dinner for the Chapel of the Four Chaplains.

The Kennedy camp studiously avoided public conflict with Protestant clergymen. Their criticisms were ignored or, as in the case of Dr. Peale, were countered by restrained statements outlining the facts as Kennedy saw them, which were issued only in response to press queries.

Votes Against Bigotry

There were signs that Kennedy's strategy not only was paying off but might reap him dividends from angry West Virginians, who would vote for him to prove their state was not a hotbed of bigotry. At the mining community of Pursglove near Morgantown, a Wisconsin atheist who had followed the campaign to West Virginia to promote anti-Catholicism (Kennedy converted him to his politics but not his religion) passed out anti-Catholic literature to miners. "It's a bunch of junk," a miner said, after glancing it over and handing it back. At Cedar Grove near Charleston, a Methodist minister introduced Kennedy. At Kermit, deep in the southern coal fields, an unemployed miner told Herb Little of the Associated Press: "My dad was a Baptist preacher. There was eight of us boys, and every one of us is for Kennedy."

The turn of events infuriated Humphrey's aides. What columnist L.T. Anderson of *The Charleston Sunday Gazette-Mail* described as "the popular psychology which suggests that a West Virginia vote against Senator Kennedy is a vote for bigotry" apparently was spreading. Ironically, its victim would be the man who, perhaps more than any other in public life, had been the champion of equality and tolerance, Hubert Humphrey.

Angered at a column on bigotry in the hills by Joseph Alsop, the co-chairman of the West Virginia Humphrey for President Committee on April 16th issued a statement accusing Kennedy supporters of "deliberately stirring up doubts as to the fairness and tolerance of our voters." Co-chairmen William Jacobs of Parkersburg and Marshall West of Oceana said the objective was "to create a climate that makes it appear unfair not to vote for Kennedy, regardless of whether or not he is qualified." Kennedy himself, they added, "seems to think everybody who doesn't want him to be President is a bigot."

Humphrey backed them up and later said that Kennedy supporters saw no bigots in West Virginia after an early poll showed their man far ahead. When a second poll indicated a close race, "all of a sudden they began seeing ugly things . . . there was intolerance and ignorance," he said. Humphrey also accused Kennedy of talking too much about the religious issue.

The day after Jacobs and West issued their statements, the executive director of West Virginians for Kennedy fired back. Matthew A. Reese, who described himself as 240 pounds of dedication to Kennedy, denied the charge and called their statement "the most ridiculous I ever heard." He accused Jacobs of not really favoring Humphrey for the Democratic nomination, and he said his statement challenged Kennedy's patriotism. Reese then detailed Kennedy's record in the Navy and in Congress. . . .

In FDR's Footsteps

If there was a bona fide issue in the West Virginia primary, neither Humphrey nor Kennedy found it after a month of strenuous campaigning. Their only disagreement was over who should be President. Both promised, once in the White House, to pursue the standard liberal solutions to the problems of depressed areas.

Humphrey, stressing that he was a man of the people who really felt the need for such programs, tried to spell them out between attacks on Kennedy's campaign expenditures. The Kennedy strategy, however, was to concentrate on two themes in an effort to convince voters that, although a Roman Catholic, Kennedy was the man most likely to live in the White House and provide the loaf of bread. The themes were:

Linking John F. Kennedy and Franklin Delano Roosevelt, no pauper himself and a patron saint in the coal fields because of his liberalism, and prophesying that JFK represented FDR's second coming.

Confidently insisting Kennedy would be the next President, with national polls offered as evidence, while arguing that Humphrey did not stand a

Republican's chance of even getting the Democratic nomination. . . . Kennedy's big gun was the namesake of the great man himself, Franklin D. Roosevelt, Jr. He tramped the state for Kennedy, leading interference on the religious issue and carrying with him, by implication, the personal endorsement of his father. "As a Protestant, I urge all my fellow Protestants not to make a religious issue in the West Virginia campaign," he said at Logan in the southern coal fields.

Campaign material boosting Kennedy was mailed from Hyde Park, New York, FDR's home, to every West Virginia Democrat whose name and address could be collected by volunteers in nearly every county. . . . The neatest FDR touch of all was a large advertisement which appeared in the daily newspapers of every major West Virginia city the day before the election. Under a sketch of FDR with his famed cigarette-holder in his mouth, this testimonial appeared: "I am positive that John F. Kennedy is the only candidate for President who can do for West Virginia in the '60s what my father did for West Virginia in the '30s.'" It was signed by FDR, Jr., with this reminder tossed in for good measure: "Vote for West Virginia! Vote for Kennedy for President tomorrow.". . .

Vote for West Virginia

The FDR advertisement was one of a series which appeared in every daily newspaper during the last week of the campaign. The other ads in the series spelled out in terse detail why West Virginia's future rested with a Kennedy victory and why Humphrey was not worth a vote.

One was so blunt that Kennedy aides almost killed it, but then decided they were playing for keeps and distributed it to every daily and weekly. It became known as the Humphrey ash-can ad and infuriated the Minnesota Senator and his supporters. On the left side of the advertisement appeared an unflattering caricature of Humphrey holding a garbage can lid. A sign read "back to Minnesota" with the senator saying "I'll take all these back to Minnesota with me," as a frowning voter hesitated to put his ballot in the garbage can. The right half of the ad depicted a confident, smiling voter casting his ballot for a confident, smiling Kennedy with the White House below and a crowd (identified as the people of West Virginia) surrounding it. "Kennedy's Our Man. Our Votes Will Count!," the headline read. . . . A follow-up ad the next day reminded voters that "when Senator Kennedy goes to the White House, his first order of business will be to give West Virginia a fair break—missing for eight long Republican years." Another ad said, "West Virginia needs a winner! This is the choice on May 10th.". . .

In Search of Salvation

In the affluent 1950s, West Virginia's one-crop economy had discarded surplus coal miners by the thousands. From 1950 to 1959, 106,000 jobs disappeared—creating the highest unemployment rate in the nation. Almost 450,000 West Virginians moved to other states, while 300,000 of the 1.8 million at home depended wholly or partly on government surplus food commodities to stay alive. Meanwhile, President Eisenhower vetoed the federal redevelopment bills designed to begin the slow process of rebuilding depressed areas.

On the eve of the election, Kennedy went before the television cameras and stressed what a victory for him would mean to West Virginia. "I pledge to the people of West Virginia tonight if I'm nominated and elected President, within sixty days of the start of my administration, I will introduce a program to the Congress for aid to West Virginia.". . .

PT Boat 109

Kennedy's war record was dusted off in an effort to establish a bond with West Virginians. War was one thing he had in common with them. Kennedy pointed out during the campaign that "more men from West Virginia lost their lives in the Korean War than from any state in the union of its size." And "more West Virginians served in World War II than from any state of its size," he said. His Catholicism and Harvard accent, with a touch of Roosevelt in it, may have been strange to them. But a state with a dozen Congressional Medal of Honor winners, and almost as many veterans' organizations as schools, could identify with Kennedy as a decorated combat veteran.

Television and radio were used primarily to spread the word of Kennedy's bravery as a PT boat commander in the South Pacific. A filmed episode of a commercial program based on his experience, in which the hero bore a strong resemblance to Kennedy, was shown on every TV station in the state. . . .

The Politics of Coal

Slightly more than half of West Virginia's Democratic voters live in a 15 county area south of the Kanawha River where most of the coal is mined. The proportion of registered Democrats in the coal counties ranges from 61 to 79% of the electorate, usually enough to assure comfortable Democratic majorities in state-wide elections. In this comparatively small region of the state Kennedy concentrated his efforts.

When the vast coal resources were opened up at the turn of the century, the cultural pattern which was to shape state politics also developed. The coal lay deep in the ground in wilderness as untamed as when Daniel Boone roamed through them. To house their miners, the coal operators carved out little feudal empires. In their company towns, the operators owned everything: the shacks in which the minors lived, the streets on which they walked, the stores, and even the law enforcement agencies.

They also controlled the politics. "I can remember when the election clerks were ordered to stuff the ballots down an outdoor privy," said a labor leader who drove a truck in the coal fields during the 1920s. But even the privies could not hold the protest ballots of 1932. Democratic political organizations emerged to capitalize on New Deal sentiment and deliver the big majorities that controlled state politics. In turn, statehouse patronage was used in an effort to keep the peace between the party's dominant labor-liberal and frustrated conservative wings. Handsome campaign kitties, built up largely by the contributions of state employees, also helped keep the county organizations loyal.

Into that factional maze of West Virginia politics stepped Humphrey and

Kennedy, who had sat beside each other in the comparative calm of the United States Senate. In Humphrey's Minnesota, personalities and issues tend to dominate a wide-open style of politics. Kennedy, however, came to West Virginia with at least some knowledge of how rough-and-tumble organizational politics is played. He received his basic training in Massachusetts where politics bears some similarity to the West Virginia brand, with disciplined organizations providing election-day insurance.

Cash and Carry

In West Virginia, the traditional electioneering techniques of the city machines that thrive in Boston or Chicago are modified to fit the state's rural environment. It takes money, lots of it, to lubricate the county organizations so that their wheels turn smoothly on election day.

Enough workers in each precinct must be paid to deliver the printed slate of organization-favored candidates to voters, and arrange to take them to the polls. Workers also check off who votes and then try to turn out those who have not before the polls close. Hiring a man's car for $40 to haul voters on election day—important in getting West Virginia's scattered rural populace to the polls—is expected to set off a chain reaction of loyalty to the county machine. Putting a man on the election-day payroll may assure the votes of a dozen relatives. In a low-income state, people always can use the extra money. And they also want future favors, such as jobs for themselves or their friends.

In the handful of organizational counties where the worst abuses of machine politics have not been softened by public outcry, vote-buying and crooked election officials still play a small part in the democratic process. Voter registration lists in those counties are bloated with the dead and departed. While West Virginia's population declined 7.2% from 1950 to 1960, the number of registered voters increased 2.4%. The 1960 Census counted 6,629 noses in Williamson, including more than 3,700 residents under voting age. But the coal field town reported 7,298 registered voters.

Direct vote-buying is the exception rather than the rule in West Virginia. It infects only a half-dozen counties, including many predominantly Negro precincts. Both sides usually buy votes, which tends to cancel out anticipated benefits. Whiskey, however, is still used in the machine counties as an inducement to good citizenship, although some politicians oppose it because booze may keep their followers from staggering to the polls. The fact that booze is still used was demonstrated by a nonchalant letter which the former Republican State Liquor Commissioner sent to the chairmen of both parties before the 1960 primary and general elections. He informed them the State Liquor Commission had stocked up on half-pints in anticipation of election-day demands and suggested they let the state of West Virginia profit from their trade rather than foreigners across its borders.

Only five of West Virginia's 55 counties have voting machines.[2] The others still use cumbersome paper ballots which in primaries resemble what Arthur Edson of the Associated Press described as "an itemized list of a mammoth auction sale." Slates[3] help guide voters through the maze. For the many citizens who come to the polls to vote for only one man, crooked election officials usually can complete their ballots without working up a sweat or risking a jail sentence. Voting machines, however, also can be manipulated. When Democratic and Republican election officials, who are appointed by county courts often controlled by political organizations, agree to take care of their own with a bi-partisan wink at each other's primary irregularities, their favored candidates can show amazing popularity at the polls.

In primaries, the money to grease the county organizations comes from businessmen who want future favors and the candidates, who are expected to make contributions based on the office they seek and their ability to pay.

"It takes money," one politician explained. "You buy the organization just like you would if you were going to build a house and hire carpenters, electricians, and plumbers. And most of the money is spent legally—on hiring cars and precinct workers." Another politician complained that he could not draw up his campaign budget in advance as businessmen do. The candidates and influence-peddlers hold out to the last minute in an effort to make sure their money will not be wasted and to find out which faction looks like the winner.

Picking Winners

But it requires more than money to win the blessings of county organizations. They also want to be with the candidates who look like winners. In state and local elections, their very survival depends on picking winners. Although their support often is crucial in primaries, the county organizations can be beaten. "I'd rather have public sentiment behind me than anything else in an election," a county leader remarked. In the petty brawling of a primary, factions can arise within a county to challenge the organization's supremacy. If they can awaken a public cynical of politics and bored by intra-party wrangling, a new organization can replace the old.

West Virginia's rural political machines try to mirror public sentiment which explains why, through the statehouse, they usually have been aligned with the labor-liberal wing of the Democratic Party. They cannot always tie up elections in neat little packages and deliver them to their candidates. In McDowell County, for example, the organization barely won the sheriff's office and lost a state Senate race in the 1960 primary. Its leaders believed if they had opposed Kennedy he still would have won by 7,000 to 8,000 votes—instead of winning with 14,336 votes to Humphrey's 2,708, a startling 84.11% of the county vote.

"John F. Kennedy could sell eggs to chickens," explained McDonough, his West Virginia campaign director, who stressed the importance of Kennedy's personal appeal in winning county organization support. "It was Kennedy himself who converted the county leaders. Expose him to ten people and he'll win nine of them.". . .

Organized Confusion

One politician described the Kennedy campaign as "organized confusion."

He laughed off reports of Kennedy's smooth organization. "They were the most disorganized bunch of people I ever saw," he said. "Their sheer numbers just steam rollered our county organizations. Everywhere the politicians went, they saw someone working for Kennedy. They sensed he was going to win and wanted to be on the winning side. On the other hand, they seldom saw any Humphrey people. But everywhere there was enthusiasm and excitement for Kennedy. They began saying that Humphrey didn't think enough of them to ask for their support."

Lines of authority were loose in the Kennedy campaign. Titles were not considered important. Key aides were expected to make decisions to avoid burdening Kennedy with too many details. Five persons could be assigned to one task, assuring that somebody got it done. Using all available manpower, voters were bombarded from all sides—by mail, by telephone calls, through the mass media, at well-publicized rallies and receptions. . . . Just as Kennedy, with an assist from his bottomless treasure chest, out-maneuvered Humphrey with the professionals, he also left him far behind in attracting the volunteers that Humphrey aides admitted were their only hope in West Virginia.

Kennedy's family, friends, and aides who followed him into West Virginia outnumbered Humphrey's about four to one. Many of the Kennedy outsiders were wealthy friends working out of devotion to him. They were stationed about the state to keep headquarters informed on local developments, boost morale of volunteers, help with advance work, and assist with the other endless campaign chores.

Robert Kennedy and O'Brien were the chief field generals, with Sorensen supervising the image-making. They put great emphasis, however, on utilizing local talent. John J. McCormack Advertising, Inc., of Huntington was hired to handle their vast advertising outlay. Two West Virginians who knew their state's politics, McDonough and Reese, were chosen as coordinators. Reese, former aide to a West Virginia congressman and state leader of the Young Democrats, became executive director of West Virginians for Kennedy. . . .

The Ambush That Failed

Stuart Symington jokingly remarked that Lyndon Johnson and he would be running for President as long as there was a breath of air in the body of Hubert Humphrey. The West Virginia primary knocked the air out of Humphrey's candidacy, and left Johnson and Symington so far behind in the presidential race that they never did catch up.

If there was a genuine effort to stop Kennedy in West Virginia, it must be rated as one of the colossal political flops of all times. No doubt many politicians wanted to stop Kennedy. But only one really tried: Senator Robert C. Byrd, a son of the coal fields who had risen from an impoverished childhood through the West Virginia Legislature to the United States Senate.

Byrd, an alumnus of the Ku Klux Klan, was among the powerful group of senators who belonged to Johnson's mutual admiration society in the Senate.

They remained loyal to the Senate majority leader on crucial votes and he always remembered them when committee assignments were passed out or other favors could be arranged.

Byrd's motives for opposing Kennedy were simple: he passionately favored Johnson and realized a West Virginia victory might give Kennedy the nomination. His reasons for failing also were simple; Johnson apparently never realized the danger he was in, and Byrd controlled no political organization. His popularity, like Eisenhower's, would not rub off on another candidate.

The difficulties of Byrd's chosen role virtually doomed him to failure. He asked West Virginia voters to help Johnson by supporting Humphrey, a presidential candidate whom he thought worthy only of the vice presidency. As Kennedy repeatedly reminded the voters, their choice lay between Humphrey and him; the others had not stirred themselves to come in and ask for West Virginia's support. "The voters in the primary had to be either for Humphrey or Kennedy," a state politician pointed out. "The stop Kennedy movement undersold Humphrey, who is a better man than that. He would have done better if his supporters had been for Humphrey rather than against Kennedy. That hurt him."

"There was some talk at one time of Johnson entering the West Virginia primary," wrote Harry G. Hoffman, editor of *The Charleston Gazette*, in his column on politics. "There also was talk of Byrd running as a favorite son in an effort to assure the state's delegation for Johnson. But both plans were abandoned without explanation."

Byrd did try to arouse enthusiasm for the Johnson candidacy by polling Democratic leaders and revealing that Johnson was their choice for President. The poll was attacked as incomplete and inaccurate. Byrd replied that some prominent Democrats who favored other candidates had not received his questionnaire because he was limited by the cost of postage.

Ignoring Humphrey's public coldness and widespread criticism of his role, Byrd toured the state buttonholing people and politicians in an effort to stop Kennedy. But his fellow citizens did not listen. They still voted for Byrd as a delegate to the Democratic National Convention, but many of them resented his plea to vote for Humphrey because he favored Johnson. . . .

Trouble-Makers, Go Home

A stop Kennedy and Humphrey movement also failed in West Virginia. Several international unions, including the Steelworkers and Auto Workers, tried to persuade both Humphrey and Kennedy to negotiate a withdrawal. They feared what looked like a certain Kennedy defeat in West Virginia might give the nomination to Johnson at Los Angeles. And West Virginia Republicans, fearful that Democratic finger-pointing at state economic woes would harm them in November, attacked both Humphrey and Kennedy for invading their soil. Harold E. Neely, the favored GOP gubernatorial candidate, accused Humphrey and Kennedy of "spreading the virus of bigotry, intolerance and hate into every corner of our state." Neeley called them trouble-makers and described the primary campaign as ungodly and phony. "The year of the locusts was mild," he continued. "This Humphrey-Kennedy pestilence is gnawing at the very hearts and minds and souls of our people. Humphrey and Kennedy, go home. . ." GOP Governor Cecil H. Underwood said Humphrey and Kennedy "are having a political feast on our poverty."

The Republican attacks gave the two presidential candidates an opportunity to provide relief from their set scripts. Both pointed out that their primary campaigns had made West Virginia's problems the concern of the nation.[4] And they advised Governor Underwood to become familiar with conditions in his own state. Humphrey said Underwood "must have a kinship with Nero, the mad fiddler who played a mean tune while Rome burned. How has he escaped hearing the cries of hungry children for so long?"

Kennedy almost was stopped in a way which no one would have wanted. Visiting a big mine at Itmann, Wyoming County, during a coal field tour on April 26th, Kennedy ignored the planned routine and walked a short distance inside the mine mouth without a safety helmet. When he climbed onto a mine car his head came perilously near a 250-watt trolley line overhead. Kennedy did not understand shouts of warning and went on. A photographer rushed forward and pushed him out of danger.

Labor Walks a Tightrope

For Hubert Humphrey, long-time champion of organized labor, there really was only one hope of winning in West Virginia: if the unions manned the barricades and hustled up some funds. Money is fundamental in politics, and Humphrey had none when he entered West Virginia. In fact, Wisconsin had left him about $75,000 in debt. But the unions and their friends refused to give him any funds to continue the campaign. Some even put pressure on him to withdraw. The fearful neutrality of most of the internationals effectively restrained their West Virginia locals. . . .

Humphrey pleaded for the support of West Virginia unions; so did Kennedy. The majority of state labor leaders undoubtedly favored Humphrey personally. And, before the campaign began, they found widespread support for him in their locals. But after his defeat in Wisconsin, the internationals considered Humphrey's candidacy hopeless. And they did not want to alienate anyone who might become President. . . .

The UMW also maintained an official policy of neutrality in response to a request Kennedy made of their international in Washington. UMW leaders actually leaned toward Symington because of his labor record as a corporation president. But, between Humphrey and Kennedy, they preferred Humphrey because of Kennedy's role in the passage of the Landrum-Griffin labor-management control bill. Their district leaders in West Virginia, who Kennedy tried to convert after asking for their international's neutrality, passed the word to the rank-and-file that they personally favored Humphrey. But no exhaustive effort was made in his behalf. And miners are famed for ignoring the political advice of their union leaders. They even ignored their beloved president emeritus, John L.

Lewis, when he gave them a choice of voting against Roosevelt or loosing him as CIO president in 1940. They voted for FDR and Lewis resigned.

Teamsters Endorse Humphrey

Angered at the persistent Kennedy attacks on their international leadership, West Virginia Teamsters did what was expected. They gave a public endorsement to Humphrey. The Kennedy camp immediately counter-attacked and charged that Teamster President James R. Hoffa ordered the endorsement. "I'm sure the people of West Virginia are not going to let Jimmy Hoffa determine who should be the Democratic nominee for President," Kennedy remarked at a rally in the steel town of Weirton. . . .

In response to the Teamsters' endorsement, Humphrey simply said he was always pleased "when I get the help of honest working people." The Kennedy strategy was clear; to turn the Teamster endorsement into a liability rather than an asset for Humphrey.

Stymied at the state level in their attempt to get union support, Kennedy aides tried to find young, aggressive union members throughout the state who would work for them as volunteers. Stanley[5] thinks they succeeded. The president and vice president of a Steelworkers local in Huntington, for example, personally endorsed Kennedy. . . .

A Familiar Snake

Humphrey's crusades of the past had an uncanny knack of failing to reward him in West Virginia. "The best thing in politics," he remarked, "is to do right. Do good for the people, and your political cash register will ring." In West Virginia, it rang up short of cash—and short of support from the very people he had championed most.

The state's 90,000 Negroes even outdid organized labor in deserting Humphrey's sinking ship. Negro political leaders estimate that about 75% of the registered Negro Democrats voted for Kennedy in the primary. . . . "West Virginia Negroes voted for Kennedy for one reason; the opposition to him because of his religion looked like the same snake that had been biting them all the time," said G.E. Ferguson, Charleston businessman and Republican leader. William L. Lonesome, a Charleston lawyer and Democratic leader, agreed.

"The feeling the Negro has of being the underdog made him respond to Kennedy's candidacy despite Humphrey's civil rights record, Ferguson continued. "The same type of thinking—that Kennedy's religion disqualified him from becoming President—keeps Negroes out of the White House, too."

Kennedy campaigners worked hard to exploit that underdog identification among West Virginia Negroes. A minister from New York City was brought in to soothe any worries about Kennedy's Catholicism on the part of the predominantly Protestant Negroes. . . .

Unpublicized meetings were arranged with Negroes throughout the state at which they were advised that minority groups must stick together if they hope to eradicate their second-class citizenship. . . . With an assist from the county organizations, Kennedy rolled up enormous majorities in Negro precincts—140 to 4 for Humphrey in Charleston's Coal Branch Heights and 62 to 5 in another largely Negro precinct near Omar in the coal county of Logan.

Sport for the Rich

"It is a sad and sobering fact of life that presidential politics in America is more than a sport for the rich or their protegés," Douglass Cater wrote in *The Reporter*. Only with the unlimited funds at his disposal could John F. Kennedy have staged the blitzkrieg which brought him victory in West Virginia. But money alone does not always assure a winner in politics, as the Johnson and Symington campaign demonstrated.

What makes the difference is how a candidate uses his money, what political party he is aligned with, and if he also has that mysterious quality called appeal. In West Virginia, Kennedy's personal appeal and his pocketbook made him unbeatable. The ways in which he used his money projected his appeal to thousands of voters and bought him a landslide through organizational support. "The Massachusetts senator bought a landslide not an election," wrote Chilton, assistant to the publisher of *The Charleston Gazette*, in *The New Leader*. "At the outset Kennedy contracted with factional organizations in machine-controlled counties where money talks . . . . ," he explained.

How much did Kennedy spend in West Virginia? After the primary, he officially reported spending $91,322.62. Humphrey filed only a pre-election report showing expenditures of $13,835.17. At that time, Kennedy reported spending only $11,211.94—a propaganda coup since Humphrey was running as the poor boy candidate. But state requirements for reporting campaign expenses are so loose and shot with exemptions that they are meaningless.

Kennedy's West Virginia tab, excluding most staff salaries and personal expenses such as the use of a private plane, probably totaled at least $250,000. His outlay for advertising came close to $100,000. Space and time were bought in every West Virginia daily and weekly newspaper and on every radio and television station. His local committees also bought newspaper advertising to publicize local rallies or TV appearances. Politicians estimate Kennedy's contributions to county machines for organizational support totaled $50,000 to $100,000. Other expenses reported to the Secretary of State, excluding advertising, exceeded $76,000.

In contrast, Humphrey spent at most $30,000 and that went largely for staff salaries. Operating on what he called "a shoestring cut in half," Humphrey never did mount a public relations offensive to help create a clear image of who he was and what he was doing in West Virginia. His expenditures for newspaper advertising and radio-TV time were more appropriate for a candidate seeking a seat in the state legislature rather than the presidency. He spent only $2,000 or $3,000 on television (done hastily in the last week of the campaign), and practically nothing on radio or newspaper advertising.

Money gave Kennedy a freedom and flexibility which Humphrey did not have. He got more rest flying back and forth to Washington for key Senate roll-calls on his private plane than Humphrey could on the commercial airlines he had to use. Faced with a deadline for their series of newspaper advertisements, Kennedy aides hired two private planes to fly the mats from Cincinnati to daily newspapers throughout the state. A Hollywood film company handled Kennedy's radio and TV production, sending a crew to West Virginia to do the bulk of the work and then relying on film shot by local photographers, which was flown to the West Coast for processing.

Kennedy's hard-won role of the underdog helped counteract Humphrey's charges that he was trying to buy the election. "I can't afford to run through this state with a little black bag and a checkbook. . . . I'm being ganged up on by wealth," said Humphrey, who during the primary estimated that Kennedy was spending from $250,000 to $500,000. "I don't have a daddy to pay the bills," Humphrey said in another stump speech. "I don't have an open checkbook." He described Kennedy's money as compounding into a "short-term area redevelopment program for West Virginia" and as "floating as freely as water in West Virginia streams—and both are a little polluted." Humphrey said the campaign boiled down to "pitting my body, my ideals, and my faith against the wealth of my opponent."

"Nobody Can Buy Him"

Kennedy made no apology for his wealth and admitted frankly that his campaign was costing a lot of money, primarily because he had to overcome voter uneasiness about his religion. And as columnist Doris Fleeson pointed out: "The Kennedys do not condescend to a less well-off public by any change of dress or manner. They come from the great world and they carry it about with them. Some observers think it is a large part of their appeal."

Winning elections with the family checkbook is an old charge against Kennedy, first raised in his Massachusetts congressional campaigns. But it obviously has not affected his political career. In fact some voters are convinced that a personal fortune is the best guarantee of a politician's honesty. "Kennedy has money," said a local Democratic committeeman in West Virginia's Northern Panhandle. "Nobody can buy him. He doesn't have to worry about industries to back him or any kind of graft.". . .

Two *Charleston Gazette* reporters, Don Marsh (a former Nieman Fellow at Harvard) and John G. Morgan (a former Reid Fellow in India), traveled the state after the primary in an effort to find out why Kennedy won. They interviewed hundreds of politicians and citizens. Their conclusion: Kennedy had not bought the election. Even most Republican leaders agreed that was true.

A Classical Operation

How had he won? "We just set up a classical political operation and pushed it to the hilt," said McDonough, Kennedy's West Virginia campaign director. "We used the local political organizations, the candidate's own organization, and fully exploited our candidate. There are only three things you can do to get somebody elected to office: enlist the help of those already in politics, enlist your friends as volunteers, and get your candidate out there where everybody can see him."

It was the way in which Kennedy and his aides operated in that classical framework which brought them victory. The candidate's personal appeal aroused the enthusiasm of volunteers and impressed county bosses. The religious issue and stop Kennedy efforts were used to pre-empt the underdog role from Humphrey.[6] Identifying Kennedy with FDR and as the next President who would help desperate West Virginia filled out his appealing image. His string of primary victories elsewhere and his glamorous national publicity also undoubtedly contributed to Kennedy's West Virginia victory.

The Kennedy camp missed few tricks. No possibility was too small to ignore. Two former great football players at West Virginia University, Joe Stydahar and Sam Huff, were brought in to give personal endorsements to Kennedy. The National Coal Policy Conference issued a statement commending Kennedy for his support of a national fuels policy. After the West Virginia Teamsters had endorsed Humphrey, the presidents of four international unions praised Kennedy's labor record in a news release issued by his Washington headquarters. . . .

Humphrey, unlike Kennedy, never convinced himself that he could become President. His campaign buttons read "It's Humphrey in '60," a slogan which was chosen so the buttons could be used in his Minnesota senatorial campaign if his bid for the presidency failed. Voters undoubtedly sensed Kennedy's confidence and Humphrey's uncertainty, which was reflected in his disorganized campaign. "Most people realized what Humphrey knew himself—he couldn't become President," a West Virginia labor leader said.

On the Road

On May 10, 1960, almost 390,000 West Virginia Democrats, 57% of those registered, entered 2,751 precincts and gave John F. Kennedy the boost he needed to capture their party's presidential nomination. Kennedy received 60.84% of the votes—236,510 to Humphrey's 152,187.

Early the next morning when the outcome was clear, Humphrey stepped before the TV cameras. "I have a brief statement," he said. "I am no longer a candidate for the Democratic presidential nomination."

Kennedy, who had flown to Washington election day, received a telephone call late that night from his brother, Robert. He boarded his private plane and flew back to Charleston. "Thanks, Hubert, for coming over," Kennedy said, as they shook hands at the photographers' request.

Then, as Humphrey left unnoticed, Kennedy went to greet his delirious supporters. "I think we're on the road now," he remarked. "I am in debt to the people of West Virginia. I believe now that you have made it possible for me to be nominated for President."

Notes

From Harry W. Ernst, "The Primary That Made A President: West Virginia 1960," *Eagleton Institute Cases in Practical Politics*, McGraw-Hill Book Company, Inc., 1-13, 15-20, 23, 25-32. Copyright 1962 by Rutgers, The State University. Used with permission of the Eagleton Institute.

[1] See Theodore H. White, *The Making of the President 1960*, (Atheneum Publishers: New York, 1961). After both Humphrey and Kennedy had entered the West Virginia primary, local polls conducted by Harris either showed Kennedy ahead with the outcome in the hands of the undecided voters or far behind, which may have prompted Kennedy's public statements that he would do well if he received only forty percent of the vote. One political writer said a poll conducted in the Huntington area just before the election convinced Kennedy he was going to lose, which he prompted his flight to Washington on election day. He did lose in the Huntington area, but swept the state. Harris apparently was unable to conduct any state-wide samplings after the campaign began and the local polls, compared to the pre-campaign state surveys that indicated victory would come easy, gave the impression Kennedy was losing ground and faced an uphill fight. All of the published straw votes conducted in West Virginia high schools and colleges, however, showed Kennedy winning easily.

[2] Today there are 22 counties using paper ballots; 20 using punch card ballots, 3 using lever machines and 10 using optical scanner. See West Virginia State Election Commission; http://www.state.wv.us/sec/voting/vsys.htm <ed.>.

[3] This is a procedure known as slating candidates. Political organizations have a list printed and distributed of candidates who have received their endorsement. To be slated, a candidate must have friends, money, be in a position to ask support for past favors, or look like a winner.

[4] After Kennedy became President, TV newsman David Brinkley credited the West Virginia primary for passage of the area redevelopment bill in Congress.

[5] Miles C. Stanley was President of the state AFL-CIO and was consulted by both Humphrey and Kennedy. . . . <ed.>.

[6] Both Humphrey and Kennedy claimed to be the genuine underdog throughout the campaign. "I'm running against tremendous odds," Humphrey said. "He (Kennedy) looks as much like an underdog as Man Mountain Dean looks like a pygmy." Edson of the Associated Press observed: "It could be the only race in history with two underdogs entered."

On Guns, Coal, and Electoral College Victory Margins: West Virginia in the 2000 Presidential Campaign

Allan S. Hammock and Lawrence J. Grossback

West Virginia does not often cast its electoral votes for Republican presidential candidates, at least not challengers. Until George W. Bush won the state in 2000, it had been seventy-two years since a nonincumbent Republican candidate had carried the state. The victory gave Bush five electoral votes, one more than his margin of victory.[1] The implication here is striking. A Gore victory pushes the Florida recount debacle off the front page, puts the Supreme Court back on the sidelines of electoral politics, and, most importantly, puts a Democrat in the White House. A blatant pro-Bush headline on the front page of the *Wall Street Journal* summed it up well, noting, "Western Civilization is greatly indebted to [West Virginia.]" (Hamburger, *Wall Street Journal*).

While western civilization's debt to West Virginia is debatable, the uniqueness of the 2000 election in West Virginia is not. The Bush victory was not the only oddity. In 2000 an incumbent governor lost. Moreover, that incumbent was a Republican, one of only two elected to that position since 1932. More impressively, Shelly Moore Capito became the first Republican elected to the U.S. House of Representatives from the second congressional district in 18 years. Capito overcame a 23-point Democratic registration advantage, a 30-point poll deficit, and the nation's highest spending House candidate (he spent $7 million, a 6 to 1 imbalance) to score a remarkable come-from-behind victory. The election of 2000 thus stands out as something of an historical puzzle (Basu, 2001). Luckily puzzles make for good story telling and good research, and that is precisely what we offer. Our goal in this paper is two-fold; we offer our version of the story of the 2000 election in West Virginia and we offer some reasons as to why and how it turned out the way it did.

Where possible we link the story of West Virginia to broader questions within the political science literature on electoral strategy, campaign effects, and voting behavior. Among the questions we explore are the following. Why did the Bush campaign target West Virginia and how does this fit with our existing understanding of campaign strategy development? How did the Bush campaign (and consequently the Gore campaign) approach the state? How did they select issues to run on? Where did they campaign and why? What drove voting patterns in the state? How did the issues, candidate appearances, and other activities affect the outcome? How was the outcome reflective of the context of West Virginia's politics, economy, and culture? What are the implications for future elections in West Virginia and presidential campaign strategies more generally?

We proceed as follows. We first place the state in the context of the national election by reviewing prominent explanations for the Bush victory and how the Bush strategists came to view West Virginia as a target of opportunity. We next explore how the Bush strategy was translated into an effective state-level campaign. In the process we offer some explanations for why Bush won, and a few for why Al Gore lost. We close with some reflections on the future of electoral politics in West Virginia.

The Federal Campaign

Florida recounts and the Supreme Court aside, the 2000 election saw some oddities outside of West Virginia as well. It is important to account for the national decisions and trends that contributed to the election's outcome before assessing how these trends manifest themselves in West Virginia. That West Virginia was a key element in Bush's victory was no accident . . . .. The Bush campaign was built around a strategy that sought to win West Virginia and a number of states that look like it; states that are small, predominantly rural, home to hunters and union workers, and a little culturally conservative (Pomper, 2001). As it turns out, when we look at a number of analyses of electoral trends following 2000, it might be more surprising that West Virginia stayed Democratic as long as it did. Two broad sets of national factors have emerged from the Bush victory, those associated with a new political geography in the United States and those associated with the Bush campaign strategy and tactics.

Pomper (2001) argues that the 2000 presidential elections signaled the final stages of a new political geography in the United States and that the Bush campaign skillfully used this new electoral map to their advantage. The new political geography mirrors the electoral vote map from the 2000 election, and Pomper goes so far as to suggest the emergence of two nations (see Cook, *The Washington Quarterly* for a similar analysis). The Democratic nation includes large states (Gore won 6 of the 9 largest) and urban areas primarily in the northeast, west coast, and Great Lakes regions. The GOP nation includes smaller rural states in the south, border, mountain and plains regions. The Bush campaign recognized this pattern and moved aggressively to develop a message targeted at states that fit the GOP pattern but had voted for Bill Clinton in recent elections. Early in the election cycle, Bush's chief strategist, Karl Rove, developed a plan to win a number of smaller states in an effort to ensure an electoral college victory even if Al Gore won the large industrial states and California. The Bush strategy was to use the "cultural conservative" mantra to hold their advantage on moral issues that play well in the south and rural areas and to appeal to more moderate voters with a renewed interest in government actions to shore up Social Security and spur the economy with tax cuts (*Newsweek*, Nov. 20, 2000, 110).

The Bush electoral strategy was one of the stories of this national election . . . The . . . campaign maintained a Republican base that was comprised of the states Bob Dole won in 1996. The states in bold (see Figure 2.2) are where the Bush campaign worked to win the election. These eleven states all voted for Bill Clinton, but were seen as either marginal Republican states or targets of opportunity because they were socially conservative, had significant rural populations, were in the south, or had significant Republican trends since 1996. Note the position of West Virginia. The Gore campaign viewed it as a base Democratic state while the Bush campaign made it a target very early on. Why they did so and how they tailored their message to the nature of the state is explained in the next section of the paper. The Bush team's confidence in winning these states (which they did) also allowed them to contest several large states such as Pennsylvania and Michigan and a variety of Democratic-leaning states such as Minnesota and New Mexico. Eventually the Bush campaign put resources into both California and the northwest in an effort to force the Gore campaign to divert resources from swing states such as Florida. Eventually the Gore campaign withdrew from Ohio and pulled their advertising from West Virginia as well. . . . In the end a series of smaller states with rural or southern leanings (West Virginia, Kentucky, Arkansas, Tennessee, Louisiana) helped push Bush to an electoral college victory.

Figure 2.2 Initial 2000 Electoral College Strategies

Gore Strategy 2000

Bush Strategy 2000	Base Republican	Marginal Republican	Battleground	Marginal Democratic	Base Democratic
Base Democratic					MA, NY, RI, CT, HI, MD, VT, DC, DE
Marginal Democratic				CA, NJ, ME	MN, WA, OR
Battleground			PA, MI, IA, WI	IL, NM	**WV**
Marginal Republican		**AZ, NC CO, GA IN, NE, SD, LA, KY, NV, AR, NH**	**FL, MO, TN, OH**		
Base Republican	AL, SC, TX, MA, VA, AK, ID, MT, UT, WY, KS, ND, SD, OK				

Source: The electoral college strategies were developed by the authors from media sources, studies, and personal analysis of the campaign.

The second set of national factors that need to be considered before reviewing what happened in West Virginia, relate more specifically to the events and tactics of the 2000 campaign. Several aspects of the Republican efforts in 2000 made them more competitive than most analysts expected given Gore's near incumbent status and the current state of the American economy. (Of course we now know that the economy was not as bright as analysts thought and that the American people caught on to this before the analysts and the economic indicators.) The Republican Party made a concerted push to win back the White House. Part of this effort included an early focus on Bush as a centrist candidate, a quiet accommodation of the Republican right early in the campaign, and a monumental fundraising effort that raised and spent the most money in the history of presidential campaigns, somewhere between $350–400 million (*Newsweek*, November 20, 2001, 50).

Two aspects of the Bush campaign would come to play a key role in West Virginia. The first was a strategy designed to reach out to workers in industrial states in the Ohio River Valley in an effort to capitalize on Al Gore's environmental reputation. The strategy, nicknamed "cars and coal," sought to reduce the Democrat's advantage with union members, autoworkers, and miners by stressing Gore's environmental stance, the gun issue, and taxes (Hamburger, *Wall Street Journal*). These efforts were targeted at states such as Michigan, Ohio, Pennsylvania, West Virginia and Kentucky. A second important national effort was in the area of getting out the vote (GOTV) . The Republican Party spent an estimated $56 million dollars on GOTV activities in the last five weeks of the campaign. In a number of battleground states the national Republican Party targeted 15% of the states' swing voters with between five and seven pieces of mail in the closing week (*Newsweek*, November 20, 2001 10).[2] As we shall show, turnout looms large as a cause of Bush's success in West Virginia.

Several other factors emerged from the 2000 campaign that made for a tight race but may have played less of a direct role in West Virginia. First is what some have called Gore's "Clinton dilemma." The Gore campaign was clearly concerned about their association with Bill Clinton in the post-impeachment era. Gore's dilemma was to take credit for a strong economy and thus convince the voters they were better off today than they were eight years ago while avoiding the stain of Clinton's various scandals. Many analysts question Gore's decision to not make better use of the economy as an issue in the campaign while also putting forth a more liberal populist message. Given West Virginia's perpetually weak economy and the importance of economic versus environmental issues, Gore's advantage may have been mitigated even if he had made better use of the issue in the state. Exit polls done in West Virginia indicated that about 53% of respondents felt their family's financial situation was either worse or the same than the same time last year, and both groups supported George Bush by a wide margin (Voter News Service). On other issues, the campaigns often fought to a draw with Al Gore winning votes on education, social security and health care. George Bush, on the other hand, did well on leadership, character traits, and taxes.

An important question in the literature on electoral college strategies is whether and how campaigns prime voters in the states they target (Shaw, 1999). West Virginia provides an important case to study this question. Contextual studies of electoral politics recognize that politics is a function of individual decisions, but individuals make decisions at a particular time and place (Huckfeldt and Sprague, 1995). These scholars note that national politics is actually played out in countless specific locations and that electoral behavior is best understood at the sub-national level. Recognition of this is key to the development of a campaign strategy within a targeted state. MacKuen and Brown (1987) provide an important base for assessing the actions of the Bush campaign in West Virginia. In a study of political context and attitude change, they found that evaluations of candidates and parties were directly influenced by what neighbors are saying while partisan identification was linked mostly to stable environmental and historical influences. Using data from the 1980 election, they found that a Democratic context or neighborhood did little to help Jimmy Carter while the mere discussion of Ronald Reagan among neighbors significantly increased people's positive evaluation of him. They speculated that the conversational environment rather than the more stable partisan climate had a greater impact on vote intentions and that Carter was hurt by being perceived as not fitting into the classic Democratic model.

A similar dynamic may have been at work in West Virginia during the 2000 campaign. The Bush campaign made a clear effort to paint Gore as an environmental extremist that cared little about the jobs of union workers in major industries. If the Bush campaign could get people talking about Bush as a viable alternative and cast Gore as outside the traditional model of the working class Democrat, they could overcome the voter's Democratic predisposition and win a state such as West Virginia. The findings of the contextual researchers point to an important causal mechanism. A campaign that stressed values and issues appropriate to the regional or state context could spur a conversational environment capable of overcoming the single party based voting cue. The question now is whether the Bush campaign did this in West Virginia and how successful were they?

The West Virginia Campaign

Although there are few "certainties" in politics, the most obvious "certainty" of the pre-2000 presidential election campaign was that Al Gore and the Democrats would carry West Virginia.[3] George W. Bush, the Republican, had absolutely no chance of winning. After all, Democrats outnumbered Republicans 2 to 1 statewide and in some counties as much as 25 to 1 (Logan), 18 to 1 (Mingo), 15 to 1 (McDowell), and 13 to 1 (Boone). Moreover, West Virginia had gone Republican in presidential contests on only three occasions since 1932 (1956, 1972 and 1984), and only four times in some 70 years (Hoover, 1928, Eisenhower, Nixon, and Reagan in their race for a second term). If ever there was a "modified one-party" state, to use Ranney's (1971) classification scheme, West Virginia was it! Yet, Bush won; and unlike Florida, it was not even a "squeaker" (Bush 53.2%; Gore 46.8%). Bush's better than 6 percent margin of victory defied the conventional wisdom that West Virginia was a "lock" for the Democrats. How could Gore have lost? The answer to this question appears to lie in the peculiar circumstances of the West Virginia campaign—that extraordinary coming together of issues, candidates, political events, and campaign initiatives and strategies that made it possible for Bush to capture West Virginia's five electoral votes and thus become president by a margin of 271 to 267 electoral votes.

King Coal and the Kingmaker

One of the keys to understanding the Bush victory in West Virginia . . . is that coal is still "King" in the state (Nyden, *Charleston Gazette-Mail*). To be sure, the number of active coal miners in West Virginia has dwindled to around 14,000 from a high of some 150,000 in the 1940s, yet, coal remains a significant part of the economy of the state (although tourism, education, and health care eclipse coal in the number of jobs produced). Anything endangering the coal industry is cause for alarm. Al Gore was widely perceived as anti-coal, which, as we shall see, was a perception that was not altogether unfounded.

It is against this backdrop of king coal that one of West Virginia's leading coal executives—James "Buck" Harless—emerged to play a significant, some say pivotal role, in the Bush campaign. Dubbed "Kingmaker" by the *Charleston Gazette* (Tuckwiller, *Gazette-Mail*, March 11, 2001), Buck Harless today is a household name among national journalists (e.g., *Washington Post, Wall Street Journal, Newsweek*), Washington, D.C. and Charleston, WV politicians and policymakers, and the man-on-the-street in West Virginia. The *Charleston Gazette* refers to him as a "one-man political machine;" the *Wall Street Journal* as "local kingmaker," and early Bush "Pioneer," a label given to those who pledged to raise $100,000 for the Bush campaign (Hamburger, *Wall Street Journal*). According to the *Journal*, Harless personally helped raise more than $275,000 for the Bush campaign in West Virginia (five times the amount raised by Gore in the state). In one of the supreme compliments ever given to Harless as regards his influence, former Secretary of State Ken Hechler, said, "Buck Harless controls the thought processes of the people of the coal fields" (Hamburger, *Wall Street Journal*). He no doubt "controls" those thought processes, because, in the words of U.S. Senator John D. Rockefeller, IV, "Harless is one of those people whose heart you feel really operates strongly on behalf of West Virginia" (quoted in Martel and Hodel, *Gazette Mail*, Aug. 13, 2000). Harless himself, has made a similar point:

> "I have spent a blessed lifetime in the state of my birth, the state I love, the town I love. I've lived in the same house for over 50 years, choosing to find ways to be successful in West Virginia rather than turning my back on my home as so many others have done, and so many tried to tempt me to do" (Harless, *Charleston Gazette*, April 1, 2001).

Harless' role in the Bush campaign simply cannot be overestimated. It was Harless who first suggested to Bush at a meeting of Bush "Pioneers" (a meeting of financial heavy hitters in Texas) that he had a real chance of carrying West Virginia. As a leading coal executive, moreover, it was easy for Harless to mobilize the coal industry for Bush (both locally and nationally). Harless enlisted William Raney, President of the West Virginia Coal Association, as a kind of aide de camp, to coordinate the coal industry in the fight to defeat Gore. Five months after Bush was sworn in as president, Bill Raney stood before the annual meeting of the Coal Association and congratulated the members on their efforts on behalf of Bush. "You did everything you could to elect a Republican president," he said, and now "you are already seeing in his actions the payback, if you will, his gratitude for what you did" (Quoted in Hamburger, *Wall Street Journal*).

Evidence of the fruits of Mr. Harless' labors can be seen in Table 2.8. Table 2.8 presents a comparison of coal and non-coal producing counties (determined by 1998 coal production numbers from the West Virginia Geological Survey) on a variety of election statistics. Al Gore won, on average, only 47% of the vote in coal producing counties, eight points worse than Bill Clinton in 1996. Despite an average Democratic registration advantage of 41%, George Bush was still able to win 16 coal counties. The only counties Al Gore won were coal producing, but he so underperformed both Bob Wise and Bill Clinton that it is clear that the Republican efforts turned much of coal country against their Democratic roots and toward George Bush.

Table 2.8 Comparing Coal to Non-Coal Counties

	Coal Producing	No Coal Production
N	29	26
Bush Percent	50%	58%
Gore Percent	47%	40%
Clinton Percent 1996	55%	46%
Gore% - Wise%	-6%	4%
Gore% - Clinton% 1996	-8%	-7%
Wise Victories	23	8
Clinton Victories 1996	25	18
Gore Victories	13	0
Democratic Registration	67%	55%
Republican Registration	26%	35%
Democratic Registration Advantage	41%	20%
2000 Democratic Margin	-3%	-18%
1996 Democratic Margin	22%	5%

Numbers are average values

Source: West Virginia Geological Survey, 1998 coal production data; West Virginia Secretary of State, 1996, 2000 elections.

Harless also was an important player, if not the single most important player, in the election of Republican Governor Cecil Underwood in 1996 (Tuckwiller, *Charleston Gazette-Mail*, March 11, 2001). However, Harless represents only one set of interests in the state—that is, business, and specifically coal, timbering, and trucking—and those interests cannot prevail electorally in the state unless the Democratic Party is split. Thus in 1996, Underwood the Republican, was elected governor when the Democratic Party failed to come together to support Charlotte Pritt, a "liberal" Democrat (Brisbin, et al.). In the same manner, many moderate and conservative Democrats abandoned their party in 2000 to support George Bush. According to Voter News Service exit polls, one-quarter of Democrats voted for Bush; and among those who considered themselves "conservative" (of both parties) 81% voted for Bush. Republican victories, therefore, depend upon defections from the majority Democratic Party. Harless was able to capitalize on the fact that there were likely to be Democratic defections in 2000, just as there were in 1996.

The Issues and the Campaign

The seeds of the Bush victory were actually planted much before the 2000 campaign itself. The single most important seed—jobs in the coalfields—was planted, ironically, not by Harless but by Republican appointee U.S. District Court Judge, Charles H. Haden. In October 1999, Judge Haden issued a court order limiting "mountaintop removal" coal mining (Ward, *Charleston Gazette-Mail*, Dec. 3, 2000). Siding with the environmentalists, Haden ruled that the practice of filling valleys with waste rock and soil, covering small streams, violated various provisions of the federal and state environmental statutes.

Judge Haden's ruling evoked a hail of protests from coal companies, coal miners and their families, state and national politicians and from those families directly and indirectly affected by the ruling. The chief lawyer for the National Mining Association, Hal Quinn, exclaimed that "the decision jeopardizes the continued viability of the coal industry in Appalachia and elsewhere." A coal industry lawyer, R. Hewett Pate, in a friend of the court brief, wrote that "the district court ruling . . . will destroy coal mining as an economically viable industry in West Virginia" (Quoted in Ward, *Gazette-Mail*, Dec. 3, 2000).

The response of the coal industry to the ruling was not unexpected. What made the ruling all the more important, however, was that it galvanized opinion in the southern coal fields, perhaps as no other issue had done in recent times. U.S. Senator Robert Byrd and the rest of the congressional delegation denounced the ruling (Ward, *Gazette-Mail*). Local governments feared the loss of tax revenue. In Logan County, coal tax revenue represents 64% of all revenue in the county (*Charleston Gazette*, May 3, 2001). A study conducted by researchers at Marshall University projected a $168 million annual loss in state taxes after five years as a result of the ruling (Seider, *Charleston Gazette*, Feb. 14, 2001). Most importantly, the president of the United Mine Workers of America, Cecil Roberts, denounced the ruling. In a major op-ed piece in the *Charleston Gazette* Roberts stated:

> "When Judge Charles Haden ruled last week to outlaw most valley fills, he single-handedly sentenced thousands of West Virginia coal miners and other industry workers to almost certain economic death . . . The members of the UMW expect me to protect their jobs, and I intend to fight for them with every available resource" (Roberts, *Charleston Gazette*, October, 1999).

Although Judge Haden's order was ultimately reversed on appeal in the U.S. 4th Circuit Court of Appeals, the political consequences were immediately evident: a broad coalition of coal companies, coal miners, businesses, government officials, community leaders, and ordinary citizens had become mobilized to fight for coal-related jobs in West Virginia. With but a few cracks (notably the UMWA leadership in the last days of the campaign), this coalition was maintained throughout the 2000 presidential election. This coalition was, of course, tailor made to respond to the Bush "cars and coal" strategy that worked to pull union support from Democratic candidates.

For many West Virginians, the mountaintop removal ruling became the defining issue of the campaign. The ruling threatened jobs, not only in the coalfields but in an array of coal-related supporting industries and services scattered throughout the state. Asked during the campaign to identify the most important problem facing West Virginia, 25% named "jobs." The next closest response was "education" with 12% (West Virginia Poll). Among those who actually went to the polls, 57% were concerned about the economy, and of that group, 61% voted for Bush and 38% for Gore (Voter News Service). For many West Virginians, therefore, it was "the economy, stupid," a factor which did not play in more prosperous states nor in the nation as a whole (Pomper, *PSQ*, 2001).

Organized Labor and the Election

The issue of mountaintop removal and its effect on jobs cut deeply into traditional Democratic strongholds in various parts of the state, but particularly in the southern coalfield counties. In some coal counties, the only game in town is coal, and to have these jobs threatened is to suffer a major economic blow. Indeed, as the 2000 campaign unfolded, the issue of jobs served to cause cracks in what is, traditionally, a solid Democratic stronghold—organized labor.

The cracks in organized labor became evident, first, in the temporary coalition of coal companies and coal miners brought about by the Haden mountaintop removal ruling. Spokespersons for each group, Bill Raney of the Coal Association and Cecil Roberts of the United Mine Workers, denounced the ruling with equal fervor, leaving no doubt that they stood with anyone who would help to reverse the decision . . .

Into this mix stepped an unlikely Bush ally—Charles "Dick" Kimbler, an unemployed former president of a UMWA local. Directly affected by a lay-off at Arch Coal Company by the District Court's ruling, Kimbler became a point person in the Bush campaign, moving about the coal fields with Bill Raney of the Coal Association and Bush operatives to make joint appearances on behalf of Bush (Hamburger, *Wall Street Journal*).

Kimbler's efforts gave credibility to the Bush campaign for West Virginia. Now Al Gore could no longer count on a solid organized labor front for support. Indeed at every Bush rally, laid-off miners held signs in support of coal, jobs, and Bush . . .

Al Gore's positions on the environment made it very difficult for the UMWA to enthusiastically join his campaign. It was well known that Gore was, at best, lukewarm to coal, and at worst, a strong supporter of the Kyoto accords, which if implemented, would effectively cripple the coal industry in the state and nation. As a consequence, the UMWA delayed its endorsement of Gore until well into the campaign (the third week of September, just six weeks before the election) . In fact, the UMWA was the last of the AFL–CIO's 68 affiliates to endorse Gore, and then only after Gore had provided written assurance on "10 points of clarification" concerning Gore's commitment to clean coal technology. Among Gore's promises was that "there would be a future for coal . . . in the nation's energy mix" (Hodel, *Register-Herald*, Sept. 21, 2001).

Gore's problems with the UMWA were compounded by an equal set of problems with the steelworkers, located primarily in the state's northern panhandle. Although the national United Steelworkers endorsed Gore, the Independent Steelworkers Union, representing 3,500 members at Weirton Steel endorsed Reform Party candidate Pat Buchanan. Gore's problems with the ISU was the fact that in 1992 and thereafter he had made promises to the steelworkers that the Clinton Administration would do something about foreign steel "dumping." Mark Glyptis, union president, made clear the contempt with which Weirton's steelworkers viewed Gore's supposed sellout of steel:

> "There wasn't any possibility of this union endorsing Al Gore. We believe he lied to the residents of the Ohio Valley . . . If he came to this town, he would be run out of this town. That's how we feel about Al Gore." (Quoted in Bundy, *Register-Herald*, Sept. 3, 2000).

In a visit to Weirton, George Bush's vice-presidential running mate, Richard Cheney, told a plant-gate crowd, "We will never lie to you . . . If our trading partners violate trade laws, we will respond swiftly and firmly" (Associated Press, *Charleston Gazette*, October 28, 2000).

Gore's problem with organized labor showed up at the polls. While Gore won most of the coal producing counties in the southern coalfields (Boone, Logan, Mingo, Wyoming, McDowell, Lincoln, Fayette, and Summers), he lost Mercer and Raleigh Counties. He also lost coal-producing Monongalia County in the north and nearly lost coal-heavy Marion and Harrison Counties, also in the north. Although able to carry Brooke County in the northern panhandle by a 500-vote margin, he lost three other counties—Hancock, Ohio, and Marshall.

Gore's weakness with organized labor is revealed first with the level of turnout in coal counties vs. non-coal counties; and second, with the actual votes garnered in 2000 vs. 1996. Turnout in coal producing, southern counties was at least 7 percentage points below that of the state as a whole and in some cases, much below. McDowell, Mingo, Lincoln, and Logan counties had turnout rates 10 percentage points or better below the state average. Moreover, turnout in coal producing counties was well below that in 1996, when at least six percent more voters went to the polls. Al Gore's total statewide vote was greatly affected by this low turnout in the southern coalfields.

Turnout

In many ways, turnout caused many of Al Gore's problems in 2000 . . . On average, counties with higher turnout had more registered Republicans, a lower Democratic registration advantage, produced less coal, and had a more rural sportsman-oriented culture as evidenced by the larger deer harvest. Al Gore lost 19 out of the 32 counties with above average turnout. The turnout statistics point to the Republican Party's ability to energize and turn out its base. Table 2.9 classifies the counties with the highest and lowest turnout according to their degree of party competition. Turnout was clearly highest in competitive and Republican leaning counties and lowest in traditionally Democratic counties. This pattern helps to explain Al Gore's poor performance.

Table 2.9 Voter Turnout and Party Competition in West Virginia

County	% Turnout	Party System
High Turnout Counties (n = 15)		
Greenbrier*	71.9	2–party competitive
Randolph*	71.3	1–party Democratic
Pleasants*	70.4	2–party competitive
Wetzel*	70.4	1–party Democratic
Wirt*	68.2	2–party competitive
Barbour*	67.8	2–party competitive
Jackson*	67.0	2–party competitive
Mason*	66.3	2–party competitive
Taylor*	66.9	2–party competitive
Wood*	65.7	2–party competitive
Tyler*	65.7	1–party Republican
Jefferson*	65.5	2–party competitive
Preston*	65.3	2–party competitive
Putnam*	65.3	2–party competitive
Hancock*	65.0	1–party Democratic
Low Turnout Counties (n = 10)		
Fayette	53.7	1–party Democratic
Wayne*	52.9	1–party Democratic
Calhoun*	52.3	1–party Democratic
Clay*	52.5	1–party Democratic
Boone	51.7	1–party Democratic
Logan	50.2	1–party Democratic
Wyoming	47.8	1–party Democratic
Lincoln	46.8	1–party Democratic
Mingo	45.6	1–party Democratic
McDowell	38.5	1–party Democratic

*Carried by Bush

Source: West Virginia Secretary of State, 2000 election returns.

Gore's problems in the southern coalfield were much greater than in the northern panhandle, particularly as it relates to voter turnout. The Independent Steelworkers in the panhandle made good on their promise to vote for Pat

Buchanan. Buchanan received more than 1100 votes from Hancock, Brooke, Ohio, and Marshall counties. Had all of these votes gone for Gore, he would have carried two of the four panhandle counties—Brooke & Hancock—instead of just one—Brooke, the latter by a small, 500-vote margin. Gore's vote, in short, would look a lot more like Wise's vote than it did. Wise won three out of four panhandle counties (losing only Ohio), obtaining 26,245 votes in the four counties. Gore received 24,342 in the four counties, a difference of 1,903. Gore's lack of credibility among steelworkers apparently cost him votes.

Guns and the NRA

Gore's problems in West Virginia were compounded by the widely held perception that Gore and the Democrats were antigun. Interviewed at a large pro-gun rally held by the NRA in Beckley, one gun enthusiast, a retired coal equipment supplier, said, "I think the Democratic Party is definitely a threat to the Second Amendment." One hand-made sign read: "Three things keep US free—God, Guns and Bush." Another said: "It's all about freedom, stupid" (Porterfield, *Raleigh-Herald*, Nov. 1, 2000).

Bush's campaign was able to exploit the gun issue in West Virginia quite effectively. Piggy-backing its campaign on an NRA rally in Beckley, the Bush campaign was able to take full advantage of the pro-gun sentiment in the immediate Beckley area and around the state. At the Beckley rally, NRA president Charlton Heston, told a wildly enthusiastic audience, "If Al Gore is elected he will have the power to hammer your gun rights into oblivion" (quoted in Porterfield, *Raleigh-Herald*, Nov. 1, 2000) . After the rally Heston said, "This is stunning. I've never seen a crowd like this" (quoted in Porterfield, Nov. 1, 2000).

Gore lost Raleigh County (Beckley) by 1,480 votes. Democrats outnumber Republicans 3 to 1 in Raleigh County . . . It may be argued that guns did not cost Gore much nationally (Dionne, *Washington Post Weekly*, February 9–25, 2001), but it obviously had an effect in West Virginia. Bush strategist Karl Rove counted on winning the vote of deer hunters, he made it a part of the culturally conservative message. When Bush was campaigning in Tennessee and surprised by the voters lining the streets, Rove commented that,

> "They relate [to Bush]. The Elvis voter is culturally conservative. Al Gore ain't culturally conservative. He doesn't relate to deer hunters" (Newsweek, November 20, 2001), 110.

The Campaign Trail: 2 is Good; 3 is Better

The Bush campaign . . . in West Virginia was masterful from the standpoint of candidate appearances, timing, and appeal. Bush made his first appearance in the state (at the Charleston War Memorial) on his way to the Republican nominating convention. He appeared for a second time in Huntington. Shortly thereafter, he said in the first televised debate, "I was in coal country yesterday in West Virginia" (Porterfield, *Raleigh-Herald*, October 5, 2000), causing one of his West Virginia campaign managers to exclaim:

"That was great . . . That was one of the most important things from an Appalachian sense. Bush came to West Virginia and gave a speech and discussed coal and was surrounded by miners. Then he goes on national television and talks about West Virginia and West Virginia's coal resources" (Quoted in Porterfield, *Raleigh-Herald*, Oct. 5, 2001).

Bush made a third visit to the state in the final days of the campaign. Before a huge crowd in Morgantown, candidate Bush confidently predicted that he would win West Virginia on election day (Smith, *Raleigh-Herald*, Nov. 4, 2000). He did. And he won Monongalia County, where there are two Democrats to every one Republican, by a margin of almost 1,000 votes.

By contrast Gore visited West Virginia only twice, and then only with some reluctance and last minute scheduling. His campaign spokesperson in West Virginia, Sarah Feinberg, said, "We're going to try to get him down to the coalfields in the southern part of the state" (*Raleigh-Herald*, Oct. 10, 2000). Gore's appearances (Charleston and Huntington) were notable for their lack of enthusiasm for the candidate. George Carenbauer, Democratic activist and former Clinton campaign manager, now sitting out the Gore campaign, summed up the Democrats' disappointment in the Gore campaign:

"I think visits make a big difference. They energize your base, to start with. They change discussion points" (*Raleigh-Herald*, Oct. 27, 2000).

The simple fact is, Gore's two visits failed to energize his base; Bush's three visits (and three visits by Cheney and visits by his parents) energized the Republicans. In the counties won by Bush, the turnout was at least 5 percentage points higher than the statewide average. In counties won by Gore, the turnout was on average 5 percentage points below the statewide average. It is reasonable to conclude that some of the difference in turnout is attributable to the difference in enthusiasm generated by the two campaigns . . .

Character Counts

George Bush entered the West Virginia campaign with one big advantage compared to Al Gore, he was a "likeable" candidate. Although a clearly partisan statement, Dave Tyson, chairman of the state Republican Party, said of his candidate:

"Bush comes across as a regular guy . . . He comes across as very humble and common" (Porterfield, *Raleigh-Herald*, Aug. 3, 2000).

Al Gore was clearly handicapped by the fact that people could not warm to him, as was evident by the lower than usual turnout among those who normally would vote Democratic. Gore's problems went far beyond the issue of likeableness. To many voters in West Virginia, Gore could not be trusted. For the steelworkers, he could not be trusted to do what he had promised. For coal miners, there was a question of whether he really believed that coal had a future in the United States, particularly since he had argued that natural gas could replace coal. For some voters, Gore was simply not to be trusted in the sense that he sometimes was guilty of embellishing the truth . . .

. . . The national polls found in regard to the character issue: on the "honesty" trait, Bush outscored Gore 80% to 15%; on the "likeableness" trait, it was Bush 59%, Gore 38% (Pomper).

Although it is doubtful that the character issue was the critical factor in the election, again, enough traditional Democratic votes were probably stripped away from Gore that the cumulative effect was to hand Gore an embarrassing loss in "sure winner" West Virginia.

Conclusions

The success of the Bush campaign in West Virginia appears to be primarily the product of a campaign tailored to the context of the state. Similar to previous studies of contextual effects, we find that Bush was able to overcome party identification by encouraging a conversational environment that portrayed Al Gore as unlike typical West Virginia Democrats and himself as a man that shares the values and priorities of the state's population. The skillful tailoring of his campaign message and the greater attention paid to the state appear to have culminated in a victory driven by an enthusiastic base and working class Democrats concerned about their jobs in the face of environmental attacks on the coal industry.

West Virginia Democrats should not take these findings well. If the two nations discussed earlier continue to emerge, West Virginia may increasingly be fertile ground for Republican candidates who often win in rural areas that respond to culturally conservative messages about the economy, guns, character, and freedom. More importantly, trends within the state do not ensure continued Democratic dominance . . . Turnout has declined steadily in the last thirty years and as we have seen, this hurts Democratic candidates more than Republicans. Democratic registration, while not dropping significantly, is six percentage points below its high in 1978. During this time, Republican registration numbers have held steady and the number of voters registering as "other" has increased to almost ten percent of the population. In the Voter News Service exit polls, 21% of West Virginia voters identified themselves as independent, 33% as Republicans, and only 46% as Democrats. These numbers, while the result of one poll, certainly suggest that the advantages of party registration for Democrats are significantly overestimated. George Bush won the independent vote in the survey by a margin of 62% to 34%. Democratic fortunes in the state appear far more contingent today than ever before. The politics following the terrorist attacks of September 11 will only heighten the degree of competitiveness if voters emphasize safety and security issues that typically favor Republicans. That, however, remains to be seen.

Notes

[1] The final tally of electoral votes was 271 to 267; however, an elector from Washington D.C. who was pledged to Al Gore cast a blank ballot in support of statehood for Washington. She carefully noted that she was doing so only because Bush was the clear winner and would have voted for Gore if her vote was necessary for him to win

the presidency. We therefore use the 271 to 267 tallies that reflect the state-by-state election outcome.

[2] We were unable to determine if West Virginia was among these states.

[3] It is interesting to note that during November and December of 1999, the editor with help from students of West Liberty State College's *Pi Sigma Alpha*, conducted a "voter preference poll" of Marshall County's registered voters. The results concerning Bush v. Gore showed that 55% of the voters would vote for Bush "if the election were held today" while only 22% would vote for Gore. (n=165)

References

Associated Press, "Logan Needs Coal Taxes, Court Told," *Charleston Gazette*, (March 3, 2001), 9.

Basu, Sandra, "Shelley Moore Capito's Uphill Climb," *Campaigns and Elections*, (May, 2001), 22.

Brisbin, Richard A. Jr., *et al.*, *West Virginia Politics and Government* (Lincoln: University of Nebraska Press, 1996), chapter 2.

Bundy, Jennifer, "Mountain State Not Solidly Behind Gore," *The Register-Herald*, (September 3, 2000), 1.

Cook, Charles E. Jr., "How Does 2000 Stack Up?" *The Washington Quarterly*, Vol. 24, (Spring, 2001), 1.

Hamburger, Tom, "Western Civilization is Greatly Indebted to Messrs. Harless, Raney, and Kimber," *Wall Street Journal*, (June 13, 2001), 1.

Harless, James H. "I'm Not the Antichrist, Mingo's Buck Harless Says," *Charleston Gazette-Mail*, (April 1, 2001).

Huckfeldt, Robert and John Sprague, *Citizens, Politics, and Social Communication*, (New York: Cambridge University Press, 1995).

MacKuen, Michael and Courtney Brown, "Political Context and Attitude Change," *American Political Science Review*, Vol. 81, (June 1987), 471–490.

Martel, Bret and Martham Bryson Hodel, "Bucking the Trend: Harless Stays Put, Amasses a Fortune," *Charleston Gazette-Mail*, (August 13, 2000), 2B.

Newsweek, "Pumping Iron, Digging Gold, Pressing Flesh," (November 20, 2000), 50.

Nyden, Paul J. "Coal Is Still Economic King in West Virginia," *Charleston Gazette-Mail*, (September 27, 1998).

Pomper, Gerald M., "The 2000 Presidential Election: Why Gore Lost," *Political Science Quarterly*, 116 (Summer, 2001), 9 201–223.

Porterfield, Mannix, "Bush Plugs Coal, Mountain State," *The Register-Herald*, (October 5, 2000), 1.

_____ "GOP Chair: Bush Will Take the State," *The Register-Herald*, (August 3, 2000), 1.

_____ "Calling All Swing States," (November 20, 2000), 110.

Ranney, Austin, "Parties in State Politics," *Politics in the American States*, second edition, Herbert Jacob and Kenneth Vines, eds. (Boston: Little Brown & Company, 1971), 84–89.

Roberts, Cecil, "It Is Not Too Late to Stop Mountaintop Mine Ruling," *Charleston Gazette*, (October 27, 1999), 5A.

Seiler, Fanny, "Impact on Mountaintop Ruling Felt Statewide, MU Group Says," *Charleston Gazette*, (February 14, 2001).

Shaw, Davon, "Presidential Electoral College Strategies," *The Journal of Politics*, 16 (November, 1999), 893–913.

Smith, Vicki, "GOP Nominee Declares He Will Win State on Election Day," *The Register-Herald*, (November 4, 2000), 1.

_____ "GOP Not Leaving State Unplowed," *The Register-Herald*, (October 20, 2000),1.

Tuckwiller, Tara, "The One-Man Political Machine," *Charleston Gazette-Mail*, (March 11, 2001), 1A.

Ward, Ken, Jr., "Appeal Challenges Ruling to Protect Streams From Mining," *Charleston Gazette-Mail*, (December 3, 2000).

Commentary:
HUMOR IN WEST VIRGINIA POLITICS

James F. Dent
Columnist and Editorial Cartoonist

When I was sitting in my political science classes at West Virginia University a number of years ago, I often wished I could turn the tables and lecture to a roomful of teachers. And finally, here I am. So take good notes. This <material> will be included in the final.

I've been asked to talk to you tonight about humor in politics.

As Finley Peter Dunne's Mr. Dooley observed: "I like political jokes. I've voted for any number of them."

Political humor can be traced back at least as far as ancient Rome. In one of his comedies, a Roman playwright had a senator declare: "When I depart this life I want incised on my memorial stone, 'Here lies a senator and an honest man.'" To which his slave replies: "What? Two men in one grave?" That joke, only slightly altered, is still kicking around.

A supposedly true story, on somewhat the same order, is about a congressman from Kentucky named Strange who told his family that he didn't want his name on his tombstone. "Just have them engrave "An Honest Politician," he said. "When people look at it, they'll say 'That's Strange.'"

There's a lot of humor, some of it intentional, in West Virginia politics. With our political history, of course, I suppose that if we didn't laugh sometimes, we'd have to cry. I remember the full-page newspaper ad taken out in a Logan newspaper by a candidate for the school board. It had a large picture of the smiling politician and above the photograph, his qualifications for office. In huge type it read: "Cleared by Grand Jury."

Some of the stories I'm going to tell you tonight are true, some are false and some I'm not altogether certain about.

That Logan County incident reminds me of one about the politician— possibly the same fellow—who attended a religious revival. The evangelist was whooping and heaving and finally the spirit got to the politician who began sweating and squirming on his bench. At last, he jumped to his feet and cried: "Preacher, preacher, I want to be saved." And the evangelist shouted, "First, brother, you must confess your sins." And the politician turned white and said, "Not while the grand jury's in session."

Someone else in the congregation yelled, "Jesus will forgive you." And the politician said, "Yes, but he's not on the grand jury."

I suppose you heard about the Charleston lady who died but requested that she be buried in Logan County because she wanted to stay active in politics.

The late William C. Marland, when he was governor, liked the story about the candidate in a hotly contested election whose campaign manager told him, "We've got to go to Boone County tomorrow." And the candidate said, "No, tomorrow we're going to Harrison County." The campaign manager said, "But they're telling lies on us in Madison." And the candidate said, "That don't matter. Even worse, they're telling the truth on us in Clarksburg."

Former governor and U.S. Senator Matthew M. Neely told the story about the immigrant produce peddler who was driving his cart along the streets in Fairmont early one morning several years ago, when the donkey dropped dead right in the traces. Well, the immigrant wasn't sure what to do. Finally he got off the cart and managed to unhitch the donkey and drag it over to the curb. Then he hauled his wagon away to see if he could find someone in authority. The donkey had departed this life, as it happened, right in front of the home of a prominent Fairmont Republican. This fellow had spent practically his entire life opposing Neely, the Democrat. So when the Republican looked out his front window and saw the corpse lying in front of his house he immediately picked up the telephone and called Neely in the governor's office in Charleston.

When Neely came on the line, the Fairmont Republican said, Governor, there's a dead jackass lying in front of my house." And Neely said, "Well, that's a job for the municipal sanitation department. Why are you calling me?" And the Republican purred: "I just thought I ought to notify the next of kin."

Running for office is hectic. I'm not sure which state politician it was who was running a statewide campaign and was a bit mixed up about where he was on one campaign appearance. As it happened, he was in Fairmont. But he thought he was in Morgantown. Anyway, after he was introduced he said what a pleasure it was to be in Monongalia County again. One of his aides hissed at him, "Marion. It's Marion." But the candidate didn't hear. He said it was a fine group of Monongalia County candidates sitting on the platform with him. And the aide whispered again, "Marion. It's Marion." The candidate still didn't hear him. Then the candidate said he particularly wished to thank the sheriff of Monongalia County for his kindness. And his aide gasped "Marion. Marion." This time the candidate heard him. "Oh," he said, "And of course I also want to thank the sheriff's lovely wife, Marion."

Herman Guy Kump was the first Democratic governor of West Virginia in twelve years when he was elected in 1932. One of Governor Kump's relatives told me that not long after the governor took office, a couple of Democrats from Mingo County came to see him. "Governor," they said, "we want to talk to you about Jim Williamson. Jim is a mighty good Democrat, Governor, and he has a lot of friends and relatives in Mingo County." The governor said that was nice. "Right now though, Governor," the visitors said, "Jim is in the penitentiary at Moundsville." The governor said that was a shame. "Yes it is," said the visitors. "Jim's not awful happy about it either. But you can get him out, Governor. You can pardon him." The governor said that was true. "But," he said, "I need a reason." "Hell, Governor," said one of the visitors in disgust. "If there'd been a reason, we coulda got one of them Republican governors to pardon him."

A military career is often a help in politics. I heard about a primary campaign for sheriff down in one of the southern coal counties not long after the second World War. There were three candidates running for the Democratic nomination. At that time in that place, the Democratic nomination was the same as election. I guess it still is. Anyway, the first candidate rose, walked to the front of the platform and held up a hook where his left hand ought to be. "I left that hand," he said, "on the beach at Normandy, fighting for this country." The second candidate displayed a wooden leg and said, "That leg was taken off at a field hospital on Saipan in the Pacific where I was protecting your liberty." The third candidate was an unprepossessing looking fellow with no evident missing limbs. Half defensively, half defiantly, he said, "Friends, I was 4-F during the war. But, if physical disability qualifies anybody for public office, I'm here to tell you that I am the most completely ruptured man in McDowell County."

Former Senator Jennings Randolph said he usually didn't place too much stock in public opinion polls. Senator Randolph said he always remembered the politician who conducted his own polls.

This fellow would get out of his car several blocks from wherever it was he was to speak and walk along the street stopping people and saying, "I'm Senator So-and-So. Would you mind telling me for whom you are going to vote in the election?" And of course most people, under these circumstances, would politely say, "Why I'm going to vote for you, of course, Senator."

When the senator heard that, he'd turn to his aide, who was trailing along behind and he'd say, "Mark it down, son. Mark it down." And the aide would mark it down on his tally sheet. Then when the senator got to the hall where he was to speak, he'd tell his audience, "Victory is in the air, friends. Why just to-night, walking down your beautiful Main Street on the way to this hall, I stopped a dozen people at random and asked how they were going to vote. And each and every one of them said they were going to cast their ballot for me and for our glorious party in November."

Well, one day the senator was conducting his poll when he stopped a rather sour faced fellow. The senator went through his routine. This time, though, the usual answer wasn't forthcoming. The man gave the politician a hard look and said: "Are you really Senator So-and-So?"

"Yes indeed I am," the senator said proudly.

"Well," said the man, "let me tell you, senator, I wouldn't vote for you if you were the only man running. You're a blowhard and a phony. You have a lousy voting record. I don't like a thing you stand for and I don't like you. In fact, I don't even want to be seen standing here talking to you." And he whirled around and stalked away.

The senator stood there for a few moments, fiddling with his necktie and clearing his throat. Then finally he turned around to his assistant and said: "Put that one down as doubtful."

Before the days of television, candidates for statewide office had to visit every county seat and major city at least two or three times to be sure of reaching as many voters as possible. Usually they could make the same speech every time because it was a rare voter who came out to more than one meeting. Someone once asked Senator M.M. Neely, "Senator is it true that you made 197 speeches in your gubernatorial campaign?" And the senator said, "Well, not exactly. Actually I made the same speech 197 times."

Speaking of getting known by the voters, a city council candidate in the last Charleston city election lost by a sizable majority. This candidate is a fellow who—well, to meet him is to loathe him. Anyway, after the election he told someone, "You know what the trouble was? You know why I lost? The trouble was that I didn't meet enough voters." And the fellow, being brutally honest, told him, "No—the trouble was that you met too many."

Some years ago when I was covering the state legislature for the *Gazette*, the Speaker of the House of Delegates was the late Ivor Boiarsky. I don't know if any of you knew Ivor. He was a very intelligent, very dedicated, very capable legislator—and very short tempered.

During one particularly close vote, Ivor discovered that one of the delegates he thought he had in his pocket was voting the wrong way. Ivor gaveled a recess and came storming out of the chamber breathing fire. "Where the hell is"—I'll make up a name here—"Jones?" he yelled. Someone said Jones had just gone into the men's room. "Shall I go get him, Ivor?" he asked.

Ivor stood there for a minute then he said, "No, let him alone. This is the first time today the s.o.b. has known what he's doing." Speaking of legislators, this past session I heard someone describe one of our more notorious state senators as being like a bull frog. When asked how that was, he explained: "What ain't stomach is head and that's mostly mouth."

Most politicians are loath to commit themselves. I remember one governor—I think it was Clarence Meadows—who was asked his position on a controversial issue.

Governor Meadows replied: "I'll be happy to tell you where I stand. Some of my friends are for that bill and some of my friends are against it. Gentlemen, I stand with my friends."

Over the years an occasional West Virginian officeholder has been caught doing things he shouldn't. There's the story of the politician who had been convicted of dipping his fingers into public funds, had served a short prison sentence and had returned home. Like many politicians who wind up on the wrong side of the bars, this fellow claimed to have found God and been Born Again while he was incarcerated. Even so, someone was surprised one Sunday morning to see the ex-official passing the collection plate in church.

He approached the head deacon and said: "I know Jones has served his time and I know he claims he's been born again. But don't you think it's tempting fate to put him so close to loose cash money?"

"We trust Brother Jones implicitly," said the deacon piously. "He sinned but he was punished for it and he has seen the error of his ways. He is living at the foot of the cross now. But we do take one small precaution. When Brother Jones takes up the collection, he has to carry the plate in one hand and a live fly in the other and bring both of them back to the pulpit undamaged."

You doubtless recall that during the last administration, then Governor Rockefeller and the legislative leadership weren't what you could call chummy. Now it wasn't the governor but it was a close associate of his who told me the story about the lady who was out walking on a beach one day when she saw a bottle half buried in the sand. She picked it up and brushed away the loose sand and she could see something moving around inside. So she pulled out the cork and a great gush of multi-colored smoke poured out of the bottle. The smoke sort of bunched up together and formed itself into the shape of a genie.

"Madam," said the genie, "I thank you for letting me out of that bottle. In return, I will be happy to grant you a wish. What do you want? Money? A Mercedes?" The woman said, "No, I don't want either of those. I have all the money I want and I own two Mercedes already." She stood there thinking for a moment. Did I say she was attractive but flat-chested? Well, she was—attractive and flat chested. Finally, she turned to the genie and she said, "I'll tell you what I really, really want. I want a couple of really, really big boobs." "No sooner said than done," said the genie and he waved an arm and POOF! There stood Clyde See and Warren McGraw.

Well, after I used this story of course I got calls from both those gentlemen. And one of them told me the story about the three doctors who were sitting around the hospital lounge talking about their most difficult cases.

"Once," said the first doctor, "a young man was brought into the hospital. He had fallen into a buzzsaw and his arms had been dreadfully mangled. I worked and worked over him and gentlemen, not only did I repair his arms but today that young man is a boxing champion."

"Well," said the second doctor, "that's pretty good but listen to this. A young woman who had been in an automobile accident was brought to me. Her face was practically destroyed. Not only did I repair the damage, gentlemen, but that young woman today is one of Hollywood's most glamorous movie stars."

They both looked at the third doctor.

"Well boys," he said, "both of those are fair amateur work. Listen to this though. A young man was out horseback riding and lightning struck him. All they could find left to bring me to work with was his checkbook and the horse's anal aperture. And today, gentlemen, that man is governor of West Virginia."

Some of you who were around Charleston in the past may have met Sam Chilton. Sam was one of Charleston's leading characters. Sam graduated from law school at Washington and Lee and immediately retired from practice.

Someone asked him once, "Sam, don't you get tired of doing nothing?" And Sam said, "Yes, yes I do. But a man can't quit just because he's tired."

The reason I bring Sam up is that he ran, eight times I think, for the Democratic nomination for Secretary of State. Sam said as far as he could determine from his study of the office, the Secretary of State did absolutely nothing and since he had a lifetime of practice at that he obviously was the most qualified man available for the job.

Speaking of the Secretary of State brings me to not the present holder of that office but his immediate predecessor. You can't discuss humor in politics in

West Virginia and not mention A. James Manchin.

As you may have suspected already, A. James Manchin is no shrinking violet. I attended WVU at the same time A. James was there. Even then, he made his presence known. He was the only student on campus, for example, who habitually wore a homburg and spats to class. He ran for—and was elected to—the House of Delegates while he was still a student. He only served one term though. A. James doesn't enjoy being a member of a group. When he holds an office he wants to hold it all by himself.

A few years ago I was in Morgantown for a homecoming football game and I ran into A. James. He was sitting, rather precariously, on top of a closed sedan getting ready to ride in the homecoming parade. I'm not sure he was actually asked to ride in the parade but you put A. James in the vicinity of a parade and he is bound to wind up in it if not actually leading it.

Anyway, I asked him why he was sitting up there on the roof of the car rather than inside where a normal person would sit. A. James looked at me pityingly. "A. James Manchin," he said—A. James often refers to himself in the third person—"A. James Manchin did not come all the way from Charleston to ride inside where no one can see him."

A. James is unable to pass as many as two people without making a speech and turning it into a political meeting. I heard the story, which I firmly believe, about how he was being driven to a meeting when he saw several cars parked outside a house. Manchin immediately ordered his driver to stop. He got out of the car, went inside and found a wake was in progress.

A. James immediately started shaking every hand he could reach and saying things like, "Oh my, yes, his passing is a dreadful loss," and "We shall all miss his counsel and his wisdom" and "He was an honor and a credit to his community and his state."

By and by he had worked his way around to that part of the room where the corpse was on view. A. James was in the middle of saying "No one, no one, will be able to take his place" when he looked down at the body, did a double take and blurted:

"My God, I actually know this man."

Here's one final Manchin story. It seems that Governor Moore, Senator Rockefeller and Manchin were on an airplane coming back from a hearing in Washington.

Suddenly the plane got into difficulty and crashed. Everyone aboard was killed.

A little bit later, Moore, Rockefeller and Manchin found themselves wandering through a sort of a swirling fog—the kind of thing you see in movies when the director wants you to know the scene isn't here on earth. Pretty soon, they entered an empty, brightly lit room with three doors on the left hand wall. A loudspeaker was mounted on the wall just above the doors.

The three were standing around trying to figure out what was going on when the loudspeaker crackled and a voice said:

"Arch A. Moore, pass through the first door."

So Moore went through the first door which shut firmly behind him. He found himself in another large room. Down at one end, a huge, black hairy thing was squatting. It raised its head and saw Moore. It began growling and getting to its feet. It was a huge gorilla.

The voice spoke from a loudspeaker in this room. "Arch A. Moore," it said, "you have sinned. And as punishment for your sins, you are sentenced to spend eternity in this room trying to get away from that monstrous gorilla."

Back in the other room, the loudspeaker crackled again. "John D. Rockefeller, IV," it said, "pass through the second door."

Rockefeller did. He also found himself in another room. And down at the other end of this room stood a monstrous black figure—a gigantic bull. It stared at Rockefeller out of its beady little red eyes and started snorting and pawing the floor, getting ready to charge.

"John D. Rockefeller, IV," said the voice on the loudspeaker, "you have sinned. And as punishment for your sins you are sentenced to remain forever in this room trying to escape from that godawful big bull."

"A. James Manchin," it said. "Go through the third door."

Manchin did. Again, he found himself in another room. He looked around. It appeared to be empty. Suddenly a door at the other end of the room opened and a second figure entered. It was a beautiful, gorgeous female. She looked around, bewildered. Manchin recognized her and drew in his breath. It was Bo Derek, the movie star.

The loudspeaker crackled again. The voice spoke:

It said: "Bo Derek, you have sinned. . . ."

A couple of months ago, a legislator gave me a copy of an article that had appeared in a publication called "State Legislatures." It was a collection of malaprops, misstatements and mixed metaphors that had sprung from the mouths of legislators in statehouses around the country. Here's a small sampling:

- "It's time to grab the bull by the tail and look it in the eye."
- "That's a horse of a different feather."
- "These are not my figures I'm quoting. These are the figures of someone who knows what he's talking about."
- "I think I know more about this bill than I understand."
- "Now we've got them right where they want us."
- "There comes a time to put principles aside and do what's right."
- "If it weren't for the rural electric associations, a lot of farmers would be watching television by candlelight."
- "My colleague is listening with a forked ear."
- "When I started speaking I was for the bill but the longer I talk the more I know I'm against it."

- "Before I give you the benefit of my remarks, I'd like to know what we're talking about."
- "I'm in favor of letting the status quo stay as it is."
- "This body is becoming entirely too laxative."
- "I misquoted myself."
- "I have already told you more than I know about this."

Well, I'm beginning to resemble the politician who was speaking to a group of voters. One fellow arrived late and took a seat in the rear of the hall. He leaned over and jabbed the fellow sitting in front of him on the shoulder.

"How long's he been speakin'?" he asked, pointing to the politician who was up front orating away.

"About 45 minutes," was the reply.

"What's he talkin' about?" Asked the first guy.

And the second fellow said, "he ain't said yet."

Actually I suppose my talk wasn't supposed to have any point. But although I don't want to be presumptuous and tell you how to teach your classes—although someone once said that man's greatest urge after sex, was to tell the other guy how to do his job—I would like to put a plug in here for humor writers.

I think if you had your students read Mark Twain on the politics of the Gilded Age or Finley Peter Dunne or Ambrose Bierce's wicked Devil's Dictionary—which has a lot of political definitions in it—or H.L. Mencken on political conventions and even Will Rogers, they might get a better perspective on the politics of the times. And I know they'd enjoy it.

As far as present day politics is concerned, Art Buchwald, Russell Baker and Mark Russell are as knowledgeable as their more sober fellow columnists--and they're a hell of a lot more entertaining.

Again, thank you for asking me here. Class dismissed.

Note

Remarks delivered at the annual banquet and meeting of the West Virginia Political Science Association, October 11, 1985, Holiday Inn University, Huntington, West Virginia.

CHAPTER THREE

Legislative
Policy-Making

INTRODUCTION

"I do solemnly swear that I will support the constitution of the State of West Virginia, and faithfully discharge the duties of Senator (or Delegate) according to the best of my ability. I will not accept or receive, directly or indirectly, any money or other valuable thing from any corporation, company, or person for any vote or influence I may give or withhold, as Senator (or Delegate) on any bill, resolution or appropriation, or for any act I may do or perform as Senator (or Delegate)."

The Legislative Oath

It was stated in the first chapter that "the constitutional place of West Virginia is revealed by clauses in the West Virginia and federal constitutions."[1] The United States Constitution (Article IV, Section 4) guarantees, for example, West Virginia and other states a "republican form of government."[2] This means that historically the dominant representative institution in West Virginia and other states is the state legislature. Since colonial times legislative supremacy in the preparation of the budget was considered to be the heart of republicanism. It is only in recent years that voters have weakened legislative prerogatives by approving of constitutional amendments giving governors fuller responsibility in budget-making,[3] longer terms of office, greater control of the executive branch and the line-item veto.

In this chapter we are concerned with the main functions of the West Virginia Legislature, its capacity, backgrounds of legislators, legislative processes and politics which are unique to the state.

Legislative Functions

The West Virginia Legislature performs three major functions: law making, representation and oversight.

Article VI of the West Virginia Constitution relates that the legislature is the major policy-making body.[4] Which means that it enacts general laws that affect all of the citizens in the state. For example, the legislature levies taxes to keep the state government operating and at the same time it is prohibited by the constitution from creating a deficit—"proposed expenditures must not exceed anticipated revenues."[5] The legislature has the authority to initiate amendments to the West Virginia Constitution,[6] and pass "special and local legislation, especially as it relates to the functions and operations of local government."[7]

The second major function of the legislature is to represent the people in the government. Typically during a legislative session, lawmakers spend considerable time answering requests from constituents ("servicing the district"). For example, citizens may want particular information from a legislator or help in getting a horse trailer registered when the Department of Motor Vehicles allegedly "lost" the citizen's papers, or assistance in getting a state job and so forth.

Legislators receive many phone calls from interest groups in their districts—teachers (WV Education Association), business, labor (United Mine Workers) and so on.

Contrary to popular perceptions that the West Virginia Legislature is largely dominated by labor unions, the Hrebenar-Thomas study (see Chapter 2) shows that business groups are very active in the legislative process.

The third major function, executive oversight,[8] is a more recent task that the West Virginia Legislature has assumed for itself. As one analyst[9] stated, it was: "before the 1970s as only dimly perceived and spasmodically practiced" in West Virginia.

The legislature has developed a number of methods for "checking up" on agency spending and implementation. For example, the Joint Legislative Rule-Making Review Committee has major responsibility for oversight. It can review proposed administrative agency rules and decide whether or not to approve them. Other methods are "sunset laws" where the legislature periodically reviews the operation of certain agencies to see if they should be terminated. Finally, with the passage of the governor's budget, the House and Senate Finance Committees meet jointly to draft the "Legislative Digest." This document states the "legislative intent" of how the agencies are supposed to spend their monies.[10] Critics have argued that the process of preparing the "Digest" gives too much discretionary authority to the legislators on the finance committees.

West Virginia Legislature Capacity

Does the West Virginia Legislature have the capacity or "tools" to do its job in state government? This important question was addressed earlier in a national study by The Citizens' Conference on State Legislatures (1973)[12] using the FAIIR system to rank all of the 50 state legislatures.

The FAIIR system means that a "good" or reformed legislature is functional, accountable, informed, independent, and representative. By "functional" the Citizens' Conference meant that a legislature has plenty of time to do its legislative business. There are no arbitrary time limits on sessions; the staff and physical facilities are adequate; and its rules and procedures enhance the smooth flow of legislation (no bottlenecks). The "accountable" category means that the public easily grasps the legislature's operations because the legislative process is open and comprehensible. The "informed" legislature is able to carefully manage its legislative work through an effective committee system, professional staffers assist the lawmakers in and out of session and there is a legislative auditor to periodically review the budgetary process of the executive branch. An "independent" legislature has the power to oversee the executive branch, regulate lobbying and see that the legislators are adequately paid. And finally, by "representative" is meant that the legislature adequately represents the demographic makeup of its constituencies.[12]

The West Virginia Legislature ranked 10th in functional, 32nd in accountable, 37th in informed, 24th in independent and 15th in representative. The rankings ranged from a high of 1 to a low of 50. The legislature was overall ranked 25th in the nation.

More current measures of capacity were noted in a recent West Virginia legislative study. One obvious measure is the amount of money that a legislature has available in its annual budget for law making, legislative pay and staffing. In this sense the more resources a state legislature has the more capable it is. West Virginia ranks 34th in the category "money spent on itself."[13]

Because it is a part-time body with sixty-day sessions, the Virginia Legislature ranks below the national median in staffing salaries and length of legislative sessions. Due to the small number of senators (34), average Senate committee assignments (5.7) are higher than the median. In the 100 member House the number of committee assignments (2.9) is about average. The legislature scores above average in legislation processing (its committee system facilitates decision-making) and is similar to other state legislatures in legislative turnover (about 20 to 24% of the Senate and House seats respectively change hands between elections). Most of the turnover is voluntary.

Legislative capacity is also measured by representation. It can be argued that state legislatures generally do a better job than other branches of government in fulfilling the democratic ideal of "representing the people." Legislatures represent far fewer people than do governors, attorneys general, congressmen, etc. Yet, the West Virginia Legislature is unrepresentative in the categories of gender, race and occupation (this is also a problem with state legislatures nationally). Only 17% and 3% respectively of the West Virginia legislators are female, or black with lawyers and businessmen dominating the occupational categories.

Party identification in the legislature also influences representativeness. As noted in the previous chapter, West Virginia is a modified one-party Democratic state. For example, prior to the May 9th, 2000 election, 63.5% of the state's 970,745 registered voters are registered as Democrats, 29.7% as Republicans and 6.8% as independents or other.[14] Democratic Party dominance is even more pronounced in the West Virginia Legislature with 75% of its House members and 85% of the Senators claiming the Democratic Party label.

Why do the Democrats so lopsidedly outnumber the Republicans in the legislature? A recent study by Christopher Mooney[15] found several possible explanations: (1) the West Virginia Constitution still provides that the county is the basis for state Senate districts whereas House districts, although not under a constitutional mandate, have traditionally followed county boundaries as well; (2) it is easier to divide the state into larger districts proportional in population than creating a plethora of smaller equal districts.

Mooney noted that Republican voters are concentrated in six counties (Doddridge, Grant, Jackson, Ritchie, Tyler and Upshur) but, otherwise are spread widely around the state.[16] He speculates that smaller legislative districts might capture more of these Republican voters and allow the G.O.P. better representation in the Legislature. Historical evidence for this can be seen in Table 2.4 (Chapter 2) with the reality that the state Senate through the years, with its larger districts, typically has fewer Republicans than the House with its smaller districts (see Figures 3.1 and 3.2).

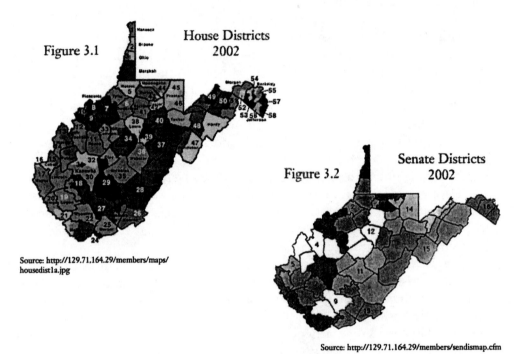

Figure 3.1 House Districts 2002

Source: http://129.71.164.29/members/maps/housedist1a.jpg

Figure 3.2 Senate Districts 2002

Source: http://129.71.164.29/members/sendismap.cfm

Another problem with the West Virginia Legislature's tradition of creating "larger" county based districts is that larger more heterogeneous districts are not as easily serviced. That is, certain groups may be ignored or have limited access to their legislators. An example of a large multi-member district is the 30th House District with over one hundred thousand citizens represented by 7 delegates. When this larger district is compared to smaller more homogeneous districts (e.g., the 5th Wetzel) it is more likely that constituents in these smaller districts will have better access to their lawmakers, and, for constituents, it is easier to get to know one delegate rather than seven. This representation problem is further complicated in the general election because the typical constituent from the large 30th district would need to consider possibly fourteen candidates rather than simply two in the smaller districts.[17]

Legislators' Backgrounds

Generally state legislators do not mirror the categoric groups that they represent. Instead, "state legislators are selected from the better-educated, more prestigiously employed, middle-class segments of the population."[18] To the extent that legislators do resemble their constituents, it is seen in the categories of race, ethnicity and religion.

The 75th Legislature follows fairly closely the national norms of other state legislatures in most of these categories except, as was noted earlier, in the percentages of Democrats and Republicans. That is, the percentages of West Virginia legislators who are Democrats, is considerably *higher* than the national average. The percentage of women in the West Virginia Legislature (17%) is slightly lower than the national average (22%), but the representation of African-Americans (2%), as a percentage of the state's population, is above the average found in most other states.

Legislative Politics

The question needs to be asked, does it make any difference in policy-making if a state legislature is dominated by the Democratic or Republican Party? It used to be argued that "healthy" party competition was correlated with more liberal education, taxation and welfare policies. However, some studies have questioned the "party competition" thesis and have claimed instead that education, taxation, welfare and highway programs are more influenced by socioeconomic factors than degree of party competition in a state legislature.

These studies[19] found that party competition is only meaningful if the parties in the legislature have strong or effective organizations and ideologically motivated activists (conservative Republicans vs. liberal Democrats) behind them. When the parties establish clear policy positions and the legislators (as members of either the majority or minority party) reflect these policy differences, then it is possible to say that the legislative parties are "policy relevant."

"Policy relevance is determined by whether or not a change in party control of state government (the governor's office and one or both houses of the legislature) is associated with changes in state welfare spending."[20] A Democratic controlled government would be generally associated with increases in welfare spending and Republican control with only slight or no increase at all.

The West Virginia Legislature may be classified as a noncompetitive, nonpolicy relevant body. This means that regardless of whether a Republican or Democrat controls the governorship the policy proposals considered by the Legislature concerning education, welfare, highways and so on are usually quite similar—fiscal austerity. This is because the state lacks the resources that other states have and the political parties do not generally reflect the class divisions in the state and instead mirror the popular cultural attitude that West Virginia is a poor state with economic problems and cannot afford tax increases and "expensive" government programs.

Table 3.1
Selected Characteristics of the West Virginia Legislature

bicameral body	100 member, House of Delegates 34 member, Senate
compensation	$15,000 per annual session $85.00 per diem for non-commuters $45.00 per diem for commuters retirement, age 60 + 5 years service
competitive seats	30 to 39% average competitive seats (def. as won by less than 60% of the vote, 1992–96)
turnover	20 to 24%, House of Delegates, 1992–2000
districts	17 Senate districts, all multi-member, with 53,699 persons per district 58 House districts, 17 multi-member, with 18,258 persons per district
staff	396 (excludes interns), 1996 rank 32
legislative work	less than one-third time (estimated proportion for a full-time job spent on legislative work, includes legislative sessions, interim committee work, constituent service and elections)
legislative bill enactments, 1999	2,724 introduced, 636 enactments, 23%

Source: National Conference of State Legislatures, 2,000; www.ncsl.org/public/trust/casebody.htm

Legislative Processes

Charles E. Lindbloom in discussing political decision-making writes: ". . . the power of various social groups . . . is less a determinant of policy outcomes than itself a result of the rules that men have made to govern the policy-making process."[21] Lindbloom is telling us that the procedures of policy-making, especially in legislative bodies, offer many opportunities to delay or defeat a bill even when a majority of lawmakers are solidly behind it.

Conversely, it must be said that these same procedures allow the leadership with control of the rules and the support of a majority to push legislation through and over the objections of a determined minority. For example, during the halfway point of the 74th Legislature, the leadership was able to pass a bill reorganizing higher education (over 200 pages) which few members had time to read or question.[22]

There are several important points in the legislative process where bills can be delayed or killed. The most obvious place to "kill a bill" is in one of the 14 standing committees in the House or in the 19 committees in the Senate. Bills that are referred by the leadership to multiple committees during the session frequently do not make it. If a bill that is "unwanted" by the leadership should survive the committee system it may be "killed with kindness" (amended to death) on the floor or it may never make it through the end-of-session logjam. This is seen when the Rules Committees of both the Senate and House, beyond the halfway mark of the legislative session, choose those bills that are most important for the "Special Calendar." It is important to note that the Speaker is the chairman of the Rules Committee in the House and the President of the Senate is the chairman of the Senate Rules Committee.

Finally, the leadership selects the members from both chambers for the Legislative Conference Committees which work out compromises when the House and Senate pass different versions of "the same" bill. The legislative leaders then, determine to a large extent which bills make it through the final hectic days of the session and which do not.

Legislative Improvement

Some ideas for improving the legislative process have been implied in the previous discussion and recommendations for reform have come from reform organizations as well.

It should be recalled that the West Virginia Legislature has better than average capacity in several areas to do its job. In legislative processing, it ranks above average when compared to other legislatures. In its committee system[23] and legislative oversight activities the legislature ranks in the middle range with other states.

Legislative salaries were increased from $6,500 to $15,000 toward the end of the 71st Legislature. Citizen reactions to the pay increase were generally negative and a number of lawmakers (including the President of the Senate, Keith Burdette), who voted for the pay increase, were defeated in the recent election by angry voters.

Three major weaknesses found by the Citizens' Conference persist. First, the legislature and the citizens should remove the constitutional restrictions on sessions. The Citizens' Conference recommends that consideration be given to annual general sessions, limited to no fewer than 90 legislative days (the legislature currently meets for an annual 60 day session). Second, the legislature should provide for single-member districts (see Table 3.1).

The reason that the Citizens' Conference and other reform groups argue for the removal of multi-member districts is that single-member districts are more accountable. Multi-member districts depart from one-person-one-vote; multi-member districts favor the majority party (voters tend to vote for one party slate or the other).

115

Third, due to the state's persisting economic problems, the legislature lags behind others in legislative resources. The legislators need more professional staff to provide them with the technical expertise that is needed to "solve" the state's problems.

The selections for this chapter deal primarily with the legislative process and politics. We start with "A Guide Through The Legislative Process" by Donald R. Andrews and James A. Hoyer which provides an overview of the legislature including "How a Bill Becomes a Law." Next we will learn from three "insiders" the realities of legislative politics. Former Delegate David McKinley (Republican, Ohio County and earlier candidate for Governor) discusses the problems of the Republican Party as the minority party in the House of Delegates. Former Delegate Patricia Bradley Pitrolo (Democrat, Hancock County) discusses stereotypes of women legislators in the House of Delegates and former Senator Thais Blatnik (Democrat, Ohio County) addresses the question, "Does the West Virginia Legislature Really Have Two Parties?"

Notes

[1] See Figure 1.1, "Federal Constitutional Provisions That Guarantee or Limit West Virginia's Powers."

[2] Defined as: "A system of government wherein laws are enacted by elected representatives of the people. Used synonymously with 'representative democracy.' Frequent elections result in a broad electorate giving limited authority to elected lawmakers, who then exercise this authority until the next election either returns them with a vote of confidence or replaces them." Joseph Dunner, Editor, *Dictionary of Political Science* (Totowa, New Jersey: Littlefield, Adams & Company, 1970), 454.

[3] This occurred in West Virginia in 1968 with the Modern Budget Amendment which gave the governor full budgetary authority.

[4] This term is used in the sense of Thomas Dye's definition: "Public policy is whatever governments choose to do or not to do." See *Understanding Public Policy*, fourth edition, (Englewood Cliffs, New Jersey: Prentice-Hall, 1981), 1.

[5] Claude J. Davis, et al., *West Virginia State and Local Government* (Morgantown: Bureau of Government Research, West Virginia University, 1963), 103; see also West Virginia Code, Chapter 8 and Article VI, Sections 39, 39a, *West Virginia Constitution.*

[6] The *West Virginia Constitution*, Article XIV provides two methods for amending the Constitution. In both methods the legislature has an important initiating role. First, Section 1 allows a constitutional convention to be called when a majority of the House of Delegates and Senate initiate such a call and when a majority of the voters ratify the proposed call in a subsequent election. A majority of the voters must finally approve all recommendations of the constitutional convention. Second, the legislature also must enact a "submission bill" for the amendment(s) to be inserted on the ballot. Submission bills may be vetoed by the governor like any other bill. And in the final analysis all amendments to the state constitution must be approved by a majority of the people voting on them.

[7] Davis, *op. cit.*, 106.

[8] See David A. Bingham and John E. Tyler, "West Virginia State Government Organization," *West Virginia Public Affairs Reporter,* II, #1 (February, 1977), 1 . . . The West

Virginia Senate is given the power to approve or disapprove the appointment of individuals by the Governor to important positions in government.

9   Christopher Mooney, et al., *West Virginia's State Government: The Legislative, Executive and Judicial Branches*, Policy Monograph Series No. 5, Institute for Public Affairs, (West Virginia University, 1993), 11.

10   *Ibid.*, 13.

11   The Citizens Conference on State Legislatures, *The Sometimes Governments: A Critical Study of the 50 American Legislatures* (New York: Bantam Books, 1971), see especially the section on West Virginia, 325–328. The Citizens Conference concluded that ideally every state legislature should be able to:
— innovate in the development of public policy;
— exercise continuing oversight over state administrative agencies and their programs;
— undertake comprehensive long-range planning for the state's economic and social development;
— evaluate and review its own performance; and
— identify and provide for future needs before they become critical (39-40).

12   *Ibid.*, 41-42.

13   Mooney, *op. cit.*, 3.

14   Ken Hechler, Office of the Secretary of State, web page:
wv.us/sec/info/stats/party/htm

15   Mooney, *op. cit.*, 10-11.

16   *Ibid.*, 10.

17   *Ibid.*

18   Thomas R. Dye, *Politics in States and Communities*, 7th edition, (Englewood Cliffs, New Jersey: Prentice Hall, Inc., 1991), 158.

19   Edward T. Jennings, "Competition Constituencies and Welfare Politics in the American States," *American Political Science Review*, 73 (June, 1979), 414–429; and Thomas R. Dye, "Party and Policy in the States," *Journal of Politics*, 46, (November, 1984), 1097–1116.

20   Dye *op cit.*, 129.

21   Charles E. Lindblom, *The Policy-Making Process* (Englewood Cliffs, New Jersey: Prentice-Hall, Inc., 1968, 34; also see Duane Lockard, *The Perverted Priorities of American Politics* (New York: The Macmillan Company, 1971) especially the classic chapter, "Congress: Prometheus Self-Bound," 123–167 and Ira Katznelson and Mark Kesselman, *The Politics of Power, A Critical Introduction to American Government*, third edition, San Diego: Harcourt Brace Jovanovich, 1987), 144–177.

22   See Tom Miller, "WV Legislature buys more time on two tough issues," *Charleston Gazette*, March 23, 2000.

23   The (14) standing committees in the House are: Agriculture and Natural Resources, Banking and Insurance, Constitutional Revision, Education, Finance, Government Organization, House Health and Human Resources, Industry, Labor, Economic Development and Small Business, Judiciary, Political Subdivisions, Redistricting, Roads and Transportation, House Rules and Veterans Affairs. The (19) standing committees in the Senate are: Agriculture, Banking and Insurance, Confirmations, Education, Energy, Industry and Mining, Enrolled Bills, Finance, Government Organization,

Health and Human Resources, Interstate Cooperation, Judiciary, Labor, Military, Natural Resources, Pensions, Rules, Small Business, and Transportation. The (11) Joint Committees are: Enrolled Bills, Legislative Rule-Making Review Committee, Government and Finance, Pensions and Retirement, Rules, Forest Management Review, Parks and Recreation, Commission on Interstate Cooperation, Employee Suggestion Award Board, Joint Committee on Technology and Commission on Special Investigations. (See: Gregory M. Gray, Clerk, *Legislature of West Virginia Manual of the Senate and House of Delegates*, Seventy-Fifth Legislature, 2001–2002, 327–330, 430–432.

Web Sites

http://www.legis.state.wv.us/
(West Virginia Legislature)
http://www.ncsl.org
(National Conference of State Legislatures)

A GUIDE THROUGH THE LEGISLATIVE PROCESS

Donald R. Andrews and James A. Hoyer

INTRODUCTION

The West Virginia Constitution sets forth an organization consisting of three branches of government having separate and, in theory, equal powers. Former Speaker of the House of Delegates, Lewis N. McManus put it this way:

> "The executive branch takes charge of the day-to-day operations of government. The judicial branch judges whether the executive branch is doing its job in accordance with the law, as well as judging legislative actions on the basis of propriety and constitutionality. The Legislature has the strong power of taxation, granted by citizens through the Constitution. This is the strongest power we possess, and if properly used, it can benefit citizens for years to come. In addition, the Legislature is the only branch with the power to appropriate funds. No public tax money can be spent without the express consent of the Legislature. These are our strongest powers, but we also pass other laws to be implemented and administered by the executive branch. The ideas for these laws come from many sources—from individuals, from interest groups or from large segments of the population which are interested in a particular activity. However, by and large, the power of the Legislature is greatest when talking about spending public money. With the power to appropriate, we have a strong, strong power."

Laws affect everyone; therefore, they are made on the basis of improving and protecting the quality of life for all state citizens, now and in the years to come. What follows is an explanation not only of how our laws are made, but also who makes them, and when and where the lawmaking process takes place.

Composition of the Legislature

West Virginia is represented by a part-time "citizen legislature." While lawmakers are elected by the people to serve as their representative voice in government, they are also professionals in other occupations. The Legislature is also bicameral, meaning that it consists of two houses, the Senate and the House of Delegates.

State citizens are represented by 34 Senators and 100 Delegates who reside in specific territories called districts. These districts are divided according to population and may change if the census figures show a growth or loss of population. Presently, West Virginia has 17 senatorial districts and 58 delegate districts. Each citizen in the state has representatives in both the Senate and the House.

Terms of Office and Eligibility Requirements

Senators are elected to four-year terms with half of the seats up for election every two years. All members of the House of Delegates are up for election every two years.

Legislators must be United States citizens and eligible to vote. Additionally, a Delegate must be a resident of his/her district for one year while a Senator must be at least 25 years of age and a resident of the state for five years. If a legislator moves out of his/her district, the seat becomes vacant.

If a vacancy occurs in either house of the Legislature, the governor appoints an individual of the same political party as the departing member to fill the seat until the next general election.

Sessions of the Legislature

Each Legislature is comprised of two sessions. For example, the 72nd Legislature consists of the 1995 and 1996 sessions.

Regular sessions begin on the second Wednesday in January of each year and last for 60 consecutive days. However, in the year a governor is inaugurated a 30-day recess is taken after the first day of the session to allow the governor time to prepare his legislative agenda, including a proposed state budget for the coming year. Then, the legislators return on the second Wednesday in February to meet for 60 consecutive days.

On the first day of the 60-day session, members of both the senate and the House hold a joint session in the House chamber at which the governor presents his legislative program along with the state's budget bill. Speaking before the full body in what is called the "State of the State Address," the governor proposes suggestions as to what key issues he believes the Legislature should act on during the session.

A regular session may be extended by concurrent resolution adopted by two-thirds vote of the membership of each house. If the session is extended, legislators cannot act on any measures except the business stated in the concurrent resolution. The governor must, by proclamation, extend the session if the budget bill is not acted upon three days prior to the constitutional expiration of the session.

There are instances when it is necessary for the Legislature to meet between regular sessions. These are termed "Extraordinary" or Special sessions. Special sessions are convened at the discretion of the governor, or when the governor receives a written request from three-fifths of the members of each house.

The governor announces the convening of a special session through a written proclamation which lists the issues the Legislature may address. This proclamation is referred to as the "call" because it calls the Legislature into session. No items outside of the call may be taken up by the Legislature during an extraordinary session.

CAUCUSES

The Senate and House of Delegates have two types of caucuses:

Party Organization Caucus—The party organization caucus is called by the respective party chairmen, for the date and time traditionally set on the first Sunday of December following a general election. They are held in the Senate and House chambers. The purpose of the party organization caucus is to officially form the party blocs and to nominate candidates for the respective elective offices of the House and Senate, i.e., Speaker and President, clerks, Sergeant-At-Arms and Doorkeepers. The minority candidates for Speaker and President become the minority Leaders of their parties.

The party organization caucus is called to order by the chairman of the executive committee of the party; who then designates a temporary chairman of the organization caucus, by tradition the member with the most continuous service. The temporary chairman then designates a secretary of the caucus to assist in the clerical business of the proceedings.

Party Caucus—A party caucus is called at the direction of the party leadership. These caucuses are designated primarily to give the parties a chance to discuss party strategy and position on issues. The caucus is generally chaired by the majority whip and the minority whip of the respective parties.

The agenda is set by the party leadership holding the caucus. Decisions made by the caucuses are not binding upon the members and caucuses are not open to the public. No formal record is published of caucus proceedings and the chamber voting machines are not used.

The standing rules of order of the House and the Senate are used in the caucus. However, the caucus may use its own tailored rules or practices, provided that such rules are in keeping with accepted parliamentary practice.

Presiding Officers

The Senate and the House of Delegates each elect a leader, or a presiding officer. The leader in the Senate is the President and in the House, the Speaker. Both leaders choose the chairs and members of the standing committees in their chambers. It should be noted, that the President of the Senate is the second ranking constitutional officer in West Virginia and he succeeds to the office of governor in the event of a vacancy (West Virginia is one of four states that does not have a lieutenant governor). The Speaker of the House of Delegates is next in line of succession.

Floor Leaders

West Virginia has a two-party system and membership in both houses includes Democrats and Republicans. Both parties have floor leaders within each house who are majority and minority leaders and majority and minority whips. These leaders serve as spokespersons for their party's political position and, as such, act as liaisons for the leadership and members of their party. The majority leader takes the more visible role during a floor session. He moves to delay or hasten the consideration of a bill, comments on legislation from the majority party perspective, and moves to recess or adjourn.

The minority leader is selected by the minority party in each body, who in turn appoints the party's minority whip. Like their majority counterparts, they serve as spokespersons for their party and act to coordinate the minority party's platform. This is sometimes done in caucus as well as on the floor.

Two additional members of the leadership team are the President Pro Tempore and the Speaker Pro Tempore. They are appointed by the President and the Speaker to assume the chair should either of the presiding officers be absent or leave their post to address the members from the floor.

Privileges of the Floor

Only current and former members of the Legislature, members of Congress, legislative personnel engaged in the proper discharge of their duties and accredited members of the press are permitted within the chambers while the Senate and House are in session. Former members who are lobbyists are not permitted in the chambers while the House and Senate are in session. Spouses also are not permitted in the chamber during sessions. House Rule 136 and Senate Rule 54 are specific as to persons admitted to the floor and members' gallery. The provisions of these rules are serious, and a violation can result in the censure of a member. Also, appropriate dress is required in the chambers.

HOW A BILL BECOMES A LAW

Bill Development

Bills are simply ideas transposed to paper and proposed to become laws. They are ideas of ways to correct or address problems in the state. While any individual or group may have an idea for a bill, only a legislator may sponsor a bill and introduce it into the legislative process.

Once a legislator decides to sponsor a bill, an initial draft of the idea may be sent to the Office of Legislative Services for final drafting in proper and consistent bill form. To draft a bill on a particular subject, the appropriate portions of the West Virginia Code are combined with the proposed changes. After the draft legislation is prepared, the sponsor reviews and submits it for introduction to the clerk of the chamber of which he/she is a member. The clerk assigns a number to a bill. Senate bills are numbered in order from 1 to 1000 and House bills are numbered from 1001. Then the presiding officer for the body names the committee or committees that will study the bill.

Bill Sponsorship

In the Senate, the rules allow for an unlimited number of joint sponsors. However, the House rules limit joint sponsorship to no more than seven members.

Introduction of a Bill

A bill is formally introduced on the floor of the House or senate when its title is read by the clerk and the Speaker or the President announces the committee reference. A bill may have more than one committee reference (a "double reference") based on its subject matter and its fiscal implications.

Introduction of Bills by Request

The House and Senate rules allow for a bill to be introduced by request. This means that a member of the Legislature may introduce a bill for a constituent or constituent group that the member may not necessarily support.

Bill Carryover

Any bill or joint resolution pending in the House at the adjournment of the First Regular Session of the Legislature or Extended First Regular Session, which has not been rejected, tabled, or postponed indefinitely, shall carry over as it was introduced to the Second Regular Session, at the request of the sponsor or cosponsors of the bill or resolution. The request must be made to the Clerk of the House not later than ten days before the commencement of the Second Regular Session. The bill or joint resolution shall retain its original number and be introduced on the first day of the Second Regular Session, and unless otherwise directed by the Speaker, shall be referred to the committee or committees to which it was originally referred.

This rule does not apply to the following cases:

1. To any bill or joint resolution when the sole sponsor, or any one of the several sponsors of the bill or resolution is not serving in the House during the Second Regular Session.

2. To supplemental appropriation or budget bills, to legislative rule-making bills, to bills to explore or continue state agencies (sunset bills), to local bills, or to any joint resolution introduced during any extraordinary session.

Committee Work

The first meeting of a committee after its appointment by the leadership is to respond to the call of the chair. Here the committee usually considers only organizational and working plans. There are currently 14 standing (plus 11 joint) committees in the House and 19 standing in the Senate, which have the responsibility to review and make recommendations on legislation referred to them regarding a particular subject (such as finance or education) . The number and titles of the standing committees differ during the different sessions of the Legislature.

After a bill is introduced on the floor of either chamber, it is sent to a committee for study. It should be noted that these standing committees and subcommittees make it possible for the hundreds of bills introduced in each house during a legislative session to receive thorough study.

A bill (question) may be referred to a committee with or without instructions. The committee may be left without restrictions or may be partly or completely restricted. Specific instructions by the body must be carried out. When a bill is referred to a committee with instructions relating to part of a bill, the committee may not recommend with reference to other parts. A committee may only propose amendments to bills referred to it and cannot actually amend or modify them. The sole power of the recommendation does not become effective until it is adopted by the body. A committee must never alter an original bill or document referred to it, but must submit proposed amendments to the body on a separate paper.

Legislation to be discussed in a committee is placed on an agenda. During the committee's discussion, amendments may be offered to the bill. If a bill in the house of origin has numerous changes made to it or if the amendments are confusing or lengthy, a committee substitute (Com. Sub.) may be offered. Once all the changes are made and agreed to by a committee—which may require several meetings—a motion is made to report the measure to the floor in one of the following ways:

- with the recommendation that it "do pass" in its original form, or with amendments suggested by the committee, or as a committee substitute; or,

- with the recommendation that the bill be rejected with no recommendation at all.

This report along with the original bill and any committee amendments are filed with the appropriate clerk so the report can be read on the floor and the bill can be placed on the calendar. Only a few bills of the many sent to committees are actually reported to the floor. Those measures which are not reported by the end of the session are considered to have "died in committee." Again, committees are the central part of the legislative process. It is in committees where most of the work in a legislative session takes place. The committee system is designed to filter out "bad" legislation and to let "good" legislation through.

Substitute Bills (Com. Sub.)

A committee may change a bill completely and substitute entirely new provisions so long as the bill remains relevant to the title and the subject of the original bill. Other than retaining the number of the original bill, a substitute bill is considered a new bill, but does not have to be referred to the committee again. However, the committee may recommend that the substitute bill be referred to a second committee. When the chamber receives a report recommending a substitute bill, it will be treated as any other bill reported from a committee.

Committee Sessions Less Formal than Floor Sessions

The rules of procedure that govern the body apply to proceedings of committees insofar as is practical and applicable. As a general rule committee proceedings are less formal and often rules are relaxed in order to encourage free discussion and not handicap the work of the committee.

Actions of Committees in Considering Bills

Bills referred to standing committees are treated as resolutions of inquiry. A committee may hold bills without taking any action, table them, disapprove them, or report them back without recommendation as to their passage, report them for reference to another committee, or report them with the recommendation that they do pass, with or without amendment.

Committee Calendar

A committee can expedite its business by authorizing the chair to prepare a schedule of bills and resolutions to be considered at each meeting. In the absence of a daily agenda or calendar, the committee may take up measures in the order in which they were referred, or take them up on motion, or upon general consent. Usually a committee considers a bill by its sections, providing an opportunity for discussion and amendment of each section before proceeding to the next. The question is not put on each section, but is reserved until consideration of the bill is completed and the question is then put on the whole measure.

Reconsideration

A committee has the right to reconsider any action taken by it under the applicable rule governing reconsideration.

Committee Meetings and Hearings

All actions of committees must be taken at an official recognized meeting. Committee meetings are open to the general public. Informal actions on matters before the committee are improper. A member cannot cast a vote, except during an official meeting of the committee. The following actions are improper: for the chair to poll members on a proposal outside of the committee meeting, for a member to request any other member to vote for him/her during any absence, for a member to inform the chair, another member, or the committee clerk how he wished to vote, except in an official meeting, or to allow a member under any circumstances to vote by proxy. Such a vote is void.

It is also not in order for a committee to report a bill or other matter which was not considered at a regular committee meeting. It is the duty of the presiding officer of the body to refuse to accept any report on a bill or other matter when he has knowledge that it was not properly considered or acted upon.

Committees do not meet while the body is in session. When it is time for the chamber to meet, it is the duty of the chair to adjourn the meeting of the committee, and for the members to attend the session.

It is not in order for a committee to report a bill or other matter which was not considered at a committee meeting regularly held. It is the duty of the presiding officer of the body to refuse to accept any report on a bill or other matter when he has knowledge that it was not properly considered and acted upon.

Minority Reports

A minority of any committee may present its views and recommendations in writing with the report of the committee. When there is a minority report presented, it should be read following the committee report and before acceptance of the committee report. A minority report and the recommendations may, by vote of the body, be substituted for, and become, the report of the committee.

Supplemental Report

A committee may submit a written supplemental report on a bill containing an analysis of the bill or a statement of the intent or purpose of the bill. Such a report may be amended by the body and by order of the body printed in the journal.

Hearings

Proposed legislation pending before committees constitutes the vehicles for establishing state-wide policy. For this reason, the public, particularly the persons directly affected by the proposed legislation, have the right to be heard. It is essential that the opportunity for public hearings and adequate facilities for such hearings be provided. The Rules of the House and Senate provide for such hearings. Adequate advance notice of such hearings should be given by public announcement.

Committees of the House and Senate may hold joint hearings on important and far reaching bills. Joint hearings avoid duplication and afford the opportunity for both houses to hear the same testimony, eliminate the necessity for witnesses to attend dual hearings and conserve available research and clerical assistance.

A public hearing is intended to give the public the opportunity to express its view regarding a measure. Members of the committee may ask questions of persons appearing before the committee, but it is not advisable to engage these persons in debate. The committee chair should not make his/her own position on a measure obvious during a hearing to avoid the appearance of being prejudiced. No final action is taken upon any measure discussed at a public hearing.

Amendments to Measures

Amendments must be put in writing in the designated format and submitted to the clerk. Committee amendments are always considered prior to other amendments. The following rules pertain to amendments and the motion to amend:

A. Takes precedence only over the motion to which it applies.

B. An amendment may be amended (amendment to an amendment), but not beyond the second degree. Thus an amendment to an amendment cannot be amended.

C. An amendment may be divided, if it contains two propositions which can stand on their own, except the motion to strike out and insert is indivisible.

D. Must be germane to the question to be amended, and the presiding officer decides the propriety of amendments, subject to appeal.

E. To table, postpone or refer an amendment to a main question is the same as tabling, postponing or referring the question itself.

Floor Action

Floor sessions in both the House and Senate are governed in large part by the rules of the body and constitutional requirements, and are conducted according to strict parliamentary procedures. A routine agenda, or Order of Business, is followed daily as the basic structure for a floor session.

Senate Daily Order of Business

1. To read, correct and approve the Journal.

2. Introduction of guests.

3. To dispose of communications from the House of Delegates and the executive.

4. To receive reports from standing committees.

5. To receive reports from select committees.

6. To receive bills, resolutions, motions and petitions.

7. To act upon unfinished business of the preceding day and resolutions lying over from the previous day; no resolution shall lose its place on the calendar by not being acted upon the day following that on which it is offered.

8. Senate and House bills on third reading.

9. Senate and House bills on second reading.

10. Senate and House bills on first reading.

11. Introduction of guests.

12. Remarks by members of the Senate.

13. Miscellaneous business.

Note: all Senate documents are printed on white paper.

House Daily Order of Business

1. To read, correct and approve the Journal.

2. To act upon leaves of absence for members.

3. To receive and consider reports from standing committees.

4. To receive and consider reports from select committees.

5. To receive and consider reports from the executive, state officials and other communications and remonstrances.

6. To receive messages from the Senate and consider amendments proposed by the Senate to bills passed by the House.

7. To receive resolutions, petitions and motions.

8. Bills introduced on motion for leave and referred to the appropriate committees.

9. To act on unfinished business of the preceding day.

10. House and Senate bills on third reading.

11. House and Senate bills on second reading.

12. House and Senate bills on first reading.

13. Miscellaneous business.

Note: All House documents are printed on green paper.

Each item of business is taken up, and dealt and dispensed with in the sequence shown. If an issue is to be brought up after the body has moved beyond the appropriate order of business, the members must agree to return to that order of business to take care of the matter.

Reading of Bills

As was mentioned earlier, bills are placed on a calendar by the clerk of each house. A calendar is actually a listing of what will be taken up on a given day, usually under three orders of business; bills on third reading, bills on second reading and bills on first reading. The reading of bills generally occurs on three separate days as stipulated in the state constitution. However, the constitutional rule may be suspended by a four-fifths vote of the membership, allowing two or three readings of a bill to take place on one day.

When a bill is read, the title or brief summary of the measure is recited by the clerk along with the bill number. If a bill is not delayed on first or second reading, the bill is "advanced" to the next reading stage once the body completes its action. A bill is read three times to accomplish three different purposes:

The **First reading** of a bill is called the information stage, informing the members that the bill will be discussed.

On **Second reading**, or amendment stage, any committee recommendations and changes proposed by individual members are discussed and acted upon. It is the amendments, and not the bill itself, that are debated on second reading. Each amendment is voted on separately, with no limit to the number of amendments which may be offered, and are adopted or rejected. After second reading, a bill is "ordered to engrossment and third reading." An engrossed version of a bill includes all adopted amendments.

Third reading is the passage stage of a bill. Debate on the merits and drawbacks of a bill occurs at this time. After the debate is completed, the bill is either passed or rejected.

If the bill is passed, it is sent to the other chamber of the Legislature where it is referred to committee and the process repeats itself.

Conference Committees

The second chamber may change a bill passed by the first body. For a bill to complete legislative action, both bodies must approve identical legislation. Therefore an agreement must be reached when changes are made.

When the first body receives the message from the second chamber that it has amended an engrossed bill, the first chamber may either accept the amendment(s) or send a message to the other chamber asking the body to "recede" from its amendment(s). The second body may back down from its position, or it may refuse to recede. If the second body refuses to recede, then a conference committee is necessary to resolve those items in a bill the two bodies disagree on in order for the bill to pass.

A conference committee is composed of an equal number of Senators, appointed by the President, and Delegates, appointed by the Speaker. As with standing committees, changes made in a bill by a conference committee are recommendations which the full bodies must act upon. Once a compromise is reached, the co-chairs of the conference committee report to their respective chambers. The conference committee report must be accepted (adopted) or rejected. If the report is adopted, the amended version of the bill must be voted on for its passage or rejection.

Once the same version of a bill is passed by both houses, it becomes an enrolled bill and is sent to the governor for his consideration.

Action by the Governor

While the Legislature is in session, the governor has five days to approve or veto a bill he receives. After the Legislature adjourns, the governor has 15 days to act on most bills before him. However, the budget bill and supplemental appropriations bills must be acted on by the governor within five days, regardless of when he receives them. If the governor does not act within these time limits, the bill automatically becomes law.

If the governor vetoes a bill, the Legislature can override the veto with a majority vote in both chambers. The exceptions to this are the budget bill and supplemental appropriations bills. A two-thirds vote of both houses is needed to override a governor's veto in these instances.

Successful Bills Become Acts of the Legislature

After a bill becomes a law, it is called an act. The "Acts of the Legislature" are published annually and reflect all of the measures which become law in a given year. The acts are inserted into the appropriate portions of the *West Virginia Code*, which is a series of books containing the laws of the state.

Resolutions

While most matters taken up by the Legislature are in the form of bills, there is another kind of legislative proposal known as a resolution. There are actually three types of resolutions, none of which require action by the governor.

A **joint resolution** is the first step to making a change in the state constitution. The adoption of a joint resolution by the Legislature means that a suggested amendment to the constitution will be placed on the ballot at the next general election or special election for the voters to decide. The Legislature only decides that the issue should be placed before the voters, not whether the change should or does occur.

Joint resolutions are referred to committee and when they are reported back, go through the same three readings as bills. Joint resolutions must be read on three separate days and must receive a two-thirds vote of the elected members in order to be adopted.

Concurrent resolutions are measures affecting the actions or procedures of both bodies. These resolutions may express the sentiments of the Legislature, authorize expenditures incidental to the session and business of the Legislature, agree upon adjournments beyond the constitutional limitation, create special joint committees, raise a joint assembly, or address other purposes on behalf of both chambers.

Simple resolutions are used to express the will or order of one house on matters in which agreement of the other house is not necessary, such as the hiring of staff for one body.

Concurrent and simple resolutions are read only once before being adopted or rejected.

Methods of Voting

In committee meetings and during floor sessions, issues are decided by members casting votes. Votes may be taken in one of three ways: roll call vote (also termed "calling for the yeas and nays,") voice vote, and division vote. The presiding officer or committee chair generally determines which method of voting will be used, unless a member requests another type of vote.

A roll call vote records how each member in attendance actually stands on an issue. In a committee meeting, each member's name is called and the vote is recorded in the minutes of the meeting. During a floor session, electronic voting machines are used and the votes are recorded on the display boards at the front of each chamber.

In an effort to save time, a voice vote is sometimes used. The presiding officer or chair simply asks all those in favor of a measure to say "aye" and all those opposed to say "no." After hearing the response, the presiding officer states the result determining which side prevails.

The third type of voting is called the division vote. When a division vote is taken, members are asked to rise at their seats. A head count is taken of those for or against the motion being voted on and the numbers are recorded without individual names.

House and Senate Journals

A daily, written record of all action taken during floor sessions is recorded for each body in the House Journal or Senate Journal, respectively. To see what took place on a particular day in either chamber, including bills acted on, the text of adopted amendments and votes cast, one may go to the appropriate journal to locate the proceedings of that day. Beyond the session activities, the journals also contain a variety of useful information by which the legislative process may be monitored. To effectively use the journals, one must first become familiar with their format.

Following the order of business for each chamber, the House and Senate journals begin with the floor action of the previous day. After this account, an abstract or bill history is listed. This is a numerical listing of bills introduced naming the sponsor(s), the short title of the bill, the date of introduction, the committee to which it is referred, the status of the bill after it is reported from the committee and any action taken by the governor. Appearing next are the topical indexes, which list bills by broad subject areas. If a person does not know the number of a bill, the subject can be located in the topical index along with the appropriate bill number. One can then find the bill number in the abstract or bill history to determine what action was taken on the measure. Other listings in the journals include resolutions, bills passed by the Legislature and bills acted on by the governor.

At the rear of each journal is the daily calendar. The calendars list legislation which will be acted on during the floor session on the day the journal is printed. In the latter part of the session, two calendars may be printed in the journals, the "regular" calendar and the "special" calendar. Only those items on the special calendar are taken up by the body.

During the latter part of a legislative session, the Rules Committees of the House and Senate set the regular and special calendars and control the flow of legislation. The Rules Committees are comprised of the leadership from both parties so decisions are open and fair. The committees ensure orderliness of legislative business and procedures during the last days of the session.

Finally, a schedule of committee meetings and public hearings appears on the last page of the journal.

In general, the minimal number of votes needed of the full membership of each house to adopt or pass a measure is: simple majority, 51 votes in the House and 18 votes in the Senate; two-thirds, requires 67 votes in the House and 23 in the Senate; and four-fifths, needs 80 in the House and 27 in the Senate.

DEFINITIONS OF LEGISLATIVE TERMS

Abrogate: to repeal a law.

Adjourn: to end a House or Senate floor session or committee meeting until another scheduled time.

Adjourn Sine Die: the final closing of a legislative session.

Adopt: approval or acceptance, usually applied to amendments, resolutions and motions.

Agenda: a list of items to be considered at a meeting.

Amendment: proposed change in pending legislation by adding, deleting or modifying material.

Appropriation: money allocated by the Legislature to various governmental departments and agencies for their operation. A supplemental appropriation is an additional allocation of funds to a specific governmental unit for a stated purpose.

Bill: a proposal for a new law, for the amendment or repeal of an existing law, or for appropriation of public money.

Budget: a financial plan that details expected revenues (income) and appropriations (expenditures) for a specific time period. The state budget covers the period of July 1 through June 30, which is called the state fiscal year. The legislation containing the state budget is referred to as the budget bill.

Caucus: an informal meeting of a group of members, usually of the same political party, to discuss policy or legislation. During a party caucus, staff, the public and the media are not permitted to attend.

Clerk: chief administrative officer of the House or the Senate elected by the members of each body.

Code: the official written laws of West Virginia, usually referred to as the Code of West Virginia, 1931, as amended.

Committee Substitute (Com. Sub.): a rewritten version of a bill recommended by a committee. Committee substitutes are generally offered when amendments to a bill are numerous or confusing and the ideas will be made clearer by rewriting the bill. A committee substitute retains the same subject and bill number as the original bill.

Committees: the various types of legislative committees are defined below:

> **Committee of the Whole:** an informal session of the entire membership of either house.

> **Conference Committee:** a committee made up of Delegates appointed by the Speaker and Senators appointed by the President to try to resolve the differences in legislative measures.

> **Interim Committee:** a group established by law or rules to work between sessions on legislative matters. The main one is the Joint Committee on Government and Finance.

> **Joint Committee:** a committee composed of members of both houses.

> **Select Committee:** a group appointed by the Speaker and the President to handle specific matters. This committee is usually dissolved when its purpose is accomplished.

Standing Committee: a committee comprised of members appointed by the Speaker and the President at the beginning of the Legislature which has continuing responsibility in a general field of legislative activity, such as finance.

Subcommittee: a portion of a committee appointed by a committee chair to research and study a particular bill or problem and to report its findings to the entire committee.

Concur: the action of one house in agreeing to or approving a proposal or action by the other body.

Discharge a Committee: to remove a bill or resolution from consideration of a committee.

Division of the Question: if an issue to be voted on has parts which can be voted on separately, it can be "divided."

Enact: to make a bill into law.

Engrossed bill: the official version of a bill that includes all adopted amendments of the house of origin attached to the original measure.

Enrolled bill: the final, official version of a bill that is agreed to by both bodies and contains all necessary signatures.

Extraordinary Session: special session of the Legislature called by the governor to deal with the specific problems arising in the state.

Fiscal Note: the financial statement required by House and Senate rules to be attached to any bill either decreasing or increasing revenues or fiscal liability of the state.

Introduction: the step by which a bill is officially started in the legislative process.

Motion: a proposal made to the presiding officer calling for a specific action. Motions are of various order, rank, precedence and class as established through parliamentary practice. **Motions commonly used in the Legislature include:**

- Lie over: to allow a bill or other matter to be considered the next day.

- Postpone Indefinitely: to delay action forever. If this motion is adopted, the matter being considered is dead for the remainder of the session.

  Previous Question: to close debate on the subject under discussion. When this motion is made, debate is interrupted and a vote is taken on whether the body wants to end debate. If the motion fails, debate continues. If the motion is adopted, a second vote is taken on the subject itself.

- Reconsideration: to retake a vote on a measure.

- Table: to set aside a matter for later consideration.

Point of Order: a member's inquiry of the chair as to the correctness of a procedure being followed.

Presiding officer: the elected leader of each legislative body; in the House the position is called Speaker and in the Senate it is called President. Committee chairs are also considered the presiding officers of their committees.

Privilege of the Floor: being permitted access to the Senate or House chamber when the legislators are in session.

Question: the main topic under discussion.

Readings: the three stages bills and joint resolutions go through on the floor of a chamber. The first reading is the information stage, the second reading is the amendment stage, and the third reading is the passage stage.

Recede: to withdraw or back down from a position on an issue.

Regular Session: the 60 consecutive days during which the Legislature meets each year, beginning on the second Wednesday in January. In the year that a governor is inaugurated, the Legislature meets on this date only long enough for each house to elect its officers for the next two-year term and to jointly publish the general election returns. It then adjourns until the second Wednesday in February for the 60-day session.

Repeal: to officially revoke a previous action.

Report Out or Report Back: when a committee prepares a report with its recommendations regarding an assigned bill and returns it to the full body for consideration.

Rules: the set of regulations and parliamentary procedures adopted separately by the House and the Senate to govern each body's actions. There are also joint rules which govern both houses.

Suspend the Rules: an action whereby a particular rule of either body is viewed as hampering efficient work on a certain issue or problem and the rule is temporarily disregarded through a vote of the members.

Sustain a Motion: the legislative method of seconding a motion, generally requiring agreement by at least one-tenth of the membership. Most motions are not sustained and the presiding officer announces when such an action is necessary.

Title: a concise statement of the contents of a bill. An even briefer summary is called a short title.

Unanimous Consent: permission granted, without exception, by either house to a member desiring to accomplish an action without making a motion. Unanimous consent is granted by members remaining silent or voicing no objection.

Unfinished Business: a matter held over from the previous day.

The Budget Bill

By September 1 of each year, each state agency must submit a budget request to the Department of Administration for the next fiscal year starting on July 1. Accordingly, the money will not be available to spend until ten months later and must be spent in approximately 670 days from the September 1 date. Reasonable requests are difficult to make that far in advance because of inflation, increase in postage, utility rates, food costs, etc.

The Department of Administration holds budget hearings with the agencies during the early Fall and budget requests are continually changed by the agencies, since they have to make adjustments to current year plans. They amend these to carry the changes into the next year, if necessary. These requests, which the governor, and then the Department of Administration, analyzes, tabulates and summarizes, form the root financial scheme for the state budget. The governor can submit an unbalanced budget but the Legislature cannot pass an unbalanced budget.

When the budget is submitted to the Legislature, following the State of the State Address, the Legislature has the authority to reroute funding as it deems preferable. The Legislature has several options when dealing with the budget. It may accept the governor's proposals at face value and enact them into law; it may meet the approximate amount of money which the governor proposes by coming up with a tax proposal of its own (in this case, the governor must amend the revenue estimates so that they are in conformity with the proposed tax increase); and, it may reject any tax proposal recommended by the governor and cut the budget requests of the various departments to fit within the estimates of revenues at their present or predictable level.

The budget bill may be finalized after the 60th day to provide sufficient time for all other legislation to be finalized as it may affect the budget. Funds do not become available for expenditure until a spending unit has filed an expenditure schedule detailing how it plans to spend its funds—general revenue, federal funds and special revenue.

Agencies have 31 days to pay bills from an old year, that is until July 31. Two weeks later, on August 15, budget requests for the following year are due, starting the entire process of developing the budget all over again.

The Budget Digest

By statute, specifically Section 18, Article 1, Chapter 4, of the *West Virginia Code*, it is mandated that a digest of the budget be prepared at the direction, and with the approval, of the members of the conference committee on the budget bill. The digest does not have the full force and effect of the law. The statute's language follows:

> "The Legislature, acting by its appropriate committees, shall consider the budget bill, the budget document and matters relating thereto, and following such consideration and upon the passage of the budget bill by the Legislature, the Legislature shall prepare a digest or summary of the budget bill containing detailed information similar to that included

135

in the budget document submitted to the Legislature by the governor but including amendments of legislative committees, and as finally enacted by the Legislature. Such digest or summary shall be prepared at the direction of and approved by members of the conference committee on the budget and shall be included on the journals of the legislature or printed as a separate document, and copies shall be furnished to the governor, commissioner of finance and administration, and the various state spending units for such use as may be deemed proper."

Lobbying

A lobbyist is a person who represents his own interests and concerns, or those of a special interest or of a special interest group or organization. The lobbyist's fundamental role is to provide accurate, needed and timely information about his, or their, position on issues before the government, particularly legislative bodies. Further, the lobbyist usually works actively to promote the passage or defeat of bills, rules and regulations, and adoption of policies.

Lobbyists and special interests have been part of the American political process since its beginning and have been viewed ambivalently for more than 200 years. As early as 1787, James Madison warned about the "mischiefs of factions."

Now special interest groups are generally viewed as an integral and beneficial part of the American political process, legitimized in the U. S. Constitution by the First Amendment guarantees of freedom of speech and the right to "petition the government for the redress of grievances." Appointed and elected officials in all levels of government frequently praise and rely upon the involvement of special interest groups as a necessary component of governmental decision and policy making, providing important information on public opinion and on the impact of policy proposals.

The First Amendment uses the word "petition." Nowhere does the U.S. Constitution use the word "lobby." When any person, as an individual or as a representative of an interest group, contacts governmental officers and elected officials about a position on legislation or other governmental matters, they are petitioning the government. They are petitioning for a redress of "grievances." They voice their objections and protests about issues at hand and request correction of the problem, or suggest a remedy to correct the problem. The remedy may be the amendment, defeat or passage of a bill by the Legislature.

How did "petitioning" get to be commonly referred to as "lobbying?" The words "lobbying" and "lobbyist" were first used in the 1830s to describe those people who frequented the lobbies of public buildings in the United States, particularly those of the federal government, and of state governments, to talk to governmental officials and legislators about issues.

To be effective in West Virginia government, lobbyists must be in the halls of the Capitol building. That is where they get the House and Senate journals, the list of bills being introduced, the calendar for the House and Senate, and the schedule of committee sessions. The Capitol is where they must be to follow and hear the formal actions of bills in which they are interested, and to hear the "scuttlebutt" about how other interest groups and legislators feel about these bills.

To be effective, lobbyists must have direct, personal contact with the legislators to persuade them that their cause is just and right. The lobbyist must know how and what the legislators are thinking, why they are thinking that way, what they are saying , and to whom they are saying it. "Seeing, hearing and talking" are three of the lobbyist's most powerful tools.

Types of Lobbyists and Political Interest Groups

The Individual: an individual may lobby and represent strictly his own interests. His statements and positions will have a very personal nature to them. This individual may use personal contacts with legislators, but will rely mainly on letters and telephone calls. The individual lobbyist who frequents the legislative hallways does so at his own expense.

Single Issue Group: these groups are comprised of individuals who share strongly held attitudes concerning a specific issue or cause. They are usually volunteers who spend their own money to lobby legislators. An example, is Mothers Against Drunk Driving (M.A.D.D.).

Civic Organization: are generally well established in communities throughout the state. They are known for their highly visible participation in public affairs and charitable causes. The League of Women Voters and the Junior League are examples. The persons who lobby for such organizations are also volunteers who live in the Capitol area. They keep their affiliated chapters abreast of legislative issues, who then contact legislators from their areas. They are usually very effective.

Professional Lobbyist (Single Client): a person (frequently a former legislator) who is employed full-time by an organization, corporation, labor union or professional association. The lobbyist keeps continuously informed on developments in the Legislature that might affect his business or organization. Additionally the person serves as his organization's spokesperson during the legislative session. The employing body provides the lobbyist with an expense account to meet the lobbying costs.

Professional Lobbyist (Multi-Client): some lobbyists represent two or more groups, businesses, or organizations during the legislative session. There are a few who represent just one organization year-round but take on additional clients during the session. These individuals must take care to insure that they do not represent conflicting interests. Each group, business or organization places the lobbyist on a retainer with a suitable agreement for expenses incurred in lobbying activities. The lobbyist is the spokesperson for each of the groups he represents.

Lobbyists that represent large organizations often plan meetings, dinners and receptions to enable many of their members to meet with legislators and personally discuss the issues.

The Tools of the Effective Lobbyist

1. Be accurate in the information provided to the legislator and know the subject well. Never knowingly supply misleading or inaccurate information. If this should happen by accident, immediately admit the error and correct it to maintain credibility.

2. Be concise while dispensing full and accurate information.

3. Be polite and professional in issue discussions.

4. Never threaten or imply a threat to a member. Intimidation simply does not work.

5. When possible, produce information in concise written form to accompany verbal expressions of positions.

6. Follow all the rules of the Senate and House of Delegates as set forth.

7. The lobbyist should become familiar with the names and titles of each legislator.

8. Lobbyists representing groups should encourage their members to write letters and make personal phone calls to legislators. These personal communications carry weight.

9. Get to know the legislative process and keep a constant watch on the legislation of interest to the group being represented. Also, be aware of the status and purpose of other major bills.

Notes

The following sources were consulted in the preparation of this article:

1   Darrell E. Holmes, Clerk of the Senate.

2   Donald L. Kopp, Clerk of the House of Delegates.

3   *A Guide Through the Legislative Process*, West Virginia Legislative Reference and Information Center.

4   *A Bill Becomes Law*, the West Virginia Legislative Reference and Information Center.

5   Donald L. Kopp, Clerk of the House of Delegates, and Gregory M. Gray, Parliamentarian and Assistant House Clerk, *Parliamentary Procedure in the House of Delegates*, "*A Handbook For Legislators,*" House Clerk's Office, (1991) .

6   Gregory M. Gray, *A Guide for Legislative Committees of the House of Delegates*, House Clerk's Office.

7   *Motions and Unanimous Consent Requests*, Senate Clerk's Office, (1993).

8   *Manual of the Senate and House of Delegates*, 72nd Legislature, 1995–1996.

9   *Orientation Manual*, 72nd Legislature, 1995–1996.

Commentary:
PROBLEMS AND PROSPECTS FACING THE REPUBLICAN PARTY IN THE HOUSE OF DELEGATES

David B. McKinley
Former Delegate, West Virginia House of Delegates

Background to the Problem

In recent years the liberal leadership within the Democratic Party in West Virginia has made a mockery of the political process in state government. This has occurred because the Republican Party has failed to elect sufficient numbers of delegates and senators to provide a two-party political system and thereby instill a means of checks and balances in the legislature.

During my eight years in the House of Delegates, our party has managed to send an average of only 21 delegates and 5 senators to Charleston. In contrast, the Democrats have amassed an average of 79 delegates and 29 senators in opposition. Unfortunately, this dismal imbalance has also extended without interruption for nearly 60 years: the House of Delegates has been controlled by the Democratic Party since the 1930 election and the Senate since 1932. This time frame becomes more relevant when you realize that our revered and beautiful State Capitol Building was not constructed until 1932, "Babe" Ruth was still hitting home runs, and Charles Lindbergh had only recently landed his plane in Paris.

The apparent inability of the Republican party to explain to the voters how the system is manipulated and to break this monopolistic control of the legislature is a serious challenge to the future of a two-party system and to the development of West Virginia's potential.

The Power Structure

One must first recognize the pyramid power structure within the system if we are to understand how the Democrats can control their own membership and, at the same time, the ebb and flow of the political process.

The first act of the respective parties in the legislature, after the general election, is to select their chosen spokesman: for the Republicans, it is the minority leader and for the majority party, it is the Speaker of the House or Senate President. These majority leaders, in turn, repay their supporters for their efforts by appointing them committee chairmen or vice chairmen. Then they name other political allies to the influential major committees. Once these individual assignments are in place, the leadership has sufficient influence to control whatever is to be addressed during each session of the legislature.

Committees in the House typically include 25 members with the political composition generally reflecting the makeup of the House; for example, the Finance Committee currently has twenty Democrats and only five Republicans. Dutifully, these committees will adopt at their first meeting the policy that the agenda is the prerogative of the chairman and thereby waive the last vestiges of independent thought. No appointed chairman would dare pass a bill out of committee that is not already blessed by the Speaker or the President. Consequently, the priorities, accomplishments and failures of the Legislature must rest at the door of the offices of the Democratic leaders.

To challenge this "authoritarian rule" has dire consequences. Democratic Delegate Dwayne Southern from Marion County chose to oppose his party's action involving the protracted deliberations of the 1987 State Budget and was summarily dismissed from the Finance Committee. This harsh action was meant to be a clear reminder to the Democratic membership not to criticize the leadership unless they are willing to suffer the political fallout. The following year Delegate Southern announced that he would not seek reelection.

This kind of retaliation underscores why electing conservative Democrats is not an adequate or reliable form of opposition to the liberal leadership. Even conservative Democrats can recognize that if they want their own legislative agenda adopted during the session, they must cooperate when solicited by their party's leadership. It is incumbent on the Republican Party therefore, to encourage strong, articulate candidates to contest for seats within the Legislature and to participate in providing vocal opposition to the current policies of the liberal leadership.

It should be clear to the reader by now that the present system of power structuring is fraught with opportunities for misuse. Either the speaker or the committee chairman has the ability to squash a bill or to delay activity until it is effectively too late to pass during a 60-day session. Another option available to a chairman is to assign a bill to a subcommittee which, like the full committee, has limited meeting times available. Remember, most committees, other than the major ones, meet approximately nine times during a session—and then only for an hour. To get on the chairman's agenda, therefore, is a major accomplishment and one that certainly enhances a bill's chances for eventual adoption.

But doesn't this control work against legislation offered by the Democratic members as well? Yes, but certainly not to the same degree. At the conclusion of a recent session, only two bills sponsored solely by Republican delegates were passed into law. The remaining bills were authored by Democrats only or co-sponsored by a Democrat.

It takes 80% of the elected membership in either the House or Senate to suspend their respective rules which otherwise restrain hasty action on legislation. If the majority party chooses to bypass this safeguard and has elected a sufficient number, the Republicans have no choice but to watch the "train" as it passes by. Bills don't have to be read, considered by any committee, or take three days to passage once the rules have been suspended. Whenever necessary, the liberal leadership has exercised this expeditious power to the detriment of the citizenry who expect full and careful deliberations to ensue.

Alternatives and Prospects for Reform

Alternatives suggested by the minority party and conservative Democrats include: removing the sponsor's name from the proposed legislation so that it will be considered strictly on its merit; not disclosing how the leadership is voting on any issue until the voting machine has locked in the votes and displays the outcome in lights; guaranteeing that a committee assignment should not be altered without due cause; and assuring that some form of action is taken on all bills that are introduced each year.

The immediate prospect for a brighter and more prosperous West Virginia would be immeasurably improved if these rules were adopted by the Legislature. No one can convince me that the Republican membership is incapable of substantive and contributing service and that the solutions for social and economic revitalization are embraced solely in the bosom of the Democratic delegates and senators.

How rational is it when West Virginia voters are swayed by national politics and ancestral bias to defeat Republican legislative incumbents with the argument that not enough is being done for education, jobs or highways when the power brokering is being managed by the opposing political party? However illogical it is to blame the minority party, it is a reoccurring nightmare at election time for Republicans—especially those that try to articulate how the liberal Democratic leadership has set the priorities about which the voters are so unsatisfied.

Historical voting patterns must be broken, straight ticket voting must be finally eliminated and our legislators elected on the issues facing our families and communities.

Partisan Politics in an Election Year

Three-term Republican Governor Moore announced early in 1988 that he would be seeking a fourth and final term in office even though this could lead to his opponents politicizing the upcoming session. Exacerbating the situation was the fact that at least two or three senators, including the President[1] of the Senate, were considering running for the Office of Governor themselves, the wife of another candidate[2] was serving in the House, and numerous campaign managers and staff personnel were in both bodies of the Legislature. As a result of this congestion in the governor's race, the 1988 session could be summarized as one in which nothing would be adopted that could benefit the Republican incumbent.

For example, take the long overdue adjustment to the gasoline tax as proposed by Governor Moore that would provide approximately $50 million annually for a statewide road maintenance and small bridge reconstruction and/or replacement program. He sought a five cent increase to the current tax and asked that it be effective on April 1, 1988 so that those vital improvements could be implemented during the year's construction season. Since the taxes are paid quarterly, that meant the State of West Virginia would have been able to initiate contracts after the second quarter or by July 1st.

With the initial blessing of the leadership in the House, the governor's program was surprisingly passed by the Finance Committee with little opposition and sent to the House for adoption. However, after reconsideration of the possible political ramifications of the bill during the unusually long waiting period before being read to the full House, the liberal Democratic leadership reversed their previous position and chose to circumvent the earlier committee vote by reassigning the bill to the Finance Committee for amendments. Despite the demands for proper maintenance of our existing secondary roads, the leadership, never-the-less, substituted a two cent increase to be used for work on bridges only and which would not be effective until July.

This meant no additional road maintenance would be forthcoming until after July of 1989 and repairs and/or replacement of bridges could not begin until after the third quarter of October 1, 1988. This regrettable action was clearly and admittedly proposed so that the incumbent governor would not have financial resources available for roadwork during an election year.

Fortunately, however, their hypocritical alternative to solving one of our state's major infrastructure deficiencies was defeated by a coalition of conservative Democrats and the five Republican members on this powerful 25 member committee. Even Highway Commissioner, William Ritchie, argued for its defeat despite the overwhelming needs because of this crass politicization of the process. He realized the unlikely nature of the legislature to increase the tax beyond the two cent increase in upcoming years so it was incumbent on us to seek an alternative. In a spirit of compromise, the Republican contingency failed in an attempt to increase the tax initially by two cents and then add one cent during each of the three succeeding years. It becomes evident that negotiating from a strength in numbers would have been far more fruitful. . . .

Constitutional Reform

To circumvent what has been a stranglehold on the legislative process in West Virginia by the current office holders (who often can be fairly charged with campaigning one way and, once elected, voting another way), the Republican Party has endorsed the concept of an amendment to the West Virginia Constitution that would allow "Initiative and Referendum" by the voters statewide.

This amendment would allow the citizens of West Virginia to prepare a petition that would be circulated statewide on any issue of concern and, if sufficient numbers sign the petition in a prescribed number of counties, the issue would be placed on the ballot at the next general election. Matters overlooked or ignored by the legislative leadership could finally be addressed in this manner. These could include right to work, state funding of abortions, dedicating lottery proceeds for education or senior citizens, and collective bargaining for public employees if the state were so inclined.

It is important to develop this alternative to jousting with the leadership and to provide in the constitution the vehicle to hear from the voters who deserve this opportunity to be heard. "Initiative and Referendum" would be an excellent outlet for those frustrated by special interest groups effecting the legislature and the timidity of elected members on certain issues.

For the past three years I have sponsored this legislation and each time it is advanced further in the legislative process. It is embraced by a growing number of thoughtful Democrats but the educational process has been slow.

Not withstanding all the roadblocks faced by Republicans in the West Virginia Legislature, we have accomplished numerous personal and collective objectives using persuasion and knowledge of procedural rules. Probably the best examples of our successes can be found in the proposition of amendments to the various bills making their way through the legislative system. In these cases, we can be the conscience of the Legislature; a voice of logic and reasonableness; or as a last resort, a warning signal. To illustrate our effectiveness, it was the small minority party that recently demanded and won the support of enough conservative Democrats to alter the proposed business tax structure in West Virginia; who exposed that state taxes are funding abortions without restrictions; and it has been the Republicans who have consistently voted for increased funding for higher and secondary education. And each year we have also challenged to support the salary increases that they espouse in their campaign for reelection. Combining our efforts in 1987 with Governor Moore, we also attempted to adopt an ambitious program to bolster our statewide educational system only to see the liberal leadership thwart the effort without an alternative.

Unfortunately the perception of our efforts is received in some quarters as obstructionist and negative. Neither can be further from the truth, but to the public, "perception" in West Virginia has a way of appearing factual after awhile.

Probably the most frustrating aspect of being a Republican in West Virginia is to observe the regions of despair and neglect in our state. Are they caused by the decisions of ruthless businessmen, out of state ownership of our land, or unfair tax treatment? Or could it be the failure of those communities to support an opposition to their presently elected officials and thereby demonstrate their dissatisfaction with their legislator's activities? It is not coincidental to find that the areas in our state that suffer the greatest indignities of poor educational programs, unsuitable housing, low economic diversification, and an inadequate highway system are those that continually elect Democrats only to local and state positions. Just imagine the attention their districts would receive if these elected officials were challenged by a two-party system that demanded accountability.

Contrast the attitudes of these depressed areas with those voters in other communities that recognize the power of opposing views and don't hesitate to elect representatives from both political camps when necessary. Politicians are prone naturally to concentrate their limited energies and time to those areas in which their opposition may develop. As a result, the needs of the electorate that historically vote only for the majority party are apparently overlooked.

Painfully I have come to this political awareness and hope that it is not too late to raise the expectations of those citizens who have been denied the opportunities enjoyed by so many other West Virginians. With a viable and numerically stronger presence in the Legislature by the Republican Party, state government would be a far better institution, our schools and communities would be rewarded with alternatives, and our people could enjoy a newly found strength at the polls.

It is also equally incumbent on the Republican Party to field candidates throughout all of West Virginia who are sensitive to the social and economic problems facing West Virginia and to gird themselves with facts and solutions as they confront the well entrenched Democratic office holders. If the minority party can thereby increase its count in the Legislature, then the prospect of cooperation will be more evident and the priorities and perverse leadership within the majority party can be reoriented.

Notes

[1] When this commentary was written (1989) the President of the Senate was Larry Tucker.

[2] The reference is to Dee Caperton <ed.>.

Commentary:
SOME THOUGHTS ON MY EXPERIENCES AS A WOMAN IN THE WEST VIRGINIA HOUSE OF DELEGATES

Patricia Bradley Pitrolo
Former Delegate, West Virginia House of Delegates

Politics is not an exact science. There is the theoretical side, the way things are supposed to be, and then there is the practical side, the way things are. In the following pages, I will try to explain one legislator's view, mine, of the practical side of West Virginia politics. My experiences are from the perspective of being a woman in the West Virginia House of Delegates and from being a member of the majority party.

I do not pretend to represent the views, opinions, or experiences of my colleagues in the West Virginia Legislature. These pages are, quite simply, a limited case study of one particular legislator presently serving in state government. It is my sincere hope that I can shed some light on the practical side of being a public servant.

Background

I was first elected to the West Virginia House of Delegates in November of 1984. I was sworn into office on the second Wednesday of January 1985 and began serving my two-year term representing the First District. I was thirty-three.

My entry into politics is a little different than most. I was asked to run for the House of Delegates by the gentleman who held the seat before me, Joe Cipriani. He had decided to run for the state Senate and his seat would be vacant. About a week before the filing deadline ended, he called me and told me that he and some other elected state officials had been talking and decided they would like me to run for the House of Delegates. I explained to Delegate Cipriani, whom I had never spoken to before, that I couldn't possibly run for the House of Delegates because I had two small children at home. He asked me to give him a chance to convince me and then talked to me for about forty-five minutes. In the end, he suggested that I talk it over with my family and let him know my decision. I followed his suggestion and obviously, I decided to run.

Prior to running for the House of Delegates, I had been very active in volunteer work in our community for about five years. I had served on several boards of directors of civic organizations and held a number of offices in these organizations. I had also been in the public eye a great deal because of my volunteer work.

So I was not really an unknown person running for public office. Additionally, I had worked with a number of elected officials on community improvement projects and always had good working relationships with these people. I assume that was why they wanted me to run for office.

I have been asked many times whether being a woman has been a help or a hindrance to my political career. I do not believe it has made any great difference. I did not campaign for office as a woman candidate. In my district, such a strategy would have been unsuccessful. I decided that those people who wanted to elect me because I was a woman would notice indeed I was a woman. Therefore, I did not need to publically announce it. I campaigned on the platform that I was the most qualified candidate for the job. I stressed my educational background, experience and active participation in community improvement projects. In me, the people already had a candidate who had been dedicated to making our area a better place in which to live, work and raise our families. It would appear to be what the people from my area wanted because I won by a comfortable margin.

Women in Legislatures

But, was my election really part of a growing trend toward equality in government? In recent years, there has been considerable talk about the growing numbers of women in state legislatures. However, the growth rate may not be as significant as some elected officials may want you to believe. To truly understand this phenomenon, one must look at some very significant information.

There are as many different forms of state legislatures as there are states. Each one is unique in an abundance of ways. Some are full-time legislatures while others, like West Virginia, are part-time legislatures. Some states provide district offices for their state legislators while others, like West Virginia, do not. And some states provide attractive salaries for legislators while others do not.

It is not the focus of this paper to research these above mentioned differences. I do believe, however, that if one were to do such a study one would find a direct correlation between the salary scale for state legislators and the percentage of women in the legislatures. In other words, state legislatures that pay little probably have an above average ratio of women. Conversely, state legislatures that pay well are still dominated by men.

I don't think we've made such great strides. I think we've just taken over a lot of jobs that men don't really want. Women must be careful not to allow our enthusiasm for statistics to blind us to the underlying facts behind these statistics. Still, we must not forget that women have significant contributions to make to state governments regardless of why they are there.

The Citizen Legislature

West Virginia has what is known as a "Citizen Legislature." This is a part-time legislature that is made up of average citizens from virtually every aspect of life in West Virginia. The fact that our legislative session is only 60 days a year makes it possible for almost anyone to participate in the legislative process. Our members include farmers, lawyers, teachers, coal miners, nurses, businessmen, homemakers, firemen, industrial workers, bus drivers, construction workers, insurance salesmen, realtors, public relations consultants, etc.

The most significant benefit of a "Citizen Legislature" is that we truly represent the people of West Virginia. Because of the abundant variety of backgrounds, we view issues from virtually every possible perspective. What a profound contribution to democracy! As I was in the beginning, I am still awed by the democratic process and how well it works.

Advantages of Women Legislators

What are the advantages that women have in the West Virginia House of Delegates? First, the Speaker of the House recognizes the political necessity of making women an active part of his leadership team, if he is to stay in power and successfully run the House the way he believes it should be run. There are 20 committees in the House of Delegates and each committee has a chair and vice-chair. Since women are an active part of the leadership team and since there are proportionally fewer women than men, it is easier for women to become either a committee chair or vice-chair.

Secondly, as a woman, I felt no need to be a "macho" legislator and I let it be known that there was much I did not understand about the job and that I needed help. That help has always been readily available.

For example, immediately after my election in November, I began writing down every question about the job that would come to mind. Over the course of the next few months, I had accumulated about ten pages of questions. I called George Gvoyich, a former legislator from my county and our present County Commissioner, and asked him if I could come to his home for advice. He was kind enough to say yes and we spent about three hours going over all of my questions. Additionally, he gave me a great deal of additional information that I had not even thought to ask for. He also contacted the House Clerk, Don Kopp, who was an old friend of his and asked Don to help me in any way he could.

On the humorous side George was quite surprised when I even asked him where the ladies lounge was in the Capitol building. I explained that during the campaign, one of my opponents had made the remark that if I were elected instead of him, it would probably take me three weeks just to find the restroom. I made sure he was wrong!

The First District has two delegates, myself and Sam Love. Sam Love was a great help to me as he was more than willing to answer all my questions and even took me on a personal tour of the Capitol my first day there.

From my perspective, the help, advice and support of George Gvoyich, Don Kopp and Sam Love were invaluable. I watched many of the other new delegates struggling to familiarize themselves with the job while pretending they knew what they were doing. They didn't want any help. I figure that my knowledge gained previous to the beginning of my first session put me about three weeks ahead of other new delegates. It was possible to begin fulfilling my legislative responsibilities immediately and comfortably.

Of course, my requests for help and advice did not end with these three gentlemen. I probably asked just about everyone there for help at one time or another. I was blessed to be around people whose capacity for giving of their time and talents was endless. Even now, as I finish my second term, I still on occasion find that I need to request help or advice from colleagues. And the best part of all of this is that no one has ever refused to help me. I often remember what Steve Bradley, my father, once told me. "Pat, I learned about 90% of what I know from listening. I learned about 10% of what I know from just doing it. But I can't remember one thing I ever learned from talking. So what you need to decide while you're young is, do you want to be smart or do you want to talk?"

Disadvantages of Women Legislators

What are the disadvantages that face women in the West Virginia House of Delegates?

Easily, the most difficult aspect of being a female legislator is the blatant and ever-present prejudice of the press toward women. Reporters follow us around like blood-hounds looking for every flaw they can find. It is as though the women of the House live in a fishbowl. If we make a reference to the fact that we miss our families during the legislative session, we are ineffective as legislators because we are too emotional to do our jobs. If we don't mention our families, we are "cold women libbers" who don't care about anything but getting to the top. One single female delegate who dated often during the legislative session was labeled "wild." Another who rarely dated was labeled a "lesbian." If any of us have marital difficulties and the press finds out about it, it is clearly our fault. If our relationships are successful, it is because of the incredible patience and understanding of our partners.

We are rarely judged by the press according to our contributions or abilities. Instead, they decide what their readers want to hear and they conform their judgement of us on what will sell newspapers. If I appear to hold the members of the House press in contempt, that is because I do. The women of the House only want to be judged on their contributions as legislators, not "placed under a microscope and dissected." The men of the House are never treated this way by the press—it is a blessing for them.

Secondly, I believe that women delegates are more prone to "burn-out" in the House than are men. With few exceptions, we are trying to be all things to all people. Generally speaking, we work longer hours than our male colleagues because we are judged more harshly by the press. Additionally, we are often trying to fulfill a week's worth of motherly obligations on our weekends. We recognize that we are lucky to be where we are, that it is an honor and we want to excel. We put entirely too much pressure on ourselves and because of that, we lose some of our best and brightest women. We need to be kinder to ourselves.

The Majority Party

In addition to being a woman in the West Virginia House of Delegates, I am also a member of the majority party. In the West Virginia House of Delegates, the Democratic Party has been the majority party since we moved into our present Capitol.

Being a member of the majority party is a distinct advantage. This advantage is most noticeable when it comes to leadership positions. There are twenty committees within the West Virginia House of Delegates. Each committee has a chairman and a vice-chairman. There is also the Majority Leader, Majority Whip, Speaker Pro Tem and Rules Committee positions. The Speaker fills all these positions with Democrats.

How is the Speaker position filled? The Speaker is elected by the members of the House of Delegates on the first day of the legislative session after an election year. Since the majority of members are Democrats, they also choose a Democratic Speaker. The Speaker's position is extremely powerful. He not only runs the formal floor sessions, he runs the House of Delegates. He hires the staff, prepares the budget and, most important for members, he chooses all committee chairmen and vice-chairmen, makes committee assignments for all members (Democrats and Republicans) and fills all House positions.

The campaign for the Speaker's position is often hotly contested and, obviously, it is very important to be on the winning side of this race. Being on the winning side can make the difference between good committee assignments or bad committee assignments. It can make the difference between seeing a lot of the bills you introduce become law or seeing them die in the system. It can ultimately make the difference between doing an effective job representing your constituents or doing a poor job.

I have always been fortunate enough to be on the winning side of the Speaker's race. As a result, during my first term I was appointed to the Banking & Insurance, the Industry & Labor and the Judiciary Committees. The Judiciary appointment was especially fortunate, since it is rare to see a freshman non-attorney appointed to Judiciary. I knew my good fortune and made the most of the opportunities given to me. In my first two years in the House of Delegates, I saw eight of the bills I introduced become laws. In my second term, seven more became laws.

The position of committee chairman is also extremely important. The committee chairman has the right to set the daily agenda for that committee. This means that the committee chairman has the right to place only those bills on the agenda that he or she wants. Sadly, bills are not always placed on the agenda according to their merit. Still, it would be highly inaccurate for me to leave you with the impression that no Republican name appears on bills passed in the West Virginia Legislature. A great many bills sponsored by Republicans are passed in our legislature. Remember, we need a four-fifths majority to suspend constitutional rules. Fortunately, strong Republican prejudice would never be tolerated by the minority party. So we work together far more often than outsiders may suspect.

Vice-chairman positions are also very helpful to individual legislators. At the beginning of my second term, I was appointed Vice-Chairman of the Banking Committee. This position provides me with a secretary, a clerk and an attorney which I share with the Chairman of Banking. Obviously, a staff makes it possible to do my job in the legislature far more efficiently than I could do by myself.

Clearly, being a member of the majority party is a distinct advantage.

Disadvantages in the Majority Party

The greatest disadvantage for the majority party is that we presently have a Republican governor. While majority members may find it far easier to get their particular legislative program through the House of Delegates and the Senate, we still need the governor's support before it can become law. It is extremely exasperating to work your bill through both houses only to see it vetoed by the governor. I speak from experience when I assure you that this does happen quite often.

In addition to the governor's control over the success or failure of our legislation, he also controls the flow of information out of the departments of state government. And you may place trust in the fact that the members of the minority party in the House and Senate are far better informed than are the majority members. The sharing of information within state government is especially important when trying to answer the questions and concerns of the people we represent.

Additionally, much of what we do in representing our constituents deals with resolving their problems with particular departments in state government. Majority party members often find executive branch commissioners and department heads much less responsive to our needs and requests than to the needs and requests of minority party members. And our constituents really don't care to hear the political reason why we failed to solve their problems. They only know that we failed.

Clearly, it would be much easier for the majority party to have a member of their party as governor.

Conclusion

I am greatly concerned that I might leave you with the impression that there is a constant war between the majority and minority parties. This is simply not true. While there are, at times, distinct battle lines drawn between us, more often than not we work together. Both parties recognize that we hold certain power over the other side. It would be counter-productive for us to always oppose each other. When we compromise, we all come out ahead. And the art of compromise is what politics is all about.

When I was first elected, I saw most issues in black or white, right or wrong terms. I saw issues only through my eyes. But as I learned to see through other people's eyes, to view issues through other perspectives, I found that there is not so much black and white in the world. There is an awful lot of gray.

From my earliest school years, I was interested in colonial history. I was fascinated by men like Thomas Jefferson and Patrick Henry and George Washington. I couldn't read enough about the formation of the United States and our democratic system of government. I have always felt a deep and profound respect for American democracy and I believed in it completely. Now, after serving four years in state government, I find myself with an even more profound respect for our democratic process. I have seen it at work and it truly does reflect the opinions and the needs of the people it represents.

The democratic process is alive and well in West Virginia and all it needs is more believers to participate in this wonderful process. But you have to participate in it for the right reasons.

If I were asked to give one piece of advice to someone considering entering politics, I would tell them to participate in the political process only as long as it brings you a sense of personal accomplishment and self-respect. Don't do it because you need the appreciation and respect of others, it seldom comes to politicians. Do it for yourself.

Commentary:
DOES THE WEST VIRGINIA LEGISLATURE REALLY HAVE TWO POLITICAL PARTIES?

Thais Blatnik
Former Senator, West Virginia Senate

Every year when an overwhelming number of Democrats are elected to the West Virginia Legislature, Republicans (and Republican newspapers) throughout the state bemoan the fact that a one-party system dooms West Virginia to poor government and economic failure.

Certainly belonging to the majority party in control of the Legislature has its benefits. All of the committees are chaired by members of the same party, and it is through committees that all legislation is passed. Moreover, the administration in power, whether it is Democrat or Republican, controls the awarding of contracts; generally Republicans fare well under a Republican governor and Democrats under a Democratic governor.

But, does a Democratic Legislature mean that typically liberal programs are passed with the overwhelming majority that the Democrats possess? The answer is no! The reason is that the Democrats are divided along ideological lines, conservatives and liberals. My contention is that liberals are in the minority.

When you identify what Republicans traditionally stand for, you can categorize the various members of the House and Senate and find that grouped together, Republicans and conservative Democrats form a majority in both houses.

If you analyze the fundamental, basic issues that Republicans cling to, and those that President Bush used so effectively in his 1988 campaign, you can see the more simple similarities between the parties.

1. There was no protest in the House, and only two small nays in the Senate on a resolution opposing flag burning, even though the United States Supreme Court had already ruled on this matter. No legislator even offered a good argument about the merits of the First Amendment.

2. A resolution prohibiting the expending of state medicare funds for abortions was resoundingly supported by both houses. This is a standard Republican issue.

But it is in the larger, more important issues where the similarities between the two parties are encountered, and they are significant. A Republican-conservative-Democratic coalition in the past few legislatures produced the following results:

1. No support for the move to consolidate the three medical schools and thus conserve money, a luxury that West Virginia can ill afford;

2. The defeat of a mammoth solid waste landfill bill that was heralded as the way to stop out-of-state garbage from being shipped into the state;

3. Easily defeated a collective bargaining bill for teachers, one that was fervently sought by the teachers' union and labor;

4. The repeated passage of pro-business bills for banking firms and insurance companies;

5. Gave tax credits to coal companies for millions of dollars, and refused to force divulgement of both companies and amounts;

6. Severely weakened an administration bill designed to control medical costs.

It would be unfair to indicate that liberals do not get their bills passed or defeated. For example, attempts to reform the workman's compensation acts typically fail; capital punishment bills never see the light of day; teacher and service personnel working regulations are continually strengthened, and there are others.

How does a bill pass or fail? Simple! By the committee to which it is assigned. Committee chairmen have the power to bottle up, or kill a bill; to love it to death (which means to burden it down with so many amendments that it loses it's original intention); or move it on to passage if they so desire.

You can predict the chances that a bill has by the ideological bent of the chairmen. Strangely, or perhaps not so strangely, chairmanships of committees like Education, Health and Human Services go to liberals, while Finance, Banking and Insurance, Small Business, Agriculture and Mining go to conservatives. The powerful Judiciary Committee chairmanship shifts between both.

In summation, while there are certain inherent benefits in being a member of the Democratic Party in the West Virginia Legislature, the major legislation is decided on by a conservative majority. In fact, in 85% of the state's legislative districts, you can espouse a Republican ideology, but must run as a Democrat to be elected. It is also true that the ideology of the governor is extremely important, for it is the administration that initiates programs and budgets. In the event of a Republican governor, it is essential that he enlist a sizable number of Democratic legislators in his camp. Governor Arch A. Moore, Jr. did that in his first and second terms and was extremely effective. He failed to do that in his third term and was a dismal failure.

CHAPTER FOUR

Executive Leadership

INTRODUCTION

Contrary to Article II of the United States Constitution which vests the executive power in the President, the Constitution of West Virginia in Article VII provides for plural executives: "The executive department shall consist of a governor, secretary of state, auditor, treasurer, commissioner of agriculture, and attorney general. . . ."[1]

This "fractionated"[2] formal structure of state executive power reveals an historical distrust of the executive branch of government that is traceable to the pre-1860s when West Virginia was part of Virginia. Rather typically the early constitutions of Virginia (1776 and 1830) "reflected the then current fear of executive autocracy by rendering the governor subservient to the legislative branch, in which the constitution makers had implicit confidence."[3]

At that time, "all executive officers were chosen by joint vote of the bicameral general assembly. The governor was selected annually and the assembly was empowered to determine his qualifications. . . ." As a check on the application of the limited powers, the constitution established an eight-member council of state whose advice was required before discretionary authority could be exercised.[4]

Some gubernatorial independence was established with the Virginia Constitution of 1851. This document provided for the popular election of the governor for a four-year term. It also abolished the council of state, but did not give the governor the power to veto legislation.[5]

The first Constitution of West Virginia (1863) provided the governor with a two-year term and the opportunity to be reelected if he wished. Otherwise, the governor's powers remained as they were under the Virginia Constitution of 1851.[6] In 1970, the Governor's Succession Amendment was ratified by the West Virginia voters. This amendment allowed governors to serve unlimited four-year terms but prohibited them from serving in the term immediately following two consecutive terms whether the terms were completed or not.

This chapter examines the evolving role of the West Virginia governorship in providing political leadership for the state. To understand this role it is necessary to consider not only the formal rules and legal constraints which affect the governor, but also the informal relationships and political pressures from others that influence him in the performance of his duties. We shall discuss: the consti-

157

tutional duties of the governor, the political powers that the governor has at his disposal, the backgrounds of West Virginia's governors and finally examine the roles of West Virginia's other (plural) state-wide elected executives.

Constitutional Duties

The Constitution of 1872 (most current constitution) and as subsequently amended, enumerates the following constitutional duties of the governor:

1. **Governor's Message.** The governor shall address the legislature on the "State of the State;"

2. **Extraordinary Legislative Sessions.** The governor may convene the legislature for extraordinary sessions;

3. **Governor to Nominate Certain Officers.** The governor nominates, and with the advice and consent of the Senate, appoints executive officials;

4. **Recess Vacancies.** The governor has the authority to fill vacancies in office that occur during the recess of the Senate;

5. **Governor's Power of Removal.** The governor shall have power to remove any officer whom he may appoint in case of incompetency, neglect of duty, gross immorality, or malfeasance in office; and he may declare his office vacant and fill the same as herein provided in other cases of vacancy;

6. **Executive May Remit Fines and Forfeitures.** The governor has the power to remit fines and penalties as prescribed by law; to commute capital punishment and grant reprieves and pardons;

7. **Governor Commander-in-Chief of Military Forces.** The governor shall be commander-in-chief of the military forces of the state, (except when they shall be called into the service of the United States) and may call out the same to execute the laws, suppress insurrection and repel invasion.

8. **Governor's Approval or Disapproval[7] of Bills Passed by Legislature.** Every bill passed by the Legislature shall be presented to the governor. . . . <see previous chapter, "How a Bill Becomes a Law," . . . . ed.>

9. **The Modern Budget Amendment** authorizes the governor to formulate the executive budget and execute the same after the Legislature appropriates the funds."[8]

An Assessment of Gubernatorial Political Power in West Virginia

It is not hard to see that *formally*, at least, the West Virginia governor has important chief executive powers. There are several caveats to this. Not all governors, or would-be governors, in West Virginia have the leadership skills or the personal wealth[9] to win that high office. And once that office is obtained, it is frequently not easy for newly elected governors to be successful in their dealings with the legislature. This is especially noticeable when legislative leaders plan to compete with the governor in the next election for his office.

Additional challenges to the governor's power may come from the other independently elected executive officials. As one analyst put it: "once elected and sworn into office, a governor soon finds he is not alone at the top of the state executive branch."[10] For example, two members of Governor Gaston Caperton's executive cabinet challenged him in the gubernatorial elections of 1992. Attorney General Mario Palumbo ran unsuccessfully against Caperton in the 1992 Democratic Primary and the Republican, Commissioner of Agriculture, Cleve Benedict was defeated by Caperton in the 1992 general election.

Other potential challengers to the governor's power are the state auditor, secretary of state and treasurer all of whom are outside of gubernatorial control. Not all of these officials carry major policy[11] or administrative responsibilities that will directly clash with the governor.[12] Several do, such as the auditor, who audits how state funds are spent and tries to determine if the legislature's intent was indeed carried out. Since the governor has the major responsibility for carrying out this intent there is a built-in potential for conflict between these two officials. Another official who is in a position to make things difficult for the governor is the attorney general. As the state's chief legal officer, he may announce contrary legal opinions concerning the governor's policies.

The question arises, who does the citizen hold accountable when things in state government seem to go awry? Presently six state-wide elected executive officials are all Democrats. The last state-wide elected Republican was Cleve Benedict who was elected Commissioner of Agriculture in the 1988 general election. Prior to the Democratic sweep in the 1992 general election, and during 1984–1988 years, the state was led by Republican Governor Arch A. Moore, the second governor (Governor Boreman, 1863–1869, was the first) to serve three terms in office.

There have been a number of attempts to change the plural executives in West Virginia. Historians note at least five major efforts at reorganization in the recent past. The first occurred in 1963 when the West Virginia Commission on Constitutional Revision recommended structural changes to the executive branch. A year later the Public Administrative Service, as consultant, studied West Virginia state government organization and made additional recommendations for change. These were not acted upon.

An important attempt to reorganize occurred in 1969 when, at that time, Governor Arch Moore worked with the state's business communities in establishing the "Governor's Management Task Force." The Task Force was able to raise over $300,000 and recommended 789 changes. "Except for those recommendations (about 76%) which could be effected by executive order, not much change occurred...."[13]

In 1986, the "Governor's Management Task Force II" report was released and the governor subsequently announced savings upon its implementation of $101 million for fiscal year 1986–1987 and $177 million for 1987–1988.[14] The report also recommended the following changes in West Virginia state government:

"• Abolish the election of the auditor, treasurer, and agriculture commissioner.

• Elect only the governor and attorney general.

• Eliminate the office of secretary of state.

• Create a board of elections.

• Establish six new secretaries reporting to the governor, with other operating agencies assigned to them. . . .

• Discontinue legislative approval of agency rules and regulations.

• Redefine the auditor's responsibility from pre-audit to post-audit. . . ."[15]

These reorganizational proposals were not acted on by the legislature.

The final attempt occurred during the 69th West Virginia Legislature in its First Extraordinary Session called by Governor Caperton (January 25–February 1, 1989), which passed "Committee Substitute for **Senate Bill No. 2.**" This measure thoroughly reorganized the executive branch of the West Virginia state government.[16] It abolished the Board of Public Works, i.e., eliminating the offices of secretary of state, treasurer and commissioner of agriculture. The only constitutional offices that would survive are the governor, attorney general, and the state auditor. The idea here was to "streamline and consolidate 150 state agencies under the administrative authority of seven appointed secretaries. . . ."[17] These "secretaries" were to administer, within the executive branch of state government, the new departments of administration; commerce, labor, and environmental resources; education and the arts; health and human resources; public safety; tax and revenue; and transportation (see Figure 4.1).[18]

The governor proposed in his February 13, 1989 "State of the State" Address that this reorganization law be presented to the voters as a constitutional amendment. At the same time he recommended a constitutional amendment to restructure the state board of education by abolishing its constitutional status and reconstituting the board under general law. The final constitutional measure was the County Organization Reform Amendment. This constitutional change would allow counties to merge with each other or with cities to form metrogovernments. The legislature was also asked to merge West Virginia and Marshall Universities into one "large" state university.

The final act of the special session was the creation of a twelve-member "independent" commission to set ethical standards for public officials, lobbyists and grass roots organizations at the state, county, and local levels of government (see Appendix, "A Summary of the West Virginia Governmental Ethics Act").

The voter's response to all of this, especially a constitutional amendment that so extensively reorganized the executive branch of West Virginia state government, was overwhelming rejection.

The official returns from the September 9 statewide special election on the three constitutional amendments follow: Amendment #1, the Educational Reorganization Amendment was defeated by a vote of 29,776 in favor and 220,286

Figure 4.1 Organization of the Executive Branch, State of West Virginia (Major Divisions and Subdivisions)

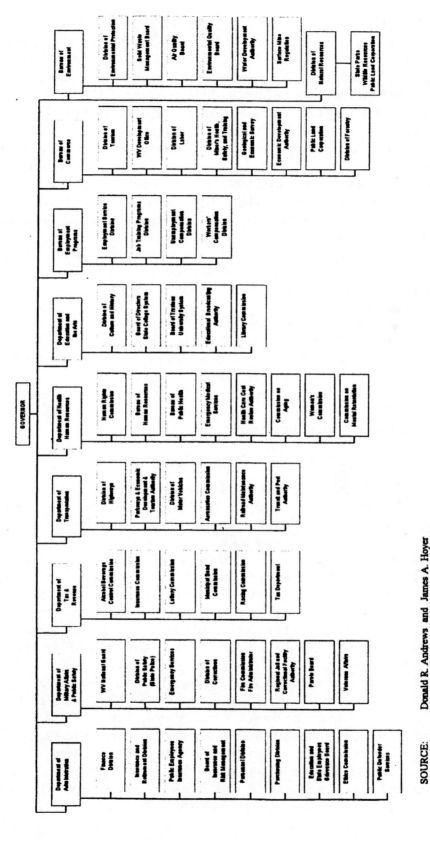

SOURCE: Donald R. Andrews and James A. Hoyer
Robert C. Byrd Institute For Government Studies
THE UNIVERSITY OF CHARLESTON

(88.1%) against. Amendment #2, the County Organization Reform Amendment, was defeated by 47,847 in favor, and 201,992 (80.8%) against the measure. The final amendment, The Better Government Amendment, which Secretary of State Ken Hechler publically opposed on the grounds that it gave the governor too much power, was defeated by 28,634 favoring it and 220,700 (88.5%) disapproving.[19] Political pundits claimed that the voters defeated the three measures to show their anger over the governor's tax increases.

Although the Caperton constitutional reforms were defeated by the voters, his cabinet system was basically retained by his successor, the Republican Cecil Underwood. Underwood, who was not expected to win in a state where the Democrats outnumber the Republicans by a two to one margin, received 51.6% of the vote to 45.8% for the Democratic candidate Charlotte Pritt, who had strong support from most of the state's labor unions (see Rausch article).[20]

Legislative leaders complained that the conservative Governor Underwood moved very slowly and had few legislative proposals. However, he did attempt extensive taxation reform with The Governor's Commission on Fair Taxation. The Commission found that the present tax system was: "too regressive, contained too many taxes, contained too many exemptions, was not adaptable to West Virginia's shifting economy, lacked sufficient revenue producing capability for local governments, used tax appeals process that were unfair and inequitable, and needs a constitutional method of funding education."[21]

These reforms were not enacted and with the return in the election of 2000 of a Democrat, Bob Wise, to the governorship, the prospects for tax reform have been placed on the "back burner."

The "Very Strong" West Virginia Governor

Before the passage of the "Modern Budget Amendment" (1968) and the "Governor's Succession Amendment" (1970), the West Virginia governorship was generally classified as "weak" in comparative studies of formal gubernatorial power.[21] For example, West Virginia ranked only an eight on Schlesinger's Index (the range was twenty for "strong" to seven for "weak").[22] It was composed of four measures of gubernatorial strength: tenure potential (can the governor succeed himself and how long is his term?), appointive powers (how many executive officials can the governor appoint?), budget powers (how much control does he and his office have over the budget process?), and veto powers (does the governor have a general veto, item veto, or item reduction, and what is the size of the legislative majority to override?).

More recent studies[23] of formal gubernatorial power reflect important changes in the West Virginia governorship. Beyle (1989) in utilizing most of Schlesinger's measures (he dropped one category, organizational power and added several new ones—legislative budget changing power and political strength in legislature) found considerable improvement in West Virginia's gubernatorial score. He overall ranked the West Virginia governorship as "very strong" in formal powers with an overall score of twenty-seven. Beyle's scores

Table 4.1 Formal Powers of the West Virginia and Selected Governorships

State	Tenure Potential	Appointment Powers	Budget Making Powers	Legis. Budget Changing Power[a]	Veto Powers	Political Strength in Legis.	Total Index
KY	3	5	4	1	4	4	21
MD	4	5	5	5	5	5	29
PA	4	5	5	1	5	3	23
VA	3	5	5	1	5	4	23
WV	**4**	**4**	**5**	**5**[a]	**4**[b]	**5**	**27**
OH	4	5	5	1	5	3	23

[a] Dilger (1993) argues for a 4 in a similar category, because the WV governor can only make uniform, across-the-board reductions after the appropriations measure has passed the legislature.

[b] Dilger, (1993) would increase this score to a 5 because the WV governor has the package, line item and reduction vetoes.

Adapted from: Virginia Gray, Herbert Jacob and Robert B. Albritton, *Politics in the American States, A Comparative Analysis*, Fifth Edition, (Glenview, IL: Scott, Foresman/ Little Brown Higher Education, 1990), 574; Robert Jay Dilger, "The Governor's Office in West Virginia," in *West Virginia's State Government: The Legislative, Executive and Judicial Branches*, Christopher Z. Mooney, *et al.*, Policy Monograph Series No. 5, Institute For Public Affairs, (West Virginia University, July, 1993), 27–58.

ranged from twenty-nine (high) to fifteen (low). West Virginia's scores in the six categories are seen in Table 4.1.

The West Virginia governorship scores a four (strong) in tenure potential because the governors are limited by the "Governor's Succession Amendment" to two consecutive four-year terms. A score of five (very strong) in tenure potential, which none of West Virginia's neighboring governorships have, would mean a four-year term with no restraint on re-election.

The West Virginia governorship is "weaker" than all of its neighbors, except Ohio, in appointive powers. West Virginia's score of four means a "moderate" rating in this category. The above score for each state is determined by the governor's power of appointment in six major functions and offices: corrections, education, health, highways, public utilities regulation, and public welfare. This category, however, is somewhat ambiguous as the national trend is to *reduce* the governors' patronage and "this has been judged . . . surprisingly, as a boon for governors because it has liberated them from an outmoded, tedious, time-consuming, and frustrating chore."[24] What really matters is the extent of the governor's appointive powers over the top level policy-making positions in his state. It was previously noted that the governor of West Virginia shares power with five other statewide elected officials, i.e., a fractionalized executive. So, regardless, of how one chooses to interpret the "moderate" appointive power rating of the West Virginia governorship, there is room for improvement.

Today most governors, West Virginia's included, have full responsibility over budgetary preparation. The West Virginia governorship scores a five (very strong) in this category. The reason why West Virginia scores so highly here is because of the "Modern Budget Amendment." This gives the governor sole responsibility for the preparation of the executive budget. The amendment also requires "the governor to make a total revenue estimate which the legislature may not exceed in the enactment of the budget unless it chooses to fund the excess through increased or new taxes."[25]

The West Virginia governorship receives four points in legislative budget-changing authority. By "legislative budget-changing authority" is meant: "the greater the power of the legislature to make changes in the governor's proposed budget, the less 'potential' budget power for the governor."[26] Because the West Virginia Legislature is required to balance the state's budget and is not allowed to increase the governor's revenue estimate without the governor's approval, West Virginia's governors have an advantage in determining the total amount of the state government's expenditures in a given year. West Virginia's "high" score reflects the fact that the Legislature may not increase the executive budget.

Finally, the West Virginia governorship receives a four in its veto power. A score of "four" represents a "strong" veto power which includes the package, item and reduction vetoes with a majority vote of the legislature to override the governor's veto (unless the bill vetoed involves the budget which requires a two-thirds vote). A score of "five" would mean these vetoes plus at least a three-fifths vote to override all vetoed legislation.

It is fair to say, with a few exceptions, that today's West Virginia governors have most of the "tools" to effectively govern the state's affairs. The question now arises, what kinds of men (there have been no women), and from what backgrounds, are attracted to the highest office in the state?

Backgrounds of West Virginia's Governors

"A basic clue to determining what a particular public office is all about, and its position within any political-power hierarchy, is to see who seeks and fills that office."[27] A recent study[28] found a "new breed" of governors in the United States. Governors today "are much younger, better educated than ever, and more thoroughly trained for their specific responsibilities."[29]

It is interesting to note that 21 (66 percent) of West Virginia's 32 governors were lawyers with business and education as the next most frequently noted occupations. The percentage of lawyer-governors in West Virginia is higher than the national average which for the years 1951 through 1981 was 49%.[30] The dominance of the legal profession in the West Virginia governorship is not surprising since successful lawyers are usually well paid and frequently have the money and connections to conduct gubernatorial campaigns.

The average age of the 32 West Virginia governors is 46.6,[31] with the recent governor, Cecil Underwood, having the distinction of being both the state's youngest and oldest governor. He was first elected governor in 1956 when he was 35 and in 1996 at age 74.

It should be recalled (see chapter 2) that West Virginia is considered a modified one-party Democratic state. Yet historically, the Republican party's control of the governorship is pretty even to that of the Democrats—15 Republicans and 17 Democrats. However, since the depression there were only two Republican governors—Cecil Underwood and Arch Moore, with the latter recently defeated in the attempt at an unprecedented fourth term.

Not surprisingly, West Virginia's governors have followed similar paths to the governor's mansion that were followed by governors in other states. That is, 52.4% of the nation's governors had previous legislative experience while 63% of West Virginia's governors had such experience.[32]

West Virginia's Other State-Wide Elected Executives

The West Virginia Constitution is unlike forty-two other state constitutions in that it does not provide for the office of lieutenant governor. The idea behind a lieutenant governorship is to provide for an orderly succession to a governor who is unable to complete a term. Since there is no lieutenant governor in West Virginia, the president of the Senate is next in line of succession, followed by the Speaker of the House of Delegates.

The West Virginia Constitution is similar to most other states with its provisions for plural executives. The attorney general, secretary of state, state treasurer, state auditor, and commissioner of agriculture are all state-wide elected offices. These officials are elected to four-year terms[33] with the governor and have no limitations on the number of terms they may serve.

The duties of these "Other State-Wide Elected Executives" follows. Generally, the attorney general (A. G.) is viewed as the legal representative of the State of West Virginia and its citizens. This means that the A. G. represents the state in cases where state government is a party in state and federal courts. The A. G. advances formal written "opinions" on legal questions when requested to do so by state government agencies, the governor,[34] local prosecutors or other public officials. The A. G.'s opinions have the force of law unless they are overturned by a court. Increasingly, West Virginia's A. G.s have worked with federal law enforcement officials in sharing information and pursuing criminals.

Some view the A.G.'s office "as a prime steppingstone to the governorship."[35] The office's role in dealing with consumer complaints, contesting national statutes and agency activities are frequently publicized and generate name recognition for activist A. G.s.

The secretary of state's office in West Virginia may also be seen as a "steppingstone to the governorship,"[36] especially if the incumbent is an activist. The West Virginia secretary of state has important election and record-keeping responsibilities. The secretary registers corporations, charitable organizations, commissions notary publics, security firms-private detectives and publishes administrative rules. It is through the election related responsibilities that the secretary of state receives name recognition. The secretary determines ballot eligibility of political parties and candidates and conducts voter registration drives.

The West Virginia treasurer is the official custodian and manager of the state's funds. "He is responsible for receiving and depositing the state's revenue in financial institutions, maintaining a record of all appropriations made by the state legislature, endorsing state checks, and investing . . . the state's . . . funds in financial institutions."[37]

The failure to make wise and profitable investments cost a recent West Virginia treasurer his job. The former treasurer, A. James Manchin was impeached in March of 1989 by the House of Delegates for losing $279 million in bad investments.

As noted earlier the state auditor, who is the official state government bookkeeper, audits how the government funds are spent. "The auditor determines if claims presented to the state for payment are valid . . . administers social security payments and a savings bond program for state employees, receives tax revenues that are collected by sheriffs, and collects and distributes public utility taxes for the state and counties."[38]

Last, but not least, is the West Virginia commissioner of agriculture. This state-wide elected executive administers the West Virginia Department of Agriculture. Although West Virginia is not known as an agricultural state, the commissioner "is responsible for inspecting agricultural products, regulating pesticides, disseminating statistical data on soils, climate, natural resources (especially water quality), and market opportunities in the state. . . ."[39]

All of these state-wide elected officials are members of the Board of Public Works, which, it should be recalled, Governor Caperton and the legislature tried to abolish with the "Better Government Amendment."

The Board of Public Works has its origins in the Virginia Constitution of 1851. At that time it consisted of three commissioners elected by the General Assembly. It was primarily created to protect the "interests" of Virginia in internal matters—taxation of railroads, toll roads, etc. The "new" State of West Virginia by legislative action made the Board part of its administrative structure in 1863. The Board actually received constitutional status with the adoption of the Budget Amendment in 1918 (see WV Constitution., Art. VI, sec. 51). Today the Board is a public corporation and is composed of seven *ex officio* members. Six of these officials are state-wide elected officials discussed above: the governor (who serves as chair), the secretary of state (secretary *ex officio*), the attorney general, auditor, treasurer, and commissioner of agriculture. The superintendent of free schools is the only non-elected member. The board has supervisory authority over the entire financial organization of the state. Its duties entail general fiscal management, budgeting, expenditure control custody of public funds, assessment, taxation and accounting.[40]

The selections for this chapter reveal the difficulties and successes experienced by several of the state's important executive officers. We start with the "Dear Ronald Letter" by former Governor Edmund "Pat" Brown which provides sound and at times humorous advice to (at that time) the newly elected governor of California, Ronald Reagan. This same letter was sent as an advisory to most of the recent West Virginia governors, including Governor Caperton, by Professor Evelyn L.K. Harris of the University of Charleston.

David Webber's study of gubernatorial transition from Governor Rockefeller to Governor Moore in 1984 shows how important cooperation between two West Virginia governors was for setting a positive tone in the beginning of the new administration. Webber points out that previous transitions were not always successful, but the smooth Rockefeller-Moore transition allowed "the new governor to hit the ground running."

Paul Lutz's selection concerning Governor Marland reveals the pitfalls inherent in executive leadership when a governor underestimates the political foes allied against his severance tax proposal. Successful gubernatorial leadership is considerably more than a good policy idea, it requires adroit selling of the policy to the opinion leaders within and outside of the legislature.

Former Secretary of State Ken Hechler reveals in his updated article the many tasks and responsibilities facing the "Chief Record Keeper of the State." The Secretary shows that his office is considerably more than record keeping: preservation of all "executive" records, issuance of charters of incorporation, implementation of the conflict of interest statutes, etc. He reveals "that in many instances, he is a policy-making official" especially in his vital role as supervisor of elections. He argues that an aggressive, independently elected secretary of state is necessary to keep voter fraud and charities' "scam" operations in West Virginia to a minimum.

Finally, the former Attorney General, Mario J. Palumbo provides an overview of the many roles and responsibilities facing the West Virginia attorney general. General Palumbo finds the responsibilities of his office much more than advising and litigating for the various agencies of state government. He has significant duties in the areas of human rights, consumer protection, antitrust matters, etc. He sees the Office of the Attorney General as critically important to the citizenry because, as he says, "the power of the office can be utilized to bring insight into important issues and change for the common good."

Notes

[1] *West Virginia Constitution*, Article VII, section 1.

[2] William Schultze, *State And Local Politics. a Political Economy Approach* (St. Paul: West Publishing Company, 1988), 136.

[3] Claude J. Davis, *et al. West Virginia State and Local Government* (Morgantown, West Virginia: Bureau of Government Research, 1963), 122–123.

[4] *Ibid.*

[5] *Ibid.*

[6] *Ibid.*, under the Constitution of 1872, some provisions were "liberalized" but no basic changes occurred.

[7] Budget or supplementary appropriation bills that are vetoed by the governor require a two-thirds vote of the Legislature to override. See "Modern Budget Amendment," Article VI, Section 51.

[8] *West Virginia Constitution*, Article VII, Sections 5–19.

[9] Thad L. Beyle writes: "The electoral campaign . . . costs money. The good news is that you can still buy West Virginia. The bad news is, boy, is it expensive (Baker, 1980)." WV gubernatorial campaigns have indeed been expensive. The state's gubernatorial campaign has revealed some of the highest expenditures per voter in the nation: Democratic candidate for governor, John D. "Jay" Rockefeller, IV spent $12 million in defeating his Republican opponent Arch A. Moore, Jr. Other expensive races were the Moore-Clyde contest in 1984 where both candidates spent $9.7 million and in 1988 Democrat Gaston Caperton spent $4.6 million. Rockefeller and Caperton liberally spent sizeable portions of their own money. See Thad Beyle, "Governors," in *Politics an the American States*, fifth edition, Virginia Gray, Herbert Jacob and Robert B. Albritton, eds. (Glenville, IL: Scott, Foresman/Little Brown Higher Education, 1990), 211–214; Also, Robert Jay Dilger, "The Governor's Office in West Virginia," in *West Virginia's State Government: The Legislative Executive and Judicial Branches*, Christopher Z. Mooney, *et al.*, Policy Monograph Series, No. 5, Institute for Public Affairs, (Morgantown: West Virginia University, 1993), 28.

[10] Beyle, *op. cit.*, 191.

[11] It is sometimes argued that secretaries of state and state treasurers do not carry major policy or administrative responsibilities and as such these officials should be appointed by the governor, See T.L. Beyle and R. Dalton, "Appointment Power: Does it Belong to the Governor?", *State Government*, (1981), 54, 2–12.

[12] See Ken Hechler, "Change for the better, We need more hellraisers," *Charleston Gazette*, January 3, 1995; Ken Ward, Jr., "McGraw's release of suit settlement in Wayne angers governor's lawyer," *Charleston Gazette*, December 12, 1994.

[13] Information provided to the editor by Thomas Tinder, Administrative Assistant to Governor Arch A. Moore, October 26, 1988.

[14] "Governor's Management Task Force II," May, 1986, 140.

[15] *Ibid.*

[16] The reorganization bill is accompanied by the "Fiscal Responsibility Act" which provides for additional taxes. "Some of the provisions of this historic tax package include making a temporary one cent increase in sales and use taxes permanent, <restoring> the sales tax on food to six percent, imposing a business and occupation tax on electric companies and power utilities, changing the rate of severance tax on coal, natural gas, and oil, as well as imposing a tax on gas stored in reservoirs throughout the state . . . a bill <increasing> gasoline prices by five cents a gallon was also passed." See "Legislative Wrap Up," West Virginia Legislature, Office of Public Information, February 3, 1989.

[17] See "Enrolled Committee Substitute for Senate Bill No. 2," (p. 4), First Extraordinary Session of the 69th West Virginia Legislature, enacted February 1, 1989. . . . It is interesting to note that the governor abolished the Secretary of Education and the Arts position in his most recent "State of the State" address. This point was made by Secretary of State Ken Hechler, in a conversation with the editor, February 11, 1989.

[18] Special thanks are extended to Joseph William Carey, former Advanceman, Office of Governor Caperton, who provided helpful background information and to Donald R. Andrews and James A. Hoyer of the Robert C. Byrd Institute, University of Charleston for creating Figure 4.1, "Organization of the Executive Branch, State of West Virginia."

[19] These data are from a "Memorandum to State Election Commission," October 4, 1989 by Ken Hechler, Secretary of State.

[20] See Stephen Good, "The Elephant Awakens in Mountain State Politics," *Insight on the News*, (June 2, 1997), 22.

[21] *Report to the Governor, The Governor's Commission on Fair Taxation*, July 2, 1998, v.

[22] David G. Temple, "The West Virginia Governorship in Changing Perspective," *The West Virginia Public Affairs Reporter*, Vol. 3, No. 1, (Morgantown, West Virginia: Bureau of Government Research, 1978), 1–4.

[23] Joseph A. Schlesinger, "The Politics of the Executive," in *Politics in the American States: Comparative Analysis*, second edition, Virginia Gray, Herbert Jacob, and Kenneth N. Vines, eds. (Boston: Little, Brown and Company, 1971), 232.

[24] K.J. Mueller, "Explaining Variation and Change in Gubernatorial Powers, 1960–1982," *Western Political Quarterly*, 38 (September, 1985), 424–31, and Thad L. Beyle, "Governors," in *Politics in The American States, A Comparative Analysis*, fifth edition, Virginia Gray, Herbert Jacob and Robert B. Albritton, eds. (Glenview, IL: Scott, Foresman/Little Brown Higher Education, 1990), 568–574.

[25] Larry Sabato, *Goodbye to Good-time Charlie. The American Governorship Transformed*, second edition, (Washington, DC: CQ Press, 1983), 88.

[26] Ann O'M. Bowman and Richard C. Kearney, *State And Local Government*, second edition, (Boston: Houghton Mifflin Company, 1993), 199.

[27] See David A. Bingham and John E. Tyler, "West Virginia State Government Organization," *The West Virginia Public Affairs Reporter*, vol. 2 #1, (Morgantown, West Virginia: Bureau of Government Research, 1977), 3–4.

[28] Beyle, *op. cit.*, 182; Also, the constitutional requirements for governor in West Virginia are: "(1) the governor must be at least 30 years old, (2) a state citizen for at least 5 years, (3) a legal resident of West Virginia, (4) an United States Citizen, and (5) a qualified voter." See Robert Jay Dilger, "The Governor's Office in West Virginia," in *West Virginia State Government: The Legislative, Executive And Judicial Branches*, Christopher Z. Mooney, *et. al.*, Policy Monograph Series, No. 5, Institute For Public Affairs, (Morgantown: West Virginia University, July, 1993), 57.

[29] Sabato, *op. cit.*, *passim*.

[30] *Ibid.*, 52

[31] *Ibid.*, 26.

[32] *Ibid.*, 34.

[33] Beyle, *op. cit.*, 183.

[34] Under a law that dates back to the state's original 1863 Code, the governor has the authority to declare the winner in statewide races where there might be a tie. See Phil Kabler, "Caperton would have broken election tie," *The Charleston Gazette*, November 14, 1996.

[35] Bowman and Kearney, *op. cit.*, 209–212.

[36] Dilger, *op. cit.*, 32.

[37] *Ibid.*

[38] *Ibid.*

[39] *Ibid.*, 33.

[40] See W.W. Kaempfer, *The Board of Public Works: West Virginia's Plural Executive* (Morgantown: Bureau of Government Research, West Virginia University, 1957).

Web Sites

http://www.nga.org
(National Governors' Association)
http://www.state.wv.us/governor/
(West Virginia Governor)
http://www.polsci.wvu/wv/wvlinks.html#daily
(West Virginia Daily Newspapers)

DEAR RONALD LETTER

Edmund G. "Pat" Brown
Former Governor of California

SACRAMENTO—Former Governor Edmund G. Brown has offered former actor Ronald Reagan, serving his first time in public office as governor of California, some sage political advice in a letter released here.

Honorable Ronald Reagan
Governor's Mansion
Sacramento, California

Dear Governor:

There's a passage in *War and Peace* that every new governor with a big majority should tack on his office wall. In it young Count Rostov, after weeks as the toast of elegant farewell parties, gallops off on his first cavalry charge and then finds real bullets snapping at his ears.

"Why, they're shooting at me," he says. "Me, whom everyone loves."

Nothing worse will happen to you in the next four years. Learn to live with that, the rest is easy.

As you must have noticed by now, the press fires the first real bullets at new governors. And the hardest lesson to learn is that it is futile to fire back. Never get into an argument with a newspaper unless you own it. A newspaper fails to get in the last word only if it goes broke in mid-debate.

Publishers in California generally will be more tolerant of a governor before he raises taxes, much as a young man will take more nonsense from a fiancee whose father is rich. But you will be amazed at how easily even a friendly publisher's tolerance is strained by trivial matters—a freeway route through his backyard; a rollback in government construction in his city; failure to follow his advice on the appointment of a judge.

I recommend a form letter for all disagreements with publishers which reads: "thank you for your sincere interest in the matter of ( )." This provides little in the way of ammunition for a new attack.

There is also not much I can tell you about the weekly news conference that you haven't already learned. You will find that while both surgeons and reporters operate with professional detachment there is only one real difference between them. Surgeons make more money for cutting you up. But their motives are the same—to make sure everything is running properly. And in the case of the press, they operate with a proxy from the voters. For the voters, news conferences are as close to a first-hand accounting of what happened to their money as they ever get. This is true unless public-relations firms prepare live two-minute television spots.

171

Invest as much time preparing for these inquisitions as you can spare, but don't feel bad if you are caught off guard. I can still hear a voice from the back of the room asking: "Governor, do you think lobbyists should be required to wear little green buttons on their lapels?" Maybe you would have a ready answer for that. I didn't.

Harrowing as they are, news conferences do provide a chance for correspondents to bore in, a practice that philosophers find a healthy thing for the democratic process. Few governors take any comfort in that. (I, on the other hand, am holding news conferences less, enjoying them more, and find myself in complete agreement with the philosophers.)

One last word about dealing with reporters. If you don't want it in the papers, don't do it. There is no such thing as a secret in state government.

In the first place, gossip, rumor and inside-information are the nickels, dimes and dollars of life in government. It's not money that determines a man's place in the government sun; it's what he knows that nobody else does. And unless he spends a little of that inside information, who's to know he has it? Then, too, most reporters would rather miss every news conference in a year than miss a single secret meeting. Finally, there is always someone at any meeting, secret or otherwise, who thinks you have it all wrong and believes the best way to straighten you out is to tell all to newsmen.

There's only one way to deal with this problem. Leak the story yourself. That way, at least, you are sure to get your version into print first.

In one of his novels, C.P. Snow writes that the difference between success and failure in politics lies in knowing which doors to push. The successful politician pushes only on unlocked doors; the failure pushes on locked doors.

You should keep as many doors—or options—unlocked as possible—keep open as many alternative approaches to problems as you can. With any luck, of course, a governor—like everyone else—eventually comes to the choice between just two answers to any question and his chances of being right are as good as the next man's—50-50. On the other hand, if you read your mail regularly you will find an enormous bloc of Californians who build a surprisingly better score, just by guessing, than the governor can with all of the facts at hand.

In the matter of those options, the script of every news conference is the same—the governor trying to keep the doors open without being evasive; the press trying to close them without resorting to physical violence.

Let's take an example of an option. You are ideologically opposed to withholding income taxes on the ground that "taxes should hurt." Over a period of weeks or months, your career budget men are bound to persuade you that California government loses about sixty million a year in taxes because ours is one of the few states in the nation that doesn't withhold income taxes. Now, it takes a monumental amount of "squeezing, cutting and trimming" to produce sixty million dollars in new revenue. Over a period of time, you may well decide—as I did—that withholding income tax is the only way to guarantee that all taxpayers pay their fair share—that many leave the state owing about sixty million dollars that must be absorbed by the rest of us.

But you have already closed a door here by declaring flatly that you oppose withholding.

After all, even Bart Starr has to use audible signals now and then, because everything can change in the few seconds it takes to get from being entitled to hear all of the arguments on both sides and that's the huddle to scrimmage. It's the same in Sacramento.

Don't spend too much time talking with people who agree with you—you already know what they think. Of course, if you listen to all sides you risk a reputation for indecision. But in the long run, the advantages of searching out contrary advice make the risk worth taking.

The current controversy over the state colleges and the university is a prime example. I think you correctly read your November majority as a mandate to cut government costs as much as possible. But don't think the mandate extended to imposing tuition.

Knock on any door in suburban California and the chances are you will find: (1) the property taxes are too high, (2) the parents of the teenagers who live there badger the youngsters day and night about good grades—good enough to qualify for the University of California where there's no tuition, and (3) paying tuition would more than wipe out any cut in property taxes. As a matter of fact, the added burden on junior colleges that tuition would mean would probably force an increase in property taxes.

Listening to the other side won't guarantee the right decision, but it raises the odds in your favor.

But the surest way to get the other side of any question (including whether the earth is really round) is to spend a lot of time with the legislature. And bear in mind that if you can't beat the legislature you are in a bad way, because you can't join 'em, either.

Even as fundamental a question as whether to counsel with key members of the senate or assembly before you submit proposals for new law has a potential for disaster.

Many people feel a governor should do so. After all, they argue, the legislature decides whether a governor's program lives or dies.

Suppose you want to raise penalties for armed robbery. You call in a group of key legislators, and start to write a bill everyone can live with. One is with you all the way, no matter what the facts. Another is against you on the same basis. "Tougher penalties mean more prisons." "We can't afford them," says the next man, "but the money would do more good if we use it on the more effective parole, not just prisons." There is bound to be one man who thinks juries will be less likely of conviction if the penalty is too high.

Finally, an old-timer in the group will say he's heard all this before; there's no chance for agreement and the matter needs two years of hard study by an interim committee. And that's the end of your bill.

Of course, you can always go ahead and submit the bill, even after a conference like that—but, believe me, hell hath no fury like a key legislator scorned. If you agree to water down the bill or make it even stronger during the conference,

173

then it is no longer your bill. Besides, if it's a program with merit, it . . . can happen only on the floor of the legislature.

Finally, if it's any consolation, neither approach will work on a lot of legislation.

Take a speed-reading course, if you haven't done so already. The memoranda with the good ideas look just like the rest of them from a distance and you have to read them all to find the right ones. There are not that many good ideas in government, as you will discover. Reading it slowly is doubly depressing. You'll find two briefcases essential (three, if you don't stuff anything in your pockets or confiscate half the space in your travel secretary's briefcase).

You will be amazed, too, at how much time you will save in meetings if you read all the memoranda before they begin. Nothing slows down a bureaucrat like having a meeting start out with a summation of the half-hour report he is about to deliver.

There is a serious side to this, too. You will find the one-hundred thousand state employees as dedicated to their work as any people you have met. They are the most able state workers in the country. They will provide you with the best-documented recommendations you have ever seen. But the final decision is yours. And the more fine print you have read, the better the decision you will make.

On the other hand, you should try to stay out of some of the controversies that people will try to force on you.

The fights over highway routes are especially devastating. The ground rules for selecting highway routes are clearly set out and none of them involves the governor. But in highways, as in every other field of government, the governor is the court of last resort. And you will seldom turn away a protest delegation with the argument that the constitution gives the highway commission sole authority to fix routes and that you lost any real influence over the commissioners the day you appointed them, because you can't fire them.

Generally, all the delegation wants is a sympathetic listener, which seems harmless enough. Then, again, after you have listened sympathetically, they will leave the office convinced that their overwhelming mass of evidence and logic has swayed you to their side. And you won't hear from them again until the commissioner's decision goes against them.

There is one other area in which you can't win. You are now in office and presumed by most voters in the best American tradition to be thinking one thing and saying another. And so when you announce in all candor that you are a favorite-son candidate for the presidency solely because it is a good way to avoid a party fight, don't expect anyone to be listening. You will be a candidate for president and you will just have to do the best you can with that posture.

Finally, don't fight the federal government too hard. After all, Lewis and Clark were on the federal payroll when they discovered Oregon; it was federal money that financed the discovery of atomic energy; and man is exploring space on tax-supported rockets. After all, if it weren't for the federal government, we wouldn't have Everett Dirksen's "Gallant Men (record album)."

I'm sorry you are leaving the mansion. You would have found it comfortable once they had put in the new freeway along Thirtieth Street and the trucks no longer were shifting gears outside the bedroom. The guests at the motels around the mansion were generally quiet, and the mechanics at the used-foreign car lot across the street didn't start running up the engines until a respectable hour.

Also, I am sorry you are selling the Grizzly. A chartered jet flies too high and too fast for you to get a good look at this great, golden state as you fly over. And that is one of the genuine satisfactions of being governor of this state—soaring over the cities and towns; the farms, the dams and canals; the colleges; the National Guard fighters on a five-minute alert; the highways; all the things that make California the leader among equals in this nation.

Its people are sometimes unpredictable. Its challenges are not. You can count on them always being there. And to govern it, you need only keep in mind Satchel Paige's wise words: never look back.

Cordially,

Edmund G. (Pat) Brown

This letter, previously published in the *Charleston Gazette*, is reprinted with the permission of Don Marsh, Editor.

1984 GUBERNATORIAL TRANSITIONS IN WEST VIRGINIA: ROCKEFELLER TO MOORE

David J. Webber

INTRODUCTION

The 1984–1985 gubernatorial transition in West Virginia from John D. (Jay) Rockefeller IV (D) to Arch A. Moore, Jr. (R) offered a particularly unusual set of circumstances that held the potential for either an unusually smooth and efficient transition or a potentially explosive one. While not presenting an opportunity for a "textbook transition"—the incoming Governor Arch Moore was replacing Jay Rockefeller who had succeeded him in 1976 —this West Virginia transition is most noteworthy because of the experience and personalities of the governors involved. Each man had previously defeated the other in an election: Moore defeated Rockefeller as he won reelection in 1972 and Rockefeller returned the favor by beating Moore to gain reelection in 1980. There were, therefore, previous political and personal factors which might have been expected to color the 1985 transition.

Nevertheless, with the principals being two experienced governors and with the incumbent moving on to the U.S. Senate, there was certainly the foundation for a smooth and professional transfer of power. Further, the political climate in West Virginia was supportive of a smooth transition. There was general agreement on the central importance of economic development as the pressing policy issue facing the newly elected governor and the upcoming legislature. Together with the new, albeit Democratic, legislative leadership, this policy consensus presented Moore with what has been called a "window of opportunity." In a report proposing several economic development programs, a group of prestigious West Virginia business leaders called for increased public-private cooperation saying:

> "The time to prepare this strategic plan, put in place the legislative program, and strengthen the economic development delivery system is during the period November 1984–April 1985. This period will offer a unique window of opportunity in West Virginia. The new governor will have a virtual mandate to breathe new life into state economic development efforts. He will meet a legislature in which many members are eager for an economic action plan. . . . The elected leaders of the state will be in a unique position to harness this momentum and chart a new economic course for the state."[1]

Gubernatorial transitions are amorphous, complex, idiosyncratic processes of administrative change. They tend to be highly uncertain and unorganized for both the incoming and outgoing governors. Previous analyses of gubernatorial transitions in other states suggest that transitions occur on three separate levels: logistical, administrative, and policy.[2] The logistical, or physical, transition refers to events establishing a viable, functioning office for the new governor. The second level, the administrative transition, focuses on gubernatorial appointments and institutionalization of the decision-making process preferred by the new governor. The policy transition level pertains to the goals, principles, and programs that the governor hopes to achieve during his term of office.[3]

While all three levels present a useful way to view the 1985 West Virginia transition, relying on this typology exclusively will result in an incomplete understanding of the Rockefeller—Moore changeover. Moore's return as governor included a fourth level: a historical or symbolic transition that includes much more than individual, specific policy initiatives or new appointments. This level of transition is a critical adjustment, a "New Frontier," and a pathbreaking transformation involving fundamental changes in a state. In this sense, West Virginia, in 1984–1985, was facing more than a "window of opportunity." The state was engaged in nothing less than a struggle to resolve its future. In part, this process was reflected in Moore's campaign slogan "West Virginia's coming back."

This analysis tries to capture the intensity and immediacy of this struggle and to identify Arch Moore's role and contribution in a historical transition. . . .

Focusing on the three other levels of transitions—logistical, administrative, and policy—an analysis of gubernatorial transition in any state would focus on at least the following questions:

1. How smooth, speedy, and efficient was the transition from one administration to the next?

2. What was the role and contribution of the outgoing governor?

3. What was the extent of conflict and/or cooperation between the incoming and outgoing administrations?

4. How did the incoming governor make the transformation from a successful campaigner to chief administrator and legislative leader?

5. What was the contribution of task forces and transition teams in preparing position papers and appointment dossiers?

6. How successful was the new governor in getting his legislative package adopted?

Compared with other states and with previous transitions in West Virginia, the 1984-85 transition offers an opportunity to examine several additional questions including:

1. Did the previous experience of the Governors Rockefeller and Moore contribute to a smooth and effective transition?

2. How did this transition compare to the previous Moore-Rockefeller one or the initial Moore transition in 1968?

3. How much new blood is there in the Moore Administration?

Among the difficulties peculiar to this transition was the possibility of the need for an eleven day interim governor as a result of Rockefeller's election to the Senate. With the gubernatorial inauguration date of January 14, 1985 and the swearing in of U.S. Senators set for January 3rd, and given the state's lack of a lieutenant governor, an eleven day gubernatorial vacancy would have created legal and practical problems.

Two unsuccessful gubernatorial primary candidates and the Governor-elect Moore became involved in the constitutional line of succession: Senate President, House Speaker, and by virtue of a 1961 law, Attorney General, State Auditor, and former governors in reverse order of service. Moore was, therefore, fifth in the line of succession. If others disqualified themselves, Moore would quickly have moved up that ordering. The most likely successor, Senate President Warren McGraw, had not only been defeated in the Democratic primary but was considered ineligible by Secretary of State A. James Manchin who maintained that since legislative terms expired November 30, there would be no Senate President or House Speaker until the next session convened on January 9th. Therefore, the Secretary of State argued, Attorney General Chauncey Browning should serve as interim governor. Browning had also been defeated in the Democratic gubernatorial primary.

A more desirable scenario would have been for Rockefeller to complete his term or for Moore to assume the governor's office early. If Rockefeller completed his term, he would have become a Senator eleven days later than his peers, and would, therefore, be the lowest ranking member of the Senate. On the other hand, if Moore began his term eleven days early, Moore would have forfeited his right to seek reelection in 1988. After much media speculation and confusion, Rockefeller elected to complete his term as Governor and began his Senate responsibilities eleven days late. According to his former executive assistant, Rockefeller did not seriously consider terminating his term as Governor earlier because of the confusing impact it would have on the state.[4]

The 1984 election <which returned> Arch Moore to the Capitol after an eight year absence offered optimism for effective government as well as a smooth transition. . . .

State Politics and Arch Moore's Political Career

West Virginia is a complex and often confusing state: it's difficult to understand and more difficult to govern. While most West Virginians take pleasure in calling themselves "Mountaineers" they are probably uncertain of their heritage. Many observers have commented on the state's turbulent history and lack of regional identity. The state's economy depends on what are now declining industries (coal, chemicals, and steel) and West Virginians generally fatalistically accept their depressed economy and other misfortunes.[5] . . .

Similar to West Virginia's economic dependence on a few industries, the state has depended on just a handful of elected officials for political leadership. Moore previously served as Governor between 1969 and 1976. He was the first Governor to succeed himself, and he was replaced by Jay Rockefeller who served from 1977 to 1984. If Moore is successful in seeking re-election to a fourth term in 1988 <Moore was defeated, ed.> . . . these two individuals would have held the governor's chair for a quarter of a century. This dependence on a few individuals is also reflected in the longevity of the state's United States Senators: Jennings Randolph was first elected to Congress in 1932 and elected to the Senate in 1958 where he served until January 1985. Robert Byrd was also elected Senator in 1958.

This paucity of potential political leaders might be explained by a number of structural characteristics. West Virginia, for example, does not have a competitive two-party system. . . . Additionally, its lack of a lieutenant-governor might deprive it of a potential source of "leaders-in-waiting" as well as a loyal critic of the sitting governor. Since both Rockefeller and Moore are such formidable personalities, the lack of a strong, visible devil's advocate undoubtedly affects the leadership style of both governors.

Moore's long string of political successes is generally considered to represent personal, not Republican Party, success. Moore has been very successful in gaining election in a Democratic state. After serving two years in the West Virginia House of Delegates, he defeated a Democratic incumbent to win a congressional seat in 1956 and was elected governor in 1968 despite a large pro-Humphrey margin in the presidential race. Moore defeated Rockefeller in 1972 to gain re-election and won election in 1984 by a 53–47 margin. His only two political defeats came in the 1980 gubernatorial race against Rockefeller, when he lost 54–45, and in 1978 when he was not able to unseat Senator Jennings Randolph.

Previous Transitions and Statutory Provisions

Generally, West Virginia does not have a history of orderly and cooperative gubernatorial transitions[6] although a major exception is the Smith to Moore transition in 1968–1969. While the atmosphere is not usually overtly hostile, incoming governors have typically received little assistance or support from retiring chief executives. Kidman (1972) reviewed four transitions (1956–1957, 1960–1961, 1964–1965, and 1968–1969) and found little institutional support or policy advising for the new governor. The 1956–1957 changeover between Governors Marland and Underwood was marked by two events that appear, almost as if by tradition, in subsequent transitions: the removal of office furnishings by the outgoing governor, and a deluge of last minute gubernatorial appointments. . . .

The cordial and cooperative transition that brought Moore into the governor's office was apparently not repeated when he turned the position over to Jay Rockefeller in 1976–1977. A week after Rockefeller was elected there still had been no contact between Moore and the new governor. Moore reportedly said that he had no intention of meeting with Rockefeller and would leave the transition to staff members from both sides.[7] The governors' wives apparently also did not cooperate. Sharon Rockefeller expressed interest in receiving an invitation to see the executive mansion but Shelly Moore indicated she would have to wait until after the first of the year commenting, "They will have four years to settle in."[8]

Additionally, the outgoing Moore Administration continued the West Virginia transition tradition of last minute appointments and furniture removal. Moore extended, after the election, civil service status to thousands of state employees to protect them from replacement by Rockefeller.[9] Also in keeping with tradition, following his inauguration Rockefeller found that his new office was without furniture, files, secretarial supplies, and properly installed telephones. Moore did reimburse the state $13,606 for his office furniture.[10]

Some of the uncertainty in these transitions would have been reduced had there been formal procedures in place to guide incoming and outgoing administrations. There is currently little guidance for either. Based on information presented in *The Book of the States*, Beyle[11] has compared the processes and provisions concerning gubernatorial transitions provided for in each of the fifty states. The eight provisions are:

1. Legislation pertaining to gubernatorial transition,
2. Appropriations available to governor-elect,
3. Governor-elect participates in preparing state budget for coming year,
4. Governor-elect hires staff to assist during transition,
5. State personnel made available to governor-elect,
6. Office space in buildings made available to governor-elect,
7. Provisions for acquainting governor-elect staff with office procedures and routine office functions, and
8. Provisions for transfer of records, files, etc.

West Virginia formally has none of these eight provisions although some informal provision of office space to the governor-elect does take place. In contrast, many other states the size of West Virginia, such as Maine, Vermont, and Wyoming, provide appropriations to the governor-elect to hire staff as well as formally involve him in preparing the state's budget for the coming year.[12]

The absence of specific budgetary appropriations for transition presents problems for a least three types of expenditures. First, the incoming governor must compensate his transition staff from private funds, or the outgoing governor, as Rockefeller did in 1984–1985, must expend a portion of the governor's contingency fund for the new staff's salaries. This depends on the co-operation between the two governors—a condition not always present in a transition. Second, the outgoing governor is expected to prepare his official papers for presentation. Without a transition budget, he must find private funding or hope that the legislature will make a specific appropriation to cover the cost of preparation and publication of the official papers. Third, practical matters like accrued vacation pay for the outgoing governor's staff are problematic. Given the state's general prohibition of lump-sum benefit payments, the new governor must carry the former governor's staff on his payroll for a period of time.[13]

One formal provision in West Virginia pertaining to gubernatorial <transition> is the Legislative Improvement Amendment to the state constitution, approved in 1970, permitting the legislature to recess for thirty days after its initial organizational meeting to allow the incoming governor time to prepare his program.[14] In effect, this gave Moore from January 14, Inauguration Day, to February 13, as a formal transition period. . . .

Post Victory, Pre-Inauguration

The day after the election Moore and Rockefeller spoke by phone with Moore reporting that the two "agreed on some common interests." "We reached a plateau of cooperation," Moore reported, "Our conversation was varied and not lengthy."[15.]

After the election, Moore retained the tough and determined demeanor that has always characterized his leadership style. The first issue Moore chose to make a stand on involved the role of the state courts in ordering state expenditures to rectify inequitable and therefore unconstitutional, policy situations. The major controversy involved school funding as a result of a 1982 court decision. Speaking to his supporters at his campaign headquarters several days after the election, Moore said he "wasn't about to be pushed around by any court order that might dictate an increase in state taxes." At one point in his speech, Moore reportedly shouted "the A-team is back!"[16]

Moore did not publicly maintain this tough posture in establishing his relationship with the new legislature, choosing instead to project a cooperative, positive image. After the organizational meetings of the legislature, at which a new Senate president and a new House speaker were selected, Moore praised the Democratic leadership as "fine and experienced lawmakers" and indicated that he hoped there would be a spirit of cooperation between the two branches of government despite party differences." He declined to discuss philosophical differences between himself and the new Democratic legislative leaders, saying: "I think we've got to approach these years as West Virginians."[17]

In following the state's two major newspapers, the *Charleston Gazette* and the *Daily Mail*, a transition observer is stunned by the absence of news about Arch Moore between the week after the election and the end of December. For a politician of Moore's reputation for attracting the limelight, this conspicuous absence suggests one of two things. First, that Moore was busy preparing for his return to power and devoted to working on policy announcements and appointments that would be worth the wait. Alternatively, as one journalist suggested to me, after seeing how close Rockefeller came to losing the Senate race, Moore was depressed with the knowledge that, as things turned out, he could have been elected to the U.S. Senate!

Rockefeller and Moore both assigned a staff member to take primary responsibility for transitional activity. Moore appointed Tom Craig, a Charleston lawyer who had served as an aide in the first Moore terms and who was a key individual in Moore's campaign effort. Rockefeller assigned Nick Lazarius, his executive assistant, to coordinate the present administration's activities. While Moore and Rockefeller did not meet during the transition, they did speak on the phone several times, Craig and Lazarius along with other staff members had several meetings.[18]

Because of the lack of state provided office space, the Moore transition staff worked out of the Moore campaign headquarters. While there was not a pre-election transition team or planning committee, the fact that Moore had previously served as governor provided him considerable preparation to become governor.[19]

During this period, outgoing Governor Rockefeller did five things to smooth the transition of power. First, he issued a directive asking all department heads and staff to cooperate fully with Governor-elect Moore's staff and transition teams. Secondly, Rockefeller's staff prepared a briefing book on current departmental policy issues. Third, George Carenbauer, counsel to Governor Rockefeller, prepared a binder listing the status of the state's numerous boards and commissions in terms of vacancies and current make-up. Fourth, Rockefeller prepared a tentative fiscal year 1986 budget as required by law. He chose not to present a formal budget to the legislature.[20] Fifth, Rockefeller provided funds from the governor's contingency fund to compensate three or four Moore staffers from the period December 1 to Inauguration Day.[21]

To inform the incoming Moore staff about the status of departmental activities, each of about 25 department heads was asked to write a memo reviewing the status of activities in their department. These memos, about two-five pages in length, were collected by Nick Lazarius and delivered as a briefing book to Tom Craig on January 11th, three days before Moore took office. Rockefeller's staff made no effort to review or edit these department head memos.[22]

These briefing memos were requested by the Moore transition coordinator, Thomas Craig. According to Craig, the intention was to have the outgoing department heads communicate to their successors, as yet un-named and not to be appointed for another month, the five or six most important issues of which the new head should be aware. A similar procedure was employed in the 1976-77 Moore to Rockefeller transition when Moore's outgoing department heads prepared issue memos.[23]

To assist him, Governor-elect Moore organized six task forces to define specific approaches and programs intended to meet his broad goals. These task forces were organized in the following key areas: commerce, energy, tax reform, the state employment security debt, workers' compensation, and the termination of the Alcoholic Beverage Commission.[24] Each task force consisted of people from the private sector who were assigned to examine a specific area of state government in terms of its relative effectiveness and efficiency. The Commerce Task Force, for example, consisted of ten private citizens and three individuals who were to join Moore's staff. Of these ten appointees, two were members of a Charleston law firm, five were from businesses, one was employed by a bank, and one was from the West Virginia University School of Engineering.

The Commerce Task Force was given two main functions:

1. To recommend how state government should be organized to enhance the economic development activities of the State of West Virginia; and

2. To recommend various programs to enhance the retention and expansion of existing West Virginia businesses and the attraction of new businesses into the State.

The Task Force prepared a 23-page report, not including six attachments diagraming alternative organizational structures for conducting economic development activities. The report reviewed the state's existing economic development structure and cited 17 specific problems and observations about current programs that the Task Force intended to correct. In addition to commenting on general problems facing economic development activities, the Task Force proposed 20 specific programs and legislative ideas and identified the necessary action required to make each one of the proposals a reality.

In his farewell address to the Legislature, Rockefeller apparently went out of his way to further cooperation with Moore. In addition to listing his own achievements, he mentioned Governor-Elect Moore several times. This was well received by the legislators who commented on the conciliatory nature of the speech. House Minority Leader Larry Swann said it was "very kind to refer to Moore in a positive way" and House Majority Leader William Wooten said he "was pleased to see Rockefeller speak of Governor-elect Moore well and thought the governor was well-advised to urge bipartisan cooperation."[25]

Administrative Transition and Appointments

On February 13th, the day of his "State of the State" address, Moore announced his major administrative appointments. These appointments were a mix of familiar faces and new names. Of the 28 appointments announced, only two had served in Moore's previous terms as governor, seven of the appointees had already been working in the departments they were chosen to head, and four were former legislators--two of whom had been defeated in bids for higher office in November. The most surprising of the appointments were three new faces from medical education, the federal government, and the private sector, who were selected to head the Department of Health, the Department of Human Services, and the Office of Economic and Community Development, respectively.

Compared to the Smith-Moore transition of 1968–1969, Arch Moore appeared more eager and ready to go in 1986. As Herb Little, a veteran state capitol reporter, commented, "Moore took over the capitol rotunda for the long-awaited announcement of 20 department-head appointments and introduction of the appointees, completing his administration in one stroke." Little called this burst of energy only "a mild warmup" for that evening's "State of the State" address. . . . Little observed that Moore had virtually disappeared since his inauguration January 14 and the "only sign that there was anybody in the Governor's Office was a freeze order on hiring and new spending, routine when the office changes party hands."[26]

Governor Moore asked for the resignations of all board and commission members. In fact, he was successful in having the legislature refrain from considering several hundred eleventh hour Rockefeller appointments. Because of the magnitude of the task, the process of appointing the members to the boards and commissions is ongoing basically on a needs basis[27] and <is> not . . . completed until the legislature convenes in January.[28] Moore reportedly . . . received some criticism from loyal Republicans for both the pace of the board and commission appointments and the governor's appointment of several Democrats to various positions.[29]

Relations with and Successes in the 1985 Legislature

At the same time West Virginia was electing Arch Moore to be governor, it elected 73 Democrats and 27 Republicans to the state House of Delegates and 40 Democrats and four Republicans to the state Senate. Both legislative chambers, thought to be more conservative than in previous years, had new leadership. Both the Senate President and House Speaker were highly regarded legislators but faced considerable opposition from conservative fragments in their own party. Mere numbers suggested that Moore faced a difficult task in persuading the heavily Democratic legislature of the merits of his policy ideas. However, the more conservative ideology of the members and the perception of a "window of opportunity" made this hurdle potentially surmountable.

Governor Moore had his way with the Democratic Legislature. The governor, legislators, and political observers all agree that Moore was very successful in persuading the legislators to adopt his package of policy initiatives and budget proposals. Moore evaluated the 1985 session in terms such as: "It was a West Virginia Legislature, we now have three of the nine building blocks we need if we are going to turn this state around," and the Legislature was "the most cooperative ever seen."[30] One reporter wrote: "Observers were saying Saturday night (the last day of the session) that Arch Moore got more out of the West Virginia Legislature in one year than Jay Rockefeller got in eight."[31]

The governor's legislative success did reduce Democratic harmony. The Energy Bill, for example, was successfully pushed through the House by a coalition of the Republican minority and conservative Democrats who generally opposed Speaker Joseph Albright. Moore had a much easier time in the Senate where President Dan Tonkovich was quite accommodating to the governor in handling both the Energy Bill and the Economic Development Bill.[32]

In the final analysis, Governor Moore obtained legislative approval for most of the policy initiatives presented in his "State of the State" address. Of the 16 proposals, the only clear disappointment for the governor was the rejection of his proposal to take the state out of liquor retailing.

Several factors contributed to Moore's legislative successes. First, the House was not as unified as the 73–27 partisan breakdown suggests. Albright was elected Speaker by a three vote margin over a conservative, "pro-business" Democrat. Second, the joint effects of a well-organized and well-prepared chief executive and the prevalent "window of opportunity" attitude tipped the benefit of the doubt towards the governor. Apparently, legislators thought Moore should be given a chance to try his programs.

Summary and Assessment

Despite Moore and Rockefeller being political adversaries for well over 15 years, the 1984 election and transition appeared remarkably harmonious. From the very beginning of the campaign, with Moore's surprising announcement that he would run for governor instead of the Senate, the two men seemed to go out of their way to avoid conflict. While Rockefeller's other transition into the U.S. Senate reduced any disappointment or frustration that a defeated or lame-duck governor might experience, Rockefeller apparently did go out of his way to avoid public displays of conflict with Moore and took the affirmative step of allocating a portion of his contingency fund to members of Moore's staff for six weeks.

Moore hit the ground running. With both the major department heads appointed and the "State of the State" address delivered on February 13, 1985, the new governor had the major pieces of his policy transition and administrative transition well in place within a month of taking office. The remainder of the policy transition was completed with the governor's overwhelming legislative successes by April 30th. Most of the administrative transition was finished by August 1st when the vast number of administrative appointments were practically complete.[33]

Moore's public support has been strong well into his third term as governor. A poll of West Virginia voters in late September 1985 found that 53% of respondents evaluated Moore as doing an excellent or good job while 43% evaluated him as doing a fair or poor job. Moore received an excellent from 30% of Republicans and 14% of Democrats.[34]

In the final analysis the Moore transition must be evaluated as a very positive one: he assembled a full crew of department heads, he identified his policy goals and saw that the Legislature adopted them, and he projected an aura of hope through his leadership. . . .

Notes

[1] West Virginia Roundtable, Inc., *Economic Development Action Plan*, (1984), *passim*.

[2] Thad L. Beyle, "Lessons from the 1982-83 Transitions," in Thad L. Beyle (ed), *Gubernatorial Transitions: The 1982 Election* (Durham: Duke University Press, 1985), 31–32.

[3] *Ibid*.

[4] Interview with Nick Lazarius, Executive Assistant to Governor Rockefeller, October 4, 1985.

[5] See Bajone and Ujifusa, *The Almanac of American Politics*, (1985).

[6] See Peter Neal Kidman, "Gubernatorial Transitions," paper presented at the Annual Meeting of the West Virginia Political Science Association, Charleston, West Virginia, October 13–14, 1972.

[7] *Charleston Gazette*, November 12, 1976.

8   *Charleston Daily Mail*, December 3, 1976.

9   *Charleston Daily Mail*, December 26, 1976.

10   *Charleston Gazette*, January 19, 1977.

11   Beyle, *op cit.*, 457–458.

12   *Ibid.*

13   Lazarius, *loc cit.*

14   Kidman, *loc cit.*

15   *Charleston Daily Mail*, November 9, 1984.

16   *Ibid.*

17   *Ibid.*

18   Lazarius, *loc cit.*

19   Interview with Thomas Craig, Transition Coordinator for Governor Moore, October 8, 1985.

20   Interview with Dan Green, former Special Assistant to Governor Rockefeller, October 2, 1985.

21   Lazarius, *loc cit.*

22   *Ibid.*

23   Craig, *loc cit.*

24   *Ibid.*

25   *Charleston Gazette*, January 10, 1985.

26   *The Dominion Post*, January 17, 1985.

27   Price, *loc cit.*

28   Craig, *loc cit.*

29   Price, *loc cit.*

30   *Parkersburg Sentinel*, April 23, 1985.

31   *Charleston Gazette*, April 14, 1985.

32   *Ibid.*

33   Craig, *loc cit.*

34   *Charleston Daily Mail*, September 25, 1985.

With permission of the author and Duke University Press.

A longer, fuller version of this paper was published in Thad Beyle (ed.) *Gubernatorial Transitions*, 1984 by Duke University Press, 1989.

Case Study:
COAL, TAXES AND POLITICAL SUICIDE: GOVERNOR MARLAND'S ABORTIVE SEVERANCE TAX PROPOSAL OF 1953

Paul F. Lutz

William Casey Marland was inaugurated as the twenty-fourth governor of West Virginia on January 19, 1953, just two months before his thirty-fourth birthday. The forty-minute ceremony took place on a temporary platform erected across the great wall in the center of the legislative hallway directly beneath the capitol dome. West Virginia Supreme Court Judge Frank C. Haymond administered the oath of office.

Following the swearing in, Governor Marland, a heavily built man standing six feet in height, delivered a fifteen-minute inaugural address. During the course of the speech, the new governor's two-year old son, John Wesley, bounced gleefully on the knee of platform dignitary John L. Lewis and to the delight of the audience also took several leisurely strolls in front of the speaker's rostrum. According to Mrs. Marland, the governor explicitly ordered that the toddler not be restrained in his movement during the ceremony. The festivities concluded with a musical program by the bands from Pinville, Oceana, Mullens, and Elkhorn High Schools.

By the time of Marland's inauguration as governor, West Virginia had begun to feel the effects of a declining economy as evidenced in falling tax returns, increased unemployment in the coal fields, and the beginning of what would be a decade of migration out of the state. Since good times prevailed in the nation as a whole, West Virginians found their economic decline confusing and frustrating.

In his brief inaugural address Marland spoke deliberately and with restraint. He reviewed the state's problems generally and emphasized the importance of roads and education as the determinants in the future growth of the state. He served notice that more tax money would be needed to meet those problems and that he would make specific recommendations in his upcoming message to the Fifty-first Legislature as to the sources from which more money might be obtained.

The new governor frankly admitted that while twenty consecutive years of Democratic leadership had been responsible for providing the state progressive government, it had also led to growth without proper planning which had caused some injurious division and overlapping of departmental responsibility within state government. In light of the above, Marland recommended "a slow surgical approach to cure the state's financial ills as opposed to the 'sword approach' of overall cuts in services."

He declared that during his administration serious attempts would be made to consolidate and streamline state government in order to effect sensible economies. Aside from these rather general remarks the new governor said little that would portend the state-wide furor that would arise from his highly controversial tax package to be presented only three days later.

Marland's seemingly innocuous inaugural address elicited similarly innocuous responses from the news media. Even the "loyal opposition," led by the *Charleston Daily Mail,* chose to draw no political blood as evidenced in its assertion: "His first appearance, his presence, his remarks were encouraging. Governor Marland is certainly no orator, but he leaves an impression of sobriety and conscientiousness of a man willing to listen and ready to learn." (This was a haunting assessment of Marland in light of his later drinking problem and irrepressible stubborness.) Perhaps a more realistic appraisal of the new governor was made by Syd Barksdale of the *Bluefield Sunset News* who wrote:

> "personally, we have confidence in the new governor. He is young, it is true, but he is wise in the ways of politics and uncommonly good in grasping the essentials of governmental problems. It remains to be seen how persuasive he can be in dealing with the legislature and how good he is at getting teamwork from his department heads."

The moment of truth came for Governor Marland only three days after his January 19th inauguration when he addressed a joint session of the Fifty-first Legislature. His address began with a lengthy explanation of his budgetary philosophy in which he reiterated his pledge to streamline state government via the "surgical approach" for greater fiscal efficiency. He then proceeded to outline specific plans for the areas of conservation, legal reform, labor, probation and parole, law enforcement, education, and roads. The last item to be explained was that of additional revenues. Marland announced a three-part tax plan designed to generate $23,250,000. Part One he declared would simply require the Legislature to obey the constitutional mandate of the people of West Virginia as expressed in the passage of the 1948 Secondary Roads Bond Issue which called for the imposition of a one-cent per gallon increase on gasoline which would realize an estimated four million dollars annually. Such monies, according to Marland, would be automatically diverted to the road fund to reduce to six million dollars the ten million dollars then needed to put the state road program on a "pay-as-you-go" basis. Part Two called for a $1,5000,000 increase in the state's share of the parimutuel horse racing tax which would go for the program of free textbooks in all elementary schools. Before moving on to Part Three of his tax plan, which was to shoulder the bulk of the additional revenues, Marland engaged in a bit of "jawboning" perhaps recognizing the gravity of his next few sentences:

> "For the bulk of the revenue for this program I would unqualifiedly recommend to you that we turn to that which West Virginia has been endowed by our Creator, and which once gone is gone forever, I speak, of course, of turning to the natural resources of West Virginia for a sever-

ance tax which will bring in an estimated income of approximately $18,000,000 based primarily on the following rates: ten cents per ton on coal, twenty-five cents per barrel of oil, gas one cent per thousand cubic feet, sand and gravel five cents per ton, along with other natural resources which will be included in the bill presented for your consideration."

The severance tax proposal came across as something of an "executive bombshell" on the unsuspecting Legislature. Reaction to the governor's tax plan, which bore heavily upon the coal industry, came fast and furious and with it came the end of one of the state's briefest gubernatorial honeymoons on record.

The following two months witnessed a political donnybrook reminiscent of West Virginia's legendary Hatfield and McCoy feud. Battle lines were drawn almost immediately with the Marland "pro-severance tax" group looking quite impressive, at least on paper, with support from the UMW, the West Virginia Federation of Labor, the West Virginia CIO, the West Virginia Education Association, and the state's seven-member Congressional delegation. The principal opponents were spokesmen for the coal industry and their "legislative lackeys," the Republican minority in both houses of the Legislature, the State Chamber of Commerce, and several influential newspapers such as the *Charleston Gazette* and *Wheeling Intelligencer.*

The very next morning following the new governor's proposal, Frank Knight, the managing editor of the *Charleston Gazette*, attacked Marland's severance tax as "irresponsible and unthinking," and declared that, "it would destroy the coal industry of West Virginia." The new chief executive wasted little time in answering the *Gazette* editorial. Three days later a lengthy rebuttal was printed in which Governor Marland chastised Knight by insisting that the newspaper's position had not been arrived at in an objective manner and was grossly biased due to the presence on the *Gazette* editorial board of Carl Andrews, Secretary of the West Virginia Coal Operators Association. In point one of his seven-point rebuttal Marland urged Knight to inform the public of Carl Andrew's direct ties with the coal industry. Knight's contention that the coal industry already contributed a "large part" to the cost of state government was countered in the governor's second point in which he wrote: "You may not know that the nine or ten million dollars paid by the coal industry in gross sales tax is not what most people consider 'large' in a government that costs over two hundred million dollars a year." Then in an apparent attempt to embarrass the coal industry and, by the same token, to incite the tax-paying public Marland retorted: "You may be interested to know that the citizens of West Virginia are contributing almost three times as much as the coal industry to the cost of government in consumer's sales tax alone." Point Three demonstrated a typical Marland tactic in which the governor used Knight's own statistics in a counter-attack. Knight stated that the coal industry paid approximately thirty million dollars in taxes every year but Marland demonstrated that only one-third of that amount went to state and local governments. The governor insisted that the state and local share of coal revenues was small since property taxes statewide were based on valuations as much as 75%

below the actual value of their holdings. Finally, Marland announced that any severance tax imposed by the state of West Virginia would become a deduction from the Federal income tax paid by the coal operator. "I should think," Marland wrote stingingly, "that even the coal operators would rather their taxes go to support an improved road and school program for the state from which their wealth is derived rather than to the federal government."

Marland took Knight to task in point four over the editor's contention that other coal producing states did not have gross sales tax or severance taxes by pointing out that such states did have "corporate income taxes" and that as an example the state of Louisiana had derived $44,600,000 from a severance tax on natural resources in 1950.

The governor's fifth point was a brief statement assuaging Knight's real or imagined fear that the Democratic Party would be destroyed if such a severance tax were adopted. "To the contrary," Marland declared, "The Democratic Party will certainly fail in West Virginia unless it acknowledges its primary responsibility to all of its citizens in the matter of roads and schools."

As to Knight's prediction that the severance tax would presage economic suicide, the governor countered this fear in point six by noting that the very people whose life blood depended on the coal industry, the UMW, had given their full support to his measure starting with President John L. Lewis. . . .

As a result of the above letter, Governor Marland clearly demonstrated to many citizens that their young chief executive was made of sterner stuff than most had suspected. Moreover, the Marland-Knight confrontation served to set the tone for two months of the most caustic political debate ever witnessed in the West Virginia Legislature.

The governor's proposal became Senate Bill number 32 and was introduced by Senate President Ralph Bean on January 27th. Although Mr. Bean lauded what he called, "the many good recommendations of the governor," when questioned by reporters about the severance tax bill he responded: "I believe the governor will find many members of this Legislature very reluctant to impose the matter." In the same vein House of Delegates Speaker William L. Flannery from coal-rich Logan County observed: "I consider the governor's proposal bold and progressive—where to get the money to finance that program, however, is the sixty-four dollar question." Bartow Jones, Republican minority leader in the Senate, assailed Marland's proposal by exclaiming: "The governor must have taken lessons from Mr. Truman, the only solution being to spend more money."

On January 29th just two days after the severance tax bill was introduced, Consolidation Coal Company President George Higginbotham emerged as a bona fide "prophet of gloom" for the coal industry in an address to the Fairmont Kiwanis Club. "It would be an attempt at economic suicide to put a tax of ten cents per ton on coal and would cause a breakdown in the industry," Higginbotham asserted. The coal executive cited two factors which had already contributed to a decrease in coal usage and the loss of 25,000 miners' jobs nationwide since 1950. The most serious threat to the coal industry, Higginbotham explained, was the increased use on the east coast of imported residual oil from South America. The second threat he cited was the completion of the "Big Inch" pipeline that could carry Texas natural gas into West Virginia and other eastern states. Furthermore, Higginbotham called attention to two side-effects of this oil and natural gas competition. First, the slackened demand for "space-heater" gas from Texas in the summer allowed the industry to dump its surpluses on West Virginia at a low rate for industrial users thus undercutting coal suppliers. Second, he asserted that the state's use of asphalt in the construction of its highways injured the coal industry since the asphalt consisted of a petroleum by-product: while if concrete were used this would result in the use of one pound of coal for every one pound of steel rods used in highway construction.

Moreover, the Consolidation Coal Company president observed that one-fourth of the working men of the state were directly employed by the coal industry and that one-half of the people of West Virginia were dependent upon the coal industry for their income. Likewise, the state derived one-third of its total income from coal. "The companies could not afford to pay the ten cents proposed tax on a ton of coal." Higginbotham concluded, "Since the companies were only making eight cents profit on a ton of coal mined and the proposed tax would put them in the red which would force them to shut down their pits." Despite the gloomy prediction above, the coal executive did reveal a sense of hope as he observed: "I am not discouraged with the future of the coal industry, and I believe the industry will take a turn upward within the next five years."

As the legislature got into full swing in February, it soon became apparent to Governor Marland and the backers of the severance tax that the bill might die in committee. Senate president Ralph Bean and Senate finance chairman Glenn Jackson from Logan County led the Senate opposition. Marland caucused daily with Senate Democrats in hopes of moving his bill to the floor, and he worked closely with Jackson, repeatedly urging him to bring the bill to vote. Marland insisted that he had 13 of the 18 member committee in his camp but Jackson contended that the votes were not there and the hearings continued.

With the severance tax proposal bogged down in committee, Marland went to work calling upon numerous "big name" supporters in hopes of breaking the logjam. Following a secret meeting on February 17th with John L. Lewis at the Greenbrier Hotel, the UMW President sent a letter to each of the 120,000 UMW members in West Virginia urging them to give all-out support to the governor's legislative program. Lewis . . . explained that the ten cents per ton tax could be charged off against the cost of production as a federal income tax deduction thus reducing for most companies the actual cost to four or five cents per ton. He also asserted that the program was a sound one designed to increase the prosperity of the state and to promote the well-being of the population. . . . Then in the strongest language of the letter he skillfully inserted the miner-absentee landlord dichotomy as he wrote: "The absentee industrial landlords of West Virginia, who for 50 years have shipped the wealth of the state elsewhere, without proper recompense to its citizens, should not oppose this tax or program." Lewis also called upon the various lobbyists and legislative agents to discontinue "their insidious opposition to Governor Marland's progressive program because in so doing they are standing with the absentee industrial landlords and fighting against the coal miners and other citizens who elected them to office and whom in honor they should serve." The UMW President concluded his rather lengthy letter by calling upon each local union to insist upon a clear and uneqivocal statement of their legislator's position on the severance tax question.

The week of February 16th proved to be the climax of the joint House-Senate Finance Committees' hearings before packed galleries. The names of those testifying read like a list of "Who's Who" in West Virginia economic and political circles. Before the week was out the committee heard from such dignitaries as Hillis Townsend, State Labor Legislative Committee Chairman, Walter Thurmond of the State Coal Operators' Association, Raymond E. Salvati, President of Island Creek Coal Company, Ernest K. Jones, Charleston president of the state Chamber of Commerce, H.K. Griffith, State Road Commissioner, Phares Reeder, Executive Secretary of the West Virginia Education Association, Congressmen Robert C. Byrd, Cleveland M. Bailey, and Robert M. Mollahan, U.S. Senator Harley Kilgore, State Treasurer William H. Ansel, Jr., UMW District Presidents George Titler, and William Blizzard, while affidavits from U.S. Senator M.M. Neeley and Representative Harley O. Staggers and Elizabeth Kee were also read into the record.

As a prelude to the final week of hearings and in an apparent attempt to sell his proposal to the public, Governor Marland released a highly detailed communique explaining all the possible ramifications of his severance tax bill. Marland once again denied that his bill would bring ruin to the coal industry of West Virginia and then produced a veritable flood of specific examples to support his argument. "I would be the last person in the world to want to do anything to the coal industry—West Virginia's great basic industry--in the matter of finances," Marland explained. He then reiterated the point made previously in John L. Lewis' letter to UMW members that since the proposed state tax could be deducted from federal income taxes the actual cost to the companies would range from "a minimum of 1.8 cents to a maximum of 7 cents per ton, with most companies paying around 4.8 cents per ton."

The governor then proceeded to ask the citizens of West Virginia to examine the gloomy predictions of the coal industry on the basis of three factors:

(1) Figures of net profit per ton after taxes.

(2) Figures showing just what it actually means in cents to these companies to pay West Virginia the ten cents in light of federal income tax requirements and deductions.

(3) Figures showing the depletion allowances that these companies allow themselves.

Unfortunately for Marland, most West Virginians could not begin to fathom the complex economic and legal questions involved and his brilliant defense of the severance tax fell on deaf ears. . . .

The February 16th hearings were held in a packed House of Delegates chamber with more than 700 persons looking on from the galleries. Hillis Townsend, a Charleston attorney and legislative spokesman for the state's "pro-severance tax" labor groups, opened the proceedings by declaring: "We're willing to take the chance because we don't believe it will adversely affect the coal industry in a substantial manner." A second backer of the tax, West Virginia Education Association Secretary Phares Reeder, told the lawmakers that there was an urgent need for an additional ten to twelve million dollars a year for educational purposes.

Newly elected First District Congressman Robert M. Mollahan philosophised "there are times when the interests of a few must make way for the general welfare and this seems to me to be one of those times." According to Mollahan, the severance tax was not aimed at either labor or the companies but at all West Virginians who were directly or indirectly concerned with the natural resources of the state. "Tax experts have made it clear," he insisted, "that the ten cents per ton proposed tax can be charged by the coal operators against production cost on federal returns and when so deducted the actual approximate cost to the operators is reduced to less than five cents per ton." Mollahan further substantiated his position by reminding the committee that the coal companies had been greatly favored by the Federal Revenue Act of 1951, which had doubled the percentage depletion rate from five percent of gross value to ten percent of the gross value thus reducing significantly the corporate tax liability of companies. . . .

The "anti-severance tax" forces were led by Raymond E. Salvati, President of Island Creek Coal Company. "We're sympathetic with the needs for more roads and schools but couldn't we try to economize in government before imposing new taxes?", he queried. A second coal industry spokesman, Ernest K. Jones, Charleston President of the state Chamber of Commerce declared: "the coal industry has been paying for some 20 years a severance tax on natural resources products in the form of a gross sales tax. This is shown by the fact that coal is taxed at nine times the rate for manufacturing and merchants." Other operator spokesmen called the proposal a reckless tax pattern in the direction of confiscation and said it would literally sever the throats of many small operators. Likewise, spokesmen for the silica sand, limestone, clay, salt brine, and lumber industries all said that they were operating on such a small margin of profit that the tax could force many of them out of business. . . .

With the end of public hearings on February 20th and with the legislature going into its final two weeks, Governor Marland began to pressure the respective finance committees to vote on the measure. When rumors began to fly that there were not nearly enough votes to get the bill out of committee, Marland appeared before a joint session of the legislature on February 23rd and made an impassioned plea for his severance tax bill which was carried live by WSAZ radio in Huntington. The governor's twenty-minute address did not include any new considerations but did prove to be an especially emotional defense of his much maligned severance tax bill. . . Marland painted a bleak future for the state if the severance tax were refused as evidenced in his concluding words which served to prick his listeners' moral and aesthetic consciences as he pleaded:

> "I say to you let's use this equitable source of revenue because whether
> we like it or not, West Virginia's hills will be stripped, the bowels of the
> earth will be mined and the refuse strewn across our valleys and our

mountains in the form of burning slate dumps. This refuse will continue to be dumped into our once clear mountain streams.

Let me freely admit to you that this decision was not an easy one for me to make. My entire life has been bound up and dependent upon the coal industry. It has been so with the Marland family for many generations. I have studied the facts and the figures for many hours, many days and many weeks, studying to see if I had reached a decision that I could conscientiously defend now and at all times. I have reached that decision, I can defend my position now and at all times. The responsibility has now passed to you—the legislature of West Virginia. Will you make a decision that you too can defend now and forever more?

According to Glenn Jackson, Senate Finance Committee Chairman, he, Marland, Ralph Bean, and John Amos met briefly following the address and the governor claimed he had 13 votes on the 18 member committee. Jackson's answer to Marland was, "Governor, it will never pass. Somebody's lying to you upstairs," to which Marland responded, "I don't believe a damn word any of you say." When the committee did finally vote a few days later the bill was killed 14-4. When told of the vote by Chairman Jackson, Marland retorted, "I don't give a goddamn, I'm for it now, I'll be for it two years from now, and four years from now."

Five days later the governor caucused with Senate Democrats for 80 minutes in what proved to be a futile attempt to salvage his tax plan. Then on March 6th all hope for the severance tax vanished when the House of delegates, in what one newspaper described as "funeral rites" for the bill, voted 56–41 to postpone further consideration indefinitely. Consequently, due to House rules, the measure could not be acted upon again until the next legislative session. Governor Marland was bitterly disappointed by the defeat of his pet program which served to cast a dark shadow over his entire term of office. Nevertheless, the youthful chief executive never wavered from his conviction that the severance tax was the most equitable way to provide the needed revenue for West Virginia's two major ills—roads and education.

In the weeks and months following the adjournment of the legislature newspapers across the state performed one post-mortem after another on the severance tax issue. Particularly significant were three editorials in the pro-Marland *Fairmont Times* in coal-rich Marion County. Even before the bill's March 6th defeat in the House of Delegates the *Times* observed that Governor Marland had been in error in that his severance tax idea had not come up as a result of campaign issues which could have been hashed and rehashed over a period of many weeks. Instead, he had delayed advocating the measure until he had been duly inaugurated. "Then," wrote Ned Smith, "he called a press conference and presented his proposals with a suddenness that was reminiscent of former President Roosevelt in the early days of his tenure of office."

A second *Times* editorial of March 10th attacked the absentee landlords' relentless opposition to the severance tax which, according to Smith, "was so formidable that one might have thought the governor proposed to seize the mines and operate them under some system of state socialism." "And furthermore," observed the *Times*, "isn't it ironical that the coal industry's prophets of disaster were once so eager to descend on West Virginia's coal reserves that Uncle John Lewis had little, or no difficulty, in getting his check-off of forty cents a ton for the miner's welfare fund, whereas the suggestion advanced by Governor Marland for a mere dime a ton for roads and schools brought forth the greatest wail that has been heard in West Virginia since the Year of the Big Wind."

A third *Times* editorial surveyed Marland's first six months in office and arrived at the somewhat overlooked conclusion that the governor at least had the courage to make such a proposal and to risk such defeat in the legislature dominated by members of his own party. "From this distance," wrote Smith, "this seems to have been a clue to Marland's character and seems to presage an intellectual independence not often seen in the executive office."

Thus, the highly controversial severance tax provided newspapers across the state with months of grist for their mills. Even as late as the "dog days" of August *Fairmont Times* editor, Ned Smith could still grind out some interesting commentary complete with a dose of hillbilly humor. In an August 25th editorial Smith reluctantly admitted that the state Chamber of Commerce had outsmarted Bill Marland in the area of etymology. He concluded that the governor had erred by using such a "big word" even though his purpose for proposing such a severance tax had been a noble one. In retrospect, Smith observed that before ever submitting the proposal to the legislature "Marland should have sent about 200 guys to the nethermost precincts of the state to tell the yeomanry that the governor had a smart plan to build new roads and schools and that he was going to get most of it from the absentee landlords, but that he would need everybody's help." According to Smith, then the ensuing battle cry should have been nothing more than "Tax the Bastids." He concluded his post-mortem on the battered severance tax corpse by relating an incident he purportedly witnessed while attending the annual North-South High School football game in Charleston:

> We have seen with our own eyes the effect of using that 'bad word.' Leaving the football stadium in Charleston recently after the North-South game where some people booed the governor (which seems to be an old Kanawha County custom), we fell in step with a couple of youngsters, and overheard this dialogue. 'Gee,' said one, 'there I was cheering the governor and you was booing him. How come you did that?' 'Why, haven't you heerd? He's guy that came up heah with that old severance tax. Hit would a ruint everbody.'

Reprinted with permission from *The Journal of the West Virginia Historical Association*, Volume 3, Number 1, (Spring, 1979), 1–16. Original footnotes are omitted <ed.>.

Commentary:
WHY WEST VIRGINIA NEEDS A SECRETARY OF STATE

Ken Hechler
Former Secretary of State of West Virginia

A man named Sam Chilton once ran seven times for secretary of state. He claimed he kept running because "it seems the job consists of doing nothing, and I'm an expert at that." He never got beyond the primary, probably because he did not consider the position to be important, and the voters treated his candidacy accordingly.

Over the years, the statutory responsibilities of the secretary of state have increased. In fact, West Virginia's secretary of state has a multitude of responsibilities of a policy-making nature which in many cases exceed those in other states. As chief election officer, aggressive efforts have been undertaken to clean up the corruption, vote buying and intimidation which have given West Virginia a bad reputation in the past. A strong focus on legislation and training has helped improve election practices and upgrade implementation of election laws at the county and municipal level, and a dedication to all public information and student participation have made elections more accessible to all West Virginians.

The computerization of the corporations division not only speeded up service in chartering an increasing number of corporations, but has helped bring to justice several fraudulent business activities. Service of process and uniform commercial code filings have been accomplished more speedily, and the new requirement for central filing of all farm liens has been implemented with optical disk technology.

Since 1985, West Virginia citizens and legitimate charities are protected by one of the toughest charity solicitation laws in the nation. The secretary of state has banned the "scam" operation of more than twenty out-of-state charities, while encouraging West Virginians "to give generously, but give wisely." In licensing security firms and private detectives, several successful court fights have strengthened the authority of the secretary of state in protecting West Virginians against firms hiring those with criminal records and engaging in questionable practices.

The commissions of over 32,000 notary publics are processed by the secretary of state. In addition to providing publications to inform and train notaries in proper procedure, the secretary of state has investigated and taken action on many complaints of improper practice. Several notary commissions have been revoked.

Major improvements have been made in the publication, indexing and codification of the administrative rules of departments and agencies, boards and commissions in the state.

By statute, the secretary of state serves as a member of the Armory Board . There are also a host of record-keeping responsibilities involved in keeping the executive journal of gubernatorial actions, processing gubernatorial proclamations and executive orders, filing copies of enrolled bills and oaths of office, and handling reprieves, pardons and commutation of sentences as well as extraditions.

Supervision of Elections

It is in the area of supervising elections that the need for an independent, elected secretary of state is greatest. One has only to reflect on the practices of Governors W. Wallace Barron and Arch A. Moore to see the danger of placing the supervision of elections under the thumb of the governor. Although there have been proposals that the election process be made "independent," and placed under an independent elections commission, West Virginia's history has shown that gubernatorially-appointed commissions have been subject to persuasive pressure from the incumbent governor. In several instances, independent commission members and chairmen have been forced out by governors when they took positions at variance with the governor.

One of the first reforms which I sought as secretary of state was to lengthen from 60 feet to 300 feet the distance from the polling place within which campaigning is authorized on election day. During the 1985 legislative session, there were screams of anguish from politicians, including the proclamation of a state senator that I was "out to destroy the Democratic Party," which had traditionally relied on last-minute activity of various sorts on the election grounds. I argued that most voters had their minds pretty well made up when they went to the polls, and that any voter deciding how to vote on the strength of a last-minute card was really casting an unintelligent vote. In 1985, some legislative leaders, especially in the Senate, bottled up the proposal, but by 1986 widespread public and editorial support forced its enactment. The effect on West Virginia politics has been dramatic, especially in southern West Virginia where harrassment of voters was a common practice. Once the law went into effect, many senior citizens announced that they were pleased to go to the polls without "running the gauntlet" and being hassled on the election grounds. The law also became very popular among candidates, some of whom had been blackmailed by numerous distributors of campaign cards who collected funds from candidates to perform what had been a somewhat useless service. The new law also forced candidates to concentrate on issues and organization prior to election day, and reduced the influence of "slates"—a favorite means of collecting money by machine factions pushing certain candidates.

WSAZ television anchor Bob Brunner challenged me prior to the enactment of the law on how I could enforce the 300 foot law when few voters observed the 60 foot law. I answered that the distance was easy to visualize, since it was the length of a football field, and indeed this proved to be the case. Thousands of voters were so enthusiastic about the 300 foot law that they helped all local officials enforce it when they observed violations.

Despite the fact the 300 foot bill had to wait until 1986, 1985 saw the passage of a huge 108 page election reform bill. Many of the reforms had been suggested in a special report which I solicited from the League of Women Voters the day after the 1984 election. Starting in 1986, anonymous contributions were prohibited, and such contributions were required either to be returned or given to the state's general revenue fund. For the first time in 1986, candidates and committees were required to file annual reports in March reflecting any contribution or expenditure activity over 500 dollars, and also to reveal the status of any loans not repaid. Other election reforms included easing the requirements for military, overseas and absentee voters to cast their ballots, while insuring that there were adequate protections against fraud.

On May 7, 1985, the town election in the city of Gilbert, Mingo County, produced many charges of vote-buying, voters being transported from outside city limits, and interference from the Mingo County courthouse machine. Of 350 voters, over 100 cast challenged ballots. Accompanied by five staff members and a court reporter, we conducted four intensive days of hearings in July. We then went directly to the West Virginia Supreme Court of Appeals to obtain a writ of prohibition against Mingo County Circuit Judge Eliot Maynard, who was replaced by Special Judge Dan O'Hanlon and a special prosecutor from the state attorney general's office. Although there were some technical difficulties in the indictments obtained against Mingo County officials, fortunately the developments coincided with federal interest in widespread drug activities in the town of Kermit (Mingo County). The former sheriff and Democratic county chairman, Johnie Owens, a target of both state and federal probes, quickly began to "sing" to federal authorities when it became apparent that the evidence the state had against him would result in him being sent to Moundsville, the state prison, instead of a federal facility. Eventually, Owens was sentenced to a fourteen-year term in federal prison.

My aggressive efforts also won the plaudits of many out-of-state media observers, including three telecasts by Ken Bode, national political correspondent of NBC News, the *Boston Globe*, *Pittsburgh Press*, *Miami Herald*, and *Los Angeles Times*. The effect of the investigation and prosecutions sent a clear message around the state that the secretary of state intended to enforce the election laws aggressively.

In addition to a wide series of additional reforms in voter access to the polls, campaign finance reporting, absentee voting and voter registration, we initiated a major drive to control campaign spending. Several United States Supreme Court decisions, commencing with *Buckley v. Valeo* in 1976, made it unconstitutional to place an absolute ceiling with enforcement penalties, unless accompanied by public financing. The state of West Virginia's poor financial situation made it unlikely that either the voters or Legislature would ever support public financing, so the initial efforts were directed toward passing state legislation which might challenge *Buckley v. Valeo* on the following grounds: (1) that campaign spending had sharply escalated since the 1976 decision; (2) that a states rights court might be more supportive of state efforts; and (3) that the freedom of speech of thousands of potential candidates was being deprived to a far greater extent than the millionaires protected by the First Amendment rationale of *Buckley v. Valeo*. Efforts culminated in 52 votes out of the 100 member House of Delegates in 1988 in support of a constitutional amendment to place the issue of a mandatory spending ceiling on the ballot in 1988. Although fifty-two votes was a majority, the vote fell short of the two-thirds necessary to place the amendment on the ballot.

The voluntary Code of Fair Campaign Practices in 1988 set a code of conduct and provided spending limits for candidates in public office. A majority of candidates agreed to adhere to the Code. In 1995 the Code was strengthened by statute. It has remained voluntary, but increased in stature by being codified.

Two feature articles in the *St. Petersburg Times* praised the West Virginia spending and ethical standards. In addition, there was a sharp total decrease in the amounts of money spent in legislative campaigns in 1988 as contrasted with 1986. For example, the grand total of primary and general elections expenditure for West Virginia Senate candidates in 1986 was $1,511,032.13; and in 1988, a comparable total for state Senate candidates was down to $899,881.04. In Kanawha County, twelve successful House of Delegates candidates spent $209,392.54 in the 1986 primary and general elections and in 1988 this total was down to $112,504.85.

As secretary of state, I have worked tirelessly to protect the integrity of the electoral process by ensuring that accurate and current voter registration rolls are maintained and to increase the participation of eligible West Virginians in the election process. The National Voter Registration Act of 1993 and the subsequent companion laws crafted by my office and enacted by the West Virginia Legislature have served to support this objective. For example, the number of locations and opportunities for eligible West Virginians to register to vote has increased tremendously and includes driver's licensing and other public offices, application availability by mail and through the Internet. A notary signature on applications is no longer necessary. The voter registration record maintenance procedures have been transferred to computer applications and uniform and nondiscriminatory methods are used to identify and remove the names of *only* those individuals who are no longer eligible to vote and it is done on a scheduled basis. Because of these changes, voting procedures now cater to the voter such as making a county voter's address or name change a mere matter of recording the changes when he or she votes. Once registered, a voter remains on the list of voters so long as he or she remains eligible to vote in that jurisdiction.

On July 9, 1986, the West Virginia Supreme Court of Appeals handed down a landmark decision[2] which ruled that campaign expenditures for temporary workers which exceeded limits which were "fairly commensurate with services rendered" amounted to vote buying. The court directed the secretary of state on the advice of the five-member Election Commission to promulgate the necessary regulations designed to bring these expenditures in line with services rendered.

In September 1986, a thirty-five dollar per day limit was placed on pay for temporary workers on election day (later raised to fifty dollars per day), along with a limitation of one worker per precinct. This limit was extended in 1988 to cover pre-election day workers also. Unfortunately, the 1989 legislature severely weakened these measures by repealing the one worker-per-precinct regulation.

In training election workers, my office has conducted regional workshops and seminars for county and municipal officials, as well as producing new training programs. Also, a large series of pamphletary training materials have been developed both for election officials, students and the general public.

As ex-officio member of the State Election Commission, I have activated a close working relationship with that advisory body, which has met an average of four times per year. Also, we took the lead in providing independent financing for the Election Commission outside of the budget and appropriations for the secretary of state. Despite proposals that the Election Commission take over the functions of the secretary of state, this would scarcely be possible unless the Commission were provided with an extensive staff to handle the daily flow of inquiries from counties and municipalities concerning application and interpretation of the election laws.

Improvement in Staffing and Office Procedures

All 37 staff members are trained to work at the polls on election day to assist in monitoring precincts where there has been trouble in the past, or when requests are made for monitoring to assist in proper enforcement of election laws. The secretary of state works closely with county clerks, as well as staffs of the sheriff, prosecuting attorney and city police. Volunteers from the League of Women Voters have assisted in answering telephones in the central office, thereby freeing full-time staff members to monitor or trouble-shoot in the field. Additional compliance efforts include investigations, initiating and defending court actions, auditing campaign finance reports for accuracy and completeness, consulting with county officials to improve procedures and developing rules and regulations to implement statutes.

Since 1985, we have continuously focused on using technology to improve services. In the corporations division, we made the first conversion of 200,000 corporations records from paper to database, and by the year 2000 the corporate data is available to the public for free on the Internet. In the Uniform Commercial Code division, manual searching of 350,000 paper records has been replaced by a modern imaging system. Development of prepaid accounts for regular customers and implementation of credit card acceptance has dramatically improved convenience and reduced turnaround time. A new computerized receipts process improves the security of incoming payments and accessibility of information about the status of those payments.

Public demand for services has increased dramatically, and the Legislature has continued to assign new duties to the secretary of state, including the registration of new business types, credit service organizations, and purchasers of future payments. The steady progress in technology has allowed the office to provide faster service and handle dramatic growth in the number of filings with only a small increase in personnel. For example, since 1985 the number of charitable organizations has increased by 600%, the number of notaries by 53%, the number of annual business registrations by 37%, the number of UCC lien filings by 40%, as well as an overall increase of paid transactions by an estimated 50%.

Use of the Internet in all divisions allows the public to access forms and a wealth of information online, as well as to request services by email.

Supervision of Charitable Organizations

During the last decade the number of charitable organizations registered with the secretary of state has increased 10 fold and there are currently over 1500 organizations registered to solicit funds in West Virginia.

Enforcement actions have centered on rogue charities that have solicited funds in West Virginia without filing a registration and on professional fund raisers that have acted unscrupulously. These enforcement actions have resulted in hundreds of organizations entering into settlement agreements to act within the provisions of the law governing charitable organizations and paying fines and court costs. For example, since July 1999, 19 charitable organizations have signed settlement agreements and paid thousand of dollars in fines because they had failed to meet the registration requirements and/or provide financial information about the organization. In one case Palatine Communications was permanently enjoined from conducting business as a profession solicitor in West Virginia because of repeated violations of the law.

On the legislative front, the Charity Reform Bill was passed in 1992 and included major revisions that closed loopholes in the definitions of organizations that were exempt from filing a charitable registration and provided for private and class actions with civil penalties. In 1995 the Commission on Charitable Organizations was dissolved under the sunset law. This was a result of the U.S. Fourth Circuit Court of Appeals decision in the Famine Relief Fund case which ruled unconstitutional the administrative procedure for denying a charity the right to solicit. The court found that the administrative hearing procedure did not afford sufficient due process before the prior restraint on speech because the burden of appealing the state's decision to deny registration rested with the charity and the charity was not allowed to solicit during the appeals process. The court did uphold other key provisions of the law that required that expenditures be related in a primary degree to the stated purpose described in the solicitations and that solicitations give a clear description of the programs for which funds are requested.

The secretary of state has joined other states and the Federal Trade Commission by taking part in nationwide crackdowns on fraudulent charities and fund-raising scams and encouraged donors to check out organizations before making donations. Additionally, the secretary has provided tips, education materials and individual charitable organization profiles for consumers upon request and on the Internet.

Administrative Law Division

Since 1985, we have made major improvements in the area of administrative law. When I took office, the records were in such shape that no one could tell precisely which rules of which agencies were in effect, including the agencies themselves. Agencies were adopting and filing rules which were in violation of the State Administrative Procedures Act. Now for the first time, an annual index of all rules is published, a usable *State Register* is printed weekly and agencies are directed to follow both the Administrative Procedures Act and the Open Governmental Proceedings Act. The computerization of the rules of all state agencies starting in 1986 enabled the publication of the first ever *West Virginia Code of State Rules*. The *Code* is printed in eleven volumes, includes 15,000 pages and is loose-leaf in nature to allow for ongoing additions and revisions. Prior administration had contended that publication of the *Code* would cost one million dollars, but the work was completed for $80,000 all of which came from subscription fees, copy fees and other agency services and assistance provided at no charge.

As access through various electronic services increased, the revenue in Administrative Law decreased so the Legislature appropriated money for this Division which enabled us to establish Internet services which include all rules, which are updated monthly, as well as the *Index* which is updated annually and the *State Register* which is updated weekly. The Division still has 140 paid subscriptions for paper copies of the *Code* and 125 paid subscriptions for paper copies to the *State Register*.

All of the historical rules have been indexed, optically scanned and we now have the ability to search for historical records from our desks rather than spend countless hours downstairs going through the files. Also an FTP connection was established between the West Virginia Education and State Employees Grievance Board and all grievance decisions are now filed, stamped and imaged electronically, reducing the amount of paper that flows through this office and giving us greater ability to more quickly assist the public.

Supervision of Private Detectives and Security Firms

Since 1985, we have also toughened enforcement of the statutes covering the licensing of private detectives and security firms. Early in 1985, the United Mine Workers filed a complaint with the secretary of state that a security firm named Southeastern Security and Investigations guarding the A.T. Massey mines in Mingo County had a felon on its payroll—in direct violation of the statute. The security firm refused to furnish a list of its employees to enable my office to conduct an investigation to determine the validity of the charge. After protracted court proceedings, the Supreme Court of Appeals directed the release of the employee list, and investigation revealed not one but six employees with felony records. I then revoked the license of Southeastern Security and Investigations, and successfully defended that action against another series of court challenges.

In addition to the Southeastern case, we brought action in Kanawha County Circuit Court against a firm which was operating an investigative business without a license, resulting in a judgment and fine against that firm. We also compelled several unlicensed private detective firms to cease conducting business.

In 1987, a former employee of the security firm of Pinkerton's . . . filed suit against the secretary of state in both his personal and official capacity, asking for $1.25 million in punitive and compensatory damages because the employee was fired from his job as a security guard at a local coal company. Acting on a complaint originally filed by the United Mine Workers that the individual had a bad employment record, my office conducted an independent investigation to verify that the employee had been separated from a large number of jobs and involved in several court cases reflecting use of excessive force as a police officer. . . The . . . suit was heard in U.S. District Court in Charleston before a jury. The jury became convinced of the secretary of state's actions, and on all counts refused to award a cent to the employee thereby vindicating our action. . . Following the decision, the *Charleston Gazette* editorialized on August 6, 1988:

> "Secretary of State Ken Hechler has won a victory that should be a lesson for government officials all over West Virginia. Mired in a lawsuit, Hechler didn't pay a settlement to get rid of his accuser, as many office holders do. Instead, the secretary fought back and defeated the suit completely."

Although the only responsibility outlined in West Virginia's Constitution for the secretary of state is that he is keeper of the Great Seal, a series of statutes have given a host of duties and responsibilities as outlined above. The secretary of state in many instances is a policy-making official, especially in his role as chief election official.

Notes

[1] See *West Virginia Code* 15-64, 29-19-3, 5-6-1, 5-4-1.
[2] *Rogers v. Hechler*, 348 S.E. 2d 299 (WV., 1986).
[3] See *West Virginia Code* 29A-1-1 *et seq.*
[4] See *West Virginia Code* 6-9A-1 *et seq.*
[5] See *West Virginia Code* 29A-2-8

Commentary:
OFFICE OF THE ATTORNEY GENERAL

Mario J. Palumbo
Former Attorney General, West Virginia

The Office of the Attorney General in state government has its origins in Anglo-American history. When the American colonies were founded, what had existed as the position of "attorney general" was brought to the colonies and developed into a more structured form. After the Revolutionary War, the office of attorney general started to appear in state constitutions.[1]

The Office of Attorney General was first created in West Virginia in the Constitution of 1863. In the Constitution, adopted in West Virginia by the Constitutional Convention of 1872, Article VII created an executive department which included the attorney general.[2] Today, the attorney general is continued in the Constitution of West Virginia in Article VII, Section 1, which provides, in part, that the attorney general ". . . shall perform such duties as may be prescribed by law." The office as created and established is a statewide office and the attorney general is elected by popular vote. He is also the state's lawyer. In addition, he has the responsibility to take a role in addressing public issues as his work with legal issues and public policy provides him the necessary background to speak with authority in this area.

The State's Lawyer

The attorney general holds an unique office in West Virginia government. He is the legal representative of the State of West Virginia and its citizens. As such, he is required to give legal advice to the governor and state agencies, to prosecute and defend suits, and to appear in court on behalf of the governor, the state, and its agencies.[3] Moreover, the attorney general is frequently called upon by the legislative branch to render legal advice and opinions.

Much like a large law firm in the private sector, the Office of the Attorney General is divided into specialized areas of practice. This structure helps develop teams of legal experts in the respective divisions of the office in an effort to provide the state with the best possible representation available. These specialized areas are: the Client Services Division, the Appellate Division, the Civil Rights Division, the Environment and Energy Division, the Consumer Protection Division, and the Antitrust Division.

The Client Services Division

As the state's legal council, the attorney general, by law, represents all state agencies and state officers. This representation entails defense of state officials in any suit brought against them or their agencies in state or federal courts. For example, this could involve defending the constitutionality of a law or challenges to the scope of the enforcement power of a law.

The Client Services Division, the largest division of the attorney general's office, is charged with the responsibility of serving as legal council to these many agencies and officers. The division also prosecutes on behalf of the state's agencies. The collection of taxes, the revocation of driver's licenses, and the enforcement of environmental statutes are examples of the many areas of practice handled by the division. Further, the division gives day-to-day legal advice to state agencies regarding the application of state and federal law to their respective departments.

The Appellate Division

Of the six divisions mentioned in this article, the one with the longest history in the attorney general's office is the Appellate Division. This division represents the state on appeals by criminal defendants from convictions in West Virginia's circuit courts. It also represents the state in *habeas corpus* proceedings—collateral attacks by a prisoner on his conviction—before the West Virginia Supreme Court of Appeals and at the federal court level.

On occasion, attorneys in this division become directly involved in criminal prosecutions at the trial level. Usually this occurs when a prosecutor is disqualified from taking a case. Accordingly, the Appellate people work closely with prosecuting attorneys throughout West Virginia.

Although the work of the division consists primarily of criminal appeals, it does provide counsel to the Legislature, the Human Rights Commission and, the Civil Service Commission. It may additionally serve as legal counsel to a circuit court judge, when he or she is named as a respondent in a writ action before the state supreme court. Finally, the division works closely with the Clerk of the West Virginia Supreme Court of Appeals in tracking the docket for the purpose of identifying cases in which the state or an agency has an interest.

The Civil Rights Division

The Civil Rights Division was created, primarily, in response to the West Virginia Supreme Court of Appeals decision, *Allen v. State Human Rights Commission*, 324 S.E. 2d 99 (1984), in which the court cemented the statutory relationship between the attorney general's office and the Human Rights Commission. The court in the Allen decision set procedural mechanisms for complainants to have their discrimination cases heard before the commission in an expeditious manner.

Some two months after the Allen decision, the Civil Rights Division was established to assist the Commission in assuring that equal opportunity exists in the areas of employment and public accommodations regardless of race, religion, color, national origin, ancestry, sex, age, blindness, handicap, or familial status. The division represents the Commission in these areas, and not individual complaints. Much like a county prosecutor, the division presents the complainant's case before a hearing examiner in an effort to seek appropriate legal remedy. . . .

The Consumer Protection Division

The Consumer Protection Division of the attorney general's office is responsible for enforcing the West Virginia Consumer Credit and Protection Act (WV Code 46A-1-101 *et seq.*), which regulates sales practices, debt collection activities, and consumer credit contracts. Such enforcement often involves federal consumer protection statutes as well because violations of these laws are often considered *per se* violations of state law. . . .

The West Virginia Consumer Credit and Protection Act gives the attorney general the authority to conduct confidential investigations and subpoena testimony and records relating to possible violations of the Act. If a violation is found, the attorney general may file a lawsuit to obtain injunctive relief, restitution for injured consumers, and assess a civil penalty. As an alternative to judicial action, the attorney general may accept an assurance of discontinuance, whereby the business whose conduct could be subject to a court order agrees to discontinue the practice in question.

One interesting component of the attorney general's influence in the area of state consumer protection laws is his rule-making authority. To date, the attorney general has promulgated legislative rules—those approved by the state legislature—in a variety of areas including lemon laws, health spa contracts and home improvements. These rules strengthen existing law and help to further protect the citizenry.

A valuable service the division performs is the mediation of consumer complaints. Paraprofessionals assigned to the division attempt to resolve individual complaints. This intermediary process opens the lines of communication between the business and consumer and often resolves the issue favorably for the consumer. Additionally, the mediation process provides the data required by the division to identify patterns of unfair and deceptive practices which trigger formal investigation and enforcement procedures.

The division protects consumers in a proactive manner by educating consumers to their rights as well as educating businesses to their responsibilities. Division representatives regularly speak to citizens groups, trade associations and appear on radio and television programs dealing with consumer issues. The division also provides consumer education materials to the public including several pamphlets published in-house.

The Environment and Energy Division

This division of the attorney general's office primarily serves as legal counsel to the state's Division of Natural Resources and Department of Energy. The representation of these two entities entails a wide range of activities including administrative law actions, civil actions, and the subsequent appeals, in state and federal courts. These suits include actions for injunctive relief to compel compliance with environmental laws, rules, permits and orders issued by the clients; penalty actions to recover money for violations of laws, rules permits and orders; and defense actions attacking the constitutionality of the environmental laws and applicability of laws in various businesses and industries.

As legal counsel to these state departments, the Environment and Energy Division is often called upon to interpret the application of state environmental laws and to assist in the preparation of contracts, forms and other administrative matters.

On behalf of the Department of Energy, the attorney general's office pursues cases involving surface and deep mining, reclamation and related water problems, bond forfeitures, health and safety issues, oil and gas industry problems, and administrative concerns. This division also offers its services on a variety of issues to the Parks and Recreation Division of the Department of Commerce, the Agriculture Department, the Environmental Sciences section of the Department of Health and several state administrative boards.

The Antitrust Division

The Antitrust Division was created in July 1968 to enforce the West Virginia Antitrust Act (WV Code 47-18-1 *et seq.*). This division enforces the Act and certain provisions of federal antitrust laws and works to keep the free market system open and fair to all. It protects the interest of the consumer and businessperson and seeks to prevent the forming of monopolies, price fixing, restraining trade, and conspiracies to divide markets or customers.

It investigates all reported violations of the state antitrust laws and seeks to institute civil enforcement proceedings against violators. Antitrust issues are generally complex in nature and require extensive investigation.

The division commences actions in either state or federal court on behalf of the State of West Virginia and, where consumers are effected, on behalf of consumers to obtain injunctive relief, to seek civil penalties and to recover the costs of the investigation. It also works with other states in presenting *amicus* briefs before the United States Supreme Court and in other federal courts where arguments are presented concerning federal antitrust laws. The Division works with the Antitrust Division of the United States Department of Justice and the Bureau of Competition of the Federal Trade Commission, often sharing information and ideas relating to antitrust enforcement. . . .

Policy-Making

The policy-making role of the Attorney General is due to his importance as a statewide leader. The Attorney General as policy-maker develops ideas and programs that go beyond simply interpreting the law and representing the state. He has a moral obligation to address issues, laws, and public policy that he determines are in the best interest of the people of West Virginia. Policy-making is of critical interest to the citizenry because the power of the office can provide insight into important issues and changes that are needed for the common good.

For example, in my role as policy-maker, I organized a group of citizens, including environmental experts, to address problems concerning solid waste. This group of approximately twenty West Virginians had meetings, did a considerable amount of research, and proposed corrective legislation. My role in this process was to solicit assistance from several notable law professors at the West Virginia University College of law. These professionals were involved in reviewing the issue and proposed legislation from a constitutional perspective. The major ideas of this combined group of concerned citizens, environmental experts and legal scholars included:

1. limiting the amount of garbage at class A landfills to 20,000 tons per month;

2. limiting the amount of garbage from outside the landfill's own area to the same amount that is generated and deposited from that area;

3. a study to determine whether a statewide composting program would substantially reduce the amount of trash generated in West Virginia.

These ideas were incorporated into a bill which was introduced in the Legislature during the 1991 regular session. Unfortunately, the bill was not enacted. I plan, however, to have the bill introduced again during the next legislative session.

Concluding Remarks

The Office of the Attorney General then is an exciting office that combines stimulating challenges in the practice of law with the intrinsic rewards of public service. As attorney general, a major goal of mine has been to attract and retain the highest level of competent and dedicated lawyers to represent the State of West Virginia. My recommendation to young citizens is to continue their education, study the law, and consider the great benefits offered by the Office of the Attorney General. The vast experience that a young lawyer gains by serving the public in the attorney general's office is unmatched in the private sector.

Notes

[1] Lynne M. Ross, *State Attorneys General, Powers and Responsibilities*, (Washington, DC: BNA Books, 1990), 3.

[2] Lyell B. Clay, *The Attorney General of West Virginia*, (Office of the Attorney General: Charleston, WV, 1957), 7–8.

[3] *State ex rel. Caryl v. MacQueen*, 385 S.E. 2d 646 (WV, 1969), 649, 650.

CHAPTER FIVE

Judicial
Policy-Making

INTRODUCTION

The West Virginia Constitution provides in Article VIII, Section 1, that the third branch of government shall be "The Judiciary" and that:

> "The judicial power of the State shall be vested solely in a supreme court of appeals and in circuit courts, and in . . . such intermediate appellate courts and magistrate courts as shall be hereafter established by the Legislature, and in the justices, judges and magistrates of such courts."

The constitution also provides that:

> "the Supreme Court of Appeals shall have original jurisdiction of proceedings in *habeas corpus*, *mandamus*, prohibition and *certiorari*[1] . . . have appellate jurisdiction in . . . civil cases at law where the matter in controversy, exclusive of interest and costs, is greater value or amount than three hundred dollars . . . ; in civil cases in equity; in controversies concerning the title or boundaries of land . . . in cases involving personal freedom or the constitutionality of a law . . . appellate jurisdiction in criminal cases . . . <and> The court shall have power to promulgate rules for all cases and proceedings, civil and criminal . . . general supervisory control over all intermediate appellate courts, circuit courts and magistrate courts. . . ."[2]

The last few of these provisions reflect a referendum that amended the West Virginia Constitution (Judicial Reorganization Amendment, 1974) which provided the Supreme Court of Appeals with administrative supervision over inferior courts and also replaced Justices of the Peace with a Magistrate system.[3]

In this introduction we are concerned with the organization and functioning of the courts as part of the political process. We are also concerned with judicial decision making in the extension of religious liberty to the Jehovah's Witnesses, a religious minority in West Virginia and the controversial Wheeling Suspension Bridge case.

Function of the Courts in West Virginia

Constitutionally, the courts in West Virginia have the authority to make important decisions that affect state government and all West Virginians. One

211

way that the court system does this is to "dispense justice through interpretation of law."[4] Although there is a clearly established hierarchy of law, e.g., "Supremacy Clause," Article VI, U.S. Constitution (see Chapter 1), and in so far as the West Virginia Constitution does not conflict with the U. S. Constitution,[5] the West Virginia Constitution is the supreme law of the state. It is this document, and statutes enacted by the legislature pursuant to it, as well as procedural rules promulgated by the Supreme Court of Appeals, that the state courts usually interpret when they invoke state law.

Law passed by the legislature supersedes much of the old English common law that was in effect in Virginia prior to the formation of West Virginia.[6] "Common law"[7] is largely judge-made law based on previous decisions, *stare decisis*, or "let the previous decision stand," and is applied by the courts in controversies where there are no relevant state statutes.

Another distinction in "state law" is the dichotomy between civil law and criminal law.[8] A large percentage of the laws in West Virginia are civil (sometimes called private)[9] which govern the relationships between private citizens in the general areas of property and individual rights. Although technically the state is not a legal party in civil law cases, it does have a role to impartially arbitrate such disputes.

Criminal laws (sometimes called public)[10] are concerned with the state's political or sovereign capacity of maintaining order and regulating its citizens. Criminal law cases involve offenses (misdemeanors and felonies; see Table 5.1) against the state and are prosecuted by the state.[11]

It might appear from the above that the courts and judges are required to "apply unambiguous and impartial law" to social disputes in a way that minimizes politics. However, such is not always the case. Rather, it is possible to argue that, as "checkers," the courts are part of the political process in West Virginia rather than distinctly separate from it. For instance, judges are selected through partisan elections and, no matter how hard they may try to avoid it, they are frequently embroiled in political controversies when they decide important questions of "who gets what, when, and how."

This is because courts in West Virginia must resolve political controversies that other branches of government are unwilling or incapable of dealing with. For example, in May 1982, the Circuit Court of Kanawha County, with special judge Arthur M. Recht presiding, ruled in *Pauley, et al. v. Bailey*, a lawsuit remanded to it from the West Virginia Supreme Court of Appeals, that the entire system of education in West Virginia should be re-constructed. Judge Recht based his ruling on the testimony of educational "experts" and the interpretation of law established in *Pauley, et al. v. Kelly et al.* (1979) that the unequal funding of county schools in West Virginia is unconstitutional because it violates the West Virginia Constitution's mandate that the schools must provide a "thorough and efficient education" for all students in the state. Moreover, he argued that "our basic law makes education's funding second in priority only to payment of the state debt, and ahead of every other function. . . ." (*Pauley et al. v. Bailey et al.*, 1982:239).

This case was re-opened in early 1995 upon a motion by the original plaintiff's attorney, Dan Hedges in Kanawha County Circuit Court, with senior status Judge Dan Robinson assigned to preside. Hedges argued: "This is the issue that has been largely, in fact, totally unaddressed by the legislature . . . the Court has given the legislature 12 years to remedy the situation."[12]

An attorney for Speaker of the House of Delegates, Chuck Chambers and President Earl Tomblin of the West Virginia Senate retorted: "Our contention is that this court is without the authority to order the legislature to make (specific) appropriations. . . . It is not a simple thing."[13]

As this manuscript goes to press, the twenty-year-old Recht decision is still not fully implemented. The parties have made some progress but implementation has been stalled with disagreement over details.[14] For example, House of Delegates speaker Bob Kiss admitted: ". . . there clearly were severe problems with school facilities, program delivery and student performance when the suit was filed . . ."[15] But . . .<he argued> the lawsuit has "perpetually concentrated on resources not on results. The state has made considerable progress through such things as the School Building Authority, and computers in the classroom initiatives."[16]

Bills have been introduced in the current session of the Legislature to revise the net enrollment cap and provide for the addition of 700 new service personnel and 200 teachers. The next hearing before Judge Recht will be about six weeks after the end of the current 2002 legislative session.[17]

State Court Organization[18]

West Virginia has three tiers of courts (see Figure 5.1).[19] The lowest courts are its courts of limited jurisdiction. These courts are called magistrate and municipal courts. The state's fifty-five counties have 154 magistrates (at least two per county) who hear cases dealing with torts, contracts, and misdemeanors, including DUI and traffic. Their felony jurisdiction is limited to preliminary matters (warrants, bail, and bindover to grand jury). In civil cases the magistrates are limited to disputes that do not exceed $5,000.[20]

Magistrates are elected to four-year terms by the people of the county and the constitution does not require that they be lawyers to hold office and it prohibits the legislature from requiring them to be lawyers. Normally the division of caseload work for a magistrate court, especially when there is more than one magistrate, is determined by the chief judge of the circuit court for that county

The constitution authorizes the legislature to allow the establishment of municipal, police or so-called mayor's courts for the state's 228 cities and towns. There are 122 municipal courts and 122 municipal judges in West Virginia.[21] These courts have limited jurisdiction in DUI, traffic, parking, and other ordinance cases. Both magistrate and municipal courts are authorized to grant jury trials.[22] Criminal defendants in magistrate courts are entitled to a jury trial, and are so entitled if the offense charged carries a jail penalty. Municipal courts are not under the administrative supervision of the Supreme Court of Appeals.

The next level of courts in West Virginia are the Circuit Courts. The state's fifty-five counties are divided into thirty-one circuits (so that there may be more

Figure 5.1 West Virginia Court Structure

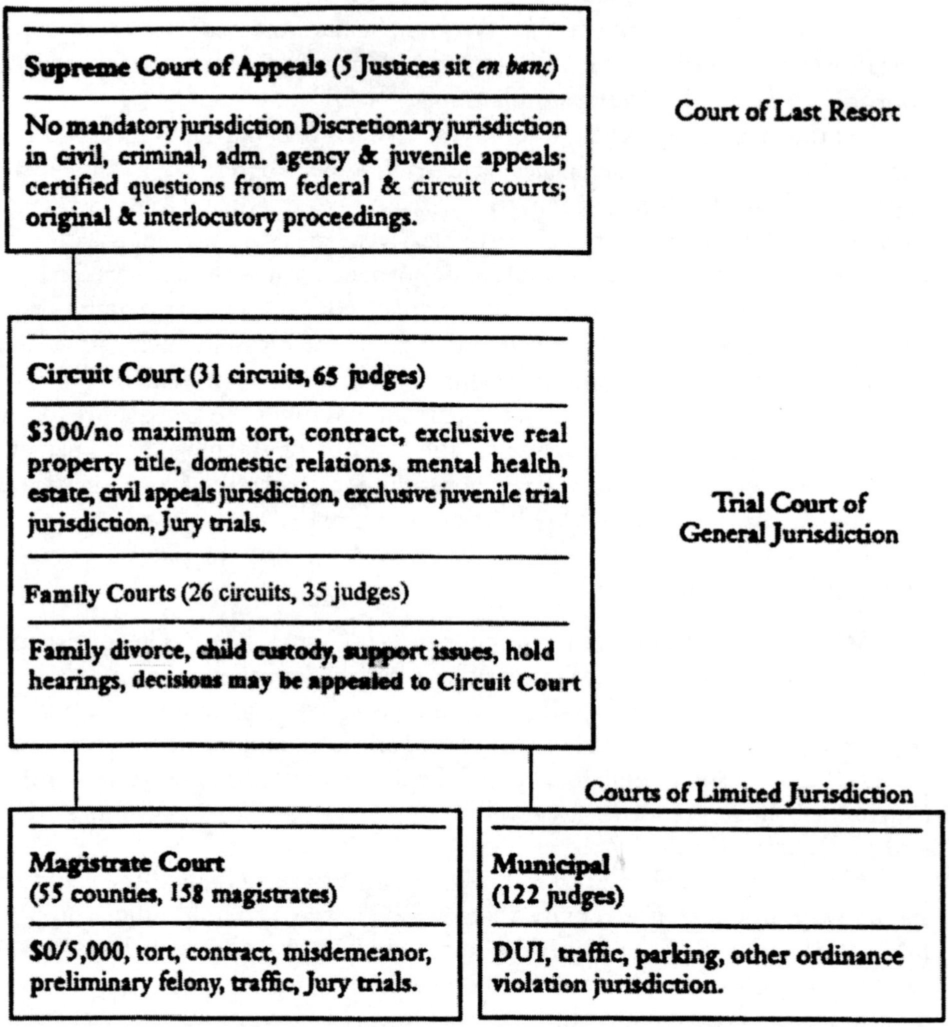

Supreme Court of Appeals (5 Justices sit *en banc*) No mandatory jurisdiction Discretionary jurisdiction in civil, criminal, adm. agency & juvenile appeals; certified questions from federal & circuit courts; original & interlocutory proceedings.	Court of Last Resort
Circuit Court (31 circuits, 65 judges) $300/no maximum tort, contract, exclusive real property title, domestic relations, mental health, estate, civil appeals jurisdiction, exclusive juvenile trial jurisdiction, Jury trials. **Family Courts** (26 circuits, 35 judges) Family divorce, child custody, support issues, hold hearings, decisions may be appealed to Circuit Court	Trial Court of General Jurisdiction

Courts of Limited Jurisdiction

Magistrate Court (55 counties, 158 magistrates) $0/5,000, tort, contract, misdemeanor, preliminary felony, traffic, Jury trials.	**Municipal** (122 judges) DUI, traffic, parking, other ordinance violation jurisdiction.

Source: David B. Rottman, *et al. State Court Organization, 1993,*(Washington, D.C.: U.S. Department of Justice, Bureau of Justice Statistics. 1995), 397; Richard A. Brisbin, Jr., "The West Virginia Judiciary," in *West Virginia's State Government: the Legislative, Executive and Judicial Branches*, Christopher Z. Mooney, *et al.*, Policy Monograph Series, No. 5, Institute for Public Affairs, West Virginia University, 1993), 61–3;http://www.state.wv.us/wvsca/wvsystem.htm

Figure 5.2

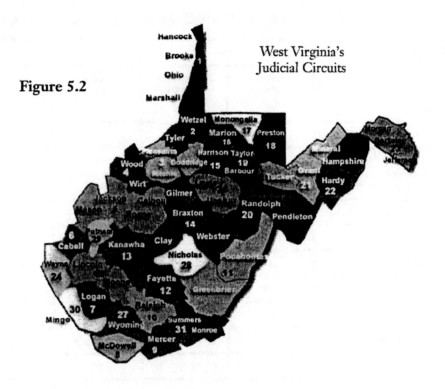

West Virginia's
Judicial Circuits

Source: http://www.state.wv.us/wvsca/circuits/map.htm

than one county in some judicial circuits). Each circuit elects at least one and some several judges for eight year terms (there are presently sixty-five judges).[23] According to the constitution, circuit judges must be members of the state bar for a least five years before being elected. These judges are required to hold at least three judicial sessions per year in each county within their circuits, called terms of court.

The circuit courts are courts of general jurisdiction and the most important cases coming before them are torts, contracts, title to real property, domestic relations, mental health, guardianship, conservatorship, estate, and civil appeals from magistrate courts.[24] These courts also hear misdemeanors (including DUI), felonies, juvenile cases, civil and criminal appeals from magistrate courts.[25] The minimum monetary jurisdiction is $300 with no maximum limit. Finally, record keeping matters within the court's county jurisdiction are handled by a circuit court clerk. The clerk is elected by the county's voters for a six-year term.[26]

In response to voters' 73% support of the Unified Family Court Amendment in the 2000 general election, the West Virginia Legislature in special session (April 4, 2001) recodified the domestic relations law. The law created an independent family court system with 26 circuits and 35 family court judges. The family court judges are required by the statute to have practiced law for at least five years.[27]

215

Figure 5.3   West Virginia Supreme Court of Appeals Case Filings

Discretionary Petition Disposition	1999		2000	
	Total Considered	Percentage Granted	Total Considered	Percentage Granted
Certified	17	35%	10	60%
Certiorari	6	67%	4	50%
Civil	456	30%	431	28.5%
Civil – Administrative	11	36%	11	.09%
Civil – Abuse & Neglect	96	11%	120	.025%
Compensation	1874	51%	2298	65%
Criminal	234	18%	194	20.6%
Habeas Corpus	108	.05%	91	.02%
Mandamus	132	30%	142	39%
Petition for Bail	16	0%	17	5.8%
Prohibition	113	27%	85	26%
TOTALS	**3063**	**40.5%**	**3403**	**51.6%**

Workload and Outcomes

The impact of the number of compensation filings in recent years is evident in the Court's 2000 workload. At both the petition and granted stage of review, 2000 marked a sharp increase in the number of cases considered and disposed.

The Court considered a total of 3,403 discretionary petitions in 2000, an increase of 340 from the 3063 petitions considered in 1999. The largest increase in the number of petitions considered was in the compensation category, where the court considered over 400 more cases in 2000 than it did in 1999, evidencing the Court's effort to keep up with the high number of filings in recent years.

Source: http://www.state.wv.us/wvsca/stats/2000/00final.htm

The family court judges currently are appointed by the governor and in 2002 they will run in partisan elections for an initial six year term. Their subsequent terms will be for eight years.[28]

The highest level of court in West Virginia is the Supreme Court of Appeals with five justices who sit *en banc* (together) to hear cases (see Figure 5.3). This court is commonly referred to as a "Court of Last Resort," and has primarily appellate jurisdiction over circuit court and administrative agency decisions. It also answers certified questions[29] from the circuit and federal courts. As noted above, the court also has original jurisdiction. Acceptance of cases for review is altogether discretionary on the part of the court.

The justices are elected on a staggered basis for twelve-year terms with a justice chosen on a seniority rotation to serve as chief justice. Each justice is required for minimum eligibility to have been a member of the state bar for ten years.[30]

Table 5.1   General Information—West Virginia Courts

Supreme Court of Appeals

How many terms does the court have?	There are two terms per year. The first term runs from the second Tuesday in January and ends in July. The second term begins on the first Wednesday in September and ends in December. The time period between terms is called *sine die* (without day).
Who makes the decision to grant/deny discretionary petitions for review?	*en banc;* majority of justices present; 3 required for quorum
Does the court use pre-argument settlement conferences?	yes
Does the court allow oral arguments in lieu of briefs?	no
Are written majority opinions required for cases requiring "decisions" on the merits?	no
Which majority opinions are published?	all
Does the court sit in cities other than the state capitol?	yes
What is the minimum age requirement?	30 (no maximum age)
Requirement to be a member of the State Bar?	yes, member 10 years
Method of initial selection to fill unexpired term until next general election?	gubernatorial appointment

Table 5.1 (continued)

Method of selection for full term?	partisan election; statewide geographic basis for selection; 12 year terms
Method of selection of chief justice?	rotation by seniority; one-year term
Who formally presents the budget to the legislature?	Supreme Court of Appeals; annual 7/1 - 6/30; WV Constitution, Art. 6, sec. 51 (4) prohibits the Legislature from decreasing any budget item relating to the judiciary.

West Virginia Trial Courts

Number of state trial court judges?

Circuit Court	65, law trained
Family Court	35, law trained
Magistrate Court	158, not req. to be lawyers
Municipal Court	0 law trained; 122 lay

What items are totally funded by the State of West Virginia to the trial courts?	judicial salaries (circuit, magistrate courts); court reporters' and probation officers' salaries; other personnel salaries (magistrate, court staff); equipment, (e.g., computers, typewriters, copiers); travel (circuit and magistrate).
What are the characteristics of felony jurisdiction in the West Virginia trial courts?	*Circuit Courts:* no minimum sentence; no minimum fine; 12 months maximum sentence for a misdemeanor; guilty pleas are accepted in this court; court may accept a guilty plea to a felony reduced to a misdemeanor; court may dismiss a felony; may pronounce sentence for a felony; this court may not bind a felony case to another court for adjudication.
	Magistrate Courts: 12 months maximum sentence length of a misdemeanor; felonies may be initially filed in this court; court may not accept a guilty plea to a felony; court may

Table 5.1 (continued)

accept a guilty plea to a
felony reduced to a misdemean-
or if charge filed originally
in magistrate court; may
dismiss a felony without
prejudice; may not pronounce
sentence for a felony; must
bind a felony case to an-
other court for adjudication.

What are the requirements and
qualifications of West Virginia
trial court judges?

Circuit Courts: must satisfy
a residency requirement; minimum age 30; 5 years as member
of state bar required.

Magistrate Courts: residency
requirement; minimum age 21;
high school diploma or equi-
valent; no law degree required,
but some training in the
rudiments of law and procedure required by statute
before assuming duties.
Magistrates are required to
attend continuing education
classes after election.

What are the methods of selection
and terms of state trial court judges?

Circuit Courts: method of
selection to fill unexpired
term until next general election
is by gubernatorial appointment;
method of selection for full term is
by partisan election; 8-year terms;
Chief judge is selected by and
serves at the pleasure of the court;
judges can succeed themselves.

Magistrate Courts: method of selection to fill unexpired term until the
next general election is by circuit
judge appointment; method of
selection for full term is by

partisan election; the geographic
basis for selection is the county;
4-year terms.

Municipal Courts: method of
selection is locally determined;

Table 5.1 (continued)

	the municipality is the basis for selection.
What are the requirements for jury size and vote for verdict?	*Circuit Courts:* 12-member juries, and unanimous decisions required for felonies; the same requirements are in place for misdemeanors; in civil trials a 6-member jury is allowed; 5/6 decision rule. *Magistrate Courts:* 6-member juries, and unanimous decisions required for misdemeanors; civil trials 6-member juries with unanimous decisions required, a smaller majority is allowed.

Family Courts

Number of family court judges?	35 judges who serve 26 family court circuits. Family court judges are first appointed by governor and then subsequently elected to 6-year terms.
What are their duties and jurisdictions?	Family court judges hear cases dealing with divorce, annulment, family support, separate maintenance, child custody, paternity and visitation
Do the family court judges follow an adversarial, due process procedure?	Yes

Source: Richard Rosswurm, Administrative Office, West Virginia Supreme Court of Appeals; David B. Rottman, *et al. State Court Organization*, 1993 (Washington, D.C.: U.S. Department of Justice, Bureau of Justice Statistics, 1995), *passim*, http://www.state.wv.us/wvsca/wvsystem.htm

The articles in this chapter deal with judicial decision making at both the appellate and local court levels. They show that the courts do not work in a vacuum, rather are affected by the institutional settings and the political process of which they are a part.

We start with Ancil Ramey's analysis of the institutional role of the Supreme Court of Appeals in its decision making. He shows that the Supreme Court of Appeals performs several highly visible roles and at least one role—administration of the judicial system—is less visible and frequently overlooked.

Next, Chuck Smith details how the Jehovah's Witnesses contributed to religious liberty in West Virginia. He traces the historical events in West Virginia that "grabbed" the attention of the nation and helped to expand the United States Supreme Court's protection of First Amendment rights.

Finally, Douglas McKay presents the background to a little known legal controversy over the famous Wheeling Suspension Bridge that lasted from 1849 to 1856. The builder of the bridge, the Wheeling and Belmont Bridge Company, was challenged in a complaint from the State of Pennsylvania that the Wheeling Suspension Bridge would obstruct the navigation of the Ohio River. McKay carefully notes that the real parties of interest were the owners of steamboat packets and the commercial shippers of Pittsburgh. Interestingly, the controversy was not resolved until the United States Congress decreed that "the bridge across the Ohio River at Wheeling" was a lawful structure.

The Wheeling Suspension Bridge and Jehovah's Witnesses cases reveal quite clearly the intergovernmental nature of judicial decision making in our federal system and how what started as local problems became important national issues.

Notes

[1] By *habeas corpus* is meant "you have the body. A writ to an official having custody of another ordering him to produce the prisoner for the purpose of allowing the court to ascertain the legality of the prisoner's detention." *Mandamus* means "a writ <that orders> an individual or organization to perform some specified action" (See Harold J. Spaeth, *An Introduction to Supreme Court Decision Making*, Revised Edition, San Francisco: Chandler Publishing Company, 1972), 77–81. Prohibition refers to ". . . a writ issued by a superior court, directed to the judge and parties of a suit in an inferior court, commanding them to cease the prosecution of the same, upon a suggestion that the cause originally, or some collateral matter arising therein, does not belong to that jurisdiction, but to the cognizance of some other court . . . ," Henry Campbell Black, *Black's Law Dictionary* (St. Paul, MN: West Publishing Company, 1968), 1377; by *certiorari* is meant "a request from the losing party in a case that the decision be reviewed by a higher court. Acceptance of the request and issuance of a writ of *certiorari* is discretionary with the higher court." Spaeth, *loc. cit.*

[2] *The Constitution of West Virginia*, Article VIII, sec. 3.

[3] David A. Bingham and John E. Tyler, "West Virginia State Government Organization," *The West Virginia Public Affairs Reporter*, Vol. 2, #1, (Morgantown, West Virginia: Bureau of Government Research, 1977), 4.

[4] See Walter Jacob, "Courts" in *Politics in the American States, a Comparative Analysis*, fourth edition, Virginia Gray, Herbert Jacob and Kenneth N. Vines, eds., (Boston: Little, Brown and Company, 1983), 222-224.

[5] There are notable exceptions to this hierarchy. In *Robbins v. Prune Yard Shopping Center*, 23 Cal. 3d 899, 592 p.2d 341 (1979), the U.S. Supreme Court found that state constitutions can create broader free speech rights than those found in the U.S. Constitution. The *Prune Yard* case is an example of "Judicial Federalism," i.e., state appellate courts are increasingly grounding their decisions on the language of their own constitutions, rather than the U.S. Constitution, suggesting that the states are finding, once again, that state constitutions are "becoming guardians of civil liberties." See Ann O'M. Bowman and Richard C. Kearney, *State and Local Government*, fourth edition (Boston & New York: Houghton Mifflin Company, 1999), 55.

[6] Claude J. Davis, *et al.*, *West Virginia State and Local Government* (Morgantown, WV: Bureau for Government Research, West Virginia University, 1963), 225.

7   "The evidence of what is common law is to be found in the decisions of the courts of justice and the treatises of learned jurists. The reports of judicial decisions contain the most certain evidence of the common law and all properly constituted courts consider it their duty to adhere to the authority of adjudicated cases." See *Michie's Jurisprudence of Virginia and West Virginia, Common Law* (Charlottesville: The Michie Company, 1951), Vol. III, sec. 9; Davis, *op. cit.*, 226.

8   See *Black's Law Dictionary*; Robert S. Summers, *et al.*, *Law: It's Nature, Functions, and Limits*, third edition, (St. Paul: West Publishing Company, 1986), *passim.*

9   Davis, *op. cit.*, 227.

10 *Ibid.*

11 *Ibid.*

12 "Lawmakers Not Excused From Recht Case," *Charleston Daily Mail*, March, 1955, 4D.

13 *Ibid.*

14 Erik Eyre, "Parties Fail to Reach Settlement on Recht Decision Lawsuit Over School Funding Court Ruling, Hung up on Details, Returns to the Courtroom Today," *Charleston Gazette*, July 31, 2000, 1C.

15 Phil Kabler, "Kiss Wants to End Monitoring," *Charleston Gazette*, January 26, 2002, 3A

16 *Ibid.*

17 *Ibid.*

18 The author is indebted to Dr. Richard Rosswurm, Administrative Office, West Virginia Supreme Court of Appeals, who reviewed an earlier draft and provided helpful materials on the organization of courts in West Virginia.

19 See David B. Rothman, *et al.*, *State Court Organization, 1993* (Washington, D.C.: U.S. Department of Justice, Bureau of Justice Statistics, 1995), 397.

20 *Ibid.*

21 *Ibid.*

22 *Ibid.*

23 http://www.state.wv.us/wvsca/wvsystem.htm

24 *Ibid.*

25 Bingham & Tyler, *loc. cit.*

26 *Ibid.*

27 Fanny Seiler, "Governor Appoints 32 Family Court Judges," *Charleston Gazette*, November 20, 2001, 4C; there are also several juvenile referees serving Kanawha, Caball and Wayne Counties. Among other duties, these referees hold detention hearings when a juvenile is arrested or detailed by the authorities. In most counties magistrates act as juvenile referees.

28 http://www.state.wv.us/wvsca/wvsystem.htm

29 Rosswurm, *loc. cit.*

30 *Ibid.*

Web Sites

http://www.ncsconline.org/
National Center for State Courts
http://www.state.wv.us/wvsca/
(West Virginia Supreme Court of Appeals)
http://www.CouncilQuest.com/
(Council Quest, a good general site on legal information)
http://www.fbi.gov
(Federal Bureau of Investigation)

Commentary:
THE IMPACT OF THE INSTITUTIONAL ROLE ON JUDICIAL DECISION-MAKING IN THE SUPREME COURT OF APPEALS OF WEST VIRGINIA

Ancil G. Ramey
Former Clerk, Supreme Court of Appeals
of West Virginia

INTRODUCTION

The institutional role of the Supreme Court of Appeals of West Virginia has a profound impact on the performance of its decision-making function. Its role defines both the manner and scope of its interpretation of constitutional, statutory, regulatory, and common law principles. Through a process of resolving individual disputes, the Supreme Court of Appeals establishes legal precedents which govern social, political, and economic behavior throughout the State of West Virginia.

As an appellate court, the Supreme Court of Appeals has four major institutional roles. First, the most obvious role is just resolution of individual disputes. Second, the most traditional role is correction of errors committed by lower tribunals. Third, the most overlooked role is administration of the judicial system. Finally, the most visible role is law development. A brief discussion of each of these institutional roles will serve to clarify the decision-making process of the Supreme Court of Appeals.

Rendition of Justice in Individual Cases

The Supreme Court of Appeals does not decide cases in a vacuum. It issues no advisory opinions on abstract legal principles. The judgements pronounced by the court are founded upon concrete disputes through an adversarial process by individual litigants. The impact on the parties before the court is an integral part of its decision-making process.

The court has additional concerns, however, outside the context of the particular case to be decided. Although it must seek to do justice in each case presented, it must avoid doing violence to the system of justice. Every decision of the court not only constitutes an authoritative resolution of the particular dispute at issue, but serves as precedent for similar disputes that may arise in the future.

Predictability is an essential element of our legal system. What may seem as injustice in an individual case, such as denial of an otherwise valid claim that was not filed within the time period prescribed by law, is essential to preservation of the system of justice.

Review of Lower Tribunals

To a large extent, the judicial process is a mechanism through which society attempts to ascertain a past set of events or "facts" and to weigh those against rules of conduct or "laws." Recognition of the fallibility of the individual to correctly ascertain "facts" and "law" has resulted in the creation of a system with a multitude of safeguards. The more serious the consequences of an erroneous determination of the "facts" or "law," the more protections are needed. For example, in a criminal prosecution, where the goal is to determine whether a particular individual performed certain acts in violation of societal rules of conduct in order that appropriate punishment, including death, may be administered, devices to enhance the quality of the process include the warrant, the indictment, the right to counsel, the right against self-incrimination, the right of confrontation, the right of trial by jury, and the right against cruel and unusual punishment. In addition to these rights, which are all found in constitutional provisions, there is the additional protection of appellate review.

The error correction role of the Supreme Court of Appeals largely involves the review of proceedings conducted by lower tribunals, including trial courts and administrative agencies, for compliance with applicable substantive and procedural rules. The effort is not to identify any possible ground for reversal of the decision rendered by the lower tribunal, but rather for prejudicial error that undermined the fairness of the particular proceedings. Appellate review further serves to prevent the arbitrary abuse of power that would undoubtedly attend unreviewable decision-making. It affords the losing party another forum within which to assert the correctness of a legal argument and serves to convey the impression that the decision ultimately rendered is consistent with fundamental legal principles.

Administration of the Judicial System

Perhaps the most overlooked aspect of the institutional role of the Supreme Court of Appeals is supervision of the system of justice. With respect to the regulatory authority of the Supreme Court of Appeals, Article VIII, Section 3 of the West Virginia Constitution provides, "The court shall have power to promulgate rules for all cases and proceedings, civil and criminal, for all of the courts of the state relating to writs, warrants, process, practice and procedure, which shall have the force and effect of law." With respect to its supervisory authority over the state judiciary, Article VIII, Section 3 of the West Virginia Constitution further provides, "The court shall have general supervisory control over all intermediate appellate courts, circuit courts and magistrate courts." These two provisions impose substantial responsibilities on the Supreme Court of Appeals with respect to maintenance of the efficiency and integrity of the legal system.

225

Pursuant to its grant of regulatory authority over the judicial process, the Supreme Court of Appeals has adopted a comprehensive set of rules. The Rules of Civil Procedure, Rules of Criminal Procedure, and Rules of Evidence control the nature and scope of circuit court proceedings. These rules determine the methodology for commencing legal actions, obtaining evidentiary materials, conducting trial proceedings, and securing enforcement of judicial decisions. Similar rules applicable to magistrate courts have been adopted. The court has also promulgated Rules for Resolution of Court Scheduling Conflicts, Rules Governing Camera Coverage of Courtroom Proceedings, and Trial Court Rules for Trial Courts of Record, which cover certain mechanical aspects of judicial proceedings. The procedural rules adopted by the Supreme Court of Appeals attempt to ensure fair, expeditious, and efficient administration of justice.

Pursuant to its grant of supervisory authority over the judicial system, the court has adopted a comprehensive body of rules for review of the conduct of lawyers and judges. No person can practice law in the State of West Virginia without the approval of the Supreme Court of Appeals. The court has adopted Rules for Admission to the Practice of Law that set forth the requirements for becoming licensed to practice law. The role of the court in regulating the legal profession does not conclude with the admission of an attorney to the practice of law. The court has promulgated Rules of Professional Conduct that establish ethical standards with which lawyers must comply or risk discipline, including disbarment. In addition to regulation of the legal profession, the Supreme Court of Appeals is charged with supervision of the state judiciary. With respect to judges, the court has adopted the Judicial Code of Ethics, enunciating ethical standards with which judges must comply or risk discipline, including removal. Fulfillment of its constitutional mandate to oversee the state judicial system is an important, yet often ignored component, of judicial decision-making by the Supreme Court of Appeals.

Law Development

The most visible role of the Supreme Court of Appeals concerns execution of its law-making function. In West Virginia, there are thirty-one judicial circuits and sixty-five circuit judges. When presented with a novel legal issue, it is highly unlikely that every circuit judge would rule the same way. Other participants in the legal system, such as members of the legislative and executive branches of government, may also have differing interpretations of the law. Without an institutional mechanism to harmonize divergent legal theories, there would be no uniformity. It is the function of the Supreme Court of Appeals to authoritatively pronounce the law for general application throughout the State of West Virginia.

There are primarily two methods by which the Supreme Court of Appeals performs its law-making function. First, it participates in the continuing development of common law, which consists of legal principles that have evolved over centuries of judicial dispute resolution. The evolution of the common law is founded in the judicial application of fairness, reason, and custom to conflicts that have arisen between individuals. Second, it interprets the language of constitutional, statutory and regulatory provisions that have been enacted by legislative bodies. The process of interpretation consists of ascertaining both the intent and purpose of the legislation. These two methods of law-making often present difficult issues for judicial resolution.

The common law does not consist of inflexible rules, but rather of broad principles of societal conduct. Changes in the common law have reflected social, political, and economic changes. For example, the liability of manufacturers for injuries caused by defective products, which is now deeply ingrained on our legal system, is a relatively recent phenomenon. Until the industrial revolution, which increased the number of products in the stream of commerce, recovery was precluded under a theory that there was no privity of contract between the purchaser and manufacturer. The change in the common law regarding products liability stirred great controversy. Today, issues such as the common law liability of individuals who transmit sexual diseases to their unsuspecting partners continue to fire debate. Many of these issues are eventually presented for resolution to the Supreme Court of Appeals. Pronouncement of the common law of the State of West Virginia on such controversial issues often subjects the court to criticism.

Interpretation of constitutional, statutory and regulatory provisions is also a method of judicial law-making by the Supreme Court of Appeals. The ultimate authority of the judiciary to determine the meaning of legislative enactments is a fundamental component of our constitutional form of government. Under the Articles of Confederation, there was no regular federal judiciary, "a circumstance," complained Alexander Hamilton in the Federalist No. 22, "which crowns the defects of the confederation." As Hamilton in that same work relates, "Laws are a dead letter without courts to expound them and define their true meaning and operation." This sentiment was reflected in the landmark case of *Marbury v. Madison*, 1 Cranch 137, 2 L. Ed. 60 (1803), where Chief Justice John Marshall stated, "It is emphatically the province and duty of the judicial department to say what the law is." This principle of judicial review, articulated by Justice Marshall for the United States Supreme Court in *Marbury v. Madison*, applies with equal force to the Supreme Court of Appeals of West Virginia.

The interpretation of constitutional, statutory, or regulatory provisions, however, presents several problems. The intended meaning or purpose of language used by the drafters of legislation is often ambiguous. Future events may change the circumstances that provided the impetus for the legislation. Occasionally, even those who participate in the adoption of particular legislation will have divergent views on its meaning. Although some legislative history may exist, such as transcripts of the debates and proceedings of the legislative body, the court must often look to rules of statutory construction that have been developed as analytical tools, such as the legal maxim *expressio unius est exclusio alterius* or "the expression of one thing is the exclusion of another," in order to interpret legislative meaning or purpose. Application of such rules of construction is, at best, an inexact science. Consequently, the interpretation afforded by the Supreme Court of Appeals, although unquestionably authoritative, remains subject to public debate.

Conclusion

Alexis De Tocqueville observed in *Democracy in America*, "Scarcely any question arises in the United States which does not become, sooner or later, a subject of judicial debate.". . . The Supreme Court of Appeals has a solemn duty to render decisions on often controversial issues, such as prison reform, equal taxation, and quality education. Moreover, the court is charged with enforcing compliance with fundamental constitutional protections, which may mandate reversal of a conviction based upon an illegally obtained confession, even where there is overwhelming evidence of guilt. Although a sometimes difficult burden to bear, the court is constantly mindful of its institutional role as it faithfully fulfills its judicial decision-making function.

WEST VIRGINIA'S JEHOVAH'S WITNESSES AND THE EXPANSION Of LEGAL PROTECTION FOR RELIGIOUS LIBERTY

Chuck Smith

INTRODUCTION

The Jehovah's Witnesses are an established fixture in the American conscious-ness. A mention of them brings to mind the picture of persistent, sometimes annoying, teams of door-to-door preachers whose aggressive prosely-tizing campaigns have made them a symbol of the troublesome irritants of daily life. Americans are less aware of the sect's valuable contribution to our laws. Yet, legal scholars recognize Jehovah's Witnesses as champions in the constitutional battle to protect religious liberty.[1]

During the 1930s and 1940s their aggressive, unconventional style of evan-gelism resulted in numerous confrontations in communities across the United States. During the period 1933 through 1951 "there were 18,866 arrests of American Witnesses and about fifteen hundred cases of mob violence against them."[2]....

A number of these attacks and incidents of discrimination took place in West Virginia.[3] Four of the confrontations that occurred resulted in important developments in law that protects religious liberty. 1) In an early example of "new judicial federalism," the Hancock County Circuit Court used the West Virginia Constitution to increase the protection of free exercise of religion beyond the protection provided by the United States Constitution. 2) In the infamous Richwood castor oil case, the U.S. District Court for Southern West Virginia expanded protection of religious liberty through judicial interpretation of federal civil rights statutes. 3) An action growing out of the firing of seven glassworkers in Clarksburg, extended the protection of the free exercise of religion through an unprecedented use of administrative law.

4) The final and best known case was an U.S. Supreme Court landmark decision that expanded the constitutional safeguards for free exercise of religion and freedom of speech. It was also a bellwether case that telegraphed the U.S. Supreme Court's move, in the early 1940s toward more expansive protection of First Amendment rights.

Salute or Be Expelled

Throughout America, children of Jehovah's Witnesses were being expelled from schools because they refused to take part in flag-salute ceremonies. In 1938, Jehovah's Witnesses families in Pennsylvania requested a federal court to issue an injunction prohibiting the Minersville School District from expelling children who refused to salute the flag. They claimed that the expulsions violated the U.S. Constitution's First Amendment provision protecting the free exercise of religion from government interference. Eventually the case made its way to the U.S. Supreme Court. On June 3, 1940 in, *Minersville School District v. Gobitis*, the Court ruled that schools did not violate the Free Exercise Clause when they expelled students who refused to salute the flag.[4] Eighteen months later the West Virginia State Board of Education adopted a resolution that required students to salute the flag and provided "that refusal to salute the Flag be regarded as an act of insubordination, and refusal shall be dealt with accordingly."[5]

Hancock County, 1941:
The State Constitution as a Safeguard of Religious Practice

High school senior Joseph Clementino resolutely entreated the Hancock County Board of Education to allow him to graduate with his class—the Weir High School Class of 1941. Over the past two months he and at least twenty-five other Jehovah's Witnesses students in West Virginia's northern-most county had been expelled from school because they refused to salute the flag. The board turned a deaf ear to the teenager's request to readmit him and his nine-year-old brother, Albert.[6] Clementino did not graduate with his class, but that was not the only cost of adhering to his religious convictions. The following year, his father and four other fathers of the expelled children were indicted for violating the state's harsh truancy law.[7]

The Hancock County Prosecuting Attorney obtained the misdemeanor truancy indictments[8] against the fathers of the expelled children in an environment hostile to Jehovah's Witnesses. National and state law, moreover, seemed to weigh heavily in favor of convicting the sectarians. The *Gobitus* decision held that such expulsions did not violate the Constitution, furthermore, the State Board of Education made student participation in flag-salute ceremonies a requirement for attending school. In addition, the previous year the West Virginia Legislature amended the school law to provide that students who were expelled for not complying with school regulations must comply with those requirement before readmission and were unlawfully absent until the requirements were met.[9]

Circuit Judge J. Harold Brennan consolidated the indictments into one case,[10] a case that appeared to be an open and shut matter. A strict application of the letter of the law would seemingly require a sure and speedy conviction.

Protecting Religious Liberty with West Virginia's Constitution.

Judge Brennan, however, was clearly uneasy with the case and explained "that he could not take upon himself 'the right to hold a religious view unreasonable.'"[11] He recognized that, in light of the *Gobitis* decision, the expulsions did not violate the national Bill of Rights. He chose, though, to base his decision on the provisions for religious liberty in the West Virginia Constitution. Today a state court occasionally rules that its state constitution protects basic rights more extensively than the national constitution,[12] but in the 1940s such rulings were quite rare. Nevertheless, Judge Brennan held that expulsion of the school children in Hancock County violated the religious liberty provisions of the state's constitution.

The West Virginia Constitution provides that "no man shall be compelled to frequent or support any religious worship, place of ministry whatsoever; nor shall any man be forced, restrained, molested or burdened in his body or goods, or otherwise suffer, on account of his religious opinions or beliefs. . . ."[13] Judge Brennan wrote that in light of this provision it would be difficult to maintain that a "court has a right to fine or imprison a man because he will not force his children to do a positive act wholly inconsistent with the religious belief of them both."[14] Judge Brennan turned to the West Virginia Constitution to safeguard religious liberties that were not protected by the Bill of Rights. The Hancock County case, however, is but one of four legal proceedings involving West Virginia Jehovah's Witnesses that significantly advanced protections for religious liberties.

Richwood Castor Oil Patriots, 1940:
Statutory Protection of Religious Freedom

The attack on the Jehovah's Witnesses in Richwood was among the most outrageous of the hundreds of brutal assaults on Jehovah's Witnesses that swept America in June of 1940. The criminal prosecution that followed the attack, however, conferred it with historical significance and the appellate decision in the case expanded the application of the federal civil rights statute. The case began when Charles Jones and C.A. Cecil began working in Richwood as door-to-door preachers. The two native-born West Virginians came from Mount Lookout, a little community at the opposite end of Nicholas County.[15] Even though the doorbell-ringing missionaries hailed from a nearby community, residents of Richwood pegged them as outsiders. Among the townspeople, speculation burgeoned concerning these apostles of the nonconformist sect.

Confrontation with the American Legion.

On Friday, June 28 Jones and Cecil were summoned to the State Police headquarters in Richwood. There, Officer Bernard McLaughlin and three members of the American Legion questioned them about their activities. The Legionnaires . . . accused the Jehovah's Witnesses of being spies and Fifth Columnists and demanded that they leave town. Late that afternoon, Jones and Cecil made their way back to Mount Lookout[16] and met with other Witnesses who agreed to accompany them to Richwood the following day.

At about 10:30 the following morning, June 29, 1940, the nine men, travelling in two cars, arrived at the Richwood Town Hall. Carlton Stull, Cecil and Jones left the others in the cars and went to the mayor's office, where Deputy Sheriff Martin Catlette confronted them. He converted the office into a makeshift jail to detain the Witnesses and asked Richwood Chief of Police, Bert Stewart to guard the office door. Deputy Catlette telephoned members of the American Legion informing them that the Jehovah's Witnesses had returned. Within an hour the news spread through Richwood and hundreds of people converged on the town hall.[17]

A Legionnaire brought the other six Witnesses into the office, which shortly thereafter fairly bristled with indignant members of American Legion Post 97. Catlette took control of the situation. He removed his deputy sheriff's badge and proclaimed, "What is done from here on will not be done in the name of the law."[18] Among the Legionnaires was a physician, who brought a stomach pump and a large container of castor oil. They forced five of the young Witnesses to drink large doses of castor oil.[19] The Legionnaires compelled the Witnesses to drink the strong laxative, to cause their humiliation and degradation.

The Legionnaires tied the Witnesses by the left wrists three or four feet apart along a rope. Their captors led the nine men out of the town hall and through a jeering mob of more than fifteen hundred people. They marched down the street to the Richwood Post Office. There, the captives refused to salute the flag, thereby confirming the mob's suspicion that Jehovah's Witnesses were indeed Fifth Columnists.[20] The Legionnaires marched the men west to the town limits. The townspeople warned them that if they returned they would be "confronted with buckshot."[21]

Seeking an Indictment

After the attack, the United States Attorney for the southern district of West Virginia learned of its nature and of the participation of the two police officers. He passed the information on to the federal Bureau of Investigation, which investigated the attack. Over the next two years, however, the prosecution of the attackers fell victim to foot-dragging and indecision by a local U.S. Attorney, the F.B.I., and high officials in the Department of Justice.[22] In Washington, the case attracted the attention of the recently created Civil Rights Section of the Department of Justice. Of the hundreds of attacks against Jehovah's Witnesses reported to the Civil Rights Section from 1939 through 1942, the Government lawyers choose the Richwood attack and several others serious assaults on Witnesses to present to grand juries; but none of the juries returned indictments.[23]

The Civil Rights Section attorneys in Washington wanted a conviction, in at least one case, involving attacks on Jehovah's Witnesses. Therefore, the Assistant Attorney General Berge directed the U.S. Attorney in West Virginia to proceed with the prosecution. . . . The U.S. Attorney accused Catlett and Stewart of a misdemeanor—depriving the Jehovah's Witnesses of their civil rights under color of state law, a violation of Title 18, Section 52 of the United States Code. A crime committed under color of law is one perpetrated by public officials while using the authority of their office.

The color of law statute's usefulness in protecting civil rights was, therefore, largely untested. . . .[24]

The Trial and Appeal

District Judge Ben Moore presided over the trial on June 2 and 3, 1942, in the United States Court in Charleston. Eight of the men who were attacked in Richfield testified at the trial. They explained why they came to Richwood and recounted what had happened to them at the hands of Catlette, Stewart, and the mob.[25] The U.S. Attorney argued that both Catlette and Stewart, as officers of the law were required to maintain the peace and protect the Witnesses in the exercise of their rights and privileges secured and protected by the Constitution and laws of the United States. Catlette's defense was that he did not act under the color of law and that the government failed to show any statute of West Virginia under which he acted. Furthermore, Catlette testified that he removed his deputy sheriff's badge and declared that he was not acting as a law officer. . . . In his testimony, Catlette emphasized that the Jehovah's Witnesses refused to salute the flag.[26] Stewart claimed that he had no connection with the attack. . . . On June 3, the jury returned a guilty verdict against both Catlette and Stewart.[27]

Catlette appealed his conviction. The Fourth Circuit of the U.S. Court of Appeals heard oral arguments in Baltimore, Maryland on November 13, 1942[28] and affirmed Judge Moore's findings. . . . Ruling against Catlette, the court rejected the contention that "an officer can divorce himself from his official capacity merely by removing his badge of office before embarking on a course of illegal conduct."[29] . . . .

Richwood's Contribution to Religious Liberty

This case resulted in several significant legal developments.[30] It was the Department of Justice's newly-established Civil Rights Section first prosecution—and one of the few ever undertaken—that used the color of law section of the civil rights statute to enforce citizens' civil rights protection of religious liberty. The case also broadened the application of color of law provision. This ruling of the Court of Appeals embraced the understanding that the color of law statute governed those instances when a public official acted in violation of the laws prescribing his powers and duties. Three years later, in its decision in *Screws v. United States*, the U.S. Supreme Court accepted this construction of the statute.[31] . . . .

Clarksburg Firings, 1941:
Defending Religious Liberty With Administrative Law

War Fever and Religious Fervor

The voice of President Franklin Roosevelt crackled from the radio in the warehouse washroom, "Yesterday, December 7, 1941—a date which will live in infamy—the United States of America was suddenly and deliberately attacked by the naval and air forces of the Empire of Japan."[32] About eighty workers in the Clarksburg plant of Pittsburgh Plate Glass Company listened intently to the six-minute speech in which the president asked the Congress to declare war on Japan. The workers' anger grew as they heard the description of Japanese attacks on Pearl Harbor, Guam, the Philippine Islands, Wake Island, and Midway Island. They were sad as the president solemnly related "that very many American lives have been lost."[33]

At the conclusion of the speech, the "Stars Spangled Banner" reverberated from the radio. As the men stood and removed their caps, they were annoyed that Clyde Seders neither stood nor removed his cap.[34] For Seders, such deference was contrary to his belief as a Jehovah's Witness. For the other men present, Seders' behavior was unpatriotic, if not outright complicity with the enemy.

Within an hour, word of Seders' nonconformity had spread throughout the plant warehouse and the workers in the shipping department refused to work with him. When plant superintendent Howard Halbach approached him, Seders told him that his religion compelled his behavior. Halbach replied that if Seders did not change his attitude he must quit or be fired. Seders quit his job at the end of the day.[35] Seders' behavior drew the attention of the workers to other Jehovah's Witnesses employed by the plant. The incident upset most of the glass workers, many of whom were veterans of World War I and members of the American Legion.[36] They chose a fellow veteran and Legionnaire, Clarence James, to be their spokesman. Accompanied by about 100 men, James asked three Jehovah's Witnesses if they would salute the flag and defend the country. The men answered that they would not.[37] . . . . Over the next few days, five more Jehovah's Witnesses were fired or resigned under pressure because other workers refused to work with them.[38] . . . .

An Appeal to Administrative Law

The matter of the firing of the Jehovah's Witnesses would have ended with the last worker's dismissal, except for the persistent, yearlong effort of Paul Schmidt to regain their jobs. Schmidt had worked as a glasscutter many years and had been employed at the Pittsburgh Plate Glass plant for more than twelve years.[39] To provide for his family and gain reinstatement to his job, Schmidt pursued several courses of action[40] But his eventual success grew from the complaint he filed with the President's Committee on Fair Employment Practice.

Paul Schmidt's complaint reached the committee by an indirect route. On January 16, 1942, he wrote to Eleanor Roosevelt complaining about the firings and beseeched her to bring the matter to the President's attention. Mrs. Roosevelt referred his letter to the committee.[41] Not until March 7, did the committee notify Schmidt that it had received word of the firings.[42] On March 10, Schmidt filed a formal complaint with the committee.[43] Within a short time the committee began its investigation. Daniel Donovan, committee field investigator, arrived in Clarksburg. . . . and concluded that the Jehovah's Witnesses lost their jobs because of their religious beliefs. Furthermore, he determined that the Pittsburgh Plate Glass managers fired or forced the Jehovah's Witnesses to quit because a large number of the workers in the warehouse were refusing to work with them.[44]

Law Enforcement by Persuasion

Soon after Donovan's investigation, the committee determined that the seven Jehovah's Witnesses had been dislodged in violation of Executive Order 8802; and it began to encourage union officials to have the union workers accept the reemployment of the Witnesses. Two unions represented the workers at Pittsburgh Plate Glass Company's Works No. 12. The glasscutters were members of a craft union, the Window Glass Cutters League of America, an affiliate union of the American Federation of Labor. Most of the workers in the plant were represented by Glass, Ceramic, and Silica Sand Workers of America, affiliated with the Congress of Industrial Organizations. The committee's top-down approach encouraged the unions to accept the reemployment of the fired workers. The presidents of both A.F.L. and C.I.O. were members of the committee, which requested them to intercede with their unions to bring the affair to an end. . . .

Over the next seven weeks a flurry of letters were exchanged between the committee and union officials and among union officials. Still there was little movement toward rehiring the Jehovah's Witnesses. When the company's intransigence continued, the committee grew impatient. At its meeting on November 24[45] the committee issues a notice that was even more forceful than other directives. It required the immediate reinstatement of the Jehovah's Witnesses to the positions they held at the time of their dismissal, with full seniority based on employment since their initial hiring. In order to increase the effect of the directive, the committee issued a news release that called the directive "an unprecedented action," and reiterated the points in its notice to Pittsburgh Plate Glass Company.[46]

Administrative Hearing

Both the company and the unions resisted the committee's directive. Pittsburgh Plate Glass Company asked the committee for a hearing reconsidering the matter.[47] On December 7 the committee agreed to provide the company and the unions the opportunity to present their arguments at its next meeting.[48] The union members did not present formal arguments; rather they were witnesses on behalf of the company's position and supported it in affidavits included in the company's brief.[49] The company argued that it should not be compelled to reinstate the Jehovah's Witnesses because that would cause a walkout of the plant's seven hundred workers thereby imperiling wartime production.[50] It discredited the religious discrimination claims of the Jehovah's Witnesses because they refuse to participate in patriotic exercises, not because of their religion. . . . and that during wartime the threshold for protecting civil liberties is lowered.[51]

The testimony of Paul Schmidt closed the hearing. Confident of a favorable outcome, he. . . . would demonstrate that he was fired because of his beliefs, rather than because he could not get along with other workers, a claim he labeled "an absurd charge."[52] He contended that he did not attend the December 18, 1941 flag ceremony at the plant because he had been warned there could be violent attacks on him and the other Witnesses. He avoided the ceremony to prevent a confrontation.[53] He also maintained that he would not have saluted the flag had he attended the ceremony.[54]

Final Negotiations

The committee determined that its earlier findings were confirmed in the hearing and it continued to press steadfastly for the reinstatement of the Jehovah's Witnesses. . . . By early March, the committee had drafted the substance of its Summary, Findings and Directions.[55] During the next two weeks the committee and the company's attorney reached an agreement on the final wording of the findings and directions.[56] The two Jehovah's Witnesses, who chose to return to work at the plant, did so without incident on Monday. March 27. Paul Schmidt and his son, Bernard reclaimed their jobs; the other five workers had secured other employment. Paul Schmidt worked at the Clarksburg plant until he retired in the mid-1950s.[57]

Significant Legal Developments

The case of the Clarksburg Jehovah's Witnesses contributed to religious liberty in several ways.[58] First, administrative law is rarely a legal means used to defend religious liberty; the Clarksburg case is probably the most significant instance of administrative law protecting the free exercise of religion. Second, the President's Committee on Fair Employment Practice relied almost entirely on persuasion to enforce public policy. The situation in the Clarksburg case limited the usefulness of the committee's usual appeals to patriotism and support for the war effort. Its arguments, therefore, focused primarily on making the injustice of discrimination evident to the company and the unions. This emphasis underscored the principle that the essential attribute of civil liberties in a democracy is to protect unpopular minorities, thus the exercise of those liberties must not rest on the assent of the majority. The committee's success highlighted the significance of persuasion as an effective means for the government to influence people's moral choices. Finally, the Clarksburg case was significant because in it the federal government made conspicuous, successful use of civil rights laws to protect persons discriminated against by private persons and enterprises. It served as an example for the need for such protection, a need that was eventually met by the Civil Rights Act of 1964.

Kanawha County, 1942: A Landmark Decision for Religious Liberty

"A Case from Charleston, West Virginia, of All Places"

During administrative hearings on the Clarksburg firings, an interesting exchange took place between the committee's council and Leland Hazard, the company's attorney. Hazard pointed out that the U.S. Supreme Court ruled in *Minersville School District v. Gobitis* (1940) that it was reasonable for states to require children of Jehovah's Witnesses to salute the flag at school. The refusal of the glass workers to salute the flag was, he argued, a similar situation. Ernest Trimble, the committee's lawyer, replied by citing a case that "came up from Charleston, Virginia of all places."[59] He was referring to *Barnette v. West Virginia State Board of Education* (1942), a decision of the U.S. District Court of the Southern District of West Virginia.[60] That court did not follow the precedent established by the U.S. Supreme Court in *Gobitis*. The *Barnette* case, a fourth incident involving West Virginia Jehovah's Witnesses, resulted in a landmark U.S. Supreme Court decision protecting religious liberty.

The Response to *Gobitis*

After the *Gobitis* ruling, refusal to participate in flag-salute ceremonies resulted in the expulsion of Jehovah's Witnesses children in a least thirty-one states.[61] This increase in the enforcement of compulsory flag-salute regulations, however, was accompanied by substantial unfavorable criticism of the Court's decision. Of the forty-two political science and law journal articles commenting on *Gobitis*, more than three-fourths were critical of the decision, ten percent supported it, and fifteen percent took no position.[62] More significantly, several state courts ruled that flag-salute ceremonies violated their state constitutions. In addition to the Hancock County Circuit Court decision above, a Minnesota trial court relied on the state constitution to restrain enforcement of the flag-salute regulations.[63] Even more dramatic, the supreme courts in Kansas and Washington expressed hostility for *Gobitis* and relied on their state constitutions to disallow mandatory flag salutes.[64]

The *Barnette* decision of the Federal District Court of Southern West Virginia presented the most notable judicial defiance of the *Gobitis* precedent. Appellate procedure requires that lower federal courts conform their rulings to the U.S. Supreme Court. Nevertheless, the Federal District Court in West Virginia disregarded *Gobitis* and found the state's compulsory flag-salute requirements violated the First Amendment's free exercise clause. The facts in *Barnette* resembled the hundreds of other flag-salute confrontations that occurred across the country. When the Jehovah's Witnesses' national legal office determined that it was again time to bring the flag-salute issue before the high court, West Virginia presented the most attractive forum for litigation. A challenge to the constitutionality of a statewide regulation could be brought before three-judge Federal District Court from which an appeal could be taken directly to the Supreme Court. The legal office chose three parents, Walter Barnette, Lucy McClure, and Paul Stull, who lived near Charleston, for a class action suit on behalf of themselves and all others similarly situated. Charleston lawyer Horace S. Meldahl filed the complaint on August 19, 1942.[65]

On August 27, District Judge Ben Moore convened the statutory three-judge court, comprised of himself, District Judge Harry E. Watkins and U.S. Court of Appeals Judge John J. Parker.[66] Hayden Covington, national legal council to the Jehovah's Witnesses, represented the parents: West Virginia Assistant Attorney General Ira J. Partlow represented the State Board of Education. At the initial hearing on Tuesday, September 14, it was soon apparent that Judge Parker disliked the regulation. He urged the board to amend its regulation to excuse students who refused to salute based on conscientious grounds. . . . The following day the board rejected a compromise position.[67] Later that day. . . . Judge Parker said that it was "unfortunate that a case of this kind should be in court," and rejected the state's reliance on *Gobitis*.[68] The court denied the state's motion to dismiss the suit and gave the defendants two weeks to file an answer.[69] Before an answer was submitted, the lawyers for both sides agreed to submit the case for a decision based on the pleadings and briefs already filed.[70] On October 6, 1942, the unanimous three-judge court enjoined the West Virginia school system "from requiring the children of the plaintiffs, or any other children having religious scruples against such action, to salute the flag."[71] Based on cues it perceived coming from the high court itself, the District Court took the unusual step of ruling contrary to a precedent of the U.S. Supreme Court.

Changing Attitudes on the Supreme Court

Justice Harlan F. Stone cast the only vote against the Court's *Gobitis* decision to uphold compulsory flag-salute laws. After that decision membership changed on the Court and some of the remaining justices modified their positions relative to constraints on religious liberty. In 1941 Chief Justice Hughes and Justice James McReynolds left the Court. President Roosevelt moved Justice Stone to the Chief Justice's chair, and filled positions left vacant by McReynolds and Stone with James F. Byrnes and Robert Jackson. In 1942, in *Jones v. Opelika* the Court upheld a law requiring a license to sell religious literature door to door. Justices Stone, Hugo Black, William Douglas and Frank Murphy voted in the minority. More notably, Black, Douglas, and Murphy, who had supported the *Gobitis* decision, joined in a special dissenting opinion in *Jones* and declared that *Gobitis* was "wrongly decided."[72] At the end of the 1941-42 term, Justice Byrnes resigned and President Roosevelt appointed Wiley Rutledge to the empty seat. On May 3, 1943, Justices Stone, Black, Douglas, Murphy, and Rutledge voted to reverse *Jones v. Opelika*.[73] The time was ripe for a reversal of *Gobitis* as well.

The U.S. Supreme Court Decision in Barnette

West Virginia's principal argument in the appeal was that *Barnette* raised no substantial federal question—*Gobitis* had settled this legal question. The state's brief quoted extensively from Justice Frankfurter's *Gobitis* opinion. Given the clear indications that at least five justices were ready to lay aside the *Gobitis* precedent, there was little else the state's lawyers could do. The American Legion's *amicus curiae* brief filed in support of the state's appeal did little more than duplicate the West Virginia argument.[74]

Hayden Covington's brief answering the state's appeal was a mixture of Jehovah's Witnesses Bible teaching and constitutional arguments. He included a fiery attack on the Court's *Gobitis* opinion; he especially rejected Frankfurter's deference to legislative policy-making authority. Such deference, he argued, allowed the legislature to define its own powers. He emphasized the nationwide persecution of Jehovah's Witnesses that followed *Gobitis* and concluded with a long list of law journal and newspaper articles that criticized the decision.[75] The American Bar Association's Committee on the Bill of Rights and the ACLU filed *amicus curiae* briefs that argued *Gobitis* was bad law and should be overruled.[76]

The Significance of Barnette

On Flag Day, June 14, 1943, the U.S. Supreme Court announced its decision in *West Virginia State Board of Education v. Barnette*.[77] The Court's six-to-three vote overturned *Minersville School District v. Gobitis* and effectively terminated the legal controversy over compulsory flag salute ceremonies in American schools. The *Barnette* decision also indirectly repudiated the many violent attacks on Jehovah's Witnesses that followed *Gobitis*. Moreover, in this case Justices Black, Douglas, Murphy, and Rutledge formed the voting bloc that served as the Court's liberal core throughout the 1940s. Likewise, the decision, and that in *Murdock v. Pennsylvania* (1943), reflected the New Deal Court's move toward broader construction of the free exercise clause. in *Barnette*, Justice Jackson enunciated what has become a guiding principle in protecting individual liberties, "If there is any star in the constitutional constellation, it is that no official, high or petty, can prescribe what shall be orthodox in politics, nationalism, religion, or other matters of opinion or force citizens to confess by word or act their faith therein."[78]

Concluding Remarks

The Uniqueness of the West Virginia Cases

All across America, meaningful developments in law resulted from hundreds of cases that grew out of the Jehovah's Witnesses practicing their faith in ways that offended or inconvenienced others. The four West Virginia cases discussed above are significant because each resulted in important expansions, in four different kinds of law, for the protection of free exercise of religion. The expulsion of children, who refused to salute the flag, from Hancock County schools resulted in the Circuit Court's use of the Constitution of West Virginia to expand protection of religious practice beyond that protected by the United States Constitution and the federal courts. The criminal prosecutions that followed the castor oil incident in Richwood resulted in developments in judicial interpretation of the federal civil rights statutes' color-of-law provisions. It was also the only successful federal prosecution in the hundreds of violent attacks on Jehovah's witnesses during the early 1940s. The firing of the Jehovah's Witnesses glassworkers in Clarksburg resulted in an unprecedented use of administrative law to protect religious liberty. The best known of the four cases, *West Virginia State Board of Education v. Barnette*, was a landmark case in defining the Bill of Rights' protections for free exercise of religion and freedom of speech. It also served as a bellwether case indicating the Court's movement toward a position of strong, unwavering rulings protecting individual liberties.

Notes

This article is based on research partially funded by the West Virginia Humanities Council, a state program of the National Endowment of the Humanities and by a grant from the West Virginia State College Research Committee.

[1] Edward F. Waite, "The Debt of Constitutional Law to Jehovah's Witnesses," *Minnesota Law Review*, 28 (1944), 209-246; Hollis W. Barber, "Religious Liberty v. Police Power—Jehovah's Witnesses," *American Political Science Review*, 41 (1947), 226-47; "Jehovah's Witnesses: Definers of Freedom," in Joan Biskupic and Elder Witt (eds.) *Congressional Quarterly's Guide to the U.S. Supreme Court*, 3rd. ed., vol. 1 (Washington, D.C.: CQ Press, 1997), 453; and Lee Epstein and Thomas G. Walker, *Constitutional Law for a Changing America, Rights, Liberties, and Justice*, 3rd ed. (Washington, D.C.: CQ Press, 1998), 101.

[2] M. James Penton, *Apocalypse Delayed: The Story of Jehovah's Witnesses* (Toronto: University of Toronto Press, 1985), 88.

[3] Robert J. O'Brien, "Persecution and Resistance: Jehovah's Witnesses and the Defense of Religious Liberty in West Virginia." an unpublished manuscript in my possession. This article examines the expulsion of Jehovah's Witnesses children from school for refusing to salute the flag in Barbour, Hancock, Harrison, Kanawha, Nicholas, Upshur, and Wood Counties. It also discusses or enumerates attacks on Jehovah's Witnesses with the complicity of government officials in Bluefield, Clarksburg, Follansbee, Holliday's Cove, Huttonsville, Keyser, Martinsburg, Morgantown, New Martinsville, Phillippi, Richwood, St. Marys, Wellsburg and Williamson, WV. Dr. O'Brien, a professor at West Virginia Wesleyan College, is writing a comprehensive book on the persecution of Jehovah's Witness.

[4] *Minersville School District v. Gobitis*, 310 U.S. 586 (1940)

[5] Quoted in *West Virginia State Board of Education v. Barnette*, 319 U.S. 624, at 621 (1943).

[6] Minutes of the Hancock County Board of Education, 22 May 1941.

[7] "Jehovah' s Witnesses Indicted," *The* (New Cumberland, WV) *Independent*, 16 April 1942, 1.

8   *State v. Frank Clementino, Sr., State v. George Maupin, State v. Joe Mercante, State v. Pete Mercante,* and *State v. Arthur Ginier*; files of the Hancock County Circuit Clerk. The grand jury returned all these indictments on April 14, 1942. Based on the number of children they had in school all the men except Ginier were named in two indictments.

9   *Acts of West Virginia 1941*, Chapter 32, pp. 148-49, codified at *West Virginia Code of 1943 Annotated*, 18-8-5a [1851(1)].

10 This Order is in the Maupin file.

11 "Judge J.H. Brennan Gives Opinion in Flag Salute Cases," *The* (New Cumberland, WV) *Independent*, 4 June 1942, *Minersville School District v. Gobitis*, 310 U.S. 580 (1940).

12 Robert D. Bursack, "Of Laboratories and Liberties: State Protections of Political and Civil Rights," *Georgia Law Review*, 10:533-64 (1976); and Ronald K. Collins, Peter J. Galie, and John Kincaid, "State High Courts, State Constitutions and Individual Rights Litigation Since 1980," *Publius*, 16:141-61 (1986).

13 Constitution of West Virginia, Article III, section 15.

14 "Memorandum of opinion," *State v. Mercante*, 1 June 1942, 12; located in the Joe Mercante file.

15 Stipulation of Facts at 2, *United States v. Catlette*, Docket no. 9390 (S.D. W.Va 1942) unreported decision. Record Group 21 National Archives and Records Administration—Mid-Atlantic Region, Philadelphia, Pa. (hereafter referred to as *United States v. Catlette*).

16 Affidavit of C.A. Cecil, 8 July 1940, American Civil Liberties Union Archives 2249:180, Seeley G. Mudd Manuscript Library, Princeton University. Hereafter materials from this collection are referred to as ACLU Archives; all such material are used by permission of the Princeton University Library.

17 Stipulation of Facts at 2-3, *United States v. Catlette*; and Stevens, *Salute!* 12-14.

18 *Ibid.*

19 Harding Legg, interview by author, tape recording, Mount Lookout, WV., 26 September 1996; Jim Comstock, "Mandatory flag-saluting has ugly history," *Charleston* (WV) *Gazette*, 16 Oct., 1988, 5; Leonard A. Stevens, *Salute the Case of the Bible vs. The Flag* (New York: Coward, McCann & Geoghegan, Inc. 1973), 13; and Stipulation of Facts at 3, *United States v. Catlette*.

20 Legg interview.

21 "2 Held Guilty in Civil Rights Case of Jehovah's Witnesses," *Charleston Gazette*, 4 June 1942, 12.

22 Robert H. Carr, *Federal Protection of Civil Rights: Quest For a Sword* (Ithaca: Cornell University Press, 1947), 156.

23 Manwaring, *Render Unto Caesar*, 177-79.

24 The U.S. Supreme Court upheld this application of the statute in *U.S. v. Classic*, 313 U.S. 299 (1941).

25 Court's Charge at 6 and 11, *United States v. Catlette*. The only victim of the attack who did not testify was C.A. Cecil.

26 *Ibid.*, 12.

27 Order on trial, guilty verdict at 1, *United States v. Catlette*.

28 Claude M. Dean to Claude L. Smith, L.R. Via, Charles M. Love, and Raoul Berger, 5

November 1942, *Catlette v. United*, Docket no. 4992. Records of the U.S. Court of Appeals for the Fourth Circuit, Record Group 276, National Archives and records Administration-Mid Atlantic region, Philadelphia, Pa. (hereinafter cited as Fourth Circuit Records).

29 *Catlette v. United States*, 132 F2d 902 (4th Cir. 1943), at 906.

30 For an extensive discussion of the legal significance of this case see Chuck Smith, "Jehovah's Witnesses and the Castor Oil Patriots: A West Virginia Contribution to Religious Liberty," *West Virginia History* 57:95-110 (1998)

31 *Screws v. United States*, 325 U.S.91 (1945). For a note mentioning that Catlette contributed to this development, see G.L. Clark, "Annotation: Validity and Construction of Statutes Making Conspiracy to Deprive or Deprivation of Constitutional Right a federal Offense," *American Law Reports* 162:1373-1401 (1946).

32 Franklin D. Roosevelt, "Address to Congress Requesting War Declaration, December 8, 1941," in Samuel Rosenman, (ed.) *The Public Papers and Addresses of Franklin D. Roosevelt*, vol. 10, (New York: Russell & Russell, 1950, reissued 1969), 514.

33 *Ibid.*

34 Affidavit of Fred Kroll, Brief of Pittsburgh Plate Glass Company, 20, The National Archives and Records Administration: Record Group 228, Committee on Fair Employment Practice, Headquarters Records/Legal division-hearings [Entry 19530-53-41-07 Box 3361], hereafter referred to as CFEP Hearing Records.

35 Verbatim transcript of proceedings, 37-39, 48, and 66, CFEP Hearing Records.

36 Affidavit of Howard L. Halbach, Brief of Pittsburgh Plate Glass Company, 18 CFEP Hearing Records.

37 Verbatim transcript of proceedings, December 21, 1942, 124, CFEP Hearing Records; and Affidavit of Clarence James, Brief of Pittsburgh Plate Glass Company, 39, CFEP Hearing Records.

38 Stanley Meredith to Harry D. Nixon, 19 December 1940, West Virginia Regional History Collection, West Virginia University Libraries, WVRHC, Glass Cutters League, general correspondence.

39 Verbatim transcript of proceedings, 142, CREP Hearing Records.

40 For a more complete description of the efforts Paul Schmidt made to regain his job see, Chuck Smith, "Paul Schmidt: A Workingman's Tenacious Pursuit of Religious Liberty," forthcoming in *Journal of Law and Religion*.

41 Paul G. Schmidt to Clifford Forster, 7 March, ACLU Archives, 2428:128.

42 *Ibid.*

43 Exhibit #11, Memorandum, Daniel R. Donovan to Lawrence W. Cramer, no date, CFEP Hearing Records.

44 *Ibid.*

45 George M. Johnson, to committee members, summary of actions taken at November 24rd meeting of the committee, 24 November 1942, CFEP Headquarters Records/office of the committee.

46 Office of War Information, War Manpower Commission, "Advance release: For Sunday Morning Papers, 29 November 1942, "National Archives and Records Administration: Record Group 228, Committee on Fair Employment Practice, Headquarters Records/Information and Public Relations Division, Press releases, 1941-1945, R-Z

[Entry 64, 530-53-50-05-box 510].

47 Agendas meeting of 7 December 1942, CFEP Headquarters Records/office of the committee.

48 Minutes, meeting of 7 December 1942, CFEP Headquarters Records/office of the committee.

49 Brief of Pittsburgh Plate Glass Company, 22-44, CFEP Hearing Records.

50 Verbatim transcript of proceedings, 17, 23, CFEP Hearing Records.

51 Brief of Pittsburgh Plate Glass Company, 3-10, CFEP Hearing Records.

52 Paul G. Schmidt to Clifford Forster, 12 December 1942. ACLU Archives 2428:147.

53 Verbatim transcript of proceedings, 143-44, CFEP Hearing Records.

54 *Ibid.*, 148.

55 "Summary of Action Taken at 1 March 1943 Meeting of the Committee," CFEP Headquarters Records/office of the committee.

56 Lawrence W. Cramer to Leland Hazard, March 5, 1943; and Lawrence W. Cramer to Leland Hazard, 15 March 1943; both in CFEP General Correspondence.

57 Francis Schmidt, interview by author, Clarksburg, WV, 12 September 1998. Francis Schmidt is the son of Paul Schmidt.

58 For a comprehensive discussion of the legal significance of this case see, Chuck Smith, "War Fever and Religious Fervor: The Firing of Jehovah's Witnesses Glassworkers in West Virginia and Administrative Protection of Religious Liberty" forthcoming in *American Journal of Legal History*.

59 Verbatim transcript of proceedings, 83, CFEP Hearing Records.

60 *Barnette v. West Virginia State Board of Education*, 47 F. Supp. 251 (S.D.W.Va. 1942).

61 Manwaring, *Render Unto Caesar*, 187.

62 *Ibid.*, 149.

63 *Brown v. Skustad*, Minnesota, St. Louis County District Court, 1942 (unreported), cited in Manwaring, *Render Unto Caesar*, 193.

64 *State v. Smith*, 127 P.2D 518 (Kan. 1942) and *Bolling v. Superior Court*, 133 P.2d 803 (Wash. 1943).

65 Complaint, 19 August 1942, *Barnette v. West Virginia State Board of Education*. National Archives and Records Administration, Mid-Atlantic Region, Phil., PA. Record Group 21, U.S. District for Southern WV, Civil Cases, Case 242, hereafter referred to as *Barnette v. WV Board of Education*.

66 Order, 27 August 1942, *Barnette v. WV Board of Education*.

67 "Board Reaffirms Flag Salute Rule," *The Charleston Gazette*, 16 September 1942, 1 and "Salute Ruling Unchanged," *The Charleston* (WV) *Daily Mail*, 16 Sept., 1942, 7.

68 *Ibid.*

69 "Salute Ruling Unchanged," *The Charleston* (WV) *Daily Mail*, 16 Sept., 1942, 7.

70 Manwaring, *Render Unto Caesar*, 212.

71 Final Decree, 6 Oct., 1942, *Barnette v. West Virginia Board of Education*.

72 316 U.S. 584 (1942), at 623-24.

73 *Murdock v. Pennsylvania*, 319 U.S. 105 (1943).

74 Manwaring, *Render Unto Caesar*, 215-17.

75 *Ibid.*, 217-20.

76 *Ibid.*, 220-24.

77 319 U.S. 624 (1943).

78 *Ibid.*, 642

Case Study:
HISTORIC BRIDGE CASE SPANNED YEARS

Douglas McKay
Attorney

Not so very many years ago the ancient Suspension Bridge in Wheeling, West Virginia, spanning the main channel of the Ohio River between its eastern shore and Wheeling Island in the center of the river, with its stately stone towers and graceful arches was named both a National Historic Landmark and a National Historic Civic Engineers Landmark. And in the current "World Almanac," it is the oldest structure listed under notable bridges in North America.

The old bridge was built between 1847 and 1849, and when completed its magnificent reach of one-thousand and ten feet between the supporting towers made it the longest span ever erected by man.

Yet this tribute to the engineering genius of Charles Ellet, Jr., the designer and contractor, and the spirit and foresight of Wheeling citizens was almost dismantled as quickly as it was constructed, for even before the first wagon was pulled across it, the bridge became the subject of a legal controversy which was to last until 1856.

In Philadelphia on the sixteenth day of August 1849, Mr. Edwin Stanton, later to be Secretary of War in Abraham Lincoln's cabinet, appeared before Mr. Justice Grier of the United States Supreme Court to move for an injunction in behalf of the State of Pennsylvania against the Wheeling and Belmont Bridge Company.

The bill stated that the Ohio River was one of the navigable rivers of the United States and was thus available for the commercial and free use of all of the citizens of all of the states of the Union; that the defendant was erecting a bridge between the main Virginia (now West Virginia) shore of the Ohio River at Wheeling to Zane's Island, crossing the channel of the Ohio River, which bridge would obstruct the navigation of the Ohio River; that the bridge was being erected under color of an act of the Virginia General Assembly which clearly provided that if such a bridge be built in this location it shall not be built in such a fashion as to be an obstruction to navigation upon the Ohio River. . . . If it does become an obstruction to navigation or a public nuisance, it shall be abated accordingly; that the bridge was only ninety-three and one-half feet above low water level at its eastern end and only sixty-two feet above low water level at its western end . . . that this bridge would not permit the passage of steamboats under it . . . and that this was preventing great volumes of commerce accustomed to ply between Pittsburgh and the ports down the river and even to foreign nations. The bill asked that an injunction be granted and that the bridge be ordered torn down.

The real parties in interest, of course, were the owners of steamboat packets and the commercial shippers of the city of Pittsburgh. It was a shrewd move on their part to get the State of Pennsylvania to file suit on their behalf as though the State of Pennsylvania were the injured party, in order to invoke the original jurisdiction of the Supreme Court of the United States under Article III, Section 2 of the Constitution. Not only would the commercial interests be represented by a powerful state, but the case would be heard and decided initially by the court of last resort.

The Wheeling and Belmont Bridge Company filed an answer stating that the sovereignty of Virginia over the Ohio River along her border was never ceded or surrendered; that the Navigable Waters Act of 1787 of the United States making such rivers as the Ohio common highways and forever free to the citizens of the United States was not intended to operate within the reserved territory and sovereignty of Virginia; that free navigation is not to be understood as one totally free from partial or incidental obstacles such as bridges; that Congress ordered a highway to be constructed from Cumberland (MD) to the Ohio River and afterwards ordered it to be extended westwardly from the western bank of the Ohio; that on March 14, 1847 the Legislature of Virginia passed an act chartering the Wheeling and Belmont Bridge Company and authorizing the latter to erect a wire suspension toll bridge at that site; that the plaintiff should have objected when bridge construction was first begun and not when it was nearly completed.

The answer of the defendant went on to add that the State of Pennsylvania has no right to be a party in a lawsuit on behalf of certain of her citizens who are the real parties in interest, and that because the bridge is an important link in an overland highway, the principles of concession and compromise should be considered.

The answer finally stated that for all useful purposes, the pipes or stacks of steamboats need not be more than forty-seven feet in height above the water . . . if the steamboat packet owners desired higher stacks, they could put them on hinges so that they could pass underneath the bridge.

Justice Grier refused to grant a preliminary injunction before the case was presented to the sitting entire Supreme Court because he felt that the plaintiff's right to prosecute this question involved a new point of law and that if the state of Pennsylvania had no right to prosecute this injunction suit, then the Supreme Court did not have original jurisdiction of the case.

Justice Grier also thought the injury would not be irremediable and that if the defendant proceeded to complete the bridge, it would gain no equity thereby but would be compelled to remove it at its expense if the decision were adverse to the defendant. Accordingly, he passed the matter on to the United States Supreme Court on the sixth day of September, 1849, and by the second day of February, 1850, the pleadings were complete.

In the meantime, in splendid partisan fashion, the Legislature of Virginia passed an act with respect to obstruction of navigation. This new act flatly declared that the bridge so erected across the Ohio River at Wheeling as aforesaid, at the height of ninety feet at the eastern abutment, ninety-three and a half feet at the highest point and sixty-two feet at the western abutment above the low water level of the Ohio River . . . was declared to be a lawful height . . . in conformity with the intent and meaning of the said 14th Section of the earlier act of March 19, 1847. A copy of this act as an exhibit was filed with the pleadings.

In regular session, the Supreme Court of the United States first entered an interlocutory order referring the matter to a Commissioner in Chancery, the Honorable R. Hyde Walworth, later late chancellor of the state of New York and directed Mr. Walworth to hold hearings and seek technical help in order to determine and report back to the court whether the bridge was or was not an obstruction of the free navigation of the Ohio River, and if it was an obstruction, what changes or alterations might be made to remove the obstruction to the free navigation of the river. . . .

The Commissioner in Chancery, who knew how to earn a fee rapidly, returned his report by the 13th of June, 1850, and after exceptions to it were filed, the matter was set down for full argument before the court on the second Monday in December of that year.

It is interesting to note that when the final arguments were presented to the full court, while Stanton was retained by the Attorney General of Pennsylvania to represent that state, the Wheeling and Belmont Bridge Company was represented by the Attorney General of Virginia, in direct contradiction of the argument of the defendant that this was a matter between private individuals and not states.

Among the many facts brought out through the testimony of experts before the Commissioner in Chancery were the following: that the usual spring and fall floods in March and December reached the height of thirty-eight feet; that floods ranging from twenty to thirty-eight feet regularly occurred in the months of January, February, March, April, May, June, July, November and December, or nine months in the space of a year; that the duration of the floods varied from two to ten days; that there were nine packets of the largest class of vessels, which class was increasing each year, which were unable to get under the Wheeling Bridge effectively at any stage of the water because of the combination of depth of the water needed to float them and the height of their chimneys, and that the larger packets had chimneys as high as eighty-four feet above the water level; that several boats had already had their stacks strike the bottom of the bridge, tearing away guys and fastenings; and that while chimneys might be hinged either near the top or near the bottom and laid down when the vessel was passing under the bridge, this was an extremely dangerous operation, the chimneys weighing two thousand to three thousand pounds each and being five feet in diameter, and being positioned above the hurricane deck, which is the deck for passengers. It was thought that if the hinging wires or mechanisms failed, the heavy chimneys would crash down through the hurricane deck all the way to the lower decks of the vessel.

Stanton, in his interminable argument which must have lasted for hours and which was highly repetitive, not only emphasized all the dangers involved, speaking dramatically of the great difficulty on a stormy night of lowering chimneys or maneuvering a ship so that it would pass under the highest part of the bridge in the narrow channel, but he also stressed the formal legal position of the plaintiff. That legal position of his was to be his undoing.

Stanton argued that the power to regulate commerce was vested exclusively in Congress and that such commerce is to be free and unfettered, and that it follows that any bridge erected by the defendant over the channel of the Ohio River, if it obstructs, interferes with or in any way regulates navigation, it is an unlawful obstruction no matter by what charter or state enactments it may be authorized or sanctioned. This matter being vested exclusively within the power of the United States Congress, it follows that any obstruction whatsoever with navigation is an encroachment upon Congressional power and thus unlawful.

The defendant's argument merely reiterated its earlier positions in the case.

The Commissioner in Chancery had reported back to the court that the bridge was indeed an obstruction to free navigation, but he had also concluded that it was practicable to alter the construction of the present bridge so that it would not be such an obstruction. He stated that the bridge should be raised so that its flooring for at least 300 feet wide over a convenient part of the channel would be at least one hundred and twenty feet above the bottom of the river.

Justice McLean issued the opinion of the majority of the court. He disposed of the objection that Pennsylvania was merely representing private citizens by declaring that from the evidence, he and the court thought that Pennsylvania had a true interest in the navigation of the Ohio River. Pennsylvania had been for years constructing canals and other forms of transportation all with a view of passing its goods and products down through the Ohio River.

But his main decision was grounded fatally upon the argument that the rights of Congress were paramount, that while it had not declared that a state, by the construction of bridges, should not obstruct the navigation of the Ohio River, Congress had regulated navigation upon such levels and had provided expressly that such navigation and commerce upon the river should be free. . . .

The justice agreed with the argument that it was too dangerous to lower chimneys, and that as to the argument that they might be constructed of a lesser height, he stated that the height of the chimney determines the speed of the packet, and that the cost in not being able to do so rapidly was too great to be borne merely for the accommodation of a road across the river.

Consequently the majority of the court, as stated by Justice McLean, believed that the bridge did obstruct the navigation of the Ohio, and that the state of Pennsylvania had been injured, and that she was entitled to the relief prayed for, that is, that the bridge should be abated, or, in the alternative, that the height of the bridge be raised to 111 feet from the low water mark for a width of at least 300 feet. In the decree which was entered, this became the injunction order given the defendant. The court then gave the defendant until the first day of February, 1853, either to remove the bridge at the expense of the defendant or to alter it as required.

Chief Justice Taney filed a dissenting opinion based principally upon the idea, that although the river is a navigable river and cannot be obstructed, Congress had provided no regulations relating to the height of bridges or what would constitute objections to navigation, and that in the absence of a congressional act, the Supreme Court has no power to act, since the matter was clearly not within the realm of common law. The dissent of Justice Daniel was more extensive but was based first upon the fact that the state had no right in this particular case to be a party in order to claim original jurisdiction... In the absence of legislation by Congress stating what is an obstruction to a river, this Supreme Court could not in legislative fashion supply special regulations or make any such declaration as to whether or not an obstruction is sufficient to deny the free navigability of the river.

He summarized his various positions as follows:

> "Believing that Pennsylvania cannot maintain this suit as a party by any just interpretation of the second section of the third article of the Constitution, vesting this court with original jurisdiction. Believing that the power which the majority of the court have assumed cannot, in this case be correctly derived to them from the competency of Congress to regulate commerce between the several states. Believing that the question of nuisance or no nuisance is intrinsically a question of fact, which, when contested, ought to be tried at law upon the circumstances of each case. . . . Seeing that the Commonwealth of Virginia, within whose territory and jurisdiction the Wheeling Bridge has been erected, has authorized and approved the erection of the bridge; and the United States under the pretext of whose authority this suit has been instituted, have by no act of theirs forbidden its erection, and do not now claim to have it abated; my opinion, upon the best lights I have been able to bring to this case, is that the bill of the complainant should be dismissed."

Subsequent to the court's decision, the defendant moved that the matter again be conferred to a commissioner for the purpose of letting the defendant determine which of many methods would be most practicable in order to satisfy the court. . . .

In this reference there was considered the following five possibilities: to elevate the bridge as required by the opinion of the court to a height of 111 feet above low water mark for a width of 300 feet; to remove the wooded bridge also owned by the defendant over the western channel of the river, to remove the flooring of the suspension bridge, so that the tallest chimneys may pass under the cables . . . to construct a draw in the wooden bridge over the western channel; or to make a draw in the suspension bridge.

All of the plans were held by the experts who testified to be unfeasible, except the elevation of the main span of the suspension bridge. Nobody seemed to know whether or not the channel on the western side of the island could carry the largest steam packets which were 250 feet in length and fifty feet in width.

The court determined that its original opinion and decree would stand.

But the defendant had not lost yet. Illustrating the power of the Commonwealth of Virginia relative to other states in the United States Congress, on the thirty-first day of August, 1852, before any action could be commenced as to the abatement of the bridge or its reconstruction to allow for greater elevation, the United States Congress passed the following act:

> "That the bridge across the Ohio River at Wheeling in the state of Virginia and at Bridgeport in the state of Ohio, abutting on Zane's Island, in said river, are hereby declared to be lawful structures in their present positions and elevations, and shall be so held and taken to be, anything in the law or of the United States to the contrary notwithstanding."

> ". . . That the said bridges be declared to be and are established post roads for the passage of the mails of the United States, and that the Wheeling and Belmont Bridge Company are authorized to have and maintain their bridges at their present site and elevation, and that the officers and crews of all vessels and boats navigating said river are re- quired to regulate the use of their said vessels, and of any pipes or chimneys belonging thereto, so as not to interfere with the elevation and construction of said bridges."

The parties to the original controversy were back in court arguing again in December 1855. The complainant, the State of Pennsylvania, had requested that contempt proceedings be taken against the Wheeling and Belmont Bridge Company for failing to tear down the bridge and remove it. The defendant claimed that the law of the United States Congress took care of the matter, and proceeded in effect the decision of the court in 1852. . . .

Justice Nelson said that although the Wheeling Bridge may be an obstruction in fact, it is not so any longer in the contemplation of law. Justice Nelson added that the court need not even pass upon whether or not Congress' power to establish post office and post roads would enable Congress to legalize the bridge. The court had already ruled that Congress alone has the power to regulate commerce on the river and can pass any laws designed to do exactly that, and Congress had passed such a law with respect to Wheeling Bridge.

The court further held that the defendant should not be held in contempt of this court since the act of Congress was passed before the defendant had an opportunity to remove the bridge and before the deadline date set by the court. And that this followed through even though in the interim the flooring of the bridge was blown into the river by a storm and defendant had defiantly proceeded to reconstruct it.

Justice McClean, who had written the majority opinion in the first application for an injunction, now wrote a long and rather bitter dissenting opinion in which, *inter alia*, he stated that the good faith of the defendant might even be questioned by this court since the defendant had procured Congress to pass an act completely setting aside the decision of this court.

Justice Grier agreed with the majority of the court at this time that the bridge company has a right to keep its bridge, but he did feel that there ought to be a contempt citation anyway against the defendant. Justices Wayne and Curtis felt the same way.

The case came to an end with the dissolution of the injunction. The Suspension Bridge at Wheeling is still standing 132 years later and still carrying traffic and serving the people of this area, while the picturesque stern or sidewheelers with their twin stacks have gone the way of the dinosaurs.

Reprinted with permission of the *News-Register*, Wheeling, West Virginia, August 16, 1987 and the author, Douglas McKay, Esquire, McKay & McKay, Wheeling, West Virginia.

CHAPTER SIX

Local Governments
and Issues

INTRODUCTION

It was noted in Chapter One, that the Tenth Amendment to the United States Constitution makes it clear that all powers not delegated to the national government, nor prohibited to the states, are reserved to the states and the people.[1] The question now arises, do local governments, which are part of the states, have any legal status under the Constitution? The answer is "no" because the Constitution says nothing about local governments, which may surprise us as local governments have been around for a long time and sometimes predate state governments. Wheeling, for example, is older than the State of West Virginia. Wheeling was incorporated as a town by the Virginia Assembly in January, 1806 and as a city in March, 1836; whereas West Virginia became a state on June 20, 1863.[2]

Actually, the Constitution recognizes two levels of governments, the national and the state which means that the states are "free" to do whatever they please with their local governments. There are no constitutional restrictions on how the states may divide or subdivide their governmental powers. In fact, states may even choose to abolish their local governments. Local governments are "legally dependent" on their respective states and as Judge John F. Dillon, put it in his famous rule:

> "It is a general and undisputed proposition of law that a municipal corporation <city or other subdivision> possesses and can exercise the following powers, and no others: First, those granted in express words; second, those necessarily or fairly implied in or incident to the power expressly granted; third, those essential to the accomplishment of the declared objects and purposes of the corporation—not simply convenient, but indispensable. Any fair, reasonable substantial doubt concerning the existence of power is resolved by the courts against the corporation, and the power is denied."[3]

The courts have additionally interpreted this arrangement of power to mean that municipalities have no inherent right of self government.[4] There are also constitutional limits on local power. What the state is forbidden from doing by the Fourteenth Amendment, so are local governments. For instance, the Wheeling City Council cannot enact an ordinance prohibiting its city newspapers from publishing the "Doonesbury" comics, because such action would be violative of the Fourteenth and First Amendments.[5]

In this chapter then, we are concerned with the legal framework, organization, and functioning of local governments in West Virginia. In particular, our focus is on some of the more important issues facing local politicians as they attempt to govern their communities in these times of increasing citizen demands and lean budgets.

Legal Framework—Municipal Corporations

Edward C. Banfield and James Q. Wilson in their "classic" *City Politics*, distinguish municipal corporations from private corporations. They write:

> ". . . Municipal corporations, . . . are artificial persons created by the state and <have> a standing in the eyes of the law. . . . The municipal corporation may be specially chartered, or it may be voluntarily organized under general acts of the state legislature. In these respects it is like a private corporation. It differs from a private corporation, however, in that it is chartered to serve public purposes only and its charter does not constitute a contract binding the state. The state can change the charter, or take it away altogether, without infringing anyone's rights. . . ."[6]

The "Municipal Home Rule Amendment" to the West Virginia Constitution prohibits the legislature from creating municipal corporations or granting charters by *special* law. Instead, the legislature has enacted a statute[7] that provides the steps that villages must follow to become incorporated:

> "To qualify for incorporation a place must be outside the limits of an existing municipality . . . the submission to the county court of a petition, signed by thirty per cent of the freeholders within the territory, accompanied by a map based on an actual survey. After a hearing to determine if the requirements of incorporation are met, the court orders a census and an enumeration of voters in the area . . . <and finally> an election on the issue. If a majority of those voting on the issue <are favorable>, a certificate of incorporation is issued by the county court. . . ."[8]

Once the municipality is created, it will be classified according to the provisions found in the "Municipal Home Rule Amendment" to the West Virginia Constitution which organized the state's local governments into four categories according to population.[9] Those communities with populations of 2,000 or more are classified as "cities" and communities with populations under 2,000 as "towns or villages."[10] "Towns and villages" are not allowed to draft charters and must adopt a Mayor-Council Plan for their municipal government.

Table 6.1 shows the classification of West Virginia Municipalities according to the "Municipal Home Rule Amendment" and *West Virginia Code*, Chapters 8 and 8A.

Table 6.1 Classification of West Virginia Municipalities

Class	Population
I	Cities with populations of 50,001 or more
II	Cities with populations of 10,001 to 50,000
III	Cities with populations of 2,001 to 10,000
IV	Towns or villages of 2,000 people or less

Source: *West Virginia Code*, Chapters 8 and 8A

The cities above that are classified as Class I, II, III are designated as "Home Rule" cities.[11] Basically, in the West Virginia context, "Home Rule" means the right of local communities to draft a charter and choose among five plans of local government: "mayor-council," "strong-mayor," "commission," "manager," and "manager-mayor" plans. Home Rule communities, according to the "Municipal Home Rule Amendment:"

> ". . . shall have power and authority to . . . amend the charter of such corporation . . . and through its legally constituted authority, may pass all laws and ordinances relating to its municipal affairs: Provided, that any charter or amendment thereto, and any such law or ordinance so adopted shall be invalid and void if inconsistent or in conflict with this Constitution or the general laws of the State then in effect, or thereafter from time to time enacted."[12]

Generally, the powers exercised by local government are seen as "express" grants of authority i.e., powers derived from the charter and ordinances (including applicable statutes). McCarthy[13] lists the "express" powers of municipalities as:

> "a. the formation of the local entity, alteration, boundary changes, internal operating problems, delegations of responsibility, elections and referenda;
>
> b. the police and zoning powers i.e., regulation of citizen conduct, business activity and land use, without compensation, to protect the public health, safety, morality and general welfare;
>
> c. the acquisition and expenditure of revenues derived from taxation, assessments, borrowing and investments."[14]

Yet, it is fair to say that in West Virginia, municipalities cannot exercise these "express" powers without serious restrictions found in the *West Virginia Code*. In effect,

> "Chapter eight and other provisions of the *West Virginia Code* clearly indicate that the procedural and substantive powers of West Virginia's cities flow from the statutes and not from individual home rule charter provisions. . . ."[15]

Do West Virginia's cities actually have any home rule at all? Probably not as was originally intended by the Municipal Home Rule Amendment. Instead, . . . "the only exceptions to the rule that "state law governs" is when the statutes clearly and expressly exempt or permit charter cities to do something differently."[16]

Organization and Functioning of Local Government

Villages and Cities

As previously noted, the *West Virginia Code* allows five types of local governments in West Virginia: the mayor-council, strong-mayor, commission, manager, and mayor-manager.[17]

The mayor-council or weak mayor-strong council type is most widely used in West Virginia because the *Code* requires its use in class IV villages and towns. The designation "weak" refers to the legal powers of the mayor in this type. The mayor is really the ceremonial head of the local government and presides over the council meetings. He shares "governing and administrative authority" with the council.

There are 707 local governments in West Virginia[18] this includes 231 municipalities, 55 counties, 55 county school districts and 366 special districts. These are strictly regulated by the *West Virginia Code*. For example the *Code*, Chapter 8 provides that these "small communities" (those with less than 2000 residents) shall have a council elected at large or by wards, a recorder, a mayor, when to hold elections, etc.[19]

It should be noted that there are variations of the popular strong-mayor and manager-council forms currently operating in West Virginia. Wheeling, until recently utilized a "weak" mayor with its manager-council form. A few years ago, Wheeling changed its charter to embrace the mayor-manager form.

The *Code* details the basic features of the strong-mayor form:

> "There shall be a mayor elected by the qualified voters of the city; and a city council elected at large or by wards, or both at large and by wards, by the qualified voters of the city; . . . The council shall be the governing body; . . . The mayor shall be the administrative authority . . . and . . . other officers and employees shall be appointed by the mayor or by his order in accordance with this charter, but such appointments by the mayor or by his order may be made subject to the approval of the council."[20]

Today, the commission form of municipal government is quite rare in West Virginia. When it is found, it generally follows the co-mingling of powers idea. That is, both administrative and legislative powers are found with the three to five member commissions that are elected at large by the voters. The *Code* prescribes that there "shall be a commissioner of public affairs, a commissioner of finance, a commissioner of public safety, a commissioner of public works, and a commissioner of streets. . ."[21] Finally, the commissioners are responsible for electing a mayor from among their membership.

The next type of municipal government in West Virginia is manager-council. Under this arrangement a five to eleven member council appoints a professional city manager to run the public affairs of the city. The council also elects a mayor from its membership to preside over council meetings. The council then, is the governing or policy-making body while the manager is the chief administrative authority. The manager is responsible to the council and serves at their pleasure. He is, in effect, a professional supervisor of the various municipal offices in the city. He hires and fires all subordinates, and is accountable to the council for the job performance of "his people."

The key to understanding the council-manager form is the important relationship that exists between the council and the manager. The line between policy formulation by the council and policy execution by the manager is not always clear. Successful city managers are frequently initiators of policy, but they must be careful that their leadership is not interpreted as offensive to the council. In the final analysis it is the manager's personality and professional skills that makes the difference in the manager-council relationship especially when the city faces difficult times.

The last type or plan of local government is the mayor-manager form. The *Code* outlines its basic features:

> "(1) There shall be a council of not less than five nor more than eleven members, elected either at large or from such geographical districts as may be established by the charter, or partly at large and partly from such geographical districts . . . (2) There shall be a mayor elected at large by the qualified voters of the municipality as may be established by the charter, who shall serve as a member and the presiding officer of the council; and a city manager who shall be appointed by the council; (3) The council shall be the governing body; and the (4) manager shall be the administrative authority. He shall manage the affairs of the city under the supervision of the council and he shall be responsible to the council. He shall appoint or employ . . . all subordinates and employees. . ."[22]

Legal Framework—Counties

With the exception of persons who live in unincorporated rural areas, most West Virginians are under the jurisdictions of both municipal and county governments.[23] This local governmental dualism is typical in most states.[24] In fact, multiple political jurisdictions are defended by Vincent Ostrom as integral to the American "compound republic."[25] That is, these overlapping jurisdictions are thought to be more responsive to the needs of the individual citizen. For example, West Virginia counties and municipalities may appear to be interdependent. Yet legally they have little to do with each other. The jurisdiction of the municipality is only found within its boundaries, whereas the county's jurisdiction includes all persons whether they are residents of a city or not. County officials do have jurisdiction within municipalities if they wish to exercise it.

Other writers are less kind to county government: "County government in the United States . . . is the dark continent of American politics . . . the last refuge

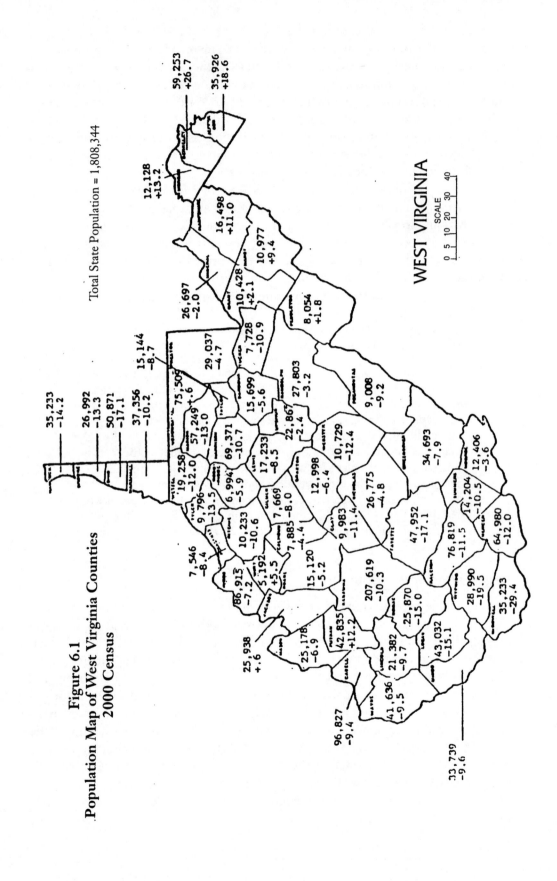

Figure 6.1
Population Map of West Virginia Counties
2000 Census

Total State Population = 1,808,344

WEST VIRGINIA

SCALE
0 5 10 20 30 40

of political incompetency."[26]

These "refuges of political incompetency" are sometimes classified as "quasi-corporations."[27]

> "Quasi-corporations . . . are involuntary territorial and political subdivisions of states. These include counties, townships, the New England town, and special districts. . . . The quasi-corporation is an administrative arm of state government, but it differs from others in that its heads may be elected from an electorate which is not of the whole state. It is subject to the legislature in the same way that other parts of the state government are. . . ."[28]

Quasi-corporations "can do only such things as are authorized by law, and in the mode prescribed."[29] Counties perform both state and local functions. For example, the sheriff and county prosecutor enforce state laws, while the county commission may supervise a county health department. "The chief feature distinguishing counties <quasi-corporations> from municipal corporations . . . is the lack of power to legislate on a local level."[30]

Organization and Functioning of Counties

West Virginia's counties have their roots in Virginia. In eighteenth century Virginia, for example, what is today West Virginia contained only four counties - Ohio, Monongalia, Hampshire and Berkeley.[31] Eventually most of these original counties were subdivided into smaller counties. In 1863 when the State of West Virginia was carved out of Virginia there were already fifty counties operating in the "new" state. Grant, Lincoln, Mineral, Mingo, and Summers were created after the separation of the state from Virginia.[32]

These early counties had "strong" governments which were run by "the justices of the peace of the county <who> sat collectively as the county court, which was the governing body of the county."[33] These early county courts exercised "distinct electoral, managerial, judicial and even military responsibilities."[34] The county populace exerted little accountability over these early officials. They were appointed by the governor until the 1851 Virginia constitutional reforms mandated that they be elected.[35]

West Virginia's first constitution (1863) established a system of townships. The township[36] is simply a subdivision of a county. The unique feature of these townships was the town meeting form of government, which is found in New England today. Elected officials such as township supervisors, the sheriff, recorder, assessor, etc., replaced the county court in handling the affairs of the townships.[37]

It is interesting to note at this time that there were two "models" of county government to choose from—the Massachusetts and Virginia models. The Massachusetts model in the beginning was not very democratic as the original counties in that state were run by officials appointed by the governor. Gradually, with constitutional reform in Massachusetts the county governments lost most of their governing power with the decline of gubernatorial authority. The counties became merely extensions of state government and the "self-governing New En-

261

gland town became the predominant unit of local government."[38] Today, counties in Massachusetts, for example, are judicial jurisdictions.

The Virginia model has persisted to the present day as a strong form of county government. It was accomplished with the idea that counties should be more than merely administrative appendages of state government. Pennsylvania early modified the Virginia model with the idea of the county commission—a board of supervisors elected by each county's citizens.[39]

With the advent of the 1872 West Virginia Constitution, the present Constitution, the county court system was restored. "The ruling body of the county was once again the county court composed of a president elected at large and justices of the peace."[40] The West Virginia constitutional reforms of 1880 established the three-member court (commission system) that is still in use, with some modifications, today.[41]

Magisterial Districts and County Commissions

The West Virginia Constitution provides that counties are subdivided into at least three but no more than ten magisterial districts of approximately equal population.[42] *The West Virginia Blue Book, 2000,* "County Register" lists 220 magisterial districts with only Mason County having ten magisterial districts.[43] These magisterial districts exist for the sole purpose that magistrates are elected from them.

Each of West Virginia's fifty-five counties is administered by the county court (retitled county commission in 1974). The Constitution of the state stipulates that every county court (county commission) shall consist of three commissioners (actually Jefferson County elects five). Any two of the commissioners constitute a quorum for the transaction of the county's business. The county commission is charged with the responsibility of electing one of its commissioners president.[44]

The county commissioners are elected to six-year staggered terms and are restricted to the requirement that no more than one may be from the same magisterial district in the county.[45] The commission is also required to hold at least four regular sessions, but may meet in special session "whenever the public interests may require it."[46]

Generally the functions of the county commission are outlined in the *Code:*

> "The county courts (county commissions), through their clerks, shall have the custody of all deeds and other papers presented for record in their counties . . . shall have jurisdiction in all matters probate. . . . They shall also, under such regulations as are now prescribed by law, have the superintendence and administration of the internal police and fiscal affairs of their counties, including the establishment and regulation of roads, ways, bridges, to lay and disburse the county levies. . ."[47]

"The authority to lay and disburse the county levies" is the most important power of the county commission.[48] Yet, this power is curtailed by the Tax Limitation Amendment of 1932 which was supposed to help West Virginians survive the Great Depression by lowering taxes. Two other tax limiting factors have also contributed to the relatively low taxes collected in West Virginia's counties: (1) property is assessed considerably below its actual value and (2) the property is only taxed on part of its assessed value.[49]

The county commissions do have other ways of raising monies especially for education and libraries. The Better Schools Amendment of 1958 gave the county commissions the authority to increase the property tax, if sixty percent of the county voters approve in a school levy election. The problem here was that many of the voters in poorer counties simply refused to support additional taxes and thus these county school systems suffered from meager funding, which contributed to low teacher salaries and inadequate school facilities.[50]

Recent events suggest that the property-tax system in West Virginia's counties is changing. The "Lincoln County Case" (Pauley, et al., v. Kelly, 1979), discussed in the previous chapter, ruled that the property-tax system for financing education in West Virginia is unconstitutional. Moreover, the court found that the county property-tax system was unfair to those children who live in poor "anti-tax levy" counties.

Because of the court's mandate and the publicity from the "Lincoln County" decision, the legislature and the voters approved a constitutional amendment to the West Virginia Constitution. The Property Tax Limitation and Homestead Exemption Amendment of 1982 provided for the following:

> "All property must be appraised (reassessed) at its 1980 value by 1985. Property is to be taxed on 60 percent of its value. The legislature can exempt (excuse) elderly property owners from paying property taxes on the first $20,000 worth of residential property. The legislature may enact a statewide excess levy, so that county school systems will be funded more equally."[51]

The Property Tax Limitation and Homestead Amendment are not fully implemented, although considerable statewide progress was made in reassessing property. A chorus of citizen complaints, and many county commission hearings for angry property owners who complained that their reassessments were too high, have underscored the point that generally West Virginians dislike tax increases. Governor Arch A. Moore, during his third term (1985–89) and perhaps reflecting this anti-tax populist view, did not actively push the reassessment process along.

The question now arises, what is the explanation of the differences in tax policy between West Virginia and its neighboring states? Thomas R. Dye presents considerable evidence to support his argument that "economic development" is the key to the variability of tax policy in the states. By economic development Dye means "three closely related components: urbanization, income and education."[52] It was noted in Chapter Two (see Table 2.1) that West Virginia ranks considerably below most states in these categories. One might expect from the previous discussion of the general reluctance of state and county officials to raise taxes to support public schools that West Virginians generally pay lower taxes than their neighbors do.

The data in Table 6.2 reveal that West Virginia does indeed rank lower than its neighboring states, except Kentucky, in per capita state-local tax revenues as a percentage of personal income. Since West Virginia ranks thirty-eighth nationally, it's citizens pay less taxes than do citizens in all but twelve of the fifty states. The *tax burden* for West Virginians is another matter. "The concept of tax burden generally refers to taxes paid in relation to personal income; because of differences among the states in income levels, states with the highest *levels of taxation* are not necessarily the same states with the highest tax burdens."[53]

West Virginia ranks twenty-third among the fifty states in its citizens' ability to pay taxes. It is easier for citizens in twenty-seven other states to pay taxes than in West Virginia.

Table 6.2 Per Capita State-Local Tax Revenue as a Percentage of Personal Income, West Virginia and Selected States

States	Per Capita State-Local Tax Revenue (national rank)	State-Local Tax Revenue as a % of Personal Income (national rank)
PA	25	34
OH	16	33
MD	22	29
KY	46	23
CT	12	16
WV	**38**	**23**
VA	44	46

Data adapted from: Thomas R. Dye, *Politics in States and Communities*, Tenth Edition, (2000), 513.

County Officers

The county commissioners share their responsibility of governing with a number of other elected officials. These include the clerk of the county commission (county clerk), the clerk of the circuit court, the assessor, the sheriff, prosecuting attorney (county prosecutor), coroner, county board of education, surveyor, etc.[54]

Organizational charts of the county commission form of government show, what was obvious to the royal thinkers in the middle ages when the English shires (counties) were first founded, that the dukes and sheriffs both made policy and administered it. Today, in many important respects, West Virginia's county officers resemble their medieval brethren. The county sheriff, for example, is still a collector of taxes in addition to his law enforcement responsibilities. He is elected to a four year term and is limited by the state constitution to two consecutive terms. Interestingly, his fellow county officers have no constitutional limitations placed on their reelection possibilities.

The data in Table 6.3 profiles West Virginia sheriffs' views on a number of issues relating to their jobs—recognition, pay, professional growth, equipment and politics[55]

Table 6.3 Job Satisfaction—West Virginia Sheriffs

Question (n=38)	Satisfied	Dissatisfied	Not Sure
"Do you enjoy being sheriff?"	87%	10%	3%
"Do you feel that WV sheriffs receive adequate recognition?"	26%	58%	3%
"Do you feel that WV sheriffs receive adequate pay?"	32%	68%	–
"Do you feel your position allows professional growth?"	19%	48%	29%
Office Space	45%	48%	1%
Office Equipment			
typewriters	58%	36%	1%
computers	45%	39%	3%
Law Enforcement Equipment			
patrol cars	42%	55%	3%
weapons	58%	38%	3%
radios	52%	45%	1%
breathalyzer equipment	74%	19%	7%
identification equipment	36%	52%	3%
teletype equipment	65%	32%	3%
Politics			
county commission	61%	39%	—
prosecutor	81%	16%	3%
city police	84%	13%	3%
State Government			
tax commissioner	84%	10%	6%
state police	81%	13%	6%
attorney general	71%	19%	7%
Local Citizens	97%	3%	—

Source: 1990 West Virginia Sheriffs Study

Inspection of Table 6.3 shows that the sheriffs in several important areas were unhappy in what F. Herzberg (1966) calls the "strong determiners" of job satisfaction—recognition, achievement, the work itself, responsibility and advancement. Only 26% of the sheriffs (n = 38) felt that they received adequate recognition and a very low percentage, 19%, registered satisfaction with the growth possibilities of their jobs. With the exceptions of office space and identification equipment, the sheriffs were generally satisfied with their working environments. Interestingly, 87% of the sheriffs said that they "enjoyed" being sheriff.

What can we make of these data? First, it needs to be stated that the sheriff is a politician. He campaigns for his job and faces the voters' judgements on election day. The open-ended responses to the questionnaires showed that some sheriffs were unhappy with the term limitation (mentioned above), others implied by their comments that they were seeking higher office. In addition, the open-ended responses revealed that the context or environment of each sheriff is unique. A few sheriffs complained that they did little law enforcement work and were primarily tax collectors. Another said that he did virtually no law enforcement, while still another sheriff did not have a patrol car. It would appear that West Virginia's sheriffs have become quite adaptable and have molded their positions to fit their personalities and perceptions of constituents' needs.

The county clerk is the chief record keeper in the county. All major county records, births, deaths, marriages, divorces, county voter registration, etc., are kept in his office. The clerk is elected on a county-wide, partisan ballot to a six-year term.

The records of the county circuit court are kept by the clerk of the circuit court. This individual is also elected, as noted above, to a six year term. The clerk of the court handles the filing of candidates who are running for public office and issues absentee ballots prior to elections. Law suits destined for the circuit court originate in the clerk's office. Clerks of county circuit courts have the additional responsibilities of issuing summons, and impaneling juries. The political survival of the clerk frequently depends upon the clerk's skill in dealing with the prosecutor, county judges and attorneys.

Another important county official is the assessor. Unlike other county officials, the county assessor is elected to a four-year term. This financial officer has the responsibility of determining the value "of all real and personal property" in the county. It was discussed earlier that the property tax policy generally followed through the years tried to provide tax relief for many "poor" West Virginians. Accordingly, some county assessors in poorer counties tended to assess property considerably less (e.g., thirty percent) than the assessed values found in the wealthier counties. However, in the Logan County case, *Killen v. Logan County*, (1982) the court required: "That all property be given an assessed valuation of one hundred percent of its appraised value under existing appraisals, and one hundred percent of market value determined by a new reappraisal. . . ."[56]

The Property Tax Limitation and Homestead Amendment (discussed earlier) provided additional sweeteners by diluting the impact of the court's decision:

> "It requires that assessed value be fixed at sixty percent of the new 'appraised value' but requires that any increase in assessed value resulting from the reappraisal be spread equally over ten years. It requires that any law raising the percentage of assessed value above sixty percent be

approved by two-thirds of the legislature rather than the simple majority required before the Logan County case. The percentage could only be decreased by a constitutional amendment. <Finally> it gives back to the legislature the authority to provide by law for the duties of the tax commissioner, assessor and county commission with respect to appraisal and assessment."[57]

The Appointed County Administrator

It should be obvious to the reader that county organization generally is in need of reform. For example, the county commissioners—supposedly the policy-making bodies of county government—have little authority to make policy because the state legislature makes and the supreme court interprets all policy for counties in West Virginia. Moreover, the counties' elected "row officers" (sheriffs, clerks, prosecuting attorneys, auditors, assessors, coroners) likewise have little policy-making authority, but plenty of clerical responsibility.

One way to centralize this decentralized, plural executive form of county government is to appoint an "administrator" or so the county commission of Cabell County thought in 1965.

The West Virginia Supreme Court of Appeals predictably did not allow such an appointment even under the "implied powers" doctrine.

> "No specific duty is imposed upon the County Court which is carried with it an inference that the County Court is empowered to employ a secretary and assistant. . . . While under its general powers and duties a County Court shall have the superintendence and administration of the internal policy and fiscal officers of its county, such functions are performed through its clerk, also an elected official. Code, 7-1-3. The secretarial and clerical duties can be and generally are performed by the County Clerk and his employees."[58]

The supreme court concluded that "power by implication" must be based upon express authority or statute and in this case neither was found.[59]

Finally in 1974, Chapter 7, Article 1, of the *West Virginia Code* was amended by the legislature to allow county commissions the authority to appoint county administrators.[60] The *West Virginia Blue Book 2000* "County Register" lists twelve counties with county administrators.

County Reorganization

Governor Gaston Caperton also proposed in his February 13, 1989 "State of the State Address" that a "County Reorganization Amendment" be added to the state constitution. This idea of this joint resolution, "would allow counties to change their form of government. It would enable them to merge and allow counties and cities to form metro governments."[61] The measure had the following provisions:

> "No new county may hereafter be formed in this state except by the consolidation of counties. The Legislature shall provide by law for the

consolidation of two or more counties or the division of a county and the consolidation of the division . . . with one or more counties. . . .

. . . . the Legislature shall provide by law for not less than three forms of county organizations and governments . . . a county manager or county executive type of organization and government; at least one form . . . shall be the form in the counties upon the date of enactment of this amendment . . . and at least one form . . . shall provide for the consolidation of the offices and functions . . . of the elected county officers . . . as they exist when this amendment takes effect. . . .

. . . . that municipal and county governments may be merged into one consolidated government with one set of officers but the county shall remain as a geographic area after such consolidation. . . ."[62]

Finally, the proposed amendment required the consent of the citizens that would be affected by the reorganizations or consolidations. It is here where the problem lies—"most consolidation efforts <historically> fail."[63] In spite of the arguments from civic leaders, academics and businessmen that consolidation and reorganization would provide more efficiency, improved and better coordinated services, county residents or suburbanites tend to reject these reform measures.[64] As discussed in Chapter 4, this is exactly what happened—the voters overwhelmingly defeated the County Reorganization Amendment.

The selections for this final chapter provide the reader with a "feel" for the varied nature of the issues and problems facing those "governments that are closest to the people."

First, Tom D. Miller, former Correspondent, *Huntington Herald-Dispatch* raises a perplexing question about the ownership of non-public lands in West Virginia. He updated an earlier study, "Who Owns West Virginia" (1974) where he found "two-thirds of the privately held land in West Virginia is owned or controlled via leases by large corporations and family trusts." His follow-up survey completed in 1988 (reported here) found little change in that pattern of out-of-state ownership.

Next, Alfred "Pinky" Clark, former Marshall County Assessor, discusses the legal, political and cultural implications involved in his decision to deny property tax exemptions to the New Vrindaban Community, located on a one hundred acre plot in Moundsville, Marshall County, West Virginia. Although he recognizes that the First Amendment guarantees the "free exercise" of religion, he argues that the amendment does not guarantee religious institutions exemptions from property taxation.

Finally, Evelyn L.K. Harris discusses the nature of the voluntary municipal consolidations with the municipalities located along both sides of the Kanawha River. Local officials and citizens in these communities worked out these creative agreements a number of years ago, to more efficiently solve environmental, law enforcement, fire protection and other problems. These activities were completed quite some time ago, and certainly before the recent passage by the legislature of the "County Reorganization Amendment" which was rejected by the voters. Today, these Kanawha Valley consolidations, more so than ever before, should serve as trend setters for other municipalities to follow.

It is appropriate to end this reader with the Harris selection because she provides insight and hope into how West Virginia's governments could finally improve, namely through the creativity and resilience of its people.

Notes

[1] The Tenth Amendment, like other amendments, has a varied interpretation by the Supreme Court. For example, "the Supreme Court from time to time held that some of the reserved powers of the states were sovereign powers and hence set a limit to the delegated powers of the national government (e.g., *Hammer v. Dagenhart*, 1918). See J.W. Peltason, *Corwin and Peltason's Understanding the Constitution*, eleventh edition, (New York: Holt, Rinehart and Winston, Inc., 1988), 215. "Today it makes no constitutional difference whether or not an act of Congress touches or governs matters otherwise subject to state regulation. Congressional regulation supersedes any conflicting state regulation." *Ibid.*, 216. Finally, in *Garcia v. San Antonio Metropolitan Transit Authority*, 469 U.S. 528 (1985), "the court held that the Tenth Amendment is not to be construed as setting any substantial judicially enforceable limits on the national government's full exercise of the powers granted to it." *Ibid.*

[2] James R. Forrester, "The Milieu of an 1855 Wheeling Ordinance Book," *Upper Ohio Valley Historical Review*. Vol. 18, (1989), 4-15.

[3] John F. Dillon, *Municipal Corporations*, fifth edition, (Boston: Little Brown & Company, 1911), Vol. I, 237.

[4] See *Trenton v. New Jersey*, 262 U.S. 182, (1923). "The city is a political subdivision of the state, created as a convenient agency . . . the state may withhold, grant, or withdraw powers and privileges as it sees fit . . . In the absence of state constitutional provisions safeguarding it to them, municipalities have no inherent right of self government which is beyond the legislative control of the state." West Virginia Supreme Court of Appeals applications of Dillon's rule may be seen in *Sheldon v. City of Wheeling*, 146 WV 691 (1961); *Hyre v. Brown*, 102 WV 505, 1926); and *Maxey v. City of Bluefield*, 151 WV 302, 151 S.E. 2d 689.

[5] See J.W. Peltason, *loc.cit.* (note 1 above); the *Wheeling News Register*, several years ago, did drop the "Doonesbury" comic strip from its "funnies section" of the paper.

[6] Edward C. Banfield and James Q. Wilson, *City Politics*, (New York: Vintage Books, 1963), 63.

[7] *West Virginia Code*, Chapters 8 and 8A.

[8] Claude J. Davis, *et al.*, *West Virginia State and Local Government*, (Morgantown, WV: Bureau for Government Research, West Virginia University, 1963), 427.

[9] *West Virginia Code*, Chapter 8, Sections 1–3.

[10] *West Virginia Code*, 8-3-2, 62–64.

[11] The newly elected Governor Gaston Caperton proposed in his February 13, 1989 "State of the State Address" to the West Virginia Legislature a constitutional amendment that would allow counties and cities real home rule including city-county mergers. See "Caperton Maps Course for West Virginia," *The Intelligencer*, February 14, 1989.

12 *The Constitution of West Virginia*, Article 6, Section, 39a.

13 See David J. McCarthy, Jr. *Local Government Law*, (St. Paul, Minnesota: West Publishing Company, 1983), *passim*.

14 *Ibid.*, 7.

15 David A. Bingham, *Manual for Drafting or Revising West Virginia City Charters*, (Morgantown, WV: Bureau for Government Research, West Virginia University, 1975), 12.

16 *Ibid.;* David A. Bingham, "No Home Rule in West Virginia," *National Civic Review*, (April, 1980), 213–214.

17 *West Virginia Code*, 8-3-2.

18 See National Association of Counties, City/County Search; http://www.nac.org/counties/queries/city1_res.cfm

19 *Code, loc. cit.*

20 As of August 1, 1987, the *West Virginia Blue Book*'s "Municipal Register" does not list a "pure" city commission form of government in West Virginia. Claude Davis, *et al.*, *West Virginia State and Local Government* (Morgantown, WV: Bureau for Government Research, West Virginia University, 1963), 434. previously listed Keyser, Parkersburg, Fairmont and Williamstown as employing the commission form. All of these cities have since changed to the strong-mayor or manager-council forms.

21 *West Virginia Code*, 8-3-2.

22 *Ibid.*

23 Robert S. Lorch, *State and Local Politics, The Great Entanglement* (Englewood Cliffs, New Jersey: Prentice-Hall, 1989), 217, uses the metaphor "mother and child" in referring to this dual arrangement of government.

24 Connecticut is an exception. Connecticut abolished counties as a unit of government in 1968 and as a result "state government . . . become<s> the metropolitan government unit in Connecticut since Connecticut transferred county functions to the state." See Steve Redburn, et al., "How Representative are Mandated Citizen Participation Processes?" *Urban Affairs Quarterly*, 15 (March, 1980), 350.

25 See Vincent Ostrom, *The Intellectual Crisis in American Public Administration* (University: University of Alabama Press, 1973), 16.

26 See Henry S. Gilbertson, *The County: The Dark Continent of American Politics* (New York: National Short Ballot Association, 1917), *passim.*; Davis, *et al., op. cit.*, 445.

27 See *Exchange Bank of Virginia v. County of Lewis*, 28 W. Va. 273 (1886).

28 Banfield and Wilson, *loc. cit.*

39 *Goshorn's Ex'rs v. County Court*, 42 WV 735, 26 S.E. 452 (1896); *Barbor v. County Court*, 85 WV 359, 101 S.E. 721 (1920).

30 Davis, *op. cit.*, 447.

31 Davis, *op. cit.*, 446.

32 *Ibid.*

33 *Ibid.*

34 Nicholas Henry, *Governing at the Grassroots, State and Local Politics*, third edition, (Englewood Cliffs, New Jersey: Prentice-Hall, 1987), 216.

35 Davis, *loc. cit.*

36 A township needs to be distinguished from the New England town. Generally, "a township is intended to be a rural government, not a city government, whereas a New England town is intended to provide government for both urban and rural areas within its boundaries . . . Townships do not practice direct democracy in the New England town hall fashion . . . The boundaries of most townships <today> are arbitrary squares, six miles to a side, no attempt having been made to encompass natural communities as New England towns do . . . Township boundaries are for the most part (except in New York, New Jersey, and Pennsylvania) the result of a monumental effort to survey the vast territory acquired by the Louisiana Purchase . . . Township government today is the least glorious of all government; the most local of all government; the most obscure of all government; and probably the most trivial, homely, and provincial of all government. Townships are being slowly extinguished by counties . . . <and> most of the functions of townships (which are basically identical to those of counties) are simply being transferred to counties." Lorch, *op. cit.*, 241–242.

37 Davis, *loc. cit.*; Henry, *loc. cit.*

38 Henry, *op. cit.*, 216–217.

39 *Ibid.*

40 Davis, *loc. cit.*

41 The 2000 census shows that West Virginia's fifty-five counties range in population from Wirt County's 5,873 to Kanawha's 200,073. The average county population is 32,098 people which clearly suggests that West Virginia is a rural state.

42 *West Virginia Constitution*, Article 8, Section 27.

43 Darell Holmes, *West Virginia Blue Book, 1996*, (Charleston, WV: Chapman Printing, 1996), 711-796.

44 *West Virginia Constitution*, Article 8, Section 22.

45 *West Virginia Code*, 7-1-1.

46 *Ibid.*, 7-1-2.

47 *Ibid.*, 7-1-3; The courts have stated that "the county court (county commission) is a corporation created by statute, and can do only such things as are authorized by law, and in the mode prescribed." *Goshorn's Ex'rs v. County Court*, 42 WV 735, 26 S.E. 452 (1896); *Barbor v. County Court*, 85 WV 359, 101 S.E. 721 (1920); "County commissioners are not authorized to exercise municipal powers in the absence of statutory authority to do so, but the constitution poses no prohibition upon the legislature which would preclude it from granting to county commissions further powers ordinarily associated with municipalities." *Op. Att'y Gen.*, Dec., 15, 1986, number 8.

48 Davis, *op. cit.*, 449.

49 William E. Coffey, Carolyn M. Karr and Frank S. Riddel, *West Virginia Government* (Charleston, WV: Education Foundation, Inc., 1983), 73–74.

50 *Ibid.*

51 Earl M. Vickers, "Summary of Property Tax Limitation and Homestead Exemption Amendment," *Joint Committee on Government and Finance*, West Virginia Legislature, 2.

52 Dye, *op. cit.*, 8.; See also, Dye, *Politics, Economics, and the Public* (Chicago: Rand McNally, 1966), Ch. 7.

53 *Ibid.*, 483.

54   For a full list of the various elected and appointed county officials, see a recent edition of the *West Virginia Blue Book*, especially the "County Register" section. For a complete discussion of the duties of these county officers see the *West Virginia Code*, Chapter 7; see also, Robert J. Dilger, "County Government in West Virginia," The *West Virginia Public Affairs Reporter*, Vol. 12, No. 3, (Morgantown, West Virginia: Institute for Public Affairs, WVU, Summer, 1995), 8-15.

55   The West Virginia Sheriffs Study was a public administration class project conducted in the Fall of 1990 by West Liberty student John Briggs. The study, with help from the author, applied F. Herzberg's ideas of job "satisfiers" and "dissatisfiers" to West Virginia sheriffs. See F. Herzberg, "The Motivation-Hygiene Theory," *Work and The Nature of Man*, (New York: World Publishing Company, 1966), 71–91. A follow-up study conducted in the Fall, of 1994, basically corroborated the results of the original study. The data are not reported because only 19 questionnaires (35%) were returned. <ed.>.

56   Vickers, *loc. cit.*

57   *Ibid.*, 3.

58   See Barry J. Goldberg, "The Appointed County Administrator in West Virginia," *The West Virginia Public Affairs Reporter*, Vol 1, No 1 (Morgantown, West Virginia: Bureau of Government Research, 1976), 3; *Arthur v. County Court of Cabell County* (1965).

59   An appointed county administrator is "defined as that person, appointed by the governing body, who is charged with the overall administrative responsibility of county government." Goldberg, *loc. cit.*

60   Goldberg, *op. cit.*, 6.

61   Willis, *loc. cit.*

62   *Ibid.*, 1000–1004.

63   Goldberg, *op. cit.*, 4.

64   See Thomas A. Henderson and Walter A. Rosenbaum, "Prospects for Consolidating Local Government: The Role of Elites in Electoral Outcomes," *American Journal of Political Science*, 17 (November, 1973), 695-720; also Vincent L. Marando and Carl Whitley, "City-County Consolidation: An Overview of Voter Response," *Urban Affairs Quarterly*, 8 (December, 1972), 181-203.

Web Sites

http://www.polsci.wvu.edu/wv/wvlinks.html#cities

(West Virginia cities)

http://www.polsci.wvu.edu/wv/wvlinks.html#counties

(West Virginia counties)

http://www.naco.org

(National Association of Counties)

http:www.nlc.org

(National League of Cities)

Case Study:
WHO OWNS WEST VIRGINIA?

Tom D. Miller
Correspondent

During Jay Rockefeller's first term as governor, he persuaded Cotiga Limited Partnership to "donate" 88 acres of land it owns in Mingo County to the state. Rockefeller wanted to use the land to build new houses for flood victims.

Actually, Rockefeller tried to buy the property for $1,000 an acre first in 1977 but Cotiga countered with an offer of $4,500 an acre. After five years of negotiations and a suit to condemn the land, the owners decided to donate it instead.

It turned out to be a good deal for Cotiga and a bad one for the state. COTIGA (Named for the valuable COal, TImber and GAs in the ground it owned) kept title to the valuable mineral rights underneath the surface and no longer had to pay property taxes.

But state government failed to follow through on its plans to build new homes on Laurel Creek and became a slum landlord, collecting nominal rents from a dozen residents living in shacks on the land.

Cotiga, with more than 40,000 acres in Mingo County, is one of two dozen well-known absentee landlords who owns or controls most of the mineral wealth in West Virginia. And it is a classic case of how people of this state sold their birthright to foreigners generations ago.

In 1884, when Mingo County was still part of Logan County, Philadelphia merchant Stuart Wood began a steady plan of buying land for 50 cents an acre. He sold sewing machines and other goods to the residents and often took land as payment for those items.

Today, a large map of Mingo County hangs in the Cotiga office in Wyndmoor, Pennsylvania, a suburb of Philadelphia, and fourth-generation heir Ted Wood scoffs at the hint his great-uncle was a peddler. And he insists his ancestors were simply good businessmen who saw the potential for the mineral-rich state more quickly than the people living there.

According to a study made by the *Herald-Dispatch* in 1974, two thirds of the privately held land in West Virginia is owned or controlled via leases by large corporations and family trusts. And in a follow-up survey in 1988, there was little change in that pattern (see Figure 6.2).

At that point, in 33 of the state's 55 counties, at least 25 percent or more of the land was held by absentee ownership. And it was becoming even more clear then that the remaining counties were being forced to subsidize welfare, educa-

Figure 6-2

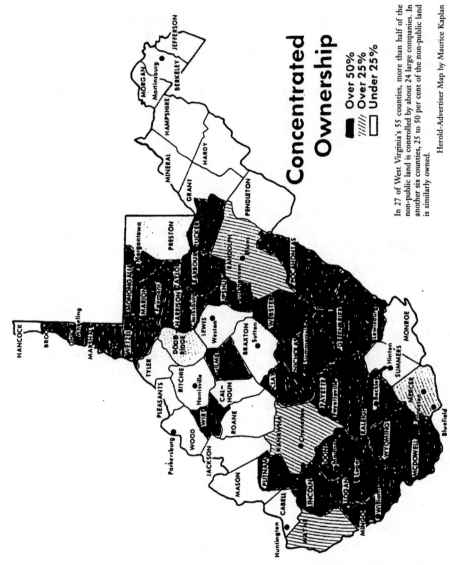

Concentrated Ownership

- ■ Over 50%
- ▨ Over 25%
- □ Under 25%

In 27 of West Virginia's 55 counties, more than half of the non-public land is controlled by about 24 large companies. In another six counties, 25 to 50 per cent of the non-public land is similarly owned.

Herold-Advertiser Map by Maurice Kaplan

tion and other state government services in these controlled counties where concentrated land ownership has stifled business, housing and even hope.

State Senator James Humphreys, D-Kanawha, is one of the few members of the state legislature who objects to this dominance.[1] He co-sponsored legislation for an excess acreage tax in 1987 when he was still a member of the House of Delegates. But it has never gotten off the ground because the land companies have always exerted a lot of influence in the Legislature.

Humphreys said as a child he can recall visiting the last day of the legislative session and "seeing a utility lobbyist with a black bag filled with money."

"That old style of influence is no longer around but they still have the ability to push their position," said Humphreys, who was chairman of the Senate Judiciary Committee.

Higher taxes on these corporate landowners has always been a goal after the 1974 study concluded that most of this mineral wealth was either totally ignored on local property tax assessments or valued at a small fraction of its worth. It has been obvious that counties with the poorest of school systems in a state woefully weak in public education are those dominated by these land barons.

The 1988 newspaper series concluded that in McDowell County, where Pocahontas Land Corporation owns a third of the land, the state spent $32 million to provide school support, roads, welfare and unemployment benefits.

This was $715 per capita for the 45,300 residents or nearly twice the amount spent on the same services for each resident of Cabell County. And on the opposite side of the ledger, tax collections in Cabell County were $877 per capita compared to $540 in McDowell County.

Tom Knight of Charleston, who sponsored the excess acreage legislation with Humphreys back in 1987 and is now a public relations lobbyist for state workers, contends these figures prove the problems associated with concentrated land ownership. "We can never be economically viable as a state until we control our own land."

But the lobbyists for the large companies, as you might suspect, don't agree. Enactment of an excess acreage tax—a levy on land holdings of 10,000 acres or more—would send out the wrong message according to Roger Sherman, public affairs forester for Westvaco. The firm has 350,000 acres in 26 counties.

Sherman said the tax is "intended to be punitive and there's a real message there for companies that might want to locate in the state and provide jobs."

They have an ally in respected economist William Miernyk of Morgantown, now retired from the West Virginia University faculty. He said he has always been "skeptical" about the claims that the absentee ownership of land causes harm to the economy.

I grew up in Colorado, another state with great mineral wealth," said Dr. Miernyk. "And Colorado grew and prospered even though some locals insisted out-of-state owners were stifling growth because most people there refused to become submissive."

It is obvious the pattern isn't going to change in the near future.

In recent years, when there has been a sale, it has been from one corporation to another. In 1987, Pocahontas Land Corporation purchased 49,650.59 acres from Royal Land Company, a subsidiary of Standard Oil of Ohio for $69 million.

Ernest F. Hays II, general land and tax attorney for Pocahontas Land Corporation, said the sale price represents about half what Sohio paid for the tract—$125 million—when it was acquired from U.S. Steel a few years earlier. He said the property taxes on the land would drop accordingly.

But Logan County Assessor J.T. Bodby, who claimed 5,000 acres of the tract is in his county, said Royal Land Company actually paid $331 million for the land in 1981 and he wanted the state tax department to help him determine the value for property tax purposes.

After it became public knowledge that coal seams were not even subject to property tax in some counties in 1974, the state tax department did institute a minerals valuation program to determine the appraised values on active mining, future valuable coal property and abandoned or mined out tracts.

But the close political relationship between the elected county assessor in some areas and the agent for the large land company has been a persistent problem that has overcome any consistent attempts to place a true market value on tracts owned by these absentee landlords.

And the close ties between the land company lobbyists and members of the state legislature is well documented.

In the 1986 election, three out of every four members of the Legislature received campaign contributions of $100 or more from the large land companies or their lobbyists.

Senator H. Truman Chafin, D-Mingo, got $10,000 including $1000 each from five coal operators and their wives, the largest amount of any member of the Senate. But Chafin, who currently is majority leader in the Senate, said he is fighting on the side of those who want to overcome this absentee ownership and in 1990 he did introduce a bill designed to tax the large land holdings.

Delegate Floyd Stiles, R-Preston, received the most in the House. Now deceased, he reported contributions of $4,600 from mineral and land interests.

And in some instances, there is no middle man and the office holder is also the land owner. Kentucky Governor Wallace Wilkinson is president of Sixth Avenue Land Company in Lexington, Kentucky and on February 18, 1983, his firm purchased 9,851 acres from Island Creek Coal Company in Logan County for $18 million, records in the Logan County Courthouse reveal.

Wilkinson also is president of Elk Creek-Lexington Coal Company, Inc. and Coal Mountain company, Inc.—both firms with West Virginia land holdings.

Governor Gaston Caperton is direct descendant of William Gaston Caperton who founded the Slab Fork Coal Company in Raleigh County. The history books identify the "Caperton Lands" in 1879 as a 90,000 tract in central West Virginia.

The late Harry Caudill, an Eastern Kentucky historian and Congressman, traced the political bosses of his region as well as those of West Virginia in his book "Theirs Be The Power." He mentions Johnson N. Camden, twice a United States Senator from West Virginia in the last century and a collaborator with John D. Rockefeller on Standard Oil Company in 1875.

Then there was Clarence Wayland Watson, president of Consolidation Coal Company and a former United States Senator from West Virginia from 1911 to 1913. Watson's brother-in-law and later chief counsel to Consol was Aretas Brooks Fleming, who was governor of West Virginia from 1888-92.

A direct descendant of Watson was former House Judiciary Chairman J.E. (Ned) Watson of Fairmont who lobbied in the Legislature for Consolidation Coal Company for years after his legislative service and was known as "Big Daddy" because of his physical size.

In the outdoor drama "Honey in the Rock" that has been presented at Beckley's Grandview State Park over many summers, the basic theme of the absentee landlord is presented when the players suggest that these out-of-state millionaires "have taken the honey (natural resources) and left us the rock."

But those associated with these companies insist they help rather than hinder the state's well-being. Consider again Cotiga and its corporate boss in surburban Philadelphia. "The last time I was down there, I had lunch with the president of Southern West Virginia Community College," said Ted Wood during a 1988 interview, "and we gave them the sign for the school."

The local land agent was in the Williamson Rotary Club and made contributions to the United Way in the community as well, Wood noted to convey his claim that Cotiga was "a good corporate citizen of West Virginia."

And John Henning, vice president of Columbia Natural Resources, will boast how his company leases 5,700 acres for the Big Ugly Public Hunting area in Lincoln County to the Department of Natural Resources and continues to pay the property taxes on those surface rights.

But he doesn't mention that the annual tax on that acreage is less than $1,200 a year.

They sell surface rights for houses but always they keep the mineral rights underneath.

Mike Burdiss, an official of the United Mine Workers of America, isn't content with these donations.

"They are placing a band-aid on arterial bleeding," said Burdiss. "They give us a ball field instead of adequate tax support."

But natives can't say they weren't warned.

At one point early in the state's history, tax officials began to ask "shall our wealth pass to strangers?" And after they had studied the issue, they made the following prophetic summation:

"The wealth of this state is immense; the development of this wealth will earn vast private fortunes far beyond the dreams even of a modern Croesus; the question is, whether this vast wealth shall belong to persons who live here and who are permanently identified with the future of West Virginia, or whether it shall pass into hands of persons who do not live here and who care nothing for our state except to pocket the treasures which lie buried in our hills.

"If the people of West Virginia can be roused to an appreciation of the situation we ourselves will gather this harvest now ripe on the lands inherited from our ancestors; on the other hand if the people are not roused to an understanding of the situation in less than 10 years, this vast wealth will have passed from our present population into the hands of non-residents and West Virginia will be almost like Ireland and her history <or> will be like that of Poland."

This vivid, succinct description of West Virginia's destiny was penned by J.M. Mason, E.A. Bennett and Joseph Bell. It appeared in the West Virginia Tax Commission's Second Report, State Development, published November 22, 1884.

Notes

Tom D. Miller graciously up-dated his 1974 report, "Who Owns West Virginia?" for this book. See Tom D. Miller, "Who Owns West Virginia?" reprint from the *Herald-Advertiser* and the *Herald-Dispatch*, Huntington, West Virginia, (December 1974), 1–28.

[1] There is considerable interest group activity for a restructuring of the tax laws in West Virginia. One such organization is Mountaineers United for Sane Taxation (MUST!) which has lobbied the legislature during the past several years for a two-tiered tax structure. This proposed tax would place a higher rate on property value than on improvements. MUST, the Henry George School of Social Science, the Center for the Study of Economics and, etc., sponsored a conference in Charleston, "Prospects for Appalachia: From Poverty to Prosperity by 2000," (Dec. 6-8, 1990) which attracted economists, state executive officials, legislators, federal officials, businessmen, assessors, etc. The conference revealed that there is a considerable interest in West Virginia's tax problems and a definite need for reform.

In a recent session of the legislature M.U.S.T. generated considerable support (although it did not pass) for a constitutional amendment:

Article X

Taxation and Finance

The State, counties, and municipalities may levy property taxes in proportion to the (1) value of land, (2) improvements therein, and (3) personal property; such taxes shall be uniform on all properties in each of these categories throughout the taxing jurisdiction. State, county and municipal legislative bodies shall determine annual rates of such taxes. Real property shall be reassessed at least every three years at full and fair market value according to procedures prescribed by law. The State may phase out the tax on personal property. The State, counties, and municipalities may set lower rates on improvements than on land. Full or partial property tax exemptions or deferrals shall be subject to approval by the legislature at intervals no longer than every five years.

Case Study:
PROBLEMS OF CHURCH AND STATE IN PROPERTY TAX EXEMPTIONS: HARE KRISHNA VERSUS THE MARSHALL COUNTY TAX ASSESSOR

Alfred "Pinky" Clark
Former Assessor, Marshall County

Under the First Amendment to the United States Constitution, Congress shall make no law respecting the establishment of religion or prohibiting the free exercise of religion. This amendment conveys two important concepts: (1) the right to practice a religion of one's choice, and the right to practice that religion in a manner separate from the affairs of the state. However, exemption from ad valorem taxes is another matter entirely. In the United States, religious institutions enjoy no inherent, national exemption from property taxation.

General Background

After the American Revolution, the state governments became sovereign regarding property within their boundaries; so, they had the right to collect taxes from landowners. Rights of ownership were vested in the individual while the states retained the rights of eminent domain, police power, reversion to the state for failure to pay taxes, and lastly, the right of property taxation. With the power to tax, the state, ironically inherits the power to exempt <those that it wishes> from property taxes.

For a church to claim an exemption from property taxation, there must be a state constitutional or statutory provision permitting the exemption (*North American Old Roman Catholic Diocese v. Havens*, 164 Miss. 119, 144 So. 473.). In addition, when a court in the United States must determine whether such an exemption exists, there is no evidentiary presumption in favor of the religious society (*Ham Evangelistic Association v. Matthews*, 300 Ky. 402, 189 S.). If there is any doubt whether the particular constitutional or statutory provision permits a property tax exemption, the court must decide that doubt against the taxpaying religious institution (*In Re Hillcrest Memorial Gardens*, 146 WV 337, 119 S.E. 2 D 753).

Therefore, the central problem with this issue in the United States is the fact that we have fifty different constitutions and statutory codes. This <complexity> results in thousands of disputes whether particular constitutional or statutory language permits property tax exemptions, and many of these cases have reached our appellate courts. Within the restrictions mentioned above, this means that a judge, or panel of judges, will generally make the final determination.

For example, a statute that existed in Massachusetts which exempted from real property taxation "places of worship" was construed to include ground that was annexed to the place of worship, which was necessary for the occupancy and enjoyment of the same (*First Baptist Church v. Pittsburgh*, 341 Pa. 568, 20 A 2 D 209). However, property that is owned by the religious society, found by a court not to be reasonably needed for the primary purpose of religious worship, will not enjoy the exemption (*Gibbons v. District of Columbia*, 116 U.S. 404, 29 L.Ed. 680, 6 S. Ct. 427).

To the other extreme, an Ohio provision that limited such an exemption to property "used exclusively for public worship" gave an opportunity for an Ohio court to chide Ohio taxing officials for their strict construction. The court said that the provision should not be so literally construed that the serving of church dinners would result in a loss of the exemption (*In Re Bond Hill—Roselawn Hebrew School*, 151 Ohio St. 70, 84 N.E. 2 D 270).

A taxing official in the United States can equitably apply or deny these property tax exemptions if he or she applies these legal principles. First, the taxing official must be knowledgeable of the language of constitutional or statutory provisions existing in his or her jurisdiction. Next, the taxing official must be aware that courts in the United States seemingly have used a "common thread" in deciding whether religious organizations are entitled to property tax exemptions—that is, a rule of "reasonableness." The exempting language should be strictly construed, but not to the extent that the primary purpose of the exemption is abused.

All of this is complicated by the fact that most of the constitutions and primary statutes regarding these exemptions were adopted by our various states in the nineteenth, or early twentieth centuries. Particular religious groups and organizations were fairly standardized and easily recognized. Since then, taxing officials have been challenged by hundreds of splinter, esoteric, and exotic collections of individuals who claim the right to stand under the umbrella of property tax exemption for "religious worship."

. . . It is small comfort to say that the law is in flux when a group, claiming to be a "religious organization," applies for property tax exemption. If any doubt of entitlement exists, the ultimate decision will be a legal one, and not an administrative one. Therefore, all legal assistance available to the taxing authority should be sought.

The West Virginia Law

Attention . . . needs to be given to my taxing jurisdiction, the State of West Virginia. The West Virginia Constitution, serving as the supreme legal document . . . , determines the taxing bodies within the state and thereby determines what entities are exempt from these taxes. As the constitutionally elected assessor of Marshall County, . . . I have found myself in a situation where the decision to determine the taxability of certain properties may have nationwide repercussions.

Assessors in West Virginia must award or deny exemptions from real and personal property taxes in accordance with the *West Virginia Code*, Chapter 11, Article 3, Section 9. The statute provides in part that the exemption must be given to ". . . property used exclusively for divine worship; parsonages, and the household goods and furniture pertaining thereto. . . ." The exempting language of the statute is modified and controlled by one of the concluding sentences of the legislation.

> "Notwithstanding any other provisions of this section, however, no language shall be construed to exempt from taxation any property owned by, or held in trust for, educational, literary, scientific, religious or other charitable corporations or organizations . . . unless such property, or the dividends, interest, rents or royalties derived therefrom is used primarily and immediately for the purposes of such corporations or organizations."

The West Virginia Supreme Court of Appeals... has provided some guidance in applying this exemption when the same has been challenged in court by taxpayers. The court has followed the national theme by noting that if any doubt arises as to the exemption, that doubt must be decided against the taxpayer who claims the exemption *(In Re: Hillcrest Memorial Gardens*, 146 WV 337, 119 S.E. 2 D 753). This is because all exemptions evade the operation of the general principle that taxation laws should be equal and uniform, and place the public burdens, as nearly as they may be, upon all property and citizens alike *(State v. Kittle*, 87 WV 526, 105 S.E. 775). However, this strict, conservative approach was <also> diluted . . . in *State v. Kittle*, when the court said that taxing officials must apply a "rational" construction to the statute. Despite the fact that the statute permitting the exemption limits it to property used "exclusively" for divine worship, our supreme court decided that the provision of West Virginia's constitution which allowed our government to exempt religious property from taxation, contemplated a use that was primary, direct and immediate, not secondary or remote *(Central Reality Co. v. Martin*, 126 WV 915, 30 S.E. 2 D 720).

The New Vrindaban Community

It was within this framework of these national <and state laws>, and court decisions, that I was required to decide the availability of a property tax exemption to a major, eastern hemisphere, religious sect which located in my jurisdiction—a small, rural county of West Virginia, primarily populated by strongly independent people whose ancestors came to this country from western and central Europe—people who take their religion seriously, but people who separate their religious lives from their secular lives.

There appears to have been one trend developing in some courts in the United States that may assist taxing authorities to determine whether an applicant is a "church" or "religious society" entitled to ad valorem property tax exemption. First, some courts have held that the group must be incorporated, associated, or otherwise organized within the state. In addition, to be recognized as a religious society, there must be meetings for worship and the group must have been formed—and the members come together—solely, or at least primarily, for religious purposes *(Parshall Christian Order, R.E. v. Board of Review*, 315 N. W. 2 D 798, Iowa).

In July, 1973, the New Vrindaban Community became incorporated in the state of West Virginia. . . . The instrument of incorporation does indeed state their mission:

> "The object of this incorporation shall be to acquire by purchase, assignment, or otherwise, all of the real estate of the international society for Krishna consciousness of West Virginia, a religious association of Marshall County, now owned by said society . . . this corporation shall build and construct housing units and other facilities, including roads and other public ways, upon said real estate. . . ."

The Krishnas do indeed emphasize "all and everything necessary" to accomplish their drive for land acquisition. From the book *The Hare Krishna Explosion,* author and Krishna devotee Hayagriva Dasa quotes Prabhupada—"I advise Kirtanananda and yourself to convert West Virginia into New Vrindaban." Dasa goes on to state the feelings of the early Krishna pioneers in West Virginia, "We ponder this. Not just the farm. Prabhupada wants the whole state."

Early attempts to buy real estate in Marshall County involve intimidation, harassment of property owners, and trespassing. Again, from the book, *The Hare Krishna Explosion,* follower Hayagriva Dasa recounts the scenario and the effects of the first Krishna "negotiating" tactics:

> "Foster grows more and more defensive and paranoid in respect to his new neighbors. Foster has taken to fire practice. He thinks it is wise to advertise himself an armory. We arrive at the goat farm, we see that Foster has thrown up picket barricades. Additional spotlights line the roof; the road gates are locked, and boards are nailed across the doors and windows. Foster's face is pale, his eyes sunken from worry and insomnia. 'All right,' Foster signs. 'I'll look into drawing up some kind of lease. Ninety-nine years! Jesus! Trouble with you people is you want to be God Almighty. . . .'"

Prior to 1984, the Hare Krishna . . . religion based on the teachings of the *Bhagavad-gita,* was given tax exempt status on its temple, <and> the Palace of Gold. Following this year, however, a change was noted by my staff. The palace, promoted as the Taj Mahal of the West was being advertised on billboards, and a colorful brochure was distributed in chamber of commerce offices and motels across the nation. Donations derived from tours and their Sankirtan rituals became mandatory for any visitor entering the Temple. . . . As part of the Sankirtan ritual, a box for donations is located at the door to the Temple. Supposedly, a donation is not required for entry, and attendance at worship services is also free of charge, although there is a suggested donation for entry into the Temple. . . .

The "Palace of Gold" has received its tax-exempt status under <the> *West Virginia Code,* 11-3-9 which stated that the structure would be given tax-exempt status if it was used "exclusively for divine worship." After wrestling with the term "exclusive" and taking into consideration how other Christian denominations use their churches for fund-raising activities, I used the authority vested in me by the *West Virginia Code* and changed the 102.82 acres, which included the Palace of Gold, to a taxable property. . . . I felt that divine worship . . . was not . . . the "exclusive" use of the palace. . . . The Hare Krishna organization appealed the taxability issue to the West Virginia Tax Commissioner... As of now, my decision . . . has been upheld pending an appeal to the Marshal County Circuit Court.

> Kaladri Das states:

> "That since this Temple was built in 1979, it has been used exclusively for religious purposes. That any contributions or solicitations derived from the aforesaid ritual are used exclusively for religious purposes and to support the aforesaid community. That the restaurant, associated with the palace, is a place where pilgrims receive sanctified foodstuffs and that any monies derived therefrom are used to support the community, although the monies derived therefrom are in no way sufficient to totally support the aforesaid community. That the so-called gift shop associated with the palace offers religious articles and souvenirs for sale and that any monies derived therefrom are used exclusively to support the aforesaid religious community."

The Krishnas had, in my professional opinion, crossed the line into tourism and the world of private enterprise. The monies collected at the palace were being used not only for the upkeep of the Palace of Gold, but also to help support the entire Krishna community.

The Krishna holistic outlook conceives of New Vrindaban as a religious community dedicated to the sole and undivided worship of its supreme being. There is no distinction between <residence> and church. . . . The Krishna train of thought does not acknowledge distinction between various segments of society. Their unification of thought and action is a beautiful outlook on life, but it does present a clash of culture and magnifies the taxation problem before us.

As the West Virginia Tax Commissioner, Herschel H. Rose, III, states in his supportive ruling of my decision to tax the Palace of Gold:

> "A difficulty with this issue is that we are dealing with both a church and a community or commune. Although they are intimately interrelated, the community is not and does not seek to be exempt from property taxation by virtue of the exemption for property used exclusively for divine worship. But because of the interrelationship, it is exceptionally difficult to distinguish what is used for religious purposes for the temple and what is used to support the commune. . . .

> ". . . It is tempting to judge the actions of the taxpayer by conventional western religious standards. The solicitation of admission fees into the temple, the operation of a gift shop, and the operation of a restaurant are all activities by western religions. But whether or not a church activity constitutes divine worship cannot be judged by some other religion's standards but must be judged by the creed of the church being reviewed. But, in my opinion, it must be judged in the context of the

political and economical system which encompasses the creed or church in question. While our constitution guarantees freedom of religion, it must have a stable and consistent method of levying taxes that keeps the tax burden divided as 'uniform and equal' as humanly possible."

My decision to place the Krishna Palace of Gold on the tax roll was one made with much research and deliberation. I took into consideration: 1) the definition of "exclusive" with regards to divine worship, 2) the concept of uniform and equal sharing of the tax burden, 3) scarcity of land with regards to my taxing jurisdiction, 4) the apparent competition with private enterprise on a daily basis, and 5) the community support received by the church. . . .

Again, let me emphasize that 1) nothing in the United States Constitution gives an institution an inherent tax-exempt status and 2) the body desiring tax-exempt status with regards to ad valorem taxes must shoulder the burden of proof to obtain this status. There are only state constitutions, statutes, and court decisions that develop trends. These trends can mold into a common thread, but the state remains sovereign in determining what is taxable and what is exempt. As an elected county assessor, the state Legislature has given me sole authority in determining taxability in my jurisdiction.

In conclusion, I must reiterate that the Hare Krishna sect has appealed the West Virginia Tax Commissioner's ruling. It is now being litigated in the Marshall County Circuit Court. I am certain that this organization has the resources and determination to take their case to the Supreme Court of the United States. The Krishnas appear to want to exist as a separate entity within an established governing body. A decision in their favor would have a monumental impact on our taxing structure and the general concept in the United States that only property owned by religious societies for religious purposes—and not materialistic purposes—should be exempt from property taxation.

As one can imagine, the shades of gray surrounding the definition of organized "religion" can be and often do become distorted and confusing. The United States is yearning for a national guideline to objectively determine the true organizational intentions of religious groups and sects. I am not advocating a strict set of rules that violates the constitutional rights of such groups, but a sound policy that serves as an advisory to state governments and the taxing officials within these states and allows for fair and impartial judgement in implementing ad valorem taxes.

CONSOLIDATION IN THE KANAWHA VALLEY—IS A "SKINNY CITY" POSSIBLE?

Evelyn L.K. Harris

The United States is a nation of fragmented governments. Much of the rationale for this lies in the hope of achieving greater accountability, as well as in the case of local governments, keeping local policy-making closer to citizen input.

As a result, America is a land of almost eighty-thousand[1] separate entities including cities, counties, public service districts; and myriads of lesser subdivisions, such as magisterial districts, townships and towns.

The Census Bureau reports that in 1980, incorporated cities held sixty-two percent of the population with eleven percent living in separately identified unincorporated places, and twenty-seven percent living in scattered rural areas. American smaller cities and towns grew faster in the seventies than did bigger cities, expanding by nearly a third over the decade.

Most of these smaller cities are bedrooms for a neighboring larger metropolis and become suburbs, ringing the larger urban center and choking off its possible expansion. Not only the expensive duplication of city services in these suburbs, but the vanishing middle class populations who formerly lived in the city and provided the necessary taxes for its support, create a major problem for local governments in America.

One wag tells us that there are three great concentrations of urban population in America: San San (San Diego to San Francisco), Chapitt (Chicago to Pittsburgh), and Boswash (Boston to Washington). West Virginia has been likened to Hogwash (Harper's Ferry to Washington).

Legal boundaries bisecting this concentration of people have lost all rational justification for their continuance. Recent research with its resulting national experimentation with different remedies for the problems of metropolitan areas has offered a wide variety of structural solutions. West Virginia, for example, can choose from: annexation, intergovernmental cooperation, city-county consolidation, governmental contracting, federated metropolis or administrative districts to cite a few. Yet, little has happened within this nation, and certainly in West Virginia to give reformers hope for the future.

At the present time, for example, there is no provision in the West Virginia Constitution for governmental consolidation of counties and municipalities of any type.[2] Consolidation amendments have been introduced periodically in the legislature since 1963, but have met with indifference or outright hostility. Part of the problem is the overwhelming difficulty of trying to alter the structure of our traditional, three-person county commission form of government. But then again, West Virginia does not have municipal home rule either.[3] This lack of constitutional authorization reduces the possibility of structural change and limits action to voluntary cooperation.

The recent revenue sharing policy of the national government encouraged fragmentation of local governments. Municipalities incorporated in order to share in the distribution of the national revenue-sharing monies. The recent termination of revenue sharing, however, triggers an economic crunch. Growing economic stringencies, caused by the skyrocketing cost of municipal liability insurance premiums and the disappearance of many local industries, among other developments, have led to a reassessment of this fragmented condition.

Recent citizen sensitivity to environmental problems, such as poor air quality, water pollution, hazardous waste, together with the more traditional environmental problem of floods necessitate a concerted effort to solve these problems. Environmental solutions require structural and policy changes which spill over the dated and uneconomic boundary lines of our local governments.

There is a draconian need for consolidation to deal with these overlapping problems. The legal boundary lines buoyed by vested interests of sheriffs, mayors, councilmen, and the traditional loyalties of residents, together with constitutional barriers, resist such rational actions as county-city consolidation, annexation or even inter-city contracts.

The history of consolidation in the Kanawha Valley of West Virginia is a beautiful example of the problems faced by citizens who believe consolidation would be a viable solution to environmental and economic problems of our local government.

The Kanawha Valley centering around the capital city, Charleston, has explored numerous efforts at consolidation. There are fifteen distinct municipalities and eleven such areas within Kanawha County alone, with spillovers in Fayette (Montgomery) and Putnam (Nitro) counties (see Table 6.4). These cities tend to cluster along the Kanawha River and up stream or creek hollows. A consolidation of these river cities strung along the meandering Kanawha would result in what has been labeled a "Skinny City."

As early as 1947, a beginning was undertaken with the formation of the Kanawha County-Charleston Health Department, a consolidation which has had a most productive and competent history of service to the region. But progress in other avenues was slow. It was not until 1959 that a minor milestone was reached, when the West Virginia Legislature permitted county commissions to establish planning commissions for overall county development.

In 1963, the legislature authorized counties to cooperate with other local governments, or even the federal government as long as there was no conflict with the state constitution. Kanawha County appointed a committee to produce plans for cooperation with its municipalities and after much consideration, in 1965, the committee recommended a voluntary metropolitan council to consist of the three county commissioners and the elected mayor of each municipality in the county.

Very little resulted from this first attempt at city-county cooperation except for the creation of a regional development authority (RDA) in 1967 with a professional director, a local architect, Clarence Moran. The Regional Development Board included representatives from each municipality, the county, and seven citizens. The authority was to concern itself with watersheds and flood control developments, sewer treatment facilities and a fire protection program. Work was started on all fronts, and progressed slowly but satisfactorily.

In the 1970s, Kanawha County participated in a state endorsed regional program to strengthen local governments. The Regional Planning and Development Act of 1971, established eleven regional councils, called COGS, to contract for planning and development services, housing projects, emergency medical services, programs for the elderly, disaster relief, sewer and water facilities and other programs needed by the region. Kanawha County, together with Boone, Clay and Putnam comprised Region III.[4] Plans were laid but the end result was the formation of many public service districts to implement the projects. Again more separate and distinct governmental entities were created to handle these needed services. Instead of consolidation or retrenchment, another layer of government was instituted.

There was a breakthrough in 1971. Charleston and Kanawha County initiated a series of functional consolidations, beginning with a combined Charleston-Kanawha County Jail. Formerly two separate jails were located across the street from each other in downtown Charleston. Following this action, a Kanawha Valley Regional Transportation Authority was established providing for bus transportation throughout the whole Kanawha valley. Moreover, the volunteer fire departments of the fifteen separate municipalities joined forces in a Mutual Aid Association to effect county-wide fire-fighting standards. A Kanawha County Ambulance Authority and even a consolidated communications center for emergency services was created in the county.

Perhaps the most hopeful development in recent years was the creation in 1985 of a Kanawha Metro Government Task Force, a twenty-nine member volunteer group created by the County Commission to study the operations of the local municipalities and public service districts and to recommend consolidation of services and governmental structures.

The Task Force was in operation for over a year consulting county officials as well as mayors and officials of the fifteen municipalities and the public service districts. Local West Virginia Delegates and Senators, as well as citizens were involved.

The Task Force recommended that public service districts should be consolidated with municipal services, intergovernmental contracts should be adopted, expansion of the Upper Kanawha Valley Mayors' Association should be undertaken, and the following services should be consolidated: Charleston and Kanawha County Ambulance Services, solid waste disposal landfills, and parks and recreation services.

The Task Force opted for the reestablishment of a voluntary Metropolitan Council with an executive director hired by Kanawha County. Hopefully the county and its municipalities would enter into intergovernmental contracts and eliminate expensive duplication of services.

The final report of the Task Force was submitted to the County Commission among much fanfare and newspaper publicity in October, 1986. To date, other than the creation of an intergovernmental service agreement for a Metro Emergency Operations Center, which was in the works at the time the Task Force was created, nothing positive has been forthcoming.

Why have so many of these attempts at structural consolidation, other than minor functional service agreements failed?

Now surely should be the time for a push toward consolidation with the overwhelming economic difficulties due to loss of federal funds, changes in the Local Severance Tax and the B & O Tax in West Virginia, and the cutbacks in major industries in the Kanawha Valley.

Consolidation of local government services should reduce operating expenses, and improve service with better use of facilities and personnel.

Can it be that urban-rural hostility or close citizen identification with local communities would stifle such forward-going programs? It is easier to understand the vested interests of myriads of local officials who would lose employment and political power networks with the elimination of city offices.

Hopefully the legislature of West Virginia with its citizen mandate for policies furthering the economic development of the state, could amend the constitution to permit flexibility in local governance by providing for county consolidation, city-county restructuring, and permit the exploring of remedies to meet local needs.

For successful change, government, business and voluntary civic organizations must work together toward common goals. Shared vision even by a Task Force is often not enough, however. Trust is essential together with both the realization by dedicated and bright people. Astute timing must also be an ingredient for a successful mix. Hopefully, West Virginia and the Kanawha Valley will find the courage to direct local governments into the twenty-first century.

Notes

Professor Harris' article was written specifically for this book.

1 The breakdown is: counties 3,043; municipalities 19,372; townships 16,629; school districts 13,726; special districts 34,683 = 87,453.

2 This article was written before the West Virginia Legislature, in its First Extraordinary Session, January 25—February 1, 1989, passed the "County Organization Reform Amendment" which proposed the merger of municipal and county governments. As noted earlier, the West Virginia voters disapproved of the amendment <ed.>.

3 David A. Bingham, "No Home Rule in West Virginia," *National Civic Review*, April, 1980, 213–214.

4 S. Poe and D. Poluga, "In the In-Between Governments: West Virginia's COGS," *West Virginia Public Affairs Reporter*, III, 2, (Summer, 1978)

Table 6.4 Population Comparisons—United States, West Virginia, County, Sub Area, Municipalities

Territory	Population 2000	Population 1990	% Change
United States (2001, est.)	284,796,887	249,632,692	8.7
West Virginia	1,808,344	1,793,477	0.83
Kanawha County	200,073	207,619	-3.63
Municipalities			
Pratt	551	640	-13.64
Cedar Grove	862	1,213	-28.94
East Bank	933	892	9.51
Montgomery	1,942	2,449	-23.15
Glasgow	783	906	-13.77
Dunbar	8,154	8,697	-6.24
Nitro	6,824	6,851	-0.42
South Charleston	13,390	13,645	-1.87
Chesapeake	1,643	1,896	-13.34
Marmet	1,693	1,879	-9.90
Charleston	53,421	57,287	-6.75
Belle	1,259	1,421	-11.40
St. Albans	11,567	11,194	3.33
Clendedin	1,116	1,203	-7.23
Handley	362	336	7.74
Sub-Area			
Cross Lanes	10,353	10,878	-4.83
Sissonville	4,399	4,290	2.54
Coal City	1,905	2,030	-6.20

Source: United States Census, 1990, 2000

APPENDIX

MAJOR CONTRIBUTORS

Donald R. Andrews (M.A.) is Director of the Robert C. Byrd Institute for Government Studies and Assistant Professor of Political Science at the University of Charleston. He planned and implemented the orientation program for newly elected members of the 72nd Legislature of West Virginia (1995). He served the State of West Virginia for over twenty-five years, ten of which were with the Office of Legislative Services, and eight as Director of the State Park System.

Thais Blatnik (Dem.) former member of the legislature having served for fifteen years. She was first elected to the House of Delegates in 1976 and to the Senate in 1988. She was the Chairwoman of the Senate Committee on Small Business. Today she is involved in civic organizations: Oglebay Institute, Ohio County Wildlife League, YWCA, Fraternal Order of Police Associates, Elm Grove Women's Club, etc. She was educated at West Liberty State College and Duquesne University.

Edmund G. "Pat" Brown (Dem.) was governor of California, 1956–66. He holds an L.L.D. from the University of San Francisco. Practiced law in San Francisco from 1927–43. Was a frequent delegate to the Democratic National Convention through the years of 1940–1964.

Alfred "Pinky" Clark (Rep.), until recently, had served twenty-two years as Marshall County Assessor and was probably the best known assessor in West Virginia. He gained national media attention for his recent decision to tax the Krishna palace (Prabhupada's Palace of Gold) in Moundsville, West Virginia. He also received considerable publicity for his three hundred mile walk from Newell to Charleston where he gathered signatures in an attempt to block the state-wide property tax reappraisal. He holds a degree from West Liberty State College.

James F. Dent (the late) was a native Charlestonian. He graduated in 1952 from West Virginia University (major in political science). He was a columnist and editorial cartoonist for the *Charleston Gazette* from 1963-1994. He has written two books: *The Dog With the Cold Nose* and *James Dent Strikes Again*.

Harry Ernst (M.S.J.) is one of the better known "political" journalists in West Virginia. His article, "The Primary That Made a President: West Virginia 1960" is considered by many to be a classic. He has had a long career in both the fields of journalism and education. He is Emeritus Professor of Journalism at West Virginia University.

James R. Forrester (Ph.D.) is a Professor of Political Science at West Liberty State College. He has presented a number of professional papers and is the author of several publications: "Reconsideration of the Diffuse Support Explanation of the Potential for Political Violence," *Humboldt Journal of Social Relations*, Fall/Winter, 1980/81; "Ethnicity in Wheeling," *Upper Ohio Valley Historical Review*, Autumn/Winter, 1981 and "The Milieu of an 1855 Wheeling Ordinance Book," *Upper Ohio Valley Historical Review*, Vol. 18, (1989).

Lawrence J. Grossback (Ph.D.) is Assistant Professor of Political Science at West Virginia University. His research interests include public opinion, political behavior, and state politics. He has published journal articles in the *West Virginia Public Affairs Reporter* and *State and Local Government Review* and his work has appeared in the edited volume, *Innovation and Entrepreneurship in State and Local Government*.

Allan S. Hammock (Ph.D.) is associate professor and chair of the Department of Political Science at West Virginia University. He currently serves as the chair of the West Virginia Election Commission and is the co-author of *West Virginia Politics and Government* and co-editor of *Points of View: Readings in American Government and Politics*.

Evelyn L.K. Harris (D.P.A.) is Emeritus Professor of Political Science and History and former head of the Department of Social Sciences at the University of Charleston. She was cited as the West Virginia Professor of the Year in 1986. She co-authored a history of the West Virginia labor movement, published articles on labor, a Library Search Manual, and devoted much time to legislative service: chair of the West Virginia Legislative Compensation Commission, involved in orientation programs for new legislators and the Frasure-Singleton Legislative Internship Program.

Ken Hechler (Dem.) Former West Virginia Secretary of State, 1984–2001. He was educated at Swarthmore College and Columbia (Ph.D., Columbia, 1940). He has had a long and distinguished record of public service: former Research Assistant, to Judge Samuel I. Rosenman and President Franklin Roosevelt in editing and annotation of *The Public Papers and Addresses of Franklin D. Roosevelt*; World War II military historian; Research Director and Special Assistant to President Harry S. Truman; published two books, *Working With Truman* and *Bridge at*

Remagen; former Associate Director American Political Science Association, Washington, D.C.; former member U.S. House of Representatives (1959–1977). He has taught at Columbia, Marshall and University of Charleston.

James A. Hoyer (MSMPA) is the Director of Special Programs and an Instructor at the University of Charleston. He served as Assistant to the Speaker of the West Virginia House of Delegates for eight years. Also, he was responsible for the management of the joint legislative staff offices from 1991 to 1993.

Paul F. Lutz (Ph.D.) was educated at Marshall and West Virginia Universities. His doctoral dissertation at WVU was on the career of Governor William C. Marland. He was formerly Chairman of the History Department, Glenville State College (WV) and is currently a history professor at Marshall University.

David B. McKinley (Rep.) former member of the House of Delegates representing the Third District (Ohio County). He had served his district since 1980; was Minority Committee Chairman of the Banking and Insurance Committee, a member of the Finance and Industry and Labor Committees. He was Chairman of the State Republican Executive Committee; and is a graduate of Purdue University (BSCE, 1969); a registered professional engineer and was awarded "Outstanding Young Engineer for the State of West Virginia, 1976" by WVSPE.

Douglas McKay graduated from Princeton University in 1942. He spent four years with the United States Army, including eighteen months in the Pacific theatre. He graduated from the University of Virginia Law School in 1949 and has practiced law in Wheeling ever since.

Tom D. Miller was chief correspondent for the *Huntington Herald-Dispatch* and the senior reporter at the state capitol. He has covered state government and politics for over 30 years. A native of Griffithsville in Lincoln County, he is a graduate of Marshall University and has been a newspaper reporter in Huntington all of his adult life. The 1974 series of newspaper articles, "Who Owns West Virginia?" received three national writing awards including the Gerald Loeb Award from UCLA for "distinguished business and financial journalism," the Pulitzer Prize of business writing.

Mario J. Palumbo (Dem.) former Attorney General of West Virginia, first elected in 1990. He was educated at Morris Harvey College and the West Virginia University College of Law. He brought extensive legislative experience to his position as "The State's Lawyer" having served twenty years in the West Virginia Senate. He chaired the important Senate Judiciary, Education and Elections committees.

Cabell Phillips was (d. 1975) the son-in-law of union leader Frank Keeney. He retired in 1972 after twenty-seven years on the Washington staff of the *New York Times*. He published a number of books and articles. Among his major works are: *Dateline: Washington, The Truman Presidency, From the Crash to the Blitz: 1929–1939,* and *The 1940s: Decade of Triumph and Trouble.*

Patricia Bradley Pitrolo (Dem.) former member of the West Virginia House of Delegates representing the First District (Hancock County) She was first elected in 1984 and served on the Judiciary, Political Subdivisions and Banking & Insurance Committees. She holds degrees from West Liberty State College (B.A.) and the West Virginia College of Graduate Studies (M.A.). Delegate Bradley resigned from the Legislature in November, 1990.

Ancil Ramey former Clerk of the Supreme Court of Appeals of West Virginia. He was educated at Marshall University (A.B., 1979) and West Virginia University receiving M.P.A. and J.D. degrees in 1983. Previously, he was a law clerk to the Honorable Darrell V. McGraw, Jr., Justice of the Supreme Court of Appeals of West Virginia.

Dave Rausch (Ph.D) is Assistant Professor of Political Science at West Texas A & M University. From 1994 to 1998, he taught at Fairmont State College. He teaches primarily courses on American political institutions and state and local government, occasionally teaching research methods. His research on legislative term limits, religion and politics, and state politics, has appeared in several journals including *Women & Politics, Oklahoma Politics, Comparative State Politics, West Virginia Public Affairs Reporter,* and *Texas Journal of Political Studies.* He is co-editor of a forthcoming collection of essays examining the effects of legislative term limits in the states.

Chuck Smith (Ph.D.) is Associate Professor of Political Science at West Virginia State College. He teaches in the areas of public law, judicial politics, and research methods. He has published articles in several journals including *University of Arkansas at Little Rock Law Journal, The Journal of Law and Religion, West Virginia History, The American Journal of Legal History,* and *State Constitutional Commentaries and Notes.* He is the author of *The New Mexico State Constitution,* Greenwood Press, 1996, and editor of *Race, Gender and Human Identity in a Diverse Society,* Tapestry Press, 1999.

Albert L. Sturm (Ph.D.) the late Professor of Political Science and Research Associate with the Bureaus for Government Research, West Virginia and Florida State Universities. He was considered an expert on state constitutional change and has a number of publications: *Methods of State Constitutional Reform,* (1954); *Major Constitutional Issues in West Virginia,* (1961); *Constitution Making in Michigan* (1963); and *West Virginia State and Local Government,* co-author, (1963).

David J. Webber (Ph.D.) is currently an Associate Professor of Political Science and a specialist in Public Policy at the University of Missouri-Columbia. He was formerly a specialist in policy analysis at West Virginia University and worked with both the Political Science and Public Administration Departments. He is the author of a number of professional papers and articles.

WEST VIRGINIA'S DECLARATION
OF INDEPENDENCE

June 17, 1861

A committee of the Second Wheeling Convention, headed by John S. Carlile, reported on June 13, "A Declaration of the People of Virginia." The report was discussed at length on the floor of the convention, amended, and unanimously adopted on June 17. Carlile, who had drafted the report with his own hand, said it was a happy coincidence and an auspicious omen that "we have fifty-six votes recorded in favor of our declaration, and we may remember that there were just 56 signers of the Declaration of Independence." Another member of the convention remarked that the date of passage was the anniversary of the Battle of Bunker Hill, while another observed that it was on June 17, 1789, that the States General declared itself the National Assembly and began the French Revolution. The declaration was engrossed on parchment and signed by all members of the Convention on June 20, 1861.

"A Declaration of the People of Virginia" is one of the most important state papers in West Virginia history. It contains a statement of principles, a strong indictment of the Virginia secession convention, an urgent recommendation for the reorganization of the Virginia government, and a list of grievances which impelled the Convention to action. An inspired paraphrase of the famous Declaration adopted at Philadelphia, July 4, 1776, the pronouncement was in a very real sense West Virginia's declaration of independence.

The true purpose of all government is to promote the welfare and provide for the protection and security of the governed, and when any form or organization of government proves inadequate for, or subversive of this purpose, it is the right, it is the duty of the latter to abolish it. The Bill of Rights of Virginia, framed in 1776, re-affirmed in 1830, and again in 1851, expressly re serves this right to a majority of her people. The act of the General Assembly, calling the Convention which assembled at Richmond in February last, without the previously expressed consent of such majority, was therefore a usurpation; and the Convention thus called has not only abused the powers nominally entrusted to it, but, with the connivance and active aid of the executive, has usurped and exercised other powers, to the manifest injury of the people, which, if permitted, will inevitably subject them to a military despotism.

The Convention, by its pretended ordinances, has required the people of Virginia to separate from and wage war against the government of the United States, and against citizens of neighboring States, with whom they have heretofore maintained friendly, social and business relations:

It has attempted to subvert the Union founded by Washington and his co-patriots, in the purer days of the republic, which has conferred unexampled prosperity upon every class of citizens, and upon every section of the country:

It has attempted to transfer the allegiance of the people to an illegal confederacy of rebellious States, and required their submission to its pretended edicts and decrees:

It has attempted to place the whole military force and military operations of the Commonwealth under the control and direction of such confederacy, for offensive as well as defensive purposes:

It has, in conjunction with the State executive, instituted wherever their usurped power extends, a reign of terror intended to suppress the free expression of the will of the people, making elections a mockery and a fraud:

The same combination, even before the passage of the pretended ordinance of secession, instituted war by the seizure and appropriation of the property of the Federal Government, and by organizing and mobilizing armies, with the avowed purpose of capturing or destroying the Capitol of the Union:

They have attempted to bring the allegiance of the people of the United States into direct conflict with their subordinate allegiance to the State, thereby making obedience to their pretended Ordinances, treason against the former.

We, therefore, the delegates here assembled in Convention to devise such measures and take such action as the safety and welfare of the loyal citizens of Virginia may demand, having maturely considered the premises, and viewing with great concern the deplorable condition to which this once happy Commonwealth must be reduced unless some regular adequate remedy is speedily adopted, and appealing to the Supreme Ruler of the Universe for the rectitude of our intentions, do hereby, in the name and on the behalf of the good people of Virginia, solemnly declare, that the preservation of their dearest rights and liberties and their security in person and property, imperatively demand the reorganization of the government of the Commonwealth, and that all acts of said Convention and Executive, tending to separate this Commonwealth from the United States, or to levy and carry on war against them, are without authority and void; and that the offices of all who adhere to the said Convention and Executive, whether legislative, executive or judicial, are vacated. *Ordinances of the Convention, Assembled at Wheeling, on the 11th of June, 1861*, 39–0.

Source: Elizabeth Cometti and Festus P. Summers (ed.), *The 35th State: A Documentary History of West Virginia* (Morgantown: West Virginia University Library, 1966). Reprinted with permission of the West Virginia University Library.

A SUMMARY OF THE
WEST VIRGINIA GOVERNMENTAL
ETHICS ACT

The West Virginia Governmental Ethics Act passed in February 1989[1] states "the Legislature believes that a code of ethics for the guidance of public officials and public employees will help them avoid conflicts between their personal interests and their public responsibilities, will improve standards of public service and will promote and strengthen the faith and confidence of the people of this state in their public officials and public employees."

WHAT IS THE ETHICS COMMISSION?

The Act established minimum ethical standards and created the West Virginia Ethics Commission to advise those covered by the Act and to investigate and adjudicate complaints of ethical misconduct. The Commission is a group of twelve part-time citizen members appointed by the Governor to serve five year terms. Commission members meet the first of each month at the Commission offices in Charleston to conduct business. A mid-month teleconference is also held to handle routine matters.

Before the Commission's advisory opinions are made public, any material which identifies the subject of the ruling is, to the fullest extent possible, deleted and his or her identity is not revealed. . . .

WHO IS COVERED BY THE ETHICS ACT?

Public officials and public employees, whether full-time or part-time, who are elected, appointed or hired to serve in State, county or municipal governments and their respective departments, agencies, boards and commissions, including county school boards.

ADVISORY OPINIONS

The primary responsibility of the Commission is to help resolve questions of ethical propriety by rendering "advisory opinions" in response to questions from public officials and employees covered by the act. Any person covered by the act may make written application to the Commission for a ruling on whether certain conduct is permissible under the Act. If the Commission rules that the conduct is ethically permissible, the person making the request is immunized against any subsequent complaint of violating the provisions of the Act.

Rulings of the Commission, set out in "advisory opinions," become public records. Copies of opinions are available to the public from the Office of the Secretary of State. . . . The cost is $2 plus ten cents per page. Any person covered by the Act can rely on the published opinions and any person acting in good faith reliance on such opinion is immune from the sanctions of the Act.

Persons covered by the Act may request advisory opinions by writing to the Commission at 1207 Quarrier St., Charleston, WV 25301. There is no particular form necessary to make a request and no specific format which must be followed. A request must be in writing.

Although the Commission is not permitted to make advisory opinions in response to phone requests, the staff can discuss any question you may have over the phone. If there is an existing advisory opinion or guideline which controls the question, they can make you aware of it at that time.

COMPLAINTS

The other major responsibility of the Commission is to investigate and re-solve ethical violations. Any citizen may make a complaint with the Commission if he or she is aware of a violation of the requirements of the Act. Once the Com-mission receives a verified complaint it initiates an investigation of the charges in the complaint.

The Commission appoints an investigative panel to determine whether there is probable cause to believe that a violation of law has occurred. The inves-tigative panel is comprised of three of the twelve members of the Commission.

The panel's proceedings are not open to the public. The person complained against may make a personal appearance before the panel and make written re-sponse to the complaint, but may not take any other part in the proceedings.

If the panel finds probable cause, the Commission's staff prepares a State-ment of Charges against the person accused. This is much like the indictment returned by a grand jury in a criminal case.

HEARING BOARD

The remaining nine members of the Commission constitute a hearing board to adjudicate the case. These members perform the role of the petit jury in a criminal case by determining the guilt or innocence of the person accused. None of these members can have taken part in the proceedings of the investiga-tive panel. Evidence is taken at public hearings.

If the Commission finds that there has been a material violation of the Act, it may impose one or more of the following sanctions:

(1) Public reprimand;

(2) Cease and desist orders;

(3) Orders of restitution for money, things of value or services taken or re-ceived in violation of the Act; or

(4) Fines not to exceed one thousand dollar per violation.

In addition to imposing such sanctions, the Commission may recommend to the appropriate governmental body that a person found to have violated the act be terminated from employment or removed from office.

BAD FAITH COMPLAINT

If the Commission finds that there has been no violation of the Act and that a complaint has been brought in bad faith, it shall order the complainant to reimburse the person complained against for all actual costs incurred, including, but not limited to, attorney fees and in addition, the person complained against shall have a cause of action and be entitled to compensatory damages, punitive damages, costs and attorney fees.

CONCILIATION AGREEMENT

The Act authorizes the Commission to enter into Conciliation Agreements with persons who are the subject of an investigation. This Agreement permits a person to acknowledge having violated the Act and accept specific penalty or a range of penalty provided by the Act. The inconvenience, expense and attendant notoriety of public hearings are avoided.

Such agreements can be entered into at any stage of an investigation. The cooperation of the accused and the savings of time and expense are matters to be considered by the Commission in establishing the penalties to be imposed. Although public hearings can be avoided by the Agreement, the Agreement itself must be made public.

CONFIDENTIALITY

The Act protects persons against public disclosure of unwarranted or frivolous complaints by requiring that all information relating to a fixed complaint be, to the extent possible, confidential until the investigative panel has found and the accused is served with the Statement of Charges.

The Commission is not permitted to disclose even the existence of a complaint until the investigative panel has determined that the complaint has sufficient merit to justify further action by the Commission. The proceedings of the investigative panel itself are not open to the public.

The Commission may, however, release any information relating to an investigation at any time if the release has been agreed to in writing by the person complained against.

The complaint and the identity of the complainant must at any time be disclosed to the person complained against upon his or her written request.

Investigations by the Commission's investigators are conducted as discretely as possible. The necessity of interviewing witnesses and obtaining records will, however, alert some members of the public to the existence of an investigation.

MINIMUM ETHICAL STANDARDS ESTABLISHED BY THE ACT

PRIVATE GAIN:

Those covered by the Act shall not use their public office or position for their own private gain or that of another.

GIFTS:

They shall not solicit gifts, except for charitable purposes, from which they derive personal benefit. They shall not solicit a gift for any purpose from a subordinate.

They shall not accept a gift from a person with an interest in their governmental activity, except that the following gifts are presumed to be acceptable:

- meals and beverages
- ceremonial gifts of insignificant value
- unsolicited gifts of nominal value
- reasonable expenses incurred in appearing at a speaking engagement
- free tickets to political, charitable or cultural events customarily given as a courtesy to the office (tickets to sports events not considered acceptable)
- purely private and personal gifts
- gifts from relatives by blood or marriage or member of the same household

Honoraria may not be accepted by elected officials, although reasonable honoraria may be accepted by all other covered persons. Nothing in the act prohibits the solicitation, giving or receipt of a lawful political contribution.

INTERESTS IN PUBLIC CONTRACTS:

The Act places certain restrictions on public contracts. It says that no:
- public official or employee or
- member of his or her immediate family or
- business with which he or she is associated may be a party to or have any interest in a contract over which he or she may have control or direct authority to enter into in his or her public capacity.

CONFIDENTIAL INFORMATION:

Covered persons may not, during or after government service, represent another in a:
- contested case
- rate-making proceeding
- license or permit application
- regulation filing or other specific matter which arose during their government service and in which they personally participated in a decision-making, advisory or staff capacity.

LIMITATION ON PRACTICE:

No elected or appointed public official or full-time staff attorney or accountant shall, while, or within six months after, serving with a government entity authorized to hear contested cases or make regulations, represent another person before that entity in the following matters:

- contested case
- rate-making proceeding
- license or permit application
- regulation filing
- to influence the expenditure of public funds

The Ethics Commission has the power to grant exemptions to the six months prohibition for good cause shown.

EMPLOYMENT BY REGULATED PERSONS PROHIBITED:

Full-time public employees and officials may not seek employment with or be employed by a person or company that is or may be regulated by the governmental body by which they are employed. This prohibition applies only to those employees and officials who exercise policymaking, nonministerial or regulatory authority.

The Ethics Commission has the power to grant exemptions for good cause shown.

LICENSING AND RATEMAKING PROCEEDINGS:

Covered persons may not take part in any license or rate-making proceedings that directly affects the license or rates of:

1. a company in which they, or the immediate members of their family, have more than a 10% interest or,

2. a person or company which has during the past year purchased more than $1,000 in goods and services from:

- the covered employee or,
- the covered employee's immediate family members or,
- a company in which they, or the immediate members of their family, have more than a 10% interest.

The Act does not prohibit a covered person from performing purely ministerial functions in regard to such proceedings. The covered persons may participate in non-ministerial functions affecting a person or company identified in 2 above, if a written acknowledgment of the customer relationship is filed with the rate-making or licensing agency.

DOUBLE DIPPING—EXPENSE REIMBURSEMENT:

Covered persons may not seek or accept reimbursement from any governmental entity, for expenses incurred in the course of their public duties which have actually been paid by a lobbyist or any other person.

HIGHER EDUCATION BLANKET EXEMPTION:

Certain members of the faculty and staff of public institutions of higher learning have been exempted by the Legislature from the Act's provisions relating to Private Gain, Gifts and Interests in Public Contracts. Those who rely on this exemption must conform to the standards established by the Board of Trustees or Board of Directors.

Note

[1] For further background see: Robert T. Hall, "The West Virginia Governmental Ethics Act," *West Virginia Public Affairs Reporter,* Vol. 6, No. 1 (Morgantown, West Virginia: Institute for Public Affairs, Winter 1989).

Source: West Virginia Ethics Commission. Reprinted and edited with permission of the WV Ethics Commission, 1207 Quarrier Street, Charleston, WV 25301.